Feminist Ethics and Natural Law
The End of the Anathemas

Feminist Ethics and Natural Law
The End of the Anathemas

CRISTINA L. H. TRAINA

GEORGETOWN UNIVERSITY PRESS / WASHINGTON, D.C.

Georgetown University Press, Washington, D.C.
© 1999 by Georgetown University Press. All rights reserved.
Printed in the United States of America

10   9   8   7   6   5   4   3   2   1   1999

Library of Congress Cataloging-in-Publication Data

Traina, Cristina L. H.
    Feminist ethics and natural law : the end of the anathemas /
Cristina L. H. Traina.
        p.   cm.—(Moral traditions & moral arguments series)
    Includes bibliographical references and index.
    ISBN 0-87840-726-X (hardcover). — ISBN 0-87840-727-8 (pbk.)
    1. Feminist ethics. 2. Natural law. I. Title. II. Series.
BJ1395.T73   1999
170′.82—dc21   98-44651

Contents

Acknowledgments

As is true of most books, the names of the people who shaped this book appear rarely, if at all, in the footnotes. First thanks go to James M. Gustafson, who inspired it; William Schweiker, who shepherded me through the dissertation that became the foundation for it; and James Keenan, who provided endless useful advice and needed encouragement during its expansion and reinvention. I also owe thanks to my colleagues at the Northwestern University Department of Religion, especially Richard Kieckhefer, without whose unfailing logistical support and genuine interest the project quite likely would not have been finished.

It is nearly impossible, for a project as protracted as this, adequately to thank all the other people who have made indispensable contributions. The text would have been poorer without the important advice of the readers for Georgetown University Press; Anne Carr and David Tracy, who helped to advise the dissertation; Lisa Sowle Cahill, Patricia Beattie Jung, Anthony Lisska, Jean Porter, and Roger Haight, all of whom read and commented on portions of it; Richard Kraut, who provided helpful bibliographic advice; Richard A. McCormick, who generously supplied a bibliography of his many articles; and Richard Gula, who offered early suggestions on casting the argument. I am thankful to my research assistant, Astella Saw, for her help with the index. Special gratitude goes to Barbara Newman and Richard Kieckhefer, who waded through entire drafts at least once, and to William George and Susan Ross, who generously read drafts of the introduction and first four chapters not once but twice, making indispensable suggestions each time. I have incorporated as much of their good advice as I could, and any remaining errors are my own. The book would have benefited from engagement with John Finnis's recent work, *Aquinas: Moral, Political, and Legal Theory* (Oxford University Press, 1998), which appeared too late to be included.

Good will, cheerleading, and happy children are essential to the completion of any large project. Shawn Madison Krahmer, Susan Ross, William

George, and Patricia Jung have been especially constant sources of encouragement. My colleagues at the Northwestern University Department of Religion have bent over backwards and in every other direction to carve out time for the project, and my parents, Dick and Polly Traina, provided a week of "writer's retreat" at a crucial point. Without the caretakers of children— my husband, William Hutchison, with the help at various stages of Debbie Camarano, Nancy Nitz, Leigh Gorski Wleklinski, and Teresa Infante—book and children would have been mutually exclusive quantities.

Finally, Bill and our children—David, Maggie, and Kate—have lived through the process of research and writing for this book twice, at least once more than should ever be demanded of any family. Bill provided endless useful comments and printing help on the first version, and all over the age of three contributed substantive and valuable technical assistance on the "home stretch." To all of them this book is lovingly and gratefully dedicated.

Introduction:
Why Feminism Needs
Natural Law

Two very different impulses might inspire a feminist critique and reconstruction of natural law ethics. The obvious one is to bring the series of volumes entitled *Feminism and...* a step closer to completion. This is an important task, but it is not necessarily systematically interesting or practically useful. This volume takes a more unlikely but more compelling path: systematic connections between these ethical traditions are so strong that responsible development of either requires careful attention to the other. In other words, in order to succeed on its own terms, contemporary natural law ethics must self-consciously adopt feminist criteria and methods of moral reflection; and in order to fulfill its own projects, feminist ethics must pay serious attention to natural law. The first claim is becoming pedestrian, but the second is surprising: why should feminism seek insight in such an unlikely place?

WHAT AILS FEMINIST ETHICS

The first part of the answer to this question is that feminist ethics needs new philosophical and theological backing. The early, imperfect foundations that grounded strong feminist moral claims have been abandoned but not replaced. Nineteenth and early twentieth century Western feminism largely embraced an essentialist anthropology of sexual complementarity: women possessed one set of valuable characteristics and men, another; the way to keep society in balance was to maintain equal respect and spheres of influence for each. Charlotte Perkins Gilman, Ellen Key, Frances Willard, and a number of suffragists took this line. [1] Essentialist feminism did and still does (for example, in official writings of the Roman Catholic hierarchy) play the theme of the angel in the house. According to this script, women have inborn capacities for tenderness and nurture that have been shut up in the home. If the doors of the household were thrown open, women's special influence would flow out into public life, transforming a world heretofore shaped only by men who,

1

though not entirely depraved, tend to be rough and mean when beyond women's gentling reach. There are plenty of problems with this theory, not least among them the empirical fact that most women do not have the energy to be angelic in both household and public square.

By the middle part of this century, feminism had begun to undergo an ideological change: the bifurcation of gender from sex. Under the various influences of existentialism, liberalism, and socialism women began to argue that what had seemed to be ingrained sex-traits and instincts were really learned behaviors, so that the shared patterns of women's experience were products not of their sex but of their common roles and positions in culture. [2] Thus Sara Ruddick has argued that the *experience of caring for small children*, which generally falls to women, is an important and neglected source of moral insight, not that *all women or all mothers* inherently possess culturally valuable, unique moral wisdom. [3] Yet through this transition two claims survived relatively intact: that women's gendered experience—especially their experience of marginalization and oppression—provided truthful and prophetic insight into the moral depravity of oppressive social institutions, and that women were a group identifiable by sex whose common flourishing could legitimately be discussed, even cross-culturally. As Margaret Farley has pointed out, it is exactly these assumptions that are no longer reliable. [4]

The first portion of this foundation to crumble was experience. Developments in recent American Christian feminist theology illustrate the problem. In 1985 the Mud Flower Collective—a group of seven Christian feminist theologians, straight and lesbian, white, African American, and Cuban American—published a book in which they began to struggle openly with the prejudice and oppression that had generated differences in their experiences and lit slow, persistent fires of mutual distrust in each of them. Women's experience, since the beginning of feminism a threat to male hegemony but a banner of unity for women, was now no longer benign for women either. [5] This was as it should have been, of course, for only dependently wealthy women had been eligible for the role of "angel in the house" upon which normative "women's experience" had been modeled up to this point. Then in 1987 Sheila Greeve Davaney sharply criticized white feminists for implying that "there is *a* perspective from which we can perceive the way things really are and that feminist experience"—the experience of the struggle for justice for women—"provides such a privileged location." [6] Rather *all* experience "is a social product and hence is relative, ambiguous, and challengeable." [7] This does not mean, Davaney argues, that "all standards and norms are arbitrary commitments"; but it does mean that "the only level that really matters [is] the level of concrete and practical consequences." [8] Four years later, feminist theologians came together at the American Academy of Religion meeting to remind each other that differences in women's experiences owe to inequalities in their social power: *women* oppress women. Women in positions of power cannot automatically claim common cause with oppressed women but should make only very circumspect and respectful use of their ideas and experiences. [9] There is, for example, something not only incongruous but also immoral about a white theologian's "borrowing" a slave spiritual in order to give voice to her own experience of psychological anguish. Finally, in 1994, Mary McClintock Fulkerson took these arguments to the conclusion at which Davaney had hinted: experience is an improper ground for feminist argument— either critical or constructive—because it necessarily draws on limited reports to make universal claims. Instead, feminists must limit themselves to examining particular emancipatory practices in their concrete social and religious contexts. [10]

We can articulate the conceptual shift by borrowing from set theory. Human difference used to be conceived of as a Venn diagram: two intersecting circles. The common human characteristics of a woman in rural India and a man in urban France fall within a substantial area of intersection. These characteristics are truly the same, despite divergences in gender, geography, and cultural experience. But if we switch to the contemporary language of standpoint, we see in three dimensions rather than two. The slightest difference in experience produces a complete reorientation of perspective. Because we now see our "common" elements from entirely different angles, each of us arrays and interprets them differently. Not only that, but people with social power install their perspective as the "real," outlawing other interpretations and so confounding the disparity with injustice. The only "common" definition of humanity is the one generated by powerful classes and institutions and inevitably reproduced by the less powerful. Experience can divide and oppress rather than unite.

The second loss is the loss of the body. One dimension of the dissolution of women's experience has been the deconstruction of sex and, with it, as articulated by Judith Butler, the loss of the material body as a concrete criterion of womanhood. Not that the physical body is a mirage. Butler is not, she quickly insists, "somatophobic." [11] She simply means to say that the body is a political construct. People who define the category "woman" are people who fulfill not only biological criteria but ideological expectations. We must ask continually what ideological assumptions "woman" binds up and whom it excludes [12] and expect that these assumptions and exclusions will change. This is as it should be, for any permanent definition of "woman" would be oppressive. [13] In addition, we ought not shoehorn ourselves or others into categories that limit us artificially. Thus sex goes the way of gender, [14] freeing us to chop sexual identity into its identifiable elements and use them, like building blocks, to experiment with constructing new combinations—a feather boa plus a gesture plus a phallus, for instance. [15] The 1990s icon, transvestite Dennis Rodman of the Chicago Bulls, embodies this buffet-style construction of sexual identity.

The terrible consequences of this deconstruction for feminism are palpable. [16] Butler catapults us right back into the mind-body dualism we have been trying to shed. Although she admits that we cannot get along without bodies—even sexed bodies—bodies are still the almost arbitrary creations of our individual and cultural minds; we create and classify them according to and in rebellion against a grammar that we have also invented. Our embodied selves can make no moral claims on us that we have not first given them. Second, she implies that freedom from the tyranny of sex and other arbitrary classifications is the most pressing moral problem we face. But do we not still need to make moral judgments about categories, as well as about the identities we construct within and against them? Is it possible to pursue the good more easily from within some categories than within others? Are any inherently wrong or evil? Is any self-construction of equal moral value, provided it is free and self-conscious? These questions are unanswerable from within Butler's framework.

Here again examples are useful. On one hand, in 1978 the post-Christian feminist philosopher Mary Daly condemned the "unspeakable atrocities of genital mutilation," a judgment that has been ratified by an international women's movement opposing the practice. [17] On the other hand, Martha Nussbaum frequently and critically illustrates the opposite point of view with the following example: at an international conference, an American economist and a French anthropologist implied that Western technology blindly imposes Western values on other cultures, insensitive to the destructive effects of those values on local traditions. The economist extolled the unity of domestic and workplace values in rural India, where the pollution of menstruation bans women equally from the kitchen and the loom, enforcing a sabbatical from both cooking and earning money. The anthropologist lamented that the British introduction of the smallpox vaccine in India had caused the decline of "the cult of Sittala Devi, the goddess to whom one used to pray in order to avert smallpox." Not only was a cult of great cultural richness lost, but the speakers implied that the British were presumptuous to impose their own hatred of death—in the form of smallpox prevention—upon Indian Hindus. [18]

It does not take much imagination to hypothesize that Mary Daly or Martha Nussbaum would condemn the Indian pollution taboo in horror and

greet the introduction of smallpox vaccines with gratitude. They would counter
Nussbaum's anonymous scholars' accusations of racial and cultural imperial-
ism with their own charges of sexism and racism. Perhaps women *have* found
some liberative silver lining in the pollution taboo—like an excuse to rest—
and perhaps the cult of Sittala Devi *did* provide comfort and meaning, but
that justifies neither the exclusion of women from paid labor nor the failure
to check preventable fatal diseases. Further, it is unlikely that Sittala Devi
would have had a following to begin with were it not that people feared a
mysterious, ugly, and dangerous illness. Likewise the unnamed economist
and anthropologist might well believe female genital mutilation—in itself a
prejudicial term—to be embedded in holistic social practices that ought not
to be disturbed thoughtlessly. We may find it disgusting, but female circumci-
sion is an element of a social system that women—who generally perform
the surgery—believe secures their welfare. And all four scholars would say they
are defending women's genuine flourishing within particular social contexts.

Butler cannot adjudicate this disagreement. She counsels resistance to
stereotypes, but as a matter of general principle: *all* categories are tyrannical.
She cannot make moral distinctions among species of resistance or types of
tyranny. On Butler's logic the category "human" would be just as necessary
but also just as tyrannical and deconstructable as "sex," and therefore just as
ineffective a critical principle. Yet if experience is not a legitimate source for
moral reflection, then the entire subject matter of practical moral reason
disappears. If we cannot talk about our experience of acts, habits, character,
and their contexts, we cannot do ethics at all.

Thus, as Margaret Farley points out, significant numbers of feminists
from all schools "articulate (or at least imply) some version of a common
morality." [19] For instance, Barbara Ehrenreich and Janet McIntosh argue that
thinkers like Butler "undermine the very bedrock of the politics they claim
to uphold." [20] This inability to make moral distinctions threatens to shipwreck
feminism precisely because feminism entails a commitment to political
liberation. [21] That is, feminism exists to free women from human oppression
and, more broadly, from all forces that prevent their flourishing. In order to
accomplish this task, feminism needs some relatively stable point of critical
leverage, some point beyond which systems and behaviors are clearly wrong.
For example, a colleague of mine curbs laissez faire relativism in his classes
by pointing out that judicial punishment of date rape depends on a solid
claim that date rape is unconditionally wrong: if there is no principled condemnation, there will be no effective judicial and educational movement against
date rape, and women's welfare will suffer. The need for a stable reference
point is especially strong in a social context inclined to exploit ambiguity,

powerlessness, and reticence. As Martha Nussbaum wryly points out, "to give up on all evaluation and, in particular, on a normative account of the human being and human functioning [is] to turn things over to the free play of forces in a world situation in which the social forces affecting the lives of women, minorities, and the poor are rarely benign." [22] Nancy Fraser's critique of Butler hits the nail on the head: deconstruction and destabilization *pave the path* to liberation, but they do not *accomplish* it:

> At the deepest level, [Butler] understands women's liberation as libera-tion *from* identity, since she views identity as inherently oppressive. It follows that deconstructive critique—critique that dereifies or unfreezes identity—is the privileged mode of feminist theorizing, whereas norma-tive, reconstructive critique is normalizing and oppressive. But this view is far too one-sided to meet the full needs of a liberatory politics. Feminists *do* need to make normative judgments and to offer emancipa-tory alternatives. We are not for "anything goes." Moreover, it is arguable that the current proliferation of identity-dereifying, fungible, commodi-fied images and significations constitutes as great a threat to women's liberation as do fixed, fundamentalist identities. ... Feminists need both deconstruction *and* reconstruction, destabilization of meaning *and* projection of utopian hope. [23]

Not only does political change of the kind feminism demands require solidarity behind strong, positive, "universally shareable" rights claims, [24] but to back up these claims we need an anthropology, a normative description of embodied human life. Further, in order to counteract Nussbaum's malevolent social forces and construct Fraser's utopia, we need not just any anthropology but a telic anthropology: one with convictions about the ends toward which human beings individually, and human society generally, are to strive. And we need methods of hammering out the concrete requirements of thriving in particular situations.

In sum, feminist ethics, and a successful feminist politics, depend upon the possibility of making some authentically common claims, rooted in com-monly held visions of women's flourishing. The post-modern claim that universal or "totalizing" ethics tend in fact to be biased, deterministic, and quite prematurely particular—and therefore subject to abuse, not to mention being based in questionable metaphysics—must be accepted, and it is worth noting that critics of radical deconstructionism like Janet McIntosh do so. [25] But an unconditional, hands-off respect for otherness is politically paralyzing, and an undifferentiated elevation of resistance is an invitation to anarchy and chaos. The continuing existence of feminism depends on finding some third path that balances the need for universal claims against the need to attend to genuine pluralism of experience and that takes the limits and possibilities of a telic "nature" seriously but not deterministically. [26]

ALTERNATIVES TO DECONSTRUCTIONISM

If Butler's version of deconstructionism does not solve this problem, neither do the other major schools of feminism. [27] What follows is a rough sketch of these alternatives, which will be treated in greater depth in the first chapter. Liberal feminism does have its virtues; [28] without its confidence in a common, transcendent human nature, the feminist argument for the equal dignity and common humanity of men and women might never have gained political currency. But it is only a short step from the liberal disjunction of fact and nature from culture and value [29] to Butler's claims about the cultural construction of "nature" and the free play of categories. Deconstruction simply takes these premises one step further: instead of the social construction of gender, we have the social construction of sex; instead of the irrelevance of the static female body—for truly the male body is the assumed standard—we have the malleability of the body. Meaning belongs to culture. The individual is the creator of value: "the essence of morality must consist in what is freely created or discovered by the moral agent in the process of reasoning itself." [30] The good to be sought is the maximization of an individual's freedom to choose among these subjectively generated goods. [31] Yet this uncritical confidence in human reason and lack of attention to human embodiment is liberal feminism's undoing. Its "thin" theory of the good gives women few grounds to press for common pursuit of any social goods beyond freedom of choice or to challenge the assumptions of an in-theory-transcendent reason. [32]

When liberalism does admit to having substantive ends, it often too quickly translates and elevates these into abstract, absolute principles: for instance, California Proposition 209, which did away with racial preference policies. Proposition 209 is based on a principle of procedural justice—that race is to be ignored in hiring and college admissions—and a conviction that justice entails applying principles inflexibly and abstractly, and without regard to context, ends, or means. Yet when Ward Connerly, the University of California regent who helped to craft Proposition 209, supported the University of California's plans to increase outreach funding to troubled high schools, critics pointed out that these plans would violate his own prohibition of preferential treatment by bestowing more money on impoverished African American and Latino schools than on wealthy, largely white schools. The result was that immediate enactment of the principle of colorblindness took precedence over the means, the context, and the good of particular persons. Had his criterion been superior education for all California students, *beginning with the disadvantaged,* then he would have begun by providing what they needed in order to accomplish that goal. [33] Principled colorblindness can be an instrument of justice only once racial parity has been accomplished.

Feminists tend to examine the suitability of means to ends more carefully than Connerly. Be that as it may, we will find ourselves in trouble if we forget to articulate the connection. It was quite clear in the early 1970s that abortion—along with family planning and elimination of public apathy toward sexual harassment and rape—was a means of preserving women's sexual freedom, existential autonomy, and holistic flourishing in an environment in which those were severely endangered. Abortion was a means subordinate to the greater goal of women's autonomous flourishing. But it is increasingly common to see references to women's right to abortion—in feminist scholarly literature, but also in a recent Supreme Court decision on assisted suicide [34]—as if it were a self-evident moral absolute, an eternal and inviolable principle, an end in itself. References to flourishing and to context are missing.

Liberalism's individualistic assumptions, as well as its arbitrary thresholds for assigning rights and its tendency to reduce ethics to the question of legal rights, also undermine feminist ends. A more holistic grounding is needed, one that accounts for historical and cross-cultural diversity in experience and even in norms without relinquishing its prophetic edge—one in which centripetal and centrifugal forces are balanced, so that diverse ethics move in orbits rather than collapsing indistinguishably into a common center or spinning off wildly and randomly to the far reaches of the universe. Some feminists have sought this grounding in a variety of naturalism: a claim that social rights and moral obligations are rooted in human ends and that there is a continuity, rather than a contradiction, between these ends and the physical and intellectual capacities of embodied human beings. [35] Lisa Sowle Cahill puts it pithily: "No consistent feminist critique can maintain that practical good and evil in matters of sex and gender are culturally constructed to their very roots and in value utterly relative to social approbation." [36] Human nature is to be not transcended but developed. Sex difference is good; the female body and sometimes even the "feminine virtues" are extolled; development of women's particular nature is consistent with their own flourishing and with that of the social whole. This is a "thick" and interdependent good: visions of holistic flourishing and the potential to fulfill them cooperatively are embedded within every person and community. To read and fulfill this purpose is to flourish, and to disregard it is to perish.

Yet human fixities do not point clearly and inexorably toward a single end, and everything depends upon which of the many possible ends is chosen. For example, naturalism has often credibly combined with an "earth mother" brand of biological determinism that identifies femininity with maternity. [37] Naturalist feminism can as easily justify permanent feminist separatism, a position that does as much violence as misogyny to Christian tenets of human equality and of the value of interdependent community. [38] It can also underwrite a theory of subordination and complementarity, as in the confusing double rhetorics of the Promisekeepers and Pope John Paul II.

A final unsuccessful alternative to deconstructionism I bring up not because of its popularity with feminists but because of its first-blush affinity to natural law. This option is inductive universalism: examining a culture, or even international cultures, to discover values, rules, or ends that, de facto, hold universally. Thinkers like Robert Merrihew Adams and John Reeder have argued that, even in a pluralist era, we can reach significant agreement on the content of moral norms through this method, [39] which enables us to form a practical "overlapping consensus" without addressing potentially divisive questions of philosophical foundations and utopian goals. [40] Consensus norms do not so much have to be argued for as (mechanically) identified: the good is simply that on which dominant norms across cultures agree. But again the advantage of such an approach proves to be its downfall: a consensus is merely an uncritical intersection of myriad moralities. For example, take the feminist claim that oppressive patriarchal values infect cultures virtually universally. According to inductive universalism, these values are as much a part of the global consensus as (e.g.) universal injunctions against murder. Unless the consensus also contained feminist values that outweighed the patriarchal ones, the only means of expunging patriarchal values from it would be to transform all the cultures that composed it.

Thus an overlapping consensus is no more appropriate a foundation for a feminist ethic of political liberation than is naturalism, deconstructionism, or liberalism. Social constructionism and liberalism, by ignoring the body or reducing it to a social construct, weaken the utterly basic material claims that embodied persons make on each other. We have vulnerabilities that cannot be theorized away. Social constructionism and liberalism are also much better at freeing us to pursue ends than they are at aiding us in judging among them or in constructing a utopian vision that will lead us toward a more just future. Although contemporary American "liberal" liberalism has made real if inadequate efforts to supply what people actually need to pursue goods, recent retrenchment on welfare and affirmative action call this commitment into question. And social constructionism especially seems at times to be all context, without principle or end. Naturalism has no reliable mechanism for interpreting the meaning of physical givens and so tends to be uncritical, deterministic, and not especially visionary; its ideal future repeats or perfects the past, rather than evolving from the present. This is an end, but an end without regard for context. Inductive universalism tells us only that the dominant classes in cultures worldwide concur, not why they do or whether their ethics are just. Here we have no principles, no end, and no context either. Deconstructionist approaches that do not artificially narrow women's choices are so reluctant to define women and women's good that they are often unable to develop and defend powerful common claims. The appreciation of human creativity and diversity that these perspectives foster is a centrifugal force that, if not countered by some strong gravitational pull, can send ethics on infinite diverse and independent trajectories. [41]

NATURAL LAW

This incapacity leaves feminist moral voices in a precarious position. The way out is to walk the line between tentativeness and absolutism: to develop descriptions credible and detailed enough to yield morally normative, prophetic claims yet flexible enough to accommodate a degree of cultural pluralism and historical change and to do so inductively, developing and refining descriptions in the midst of the cross-cultural struggle for concrete flourishing. [42] It is here that the Roman Catholic natural law tradition can prove truly helpful.

Admittedly natural law is an unlikely ally. The *Summa Theologiae* of Thomas Aquinas, the recognized father of Roman Catholic natural law thought, contains more misogynistic claims than we would care to count. [43] For example, Thomas dusted off and reiterated Aristotle's biology, including Aristotle's opinion that semen contained the seed of a complete human person in the image of the father. Therefore women were misbegotten males, members of a class of defectives, beings in whom something had gone wrong—doubtless in their mothers' faulty wombs, after they had left the safe and perfect haven of their father's loins. Not only that, but in women, the body was proportionately more influential than the intellect. Because union with God was a purely intellectual accomplishment, whether before or after death, living women were spiritually handicapped from the beginning: they must overcome their femininity before they could begin to scale the obstacles that stood in the way of even an ordinary man's path to God. Neither was women's subordination to men, as contemporary Christian feminists might argue, simply a consequence of the Fall. Thomas looked to the second creation narrative in Genesis for proof that their inferiority was divinely premeditated: Eve is taken from

Adam's side—that is, from his body—rather than from his head—where his intellect resides. To this subordination all sorts of (to us) horrifying ethical conclusions can be traced—like the matter-of-fact treatment of rape as an offense not just against a woman but at least equally against the man to whom she is subject. [44] And all of these claims rest on premises that remain integral to the subsequent natural law tradition. Certainly even within Thomas's corpus there are claims about the goodness and necessity of embodiment and about the equality of persons that implicitly or even explicitly moderate his misogynism; for instance, Thomas insists that God chose not to make woman from man's feet precisely so that he would not despise her. [45] Yet even so great a fan of Thomas as Jean Porter goes no further than to claim that "it is possible to extend his general social thought in a feminist direction, without flatly contradicting his views on women." [46]

More recent versions of natural law ethics have their faults as well, including a sometimes unsubstantiated reputation for deducing moral arguments from changeless universal moral norms and applying them inflexibly to impossibly diverse situations. Twentieth century revisionist natural law attempted to allow for greater diversity in concrete conclusions by centering its anthropology on rational self-transcendence, a move that strikes feminists as still rather modern, abstract, and unappreciative of genuine difference. Clearly if natural law is to be useful to feminism, it will have to be not all of natural law, but natural law critically retrieved. But what features of the natural law would lie at the center of such a retrieval?

Even feminists who subscribe to an anthropology of transcendence tend to situate moral discourse in the concrete rather than the transcendent: in embodiment, experience, and engagement over practical issues that arise in shared life. Women's moral wisdom can come to the table, and women's rights can be championed universally, only when women's integral flourishing and knowledge are indisputably respected and shared practical concerns guide debate. But as Lisa Sowle Cahill, Jean Porter, Margaret Farley, and Cynthia S. W. Crysdale have demonstrated, natural law fulfills exactly these criteria. It has historically employed an inductive method highly dependent on reflection upon experience; it has sought to provide guidance on common practical issues of the sort that hold promise for bridging gaps created by cultural differences; and although its method has complemented a now marginalized metaphysic, it can—thanks to its practicality and its reliance on human experience—also take part in a contemporary conversation that is more agnostic about origins and final ends. [47] The foci around which such a combined ethic must orbit are the substantively described dignity of women (including its connections to the dignity of men and of the ecosystem) and the concrete, practical concerns of life in the de facto global community.

We begin with Cahill's insight, strongly informed by Martha Nussbaum, that the most promising approaches to both natural law and feminist ethics are those that hold human givenness—especially gendered givenness—in tension with human self-creativity and that raise integral, interdependent individual and communal flourishing as their critical standard. Natural law and feminist ethics share a concern for an implicit or explicit theory of value (in this case, a normative description of flourishing) and a method (a technique for analyzing concrete states of affairs and for deciding how and when to pursue particular, sometimes conflicting, incarnations of flourishing). Indispensable here is a means of knitting together standards for systematic, *social justice*—for instance, for political and economic structures that justly account for women's particular needs as bearers of children—with probing discussions of *individual* moral integrity and accountability. This entails developing tentative but "thick" and telic descriptions of human being and thriving: What are the characteristics and requirements of individual flourishing? of social or even global flourishing? What are the connections between them? It also entails refusing to shy away from the crucial task of cultivating the methods of practical moral reason that alone can meaningfully connect the individual's moral sense of self with action in the world.

Thus these thinkers point toward an even stronger claim: feminist reconstructions of natural law are "more adequate" than earlier versions of it not only by feminist and natural law standards but also before the demands of contemporary global moral conversation. The intersection of natural law and feminist ethics is not merely systematically curious or even mutually illuminating; rather, it holds the greatest promise for culturally sensitive, flexible, yet tough and prophetic contemporary moral reflection.

This book carves out a particular and narrow segment of that claim: a case for a natural law method, critically reconstructed along feminist lines, that would be not only more useful to a prophetic and constructive feminist discourse than the philosophical models feminism currently employs but also more fitted than natural law revisionism to traditional natural law goals. In fact, as the core of the book will show, revisionist Roman Catholic natural law thought is deficient according to its own standards unless it meets feminist criteria. A feminist reconstruction of natural law remains natural law.

FURTHER GROUNDING FOR NATURAL LAW FEMINISM

The position to be justified is a theological naturalism modified by contemporary hermeneutics. The claim that this approach satisfies the systematic demands of both the feminist and the natural law moral traditions will be developed in the following chapters, but the additional assertion that it provides a satisfying option in the conversation beyond these constituencies will not. Thus my claim deserves a bit more attention here. For in an historicist and pluralist era, which has all but discredited such terms, even to allude to universals or nature or givenness is touchy business. I have stressed one pressing practical reason for doing so: without them one cannot make rights arguments stick. [48] But this is a philosophically inadequate case for a claim that runs against the postmodern philosophical grain. [49] First, one must show that such an ethic can be coherent, that it can make sense of the world and human action in it. Second, for somewhat different reasons, both feminist and natural law thinkers emphasize the need for ethical method to be rooted in general, human ways of seeing and thinking; one must thus show that an ethic making use of nature and the universal does not systematically privilege insights of a particular group. Rather, persuasive moral argument highlights and interprets in rigorous but familiar ways information in principle available to all. [50] Again, philosophical precision is crucial.

Comprehensive attention to contemporary philosophical debates over naturalism would fill volumes and so is outside the purview of this book. Here I can simply point to evidence that a particular kind of ethical naturalism is gaining philosophical credibility. Stated positively, the new naturalism claims that, universally, the psychological, environmental, and bodily circumstances of human life provide loose criteria for human flourishing, and human flourishing has central (though not exclusive) normative importance. Stated negatively, it claims that these conditions set limits on—without prescribing comprehensively the direction of—genuinely good philosophical, personal, and social transformation. This sort of naturalism is philosophically credible, I claim, if morally and methodologically normative definitions of nature—particularly human nature—are understood as open, tentative, and inductively defined—hence, subject to revision inspired by reflection on experience—rather than as closed, fixed, and deductively determined. The conviction that anthropological givens inevitably affect us profoundly yet "can be modified, overridden or reversed by other influences" requires tough thinking, "a high tolerance of ambiguity," and anticipation of continuing, reciprocal transformation of moral norms and of our comprehensive view of the world and human life. [51] In short, we must make universal claims, but we must make them with both conviction and humility.

Significant to the philosophical credibility of these positions is the recent reconsideration of the relationship between the "is," or empirical fact, and the "ought," or moral dictum: in what way do existing realities—whether necessary or contingent—dictate moral ideals or ranges of moral possibilities?

This is another way of asking about the limits of human self-transformation: which dimensions of our situation present givens that are untransgressable limits, and which, invitations to creative transformation?

We are used to believing that resurrecting the fact-value connection is backward and logically fallacious. The philosophical tradition evolving from the work of Hume, which insisted on the strict separation of scientific and moral knowledge, forbade adducement of "nature" as an authoritative moral warrant. [52] Since the development of modern hermeneutical theory, philosophers have pointed out that, even if an "essential" or "core" human nature exists, it cannot be known with any certainty, finality, or comprehensiveness; they have agreed that such an elusive "nature" is an inadequate and misleading foundation for morality. [53]

But as I will show in chapter 4, there is growing contemporary awareness of the phenomenological interdependence of descriptive and evaluative knowledge—of scientific (or factual) and moral characterizations. These sorts of knowledge and their languages are interdependent because scientific and moral knowledge arise simultaneously. "Empirical" description is in fact always already imbued with moral meaning. This epistemological development has given new credence to the idea that our descriptions of human nature *are* important sources of information about what human beings should do and become.

More accurately put, these descriptions are important sources of information about what we collectively have *believed* we should do and become. For such descriptions are not exclusive or unassailable. Human-being-as-it-is is not necessarily equivalent to human-being-as-it-should-be; for example, a phenomenological description of women's being, here and now, is not yet a normative description of women's "nature." Rather, a proper normative description of women is telic or prospective or anticipatory. It must include an ideal of women's unrealized integral flourishing. It must answer the question, what can and ought women to be? [54] The dependence of the prescriptive "ought" upon the descriptive "is" must be reciprocal rather than merely deductive. The boundary between descriptions of what is the case and indications of what ought to be done or accomplished is osmotic rather than impermeable. [55] So feminism holds that flourishing is good, and whatever contributes to flourishing (practically and morally informed description) is morally required (ontologically and teleologically informed prescription). [56] The "is" that guides the "ought" includes a hopeful, prescriptive "should be."

Moral realism—the claim that moral statements and judgments can properly be factual in an objective sense [57]—is also a live option. Substantive realism—the claim that clear universal moral norms exist somewhere and simply await discovery—ultimately amounts to an assertion; it does not tell us how to decide which moral explorer's booty of norms is authentic or why we should adhere to them. [58] But procedural realism—which places its confidence in methods of moral discernment rather than in particular lists of material moral norms—may hold more promise. It must still answer the question "why be moral?"; for instance, David Brink's utilitarian version must explain why we are to seek certain sorts of goods. Yet it avoids the arid, technical cast of strict realism because its procedure involves reflection on concrete practices rather than merely theoretical searches for abstract norms. If there are norms "out there," they must be the norms "in here," discovered in the effort to live virtuously in a complex world.

If both moral realism and some sort of carefully redescribed naturalism are tenable, then in the plural global conversation critically examined claims about "what is generally the case" for human beings are still relevant for ethics. Physical—and now historical and psychological—structures of human life have prescriptive significance. For Korsgaard, for instance, human beings are "deeply social": to be human is to be a member of a community, to have shaping traditions and practical roles that form one's identity. [59] Cahill points out that all human societies must organize sexuality and kin relations. The sheer existence of sociality and sexuality does not dictate the details of this moral arrangement, but it does dictate that there be a moral arrangement. [60] Human being is in some sense indicative for human doing, as long as moralists do not claim inherent comprehensiveness and historical finality for their particular descriptions and norms.

In addition, philosophers are experimenting with new, more tentative ways of stating moral universals that do not run roughshod over genuine divergences in history, culture, or conviction. I have already mentioned Robert Merrihew Adams's and John Reeder's argument for the possibility of significant consensus on the content of moral norms even in a pluralist era. [61] Inspired by John Rawls, they claim that inductive reasoning, attention to concrete moral exemplars, and "appeals to general features of human nature" enable us to reach agreement on core moral norms across philosophical lines and yet bypass foundational questions. [62] As we have seen, such a consensus would be merely a foundationless, universal intersection of myriad ethics, each of which has its own context, foundations, methods, and peculiar norms. It is not an ethic in its own right. And yet it does permit comprehensive, ontologically grounded ethics like natural law to participate in the common debate about moral particulars without either jettisoning their foundational claims or demanding that others adhere to them.

For hermeneutic theory has bolstered the credibility of self-consciously religious ethics. As we have seen, the norms of an "overlapping consensus" are not generated by a universal moral theory and do not get their authority from the fact of universal agreement. Working from the now clichéd claim that all statements of fact both assume and support a worldview, Basil Mitchell points out that moral judgments are no exception; every ethic assumes, if it does not explicate, a vision of the significance of human life, relationship, and possibility. [63] Every ethic has, in other words, an implicit or explicit worldview. [64] Because the authority and warrants for particular moral claims come from the comprehensive vision of the community that generated them the content of the consensus depends ultimately upon these particular comprehensive visions. Even for those who have given up on universal foundations for ethics, moral theories and worldviews—especially religious ones—remain important to the broader discussion of norms and methods.

Because like most religious ethicists natural law thinkers tend to lay out their worldviews clearly and draw careful connections between these and their ethics, they are especially well positioned to take part in contemporary critical discussions of universal or "consensus" norms. They make a point of detecting and hammering out disagreements between the metaethical, normative, and moral levels—the "whys," "whats," and "hows"—of their ethics and of arguing earnestly and prophetically in support of their positions. They are likely, in other words, to bring authentic, carefully crafted norms to the common discussion.

In the end, moral action and moral reason "relate to some conception of human nature and its possibilities." [65] This conception must be not only internally coherent but also answerable to an experience of human life and flourishing. [66] Moral reflection thus grows out of the dialectical relationship between the events of human life and the dynamic picture through which we make sense of them. [67] It is the constant give and take between—on one hand—our evolving experiences of what is appropriate, helpful, and healthy (what is "natural") to human beings and of what sorts of behavior, actions, and conditions tend to promote this "natural" flourishing and—on the other hand—our tentative theoretical descriptions of these ends and means and our methods of adjudication. As long as the experiential and the theoretical are mutually critical, an ethic of reasonable argument based in human nature is not only philosophically plausible but also philosophically preferable. A critical feminist revitalization of the traditional Roman Catholic version of ethical naturalism meets these criteria. More will be said about this in later chapters. But the acute task for both approaches, and for this synthesis, is to articulate more clearly in what sense and at what level of the moral discussion human nature is morally normative.

THE SHAPE OF THE ARGUMENT

The scope of the historical and critical discussion in the following chapters is not comprehensive. My concern is to highlight claims and patterns of reasoning that both authentically reflect insights indispensable to the natural law tradition and have some significance for an attempt to speak of shared values and norms in an era of pluralism. I especially emphasize the significance of anthropology to claims about the content of flourishing and to the evaluation of methods and procedures of ethical reflection. Other important and pressing questions—for instance, the need to bring feminist insight to bear on the epistemological connections between faith and reason—must be left for my own or others' later reflections. [68] My aim is to show that central natural law claims, critically corrected by feminism, meet the requirements of contemporary moral reflection by balancing novelty, variety, and creativity with claims about continuity and universality.

Chapter 1 explores the schools of feminist ethics examined briefly in the introduction, but with an eye less to debunking any of them than to articulating and preserving the indispensable insights each contributes to feminist moral reflection generally. These contributions anchor the criticism and reconstruction of natural law that is the project of the book. I also explain the way in which the tension between creativity and givenness—a crucial relationship in any ethic in which anthropology has a substantial normative role—is expressed in contemporary feminist epistemology. The pivotal role of experience in the maintenance of this tension and in the formation of normative moral claims, as well as its implications for issues of pluralism and authority, is explained. Finally, I point to Martha Nussbaum's "thick vague theory of the good" as an example of a normative anthropology that is also telic, inductive, and flexible. Because this chapter deals in detail with methodological and foundational debates within feminist ethics, a reader unfamiliar with that tradition might prefer to go directly to the concluding pages of the chapter.

In chapters 2 and 3, I examine classical texts from the natural law tradition in an effort to identify authentic insights useful for its renewal or criticism. The points of reference are Thomas Aquinas's *Summa Theologiae*, the casuistical tradition of moral theology, and twentieth century Roman Catholic academic and ecclesiastical theology. Here I substantiate historically my claim about the integrative pattern that inheres in that tradition: a telic theological anthropology in which practical moral reason, individual moral integrity, and life in community cohere. I identify and defend the systematic connections between givenness and openness or creativity and between universality and particularity. I also establish the historical theological backing for the contemporary identification of human and Christian ethics and address some of the recent and contemporary cultural and philosophical challenges to natural law ethics. Finally, I point out the tension between natural law's basic epistemological claims and official methods on one hand, and the institutional use—what I call procedure—of natural law reasoning in the Roman Catholic Church on the other. Both chapters treat issues internal to the Roman Catholic tradition of natural law criticism, and a reader simply wishing to know what my interpretation of the tradition yields for a feminist reconstruction of natural law might profitably skip to the concluding summaries of each of these chapters.

Chapter 4 returns to feminist ethics, articulating the systematic connections between feminist and natural law ethics and summarizing the criteria that the feminist moral discussion as a whole brings to the critique and reconstruction of natural law.

Supplied with more refined critical tools from both traditions, I return in chapters 5 through 7 to analyze the work of three representative Roman Catholic moral thinkers: Josef Fuchs, Gustavo Gutiérrez, and Richard McCormick. My initial emphasis is upon the criteria introduced in chapters 2 and 3: how do they try to meet contemporary challenges to natural law? to what degree do they accomplish and to what degree do they fall short of the criteria I have identified as central to the natural law tradition? I argue that each neglects at least one important criterion.

Chapter 8 mounts a specifically feminist critique of all three authors but ties it to the foregoing natural law and feminist criteria. Although each author is commended for working at least partly out of concern for issues that also inform feminism, each falls short by these measures as well, and the former shortfall is due at least in part to the latter. A reader interested primarily in the constructive argument may wish to skip to the final chapter.

The conclusion reconstructs the integrative pattern identified in chapters 2 and 3, drawing upon both the feminist criteria developed in chapter 4 and the insights gained from applying both sets of criteria in chapters 5 through 8. The central methods and claims of natural law ethics, taken in their full historical and theological context, are methodologically consistent with the feminist moral hermeneutic and even require adoption of some elements of feminist ethical method. Even more importantly, reconstructed, practical, principled natural law reasoning is an indispensable element in a larger process of moral discernment. A comparison of traditionalist natural law, feminist, and feminist natural law approaches to questions about reproductive technology illustrates some of the advantages of a natural law feminist approach, as well as the special challenges it faces.

NOTES

1. Ellen Key, *Love and Ethics* (New York: B. W. Huebsch, 1912); Ellen Key, *War, Peace, and the Future: A Consideration of Nationalism and Internationalism, and of the Relation of Women to War*, trans. Hildegard Norberg (New York: G. P. Putnam's Sons; London, The Knickerbocker Press, 1916); Charlotte Perkins Gilman, *The Man-Made World: Or, Our Androcentric Culture* (New York: Charlton Company, 1911; Source Book Press, 1970); Frances Elizabeth Willard, *The Ideal of "The New Woman" According to the Woman's Christian Temperance Union*, ed. and intro. Carolyn De Swarte Gifford (New York: Garland, 1987).

2. For example, Simone de Beauvoir, *The Second Sex,* trans. and ed. by H. M. Parshley (New York: Vintage Books, 1974); Shulamith Firestone, *The Dialectic of Sex: The Case for Feminist Revolution* (New York: William Morrow, 1970); Rosemary Radford Ruether, *Sexism and God-Talk: Toward a Feminist Theology* (Boston: Beacon Press, 1983).

3. Sara Ruddick, *Maternal Thinking: Toward a Politics of Peace* (Boston: Beacon Press, 1989).

4. Margaret A. Farley, "Feminism and Universal Morality," in *Prospects for a Common Morality*, ed. Gene Outka and John P. Reeder, Jr. (Princeton, NJ: Princeton University Press, 1993), 176–77.

5. The Mud Flower Collective, *God's Fierce Whimsy* (New York: Pilgrim Press, 1985). Katie G. Cannon, Beverly W. Harrison, Carter Heyward, Ada María Isasi-Díaz, Delores S. Williams, Mary D. Pellauer, and Nancy D. Richardson.

6. Sheila Greeve Davaney, "The Limits of the Appeal to Women's Experience," in *Shaping New Vision: Gender and Values in American Culture*, ed. Clarissa W. Atkinson, Constance H. Buchanan, and Margaret R. Miles, The Harvard Women's Studies in Religion Series, no. 5, 31–50 (Ann Arbor, MI: UMI Research Press, 1987), 42. Italics added.

7. Ibid., 46.

8. Ibid., 47.

9. Toinette M. Eugene, Ada María Isasi-Díaz, Kwok Pui-lan, Judith Plaskow, Mary E. Hunt, Emilie M. Townes, and Ellen M. Umansky, "Appropriation and Reciprocity in Womanist/Mujerista/Feminist Work," *Journal of Feminist Studies in Religion* 8 (Fall 1992): 91–122. See also the essays on difference and womanist method in vol. 9 of the same journal (single issue), also from the 1991 meeting of the American Academy of Religion.

10. "Until the shift from women's experience to women's faith practices in discursive totalities is accomplished, feminist theology presents its own ruminations as a form of realist representation, not necessarily emancipatory discourse" (Mary

McClintock Fulkerson, *Changing the Subject: Women's Discourses and Feminist Theology* [Minneapolis: Fortress Press, 1994], 115). For a critical analysis of one emancipatory discourse see R. Marie Griffith, *God's Daughters: Evangelical Women and the Power of Submission* (Berkeley: University of California Press, 1997).

11. Judith Butler, *Bodies That Matter: On the Discursive Limits of "Sex"* (New York and London: Routledge, 1993), 10.

12. Butler, *Bodies That Matter*, 221–22.

13. Judith Butler, "Contingent Foundations: Feminism and the Question of 'Postmodernism,'" in *Feminist Contentions: A Philosophical Exchange*, ed. Linda Nicholson (New York: Routledge, 1995), 50–54. In the same volume see also Seyla Benhabib, "The Generalized and the Concrete Other," 80–81.

14. Butler, *Bodies That Matter*, 221, 93, 6. But although sex categories shift constantly, the social and political need to classify people by sex is constant. So if sex is a "permanent site of contest," Butler avers, it is still not a matter of utter "free play": "if sex is a fiction, it is one within whose necessities we live, without which life itself would be unthinkable" (6). Butler's unwillingness to imagine that the whole system of sex categorization might be dispensable seems odd in view of her campaign for destabilization of all classification schemes. It's not clear why human beings need the category "sex" at all.

15. The new combinations shock and fascinate because their rebellion against cultural images of men and women, male and female, is constructed from those same images. Otherwise, they would not be recognizable as rebellions against sex or gender constructs. Butler, *Bodies That Matter*, 133, 137.

16. This critique is indebted in a number of ways to Susan Frank Parsons, *Feminism and Christian Ethics*, New Studies in Christian Ethics (Cambridge: Cambridge University Press, 1996), 93–120.

17. Mary Daly, *Gyn/Ecology: The Metaethics of Radical Feminism* (Boston: Beacon Press, 1978), 155 (see all of chapter 5).

18. Martha C. Nussbaum, "Human Functioning and Social Justice: In Defense of Aristotelian Essentialism," *Political Theory* 20, no. 2 (May 1992): 203.

19. Farley, "Feminism and Universal Morality," 170.

20. Barbara Ehrenreich and Janet McIntosh, "The New Creationism: Biology under Attack," *The Nation* (9 June 1997): 15.

21. "The practical goals of feminist ethics, then, are the following: first, to articulate moral critiques of actions and practices that perpetuate women's subordination; second, to prescribe morally justifiable ways of resisting such actions and practices; and third, to envision morally desirable alternatives that will promote women's emancipation" (Alison M. Jaggar, "Feminist Ethics," in *The Encyclopedia of Ethics*, ed. Lawrence C. Becker and Charlotte B. Becker, vol. 1. [New York: Garland, 1992], 361).

22. Nussbaum, "Human Functioning," 212.

23. Nancy Fraser, "False Antitheses: A Response to Seyla Benhabib and Judith Butler," in *Feminist Contentions: A Philosophical Exchange*, ed. Linda Nicholson (New York: Routledge, 1995), 71.

24. Farley, "Feminism and Universal Morality," 170–71.

25. Janet McIntosh, letter to the editor, *Atlantic Monthly* 281, no. 6 (June 1998): 8–9.

26. See Ehrenreich and McIntosh, "The New Creationism," 15; and Farley, "Feminism and Universal Morality," 170–71.

27. For a particularly useful expansion of this claim, see Parsons, *Feminism*.

28. See Parsons, *Feminism*, 14–65. Some early socialist feminists betrayed liberal roots: substituting technological for experimental reasoning, they proposed not transcending biological difference but eradicating it. See for example Firestone, *Dialectic of Sex*, 10.

29. On the liberal view, facts are objective descriptions of a natural world that, if no longer seen as completely predictable and mechanical, is not a source of meaning. Judith Webb Kay, "Human Nature and the Natural Law Tradition," Ph.D. diss., Graduate Theological Union, 1988, 104.

30. Susan F. Parsons, "The Intersection of Feminism and Theological Ethics: A Philosophical Approach," *Modern Theology* 4 (April 1988): 252–53.

31. Ibid., 254; Kay, "Human Nature," 114. Kay (37–43) points out that Enlightenment thinkers, unlike most feminists, also developed emotivist moral theories.

32. Kay, "Human Nature," 115. On this view any sort of ethical naturalism substitutes the deterministic laws of the physical natural order for free and self-determining reason (ibid., 111).

33. Ethan Watters, "Ward Connerly Won the Battle—Now He's Facing the War," *Mother Jones* 22, no. 6 (November/December 1997): 73.

34. *Washington v. Glucksberg*, 1997.

35. See Parsons, *Feminism*, 121–74.

36. Lisa Sowle Cahill, *Sex, Gender, and Christian Ethics*, New Studies in Christian Ethics (Cambridge: Cambridge University Press, 1996), 67.

37. Parsons, *Feminism*, 160–61, and "Intersection," 261–63; see also Lisa Sowle Cahill, "Feminist Ethics," *Theological Studies* 51 (1990): 53.

38. For an argument for separatism, see Sarah Lucia Hoagland, *Lesbian Ethics: Toward New Value* (Palo Alto: Institute of Lesbian Studies, 1988), 1–23. Rosemary Radford Ruether has argued for temporary or partial separation but against male-female dualism; see *Women-Church: Theology and Practice of Feminist Liturgical Communities* (San Francisco: Harper and Row, 1985); and idem, *Gaia and God: An Ecofeminist Theology of Earth Healing* (San Francisco: Harper and Row, 1992). See also Paul Lauritzen, "A Feminist Ethic and the New Romanticism—Mothering as a Model of Moral Relations," *Hypatia* 4 (Summer 1989): 41.

39. John P. Reeder, Jr., "Foundations without Foundationalism," in *Prospects for a Common Morality*, ed. Outka and Reeder, 191–214; Robert Merrihew Adams, "Religious Ethics in a Pluralistic Society," in *Prospects*, ed. Outka and Reeder, 93–113.

40. See also Albert R. Jonsen and Stephen Toulmin, *The Abuse of Casuistry: A History of Moral Reasoning* (Berkeley: University of California Press, 1988).

41. Feminist criticism of communitarianism reflects this concern: if a community's moral reflection and practice are subject only to internal criticism, no force pulls it into critical or constructive relationship with other communities; it is morally self-sufficient, impervious to criticism or engagement from without.

42. See Nussbaum, "Human Functioning"; idem, "Non-Relative Virtues: An Aristotelian Approach," *Midwest Studies in Philosophy*, vol. 13: *Ethical Theory: Character and Virtue*, ed. Peter A. French, Theodore E. Uehling, Jr., and Howard K. Wettstein (Notre Dame: University of Notre Dame Press, 1988), 32–53.

43. For the examples below, see Eleanor Commo McLaughlin's still-worthy essay "Equality of Souls, Inequality of Sexes: Woman in Medieval Theology," in *Religion and Sexism: Images of Women in the Jewish and Christian Traditions*, ed. Rosemary

Radford Ruether, 213–66 (New York: Simon and Schuster, 1974), 215–18; and Kari Elisabeth Børreson, *Subordination and Equivalence: The Nature and Rôle of Women in Augustine and Thomas Aquinas*, trans. Charles H. Talbot (Washington, DC: University Press of America, 1981), especially 147–96.

44. See Cristina L. H. Traina, "Oh, Susanna: The New Absolutism and Natural Law," *Journal of the American Academy of Religion* 65 (1997); see Saint Thomas Aquinas, *Summa Theologiae*, 5 vols., trans. the Fathers of the English Dominican Province (n.p.: Benziger Brothers, 1948; reprint, Westminster, MD: Christian Classics, 1981), 375; see, II-II, q. 154, a. 7.

45. *ST* I 92.3.

46. Jean Porter, "At the Limits of Liberalism: Thomas Aquinas and the Prospects for a Catholic Feminism," *Theology Digest* 41 (Winter 1994): 316.

47. See Jean Porter, *The Recovery of Virtue: The Relevance of Aquinas for Christian Ethics* (Louisville: Westminster/John Knox Press, 1990), and Cahill, *Sex, Gender*.

48. See Henry B. Veatch, *Swimming against the Current in Contemporary Philosophy*, Studies in Philosophy and the History of Philosophy (Washington, DC: Catholic University of America Press, 1990), 265, quoted in Anthony Lisska, *Aquinas's Theory of Natural Law: An Analytic Reconstruction* (Oxford: Clarendon Press, 1996), 182; see also Lisska, *Aquinas's Theory*, 224.

49. Kantian thinkers still hold that a moral demand is a universal demand. But it is not clear that they have moved beyond modernism. For instance, few postmodernist authors would agree with Christine Korsgaard that value is something we project or create *but* that we see matter as "really real" (Christine M. Korsgaard, "Excellence and Obligation," in *The Sources of Normativity*, ed. by Onora O'Neill, with responses by G. A. Cohen, Raymond Geuss, Thomas Nagel, and Bernard Williams [Cambridge: Cambridge University Press, 1996], 1–5).

50. See Henry Davis, S.J., *Moral and Pastoral Theology*, vol. 1, *Human Acts, Law, Sin, Virtue*, 5th ed., Heythrop Series, no. 2 (New York: Sheed and Ward, 1946), 1. Moral theology assumes, even if it does not directly employ in its arguments, revelation, tradition, and the supernatural, and "ethics considers what is right or wrong, in so far as human reason unaided by Revelation can judge." On the other hand, Sarah Lucia Hoagland's eschewal of classical philosophical categories does not prevent her from critically applying the experience of a definable, secular community to traditional philosophical ethics. Common experience provides the critical standard. See Hoagland, *Lesbian Ethics*, xiii.

51. Quoted material from Richard Dawkins and Phoebe Ellsworth, respectively, quoted without citation in Ehrenreich and McIntosh, "New Creationism," 15.

52. David O. Brink, *Moral Realism and the Foundations of Ethics*, Cambridge Studies in Philosophy (Cambridge: Cambridge University Press, 1989), 145–46.

53. See Morton White, *What Is and What Ought to Be Done: An Essay on Ethics and Epistemology* (New York: Oxford University Press, 1981); and Jeffrey Stout, *Ethics after Babel: The Languages of Morals and Their Discontents* (Boston: Beacon Press, 1988), 46ff. The virtue theories of Alasdair MacIntyre and Edmund Pincoffs are also in part efforts to find a basis for ethics which transcends the is/ought distinction as it was originally defined. See Alasdair MacIntyre, *After Virtue: A Study in Moral Theory*, 2nd ed. (Notre Dame: Notre Dame University Press, 1984); and Edmund L. Pincoffs, *Quandaries and Virtues: Against Reductivism in Ethics* (Lawrence, KS: University Press of Kansas, 1986).

54. Reeder, "Foundations without Foundationalism," 199.

55. Brink, *Moral Realism,* 9.

56. Parsons, "Intersection," 258–62; Anthony Battaglia, *Toward a Reformulation of Natural Law,* with a Foreword by James P. Mackey (New York: Seabury Press, 1981), 133–34; Basil Mitchell, *Morality: Religious and Secular: The Dilemma of the Traditional Conscience* (Oxford: Clarendon Press, 1980), 118–20; and Roger Sperry, "Changed Concepts of Brain and Consciousness: Some Value Implications," *Perkins Journal of Theology* 36 (Summer 1983): 22. See also Rosemary Radford Ruether on Freud, *New Woman/New Earth: Sexist Ideologies and Human Liberation* (New York: Seabury Press, 1975), 148–49. On descriptivism and the criterion of flourishing see William Donald Hudson, *Modern Moral Philosophy* (New York: Doubleday and Company, 1970), 318–29.

57. The definition comes from Brink, *Moral Realism,* 6–7.

58. See Korsgaard, *Sources,* 28–48.

59. Korsgaard, *The Sources of Normativity,* chapter 4.

60. Cahill, *Sex, Gender,* 102–7.

61. Reeder, "Foundations"; Adams, "Religious Ethics."

62. See Reeder, "Foundations," 205; see also Jonsen and Toulmin, *The Abuse of Casuistry.*

63. Mitchell, *Morality,* 97–98, 118–20. Mitchell uses variously the terms "metaphysical" and "religious description," "vision of life," etc.; here I have substituted "worldview."

64. See also MacIntyre, *After Virtue,* 1–5. Glenn Tinder explores the same question in a different context in "Can We Be Good without God? On the Political Meaning of Christianity," *The Atlantic* (December 1989): 69–85.

65. Mitchell, *Morality,* 119.

66. Ibid., 105. See also Hudson, *Modern Moral Philosophy,* chapter 6.

67. Mitchell, *Morality,* 151ff. On the "always already interpreted" quality of experience, see for instance Hans-Georg Gadamer, *Truth and Method,* 2nd ed. (New York: Crossroad, 1982), especially 345–66.

68. Chapter 7 touches on an analogous approach to these issues, liberation theology. See also Susan A. Ross, *Extravagant Affections: A Feminist Sacramental Theology* (New York: Continuum, 1998).

1

The Shape of Feminist Moral Discourse

When my husband and I married, we owned a nearly-antique, air-cooled Volkswagen Fastback that we tuned ourselves—every three thousand miles. This involved sliding under the car with feeler gauges to adjust the valves; changing spark plugs; filing or replacing the ignition points; and setting the points to precisely the right sparking distance while we held the crankcase pulley at top dead center with the special wrench my husband had designed just for that purpose. It was a set of skills I was especially proud of perfecting.

Enamored of the perspicuity of VW engineering, we eventually moved up to a used Jetta—and utter bewilderment. It was hard to believe two cars could be so different. The Jetta had no points; its valves virtually never needed adjustment; its timing was controlled by a computer in a tiny black box; and it had this baffling thing called a radiator. Our feeler gauges were nearly archaic, and our custom-made wrench was useless. It seemed that almost nothing we knew about caring for our old car's engine applied to this one. Nor were we very quick to understand what it did need, a fact we soon proved by cracking the engine block during a misguided attempt to flush a warm radiator with cold water!

Not all attempts to apply old wisdom to new situations—or to substitute, as we did, finger-crossing for knowledge—are quite so thoroughly destructive. Nor, unfortunately, are they so immediately and catastrophically costly to their practitioners. If they were, we might learn humility and caution more quickly. But generally the ill effects of ethicists' ignorance are felt soonest and most strongly by others who are distant, whose complaints we have learned to ignore, and whose precise differences from ourselves we have failed to recognize. This is the starting point of feminist ethics: traditional academic ethics of almost any kind, designed with the good of its predominantly male practitioners in mind, yields suffering for women (and often other men) whose good it does not truly consider and who have no say in its formulation. Accomplishing women's flourishing, then, is not just a matter of ethicists' applying existing methods more meticulously, or even of a new round of casuistic reflection. Moral reflection with women's welfare at the center requires new practitioners bearing new tools, logics, and skills. Our task is to begin to describe—in more detail than in the introduction—the concrete shape of these requirements. Articulating them with an eye to criticism of natural law must wait until after the description of historical natural law in chapters 2 and 3. Here we deal with feminism on its own terms: what are the unique and collective insights of the schools of feminist ethics? Most important, what are the criteria of a responsible moral epistemology?

Broadly speaking, *feminism* is a practical and intellectual dedication to the discovery and uprooting of ideologies, relationships, and institutions that thwart women's flourishing and to the creation of new ideologies, relationships, and institutions that promote it. But in academia this is the age of *feminisms*, not all of which even go by that name. [1] So in order to make any responsible claims about feminism in general, we must demonstrate that these feminisms intersect significantly, contribute mutually corrective cautions, or both. What we are seeking is not a foundationalist definition of universal feminism but a flexible and broadly applicable set of criteria—drawn from the various quarters of feminist conversation—to guide feminist reflection and action generally. This discussion of schools of feminism is a prerequisite to careful description of women's flourishing, which receives more extensive treatment below and in chapter 4.

ONE VIEW OF THE FEMINIST LANDSCAPE

As we have seen, feminists tend to divide their allegiances between naturalism and transformative rationalism. [2] Some liberal feminists, aware that bodily difference is a common justification for men's oppression of women, have chosen to deny any sort of moral authority to bodily nature and instead seek common ground with men in neutral, universal, transcendent reason. Other separatist, romantic, or naturalist feminists have done the opposite, seeking to raise esteem for women's unique, embodied experience. They have embraced nature, extracting new norms, methods of reflection, and procedures for discourse explicitly from women's bodies and the experiences they afford and setting them up as correctives or supplements to an artificially abstract reason.

But the intrafeminist debate has a third focus to which we must attend especially carefully because, as we will see, it has no developed analogue in natural law. Social constructionists argue that if reason or nature is a refuge, it is one we have created, and it is therefore not fixed. [3] Because cultures manufacture and manipulate descriptions of "unchangeable" nature and "universal" reason at whim, to conform nature to reason or vice versa is simply to mold one derivative, suspect standard to another. Real transformation entails new, liberative visions of both. [4] Rather than assuming that social constructionism supersedes the other two approaches, however, we need to respect the coherence of all three with our initial definition of feminism and discover what tools they provide, together and separately, for feminist moral reflection. Susan Parsons's version of this typology is an important guide here because, despite its nearly exclusive focus on white feminist academic ethics, it attends carefully to the connections between feminist positions and the rest of the Western intellectual tradition and illuminates questions of method in a way that should be useful to all feminist moral reflection. [5]

LIBERAL FEMINISM.   Susan Parsons and Judith Webb Kay, among others, have both drawn careful connections between liberal feminism and classical liberalism. The political and moral equality of persons lies at the center of each, founded on equally basic convictions about their common humanity and dignity. [6] Much of Beverly Wildung Harrison's work illustrates this position. [7] Independent of their position in society, individuals are inherently autonomous, worthy of respect, and possessed of rights. Although nature for liberal feminists may be a bit more orderly and understandable than the raw, wild, disorganized physical matter their Enlightenment predecessors discerned, they still draw a sharp distinction between it and reason: the abstract, universal, scientific ordering principle of truly human culture. But they are also aware that the criterion of common humanity that grounds liberal notions of human rights, the capacity for abstract reason, has sidelined women, whom it often dismisses as deficient abstract reasoners. So rather than lumping characteristics of gender (social roles, modes of thinking, etc.) with raw, immutable differences in biological sex, liberal feminists argue that prevailing gender characteristics are simply the historical creations of an imperfectly enlightened culture; gender differences that seem "natural" can therefore be eliminated through the cultural processes of reeducation and socialization. [8] Thus liberal feminism uses the public slogans of reason, rights, and common humanity to argue for reforms in gender relations.

Liberal feminist moral philosophy adopts the liberal tradition's peculiar understandings of fact and nature and their disjunction from both culture and value. On the liberal view facts are objective descriptions of a natural world that, if no longer seen as completely predictable and mechanical, is not a source of meaning. [9] Meaning belongs to culture, the sphere of creativity, reason, and dynamism. Human goods are not universally given but subjectively and individually chosen. The individual is the creator of value: "the essence of morality must consist in what is freely created or discovered by the moral agent in the process of reasoning itself." [10] The maximization of value is the maximization of individuals' freedom to choose among these subjectively generated goods. [11] On this view any sort of ethical naturalism violates both fact-value and nature-culture distinctions, substituting the deterministic laws of the physical natural order for free and self-determining reason. [12]

Liberal feminism has undeniable advantages. Both its stress on equality grounded in common, rational humanity and its esteem for autonomous, responsible individuals yield powerful tools of social criticism. Individuals are existentially free and self-determining and possess, as the American Declaration of Independence states, inalienable rights; thus women should "extricate themselves from webs of social interdependence" and "realize some degree of autonomy." [13] Universal reason is "a lever with which to prize open unfair practices and oppressive structures," [14] a transcendent ground that provides both hope and foundation for resolution of concrete conflicts. Liberalism proper's optimistic preference for reform over revolution or separatism encourages a pragmatic effort to work with familiar concepts and within the existing system. [15] Neither should its individualism or suspicion of passion and revolution be exaggerated, as Annette Baier points out in her well-known essay on Hume; sentiment, community, and change are not foreign to it. [16] Finally, liberal feminism tolerates neither determinism nor ossification of human institutions and behavior.

Yet despite liberalism's indispensable emphasis upon rights and individual dignity, the liberal bifurcation of value from fact undermines the liberal feminist project in several ways. First, it entails an uncritical confidence in human reason that is evident in its uncritical view of science. If scientific descriptions of nature are changeless and ahistorical, then scientific knowledge belongs not to culture but to nature and is therefore immune to the sort of reproach and correction that can be applied to cultural constructs. But a science arbitrarily protected from cultural forces is also both impervious and useless to feminist criticism. [17]

Second, the bifurcation of fact and value promotes a "thin" rather than a "thick" theory of the good; for if self-determination is the highest good, one can at best argue for women's freedom to pursue their chosen moral values, whatever they may be, despite gross inequities in the opportunity, education, and resources with which they begin. [18] Then feminists have few grounds on which to persuade human society that it has a moral obligation to pursue a rich, integral, common vision of women's good. Worse, embracing this belief eventually yields moral disability. For Baier, who regards Hume more highly than she does the liberal tradition generally associated with him, "liberal morality, if unsupplemented, may *unfit* people to be anything other than what its justifying theories suppose them to be, ones who have no interest in each other." [19]

Third, as Susan Parsons points out, the bifurcation overlooks the "dual logical force of language": "our knowledge of the world—how we describe it—is inherently associated with our understanding and acknowledgment of value—how we assess it." [20] Our descriptions of reality are filtered through our moral (and other) commitments.

Fourth, liberalism also ignores embodiment, disbelieving that the female body in particular might bring anything uniquely valuable to the human project of living well. A classic instance, Baier notes, is the liberal description of personhood: "to be a person is ... to spring forth from some fertile noumenal field of Ares fully formed and upright." [21] In Baier's view this is the fantasy of "the Y chromosome trying to disown itself," or perhaps more accurately, to disown its mother; for "it is navels too that are essential to such persons as we have any knowledge of," and "metaphysics, so far, has had little to say about navels." [22] In turn liberal feminism—like socialist feminism, its close cousin in this respect—can imply that women's biology is either insignificant or inferior to men's. [23]

Fifth, as Kay points out, liberal feminism erroneously assumes that creation of *external* conditions for moral autonomy is sufficient to undo women's oppression. Women continue to be victims of *internalized* oppression—the habituated short-circuiting of their powers of moral discernment and choice that results from previous social conditioning—even when they are freed from external constraints. [24] Liberal feminism has no systematic means of recognizing this sort of oppression because it has no means of passing moral judgment upon an apparently free choice; as long as it is objectively possible for a woman to become a bank manager, liberal feminism cannot claim that she is "oppressed" or "degraded" if she continues willingly in her minimum-wage cashier's job, for example. [25] Only a rich, teleological view of human being gives one the leverage to make a distinction between the "is" of human being and the "seems" of internalized oppression and to translate the former into moral criteria that can condemn and transform the latter. [26]

Finally, some strains of liberal feminism overemphasize individual self-determination and detachment by denigrating affectivity, overlooking inequities in the distribution of power, and idealizing impersonal and dispassionate expressions of love, [27] blind once again to the values women thought they had begun to recover for themselves.

NATURALIST FEMINISM. Against liberalism, naturalist feminism insists that nature is neither dangerously chaotic nor devoid of moral significance. Nature is within us as well as outside us, inescapably influencing our experiences and limiting our ends and actions. Yet the exegesis of this claim sends naturalist feminists off in two directions not fully distinguished by Parsons: biological and telic naturalism. Biological naturalism maps the functioning of bodies and societies (preferably purified of all cultural and especially technological interventions) onto moral norms, extrapolating moral commands from physical and social givens. Form leads to function, which leads to norm: because breasts produce milk, mothers should breast-feed their children. [28] In telic naturalism, however, the future is normative. Norms are drawn from a picture of human being or society not in its current imperfection but as it is intended to be. Perhaps, for instance, human ingenuity can devise modes of nutrition to replace breast-feeding, improving women's lives by permitting greater flexibility in infant care. Of course, everything depends upon how the normative picture is painted. Because one naturalism can bleed into the other—messages about women's future might be read from their present roles or capacities— the division between telic and biological naturalism is only a distinction, but it is a significant one.

In contrast to liberal feminism's focus upon men's and women's common rational transcendence of the body, all naturalist feminism fixes on bodily differences and the divergence in experience these can entail. Bodily differences are real and are normatively significant: women's natures are to be not transcended or replaced but celebrated and perfected. The "feminine virtues" that liberal feminism decries as the fabricated instruments of misogynist oppression—for example, affection and emotional perceptiveness, neither of which has an obvious place in liberal discussions of dispassionate justice—it revives as true virtues, though not always as specifically feminine ones. Yet—and here naturalist feminism departs from raw biological determinism—acknowledgment of fundamental differences between the sexes must not underwrite hierarchical ranking of one sex above the other.

Naturalist feminism also rejects the liberal bifurcation of fact and value. For liberals, the good is "thin" and individualistic: freedom to develop one's gifts and pursue one's dreams. Of course, liberals assume that well-used freedom has personal and social benefits, but these are happy side effects. Naturalism, on the other hand, produces a "thick" and interdependent good: visions of holistic flourishing and the potential to fulfill them cooperatively are embedded within every person and community. Human nature is to be not transcended but developed. According to biological naturalists, human nature holds moral trajectories, like seeds, within; for telic naturalists, nature in general anticipates a higher end, divine or otherwise. In either case, to read and fulfill this purpose is to flourish, and to disregard it is to perish. Concern over environmental destruction inspires even some liberal and socialist feminists, like Beverly Wildung Harrison, to a partial naturalism:

> What a feminist theological critique demands . . . is not a complete rejection of human historical agency but a profound recovery of a sense that we are, ourselves, species-dependent, in nature, culture, and history. As natural, historical, and cultural creators, we are profoundly dependent on each other and the rest of the natural/historical/cultural order. There is in fact a clear dialectic between our responsibility to nature and our capacity to become fresh, creative, and humane historical-cultural agents. If we do not recover a new respect for our deep interdependence as natural/historical and cultural beings, understanding our reciprocity with each other and nature as a dimension and condition of our freedom, all of us are doomed. [29]

In any case, humanness is not opposed to biological nature. The latter is, Baier says, "the source of strengths as well as weaknesses." [30]

From this perspective "biology determines destiny" in some sense; the fact of one's sex is, like all other givens, "inescapably relevant" to one's self-understanding and moral reflection. [31] Because naturalist feminism does not overturn or ignore sexual difference, it sees women as already worthy moral subjects who deserve respect precisely as whole, embodied persons, not just as rational minds. But gender distinctions are not absolute, for infinitely more unites the sexes than divides them. So naturalist feminism holds out hope, if not for universal, transcendent norms, at least for a concrete, cross-cultural "natural basis for moral behaviour. . . . linked with embodiment." [32] In general, naturalism unites what liberalism divides: "moral epistemology" is a matter not of transcending illumination but of "a deepening awareness of what is already the case"; moral discernment thus involves not rising above the pedestrian but discerning the ends embedded in or anticipated by ordinary existence; and the person is not an isolated consciousness but "a unity of mind, body, and spirit," deeply and intimately connected to a community. [33] This rich setting proffers an equally rich and textured vision of the good.

Equally important, naturalism accounts morally for the fact that, despite "fantasies of freedom from our own actual history" that underwrite our apparent transcendence or construction of nature, knowledge is real and freedom has limits. [34] As Lorraine Code argues in a slightly different context,

People need to be able to explain the world and to explain their circumstances as part of it; hence they need to be able to assume its "reality" in some minimal sense. The fact of the world's intractability to intervention and wishful thinking is the strongest evidence of its independence from human knowers. Earthquakes, trees, disease, attitudes, and social arrangements are *there*, requiring different kinds of reaction and (sometimes) intervention. . . . A reconstructed epistemological project has to retain an empirical-realist core that can negotiate the fixities and less stable constructs of the physical-social world, while refusing to endorse the objectivism of the positivist legacy or the subjectivism of radical relativism. [35]

Liberalism either professes to transcend these "fixities" and "intractables" or merely ignores them; social constructionism denies their independent existence; naturalism alone acknowledges their moral import, even if sometimes only by meekly accepting them.

Here lie both naturalism's strength and its chronic methodological weakness: everything depends upon how one defines the human end. That is not to say that all ends cohere equally well with human fixities, or that no relative distinctions can be made between competing accounts of the human good. It is to say—and we will return to this in our discussion of epistemology— that human fixities do not point clearly and inexorably toward a single, richly described end. As we have noted, biological naturalism has often credibly combined a hierarchical ontological dualism with a deterministic, "crude authoritarian realism" that both violates women and eschews nuanced moral philosophical reflection. [36] It can also justify permanent feminist separatism [37] or a theory of separate-but-equal complementarity, as (perhaps trivially) in the Total Woman movement and more seriously in the writings of Pope John Paul II. [38] Naturalism can avoid these pitfalls only through a strong, clear, comprehensive articulation of the human telos informed by a healthy dose of liberalism's equal regard for individuals.

Naturalism's pedigree raises related cautions. Its traditional romantic worship of embodiment is often flatly anti-intellectual. Supported by Enlightenment assumptions about the perspicuity of natural processes and the reproducibility of scientific observation, naturalism has assumed that particular moral insights hold everywhere and always, independent of the circumstances of their origins. Thus it can be prematurely universalistic, assuming that nature's structure, methodological significance, and concrete moral dictates are identical everywhere and that local culture (ideally developed by natural communities in particular settings) contributes no flavors strong enough to upset the savor of the whole dish. It also risks naive antihistoricism: all of nature is equally permanent, intractable, and morally normative; human activity occurs within nature's existing, permanent limits without altering nature itself. Naturalism's focus on bodily differences encourages it either to focus on sexual oppression at the expense of race and class oppression or to develop twisted "natural" justifications for the latter. One important side effect of this move is the flattening of the landscape of women's discourse; deep differences among women become insignificant. [39]

SOCIAL CONSTRUCTIONISM.   Liberals and naturalists presuppose a stable anthropology: they ask whether there are basic, perduring differences between men and women and whether, if there are, these differences ought to be emphasized, accommodated, or overcome. But social constructionists object that men, women, humanity, nature, and anything else that liberalism or naturalism counts as basic are not independently existing essences but categories that human beings have created. It is not just that any description is an interpretation, a "take" on a real object; rather, the speaker constructs the object in the act of naming it or—in the case of sexual identity—constructs her sex in the act of performing it. [40] Nature is a human creation. But, even more radically, so is the speaker: an argument that begins "nature tells us. . . ." informs us not about the identities and structures of existents but about the situation, interests, and power of the speaker. Subjects—speakers—and their outlooks are constituted by the intersection of their social identities (class, race, gender, etc.), by dynamic external connections rather than by a stable internal core.

Social constructionism is not a unified school but a claim common to a number of philosophical approaches—poststructuralism, critical theory, deconstructionism, and all views bearing the postmodern moniker—that struggle with questions of meaning and justice in a world they believe is bereft of changeless essences or moral norms. [41] These "essences" and "absolutes," like everything else, are socially generated, exposed as systems of names and explanations the powerful invent in order to protect social arrangements that favor them. [42] When the authority of these ideas is destroyed, their injustice shows clearly. So the purpose of destabilizing subjects and norms is an ethical one: to pull the rug out from under regnant ways of thinking in order to overturn the oppressive structures that they were designed to justify.

Unlike liberalism social constructionism unites fact and value, but unlike naturalism—in which values often reduce to facts—facts merely articulate values: any "is" is simply a mask for an "ought" someone wants to preserve. Even more radically, speakers—more accurately, powerful communities of speakers—manufacture both facts *and* values to their own specifications: "What one should do may be derived from *a social understanding* of who one is."[43] Because the "is" of social constructionism is unstable, the "ought" is also. Values have no "transcendent source," no ultimate referent; they are simply expressions of the tasks and roles generated by social institutions.[44]

Thus values themselves require evaluation, for they are only as liberating and trustworthy as the social institutions that generate them. Social constructionism demands that we examine critically not only obviously misogynist values—the premium on female virginity, for instance—but also more widely accepted ideals like industry, self-reliance, and thriftiness, which are virtues particularly in small-government, free-market capitalism. This is the most radical enterprise possible because it is not merely a matter of criticizing one system with an eye to its replacement by another; it entails giving up altogether on systems and the "grand narratives" that justify them. Social constructionism bets that a variety of (what we now think of as) marginal critical voices will produce more freedom and justice than a single, organized, complacent, artificially unified system. That is not to say all social constructionist feminists eschew a search for consensus; Seyla Benhabib, for instance, has no argument with commonly held norms and traditions as long as they are revisable and as long as their development is genuinely utopian, dialogical, and participatory.[45] But, like Reeder's and Adams's, this is a foundationless consensus.

The great contribution of social constructionism is its incessant investigation of the political and systematic interests behind statements of fact and value. Social constructionism aims to criticize without creating a new orthodoxy. By shaking off accustomed visions of ourselves and the world, it suggests, we may finally cease having to confront the same old problems in the same old formulations. There can be no transcendent sacred cows—no ideas exempt from investigation—because authority is culturally and collectively bestowed, not inherent. Traditional approaches to feminism, too, are suspect, for—as noted above—both liberal and naturalist celebration of women's dignity can disguise oppressive patterns of relationship and artificially simplistic anthropologies. Suspicious of all concentrations of power, social constructionist feminism accommodates variation along infinite axes, producing a loose, plural, critical anthropology.[46]

The difficulty for ethics is that social constructionism harbors a debilitating skepticism. It turns its deconstructive gaze equally in every direction. It can more easily identify a community's hidden interests than judge whether they are in any sense more just than those of another. This moral paralysis is dangerous because an unmodified social constructionism can quite easily become a new grand scheme, fragmenting cultures and identities so thoroughly that terms like "rights" or "goods" have little meaning. For race, gender, class, and other variables multiply descriptions of the human rapidly enough to reduce our power to glean basic moral claims from anthropology. [47] Therefore social constructionism sits uncomfortably with the feminist commitment to establish a new social order in which individual women will flourish. On the verge of tasting the good life, women suddenly discover that the definition of that life has changed, that their precise share in it depends upon unmanageably various factors, that there are no universal subsistence standards to which they are entitled, that the category "woman" no longer exists. [48] Feminists can be forgiven for wondering whether the deconstruction of women is yet another ill-disguised detour away from participation in the social good.

Judith Butler is on one hand quick to correct this impression: categories like "woman" must be deconstructed not because they are rhetorically obsolete but in order to remind us that "womanhood" is not definable once-for-all, that any permanent definition of "woman" would be exclusive and oppressive. [49] To claim that "woman" is a political construct is simply to remind ourselves to ask continually what ideological assumptions it binds up and whom it excludes. [50] Sex is a "permanent site of contest," but it is not something about which we have utter "free play"; "if sex is a fiction, it is one within whose necessities we live, without which life itself would be unthinkable." [51]

Yet on the other hand, in *Bodies That Matter,* sex categories become so fluid and amorphous that they seem drained of all rhetorical or political power, and the "necessity" to which Butler points seems itself to fade into a cultural construct as arbitrary and dispensable as "race" or "class." The problem is that if we swing too far toward the belief that we construct "woman" and "man," we tend to ignore the irreducible bodily differences that are of such utter significance to women's basic human welfare. Bodies are invented in the sense of being "seen-as," being judged good or bad, but they are not *wholly* constructed. Women make moral demands that derive directly from their irreducible bodily existence as women. Of course we must not then become biological determinists, limiting women to the tasks of which male bodies are incapable. That most women *can* bear children does not imply that they *ought* or that this capacity defines or exhausts their identity. It does imply that now and in any conceivable future their flourishing depends upon certain particular protections and benefits that do not apply to men. In short, bodily sex may be inherently *insufficient* to define womanhood, but that does not mean that bodily sex is not a *necessary* element of it. Any adequate anthropology must take account of this fact. [52]

Two further potential anthropological problems arise from social constructionism's heavy dependence on language and performance. A thing is created, comes into existence, when it is named or acted out; hence Hoagland's refusal to use the word "woman" in any but a pejorative sense: it defines a category of people by the oppression and exclusion they both suffer and inflict. [53] The power to name or create a role is the power to control. Thence comes social constructionist feminism's insistence that we respect or even privilege the language of those who have been among the named rather than the namers. But a focus on language also raises issues parallel to those troubling liberalism's focus on reason: it intimates that those who have, if not the power, the intellectual capacity to name are more fully human and so raises questions about the moral subjectivity and rights of children and the infirm. In addition, its alternative to a single "divine" law with insidious partisan interests is—if ideally inclusive of many perspectives—still a highly anthropocentric standard: the world is what it means to us. It recognizes neither the nonhuman cosmic, geological, and biological processes that exist independently of our classification of them nor the strict limits they set on credible performance and language.

Social constructionism is vulnerable in other ways as well. It can too easily underwrite unjust differences in treatment. In addition, individuals become transparent for their factions, and these in turn fade into the competition for air time in the dominant public discourse. This disappearance of the individual—her determination by the culture—makes it difficult to hold particular persons responsible, as liberalism and some naturalisms do, for love or care. [54] With the loss of realism goes "loss of any fixed base from which to engage in moral assessment" [55] like minimal standards of justice or visions of flourishing. [56] Interior measures are ultimately of little help either, for social constructionism understands the influence of the subject's choices of values and ends upon her analysis and description of the real, but it does not tell us what values and ends she is right to prefer. Without basic standards or values, it is difficult to imagine what liberation could mean: from and for what are women to be freed? How can we even recognize or condemn their oppression? In short, although social constructionism grounds a healthy, much needed ethical critique, it cannot by itself produce an ethic.

Finally, like liberalism and naturalism, social constructionism remains largely an elitist, scholarly conversation. Unlike them, it depends systematically on contributions from all quarters. But because it yields neither immutable moral norms nor a stable nature, people outside academia may be uncomfortable with its rhetoric and criteria—as well as unlikely to be heard within the theoretically inclusive academic conversation.

COMMON GROUND.   What can we draw from this typology? The answer comes in two stages. First, the exercise of creating a typology masks significant areas of agreement; feminists concur explicitly on some central points and tacitly on others. Second, it would not be possible or desirable to create a single feminist ethic, even if all branches of feminism were equipped for or interested in such a task. But as Parsons has pointed out, the fact that all the positions suffer from blind spots hardly prevents each from contributing uniquely penetrating insights that correct weaknesses in the others. Rich, comprehensive feminist ethical discourse depends upon the contributions of all feminist perspectives.

The points of agreement across the categories are deceptively elementary. Each is committed to women's integral flourishing; to the conviction that it is possible to judge whether women are flourishing; to the judgment that the current state of affairs thwarts women's flourishing; to the identification of beliefs and institutions that create and justify this oppression; and to the transformation of these forces and systems. Even feminist deconstructionists must concur implicitly; there would be no point in revealing the oppressive gender biases in "neutral" codes if women's flourishing were completely irrelevant. They agree neither on the relative importance of the dimensions of women's flourishing, nor on the precise causes of women's oppression, nor on their remedies. But confidence that these exist and can be identified reliably in context runs across the categories. In the analysis of oppression, disagreements develop not over the sources of oppression—all concur that oppression combines psychological, social, and economic factors—but only over the relative magnitude of their influence.

The first important point of mutual correction is a critical and self-critical realism. It is impossible even to identify oppression without an understanding of injustice; it is impossible to define injustice without a clear sense of fairness and right; rights are senseless without descriptions of basic goals, capacities, and needs; and all of these take shape within the practical give-and-take of daily life. [57] Yet uncritical biological or even sociobiological naturalism is clearly an inadequate basis for feminist moral reflection. If one wants to glean nature's moral wisdom, one must begin either with a very clear vision of the human end or with rigorous methods for discerning it from the details of historical and contemporary human flourishing. In practice, feminist social constructionism and liberalism tacitly concur with naturalism: the goal of the feminist ethical project is an autonomous, integrated self in a just and interdependent community. Because this implicit goal runs counter to social constructionism's critical theoretical stance, feminist ethics cannot follow social constructionism to its logical conclusion. If women are to identify and resist the definitions that have oppressed them, they must adopt, implicitly or explicitly, some realist sense of their endowments and vision of their possibilities for flourishing. These endowments and possibilities are more varied than uncritical naturalism assumes, more concrete and earthly than liberalism intimates, but not, as social constructionism at times suggests, limitless—else there would be no standard by which to gauge oppression. [58] As John Reeder points out,

> While feminist thinkers, for example, would be the last to assert they have discovered an ahistorical essence, many do argue against one cultural construction of the self in favor of another; their moral protest is anchored in a revised view of our limitations and possibilities. . . . They make substantive proposals against the background of a revised view of moral capacities and limitations: we *can* be certain sorts of people if we want to be. [59]

Or, in the words of Susan Parsons, if we are involved in creating the real, "this is not the same as creating by our choice alone how we would like things to be." [60]

But neither will an uncritical feminist naturalism succeed. Social constructionism reminds us to be suspicious of the motives behind our own moral reasons [61] and to distinguish between the variously described boundaries within which human life will likely always move (for instance, the need for air, food, water, exercise, shelter, constructive social contact) and the institutions we create to provide for them (particular gender roles, political systems, and family structures). [62] Out of recognition for perspectivalism, postmodern realism must be self-critical as well; it must never draw lines in permanent ink.

Nature, in other words, is both given and made. [63] Human nature and human reason, however defined, are no longer opposed. Human nature *is* human being-in-culture, reason *is* embodied, contextual thinking, and so on. Neither is nonnegotiable or autonomous. That the meanings of the fixities are malleable means neither that the fixities do not perdure—that they will not be conditions of human life for the foreseeable future—nor that any universal or permanent description can be made of them. Feminism must include in its vision and methods strong, concrete claims about women's flourishing and their right to it and must be prepared to examine carefully the political assumptions and implications of all "natural" claims [64]—even and especially those that come from within its ranks. A viable feminism is transformative without being relativistic; it can steer between authoritarian foundationalism and utter moral disintegration. [65] Thus Parsons combines the languages of naturalism and deconstruction when she argues for a critical naturalism "constituting a hermeneutic of nature, rather than a law of nature." [66]

But feminist ethics' tacit reliance on dimensions of naturalism and social constructionism hardly excludes the contributions of liberalism, without which the ideas of a right to flourishing and a capacity to recognize it would have little theoretical support. Both individual moral agency and the vision that inspires social transformation rely upon the human ability to transcend the nearly overwhelming power of the dominant social vision. The open-ended feminist argument for women's right to flourish rests upon a claim about their existential dignity, also an Enlightenment inheritance. Only faith in common dignity and hope in future justice can sustain the painful and difficult feminist conversation about women's role in the oppression of other women. [67] And, as Rosemary Ruether has pointed out, the claim to rights and dignity can inspire radical transformation, especially if the right claimed is not simply participation in the existing social good but pursuit of an alternative vision. [68]

One further difficulty arises across the categories. All three intimate that women's genuine flourishing and moral agency wait on the deep transformation of social structures. This claim can be problematic on three fronts. First, it can limit moral agency, reducing the individual to a pawn of social forces and removing her capacity to challenge the social order. [69] Second—problematic from both Christian theological and hardnosed historical perspectives— it can imply that complete liberation from oppressive forces and behavior (in short, an end to sin) is humanly possible and is a reward to which we are entitled. Third, although it supplies crucial visions and criticisms, it sometimes provides little guidance for functioning with integrity in a still imperfect world. Here womanist ethics, left out of Parsons's typology, supplies some essential correctives. While fighting for justice, we need also to cultivate the virtues needed to survive and flourish under injustice [70] and within the limits not only of our bodies, our psyches, and the nonhuman, "natural" world but also of human events larger than ourselves—like wars and famines—whose oppressive meanings we can interpret but over whose existence we exercise little immediate control. [71] Finally, as womanists and *mujeristas* add, just as men must not define women's welfare and liberation, neither should more powerful, majority feminists define the welfare and liberation of all women. Feminism itself must be self-critical. [72]

The feminism within these feminisms, though still formal, has more shape than when we began. It is committed to women's flourishing; to a critical realism that operates within the limitations and goals of human histori- cal existence; to an historical, social, and mutually critical view of nature and reason; to the rights and dignity of individuals; to confident, prophetic transformation of and survival in an imperfect world; to inclusiveness, self-criticism, and humility.

KNOWING AND BEING

If feminism provided only formal criteria for ethics, it could easily be defused by challenges to its method or by pointed and limited descriptions of gender difference. The route to a powerful feminist critique lies through two further developments implied in the discussion to this point: a preferential option for women, with its accompanying epistemological claims, and a feminist anthropology.

Epistemology.   The inspiration for feminist epistemology is the simple question *why* and *how* women's voices challenge the methods and assumptions of the existing moral canon. Just as there is no univocal feminism, there is no single, authoritative feminist epistemology; but—as in feminism generally—common convictions arise out of the conversation. Feminist epistemology begins with the social constructionist claim that both knowledge and the procedures for gaining and verifying it are communally produced. Hence diverse communities produce different accounts of knowledge. Questions about what is known are really questions about knowing subjects: who knows? to what communities is she answerable? what standards shape her knowing? [73] Feminists note, for example, that in the post-Enlightenment West, many or most women's actual descriptions of human being, modes of moral reasoning, and views on the shape and purpose of the moral life radically contradict the accounts of male philosophers and scientists more typically analyzed by scholars. [74] Many scholarly methods, modeled on the experimental methods of the natural sciences, pretend to be universal, abstract, and deductive; they produce discrete truths, third-person packets of facts about the world and the human beings who inhabit it. In the Enlightenment tradition, sense knowledge is information received through any of the five senses; events of sense knowledge are analyzed discretely. "Women's ways of knowing," on the other hand, count emotions, relationships, skills, and embodied, particular, practical experience generally as legitimate and essential sources of knowledge; they produce a wisdom born of a whole history of particular experiences, a history that may bear close resemblance to other histories but that cannot easily be duplicated. [75] In contrast to Enlightenment sense knowledge, feminist embodied experience is the experience of the whole self in its social context; it is normally analyzed narratively. This sort of wisdom is, at least initially, first-person wisdom, difficult to articulate concisely and nearly impossible to pass on in a scientific article.

So far, this claim demonstrates only epistemological pluralism: most women have ways of reasoning and knowing that apparently intersect only slightly with those of male academic scientists and philosophers. But feminist epistemologists, occupying both realms, make a more radical claim: that Western scholarly epistemology is not only exclusive but also inadequate even to the needs of the scholarly community. The modern attempt to reduce sense knowledge to demonstrable, neutral propositions is simply bad and rather novel epistemology; [76] indeed, the now hackneyed distinction between male rationality and female sentimentality did not become a commonplace until the eighteenth century in the English-speaking world. [77] The deeper implication is that women's ways are *human* ways, inevitably practiced also by male academics but either dismissed as trivial or cloaked misleadingly in scientific and philosophical propositions. Thus claims for women's epistemological privilege are not properly simple essentialist claims about women's inherently superior moral insight. [78]

Thus in addition to gathering information about women's flourishing, feminist epistemology sees itself as correcting the still current, overweening authority of artificially stunted Enlightenment ideals of reason by carving out space for public remedial education in modes of moral reflection currently practiced and honored mainly by women. How and what have *women*—as a distinct epistemological community—known? Feminists consider it imperative to develop models *of* these "women's ways" of moral thought before attempting to create a more human model *for* anyone. [79] These tasks commission women's *epistemological privilege*: a methodological principle that grants first hearing to women's accounts of their own experience of themselves and the world around them. The point is not to remove authority from one set of knowers in order to bestow it on another—here authority remains concentrated—but to enlarge and transform "the structures of cognitive authority" in order to expand our vision of both knowers and knowledge in the interest of women's good. [80]

What sort of authority does epistemological privilege recognize in women's reflections? Certainly to encourage women to describe and trust their own moral reason presupposes confidence in the truth and worth of their ethical insights, in a certain basic wholeness and clarity of vision. Carol Gilligan, as we will see below, relied on such an assessment of women's moral integrity when she argued that a working, healthy construal of morality as caring is identifiable in *what many women actually say and do*. Yet at the same time feminism's social and historical critical edge demands that this confidence be qualified. A woman's account is not necessarily a feminist account. For not all experience is equal. Because, like sensation, experience and emotion are interpreted socially—we are *taught* what constitutes experience and which sorts of emotions are appropriate in what circumstances—the validity of the moral reflection based on them will depend upon the degree to which the social arrangements supporting and sustained by these learned patterns encourage women's flourishing. [81] On the one hand, women's ways of knowing may actually be women's ways of coping, distorted and stunted by their circumstances. Even in the best conditions women's apparently biologically determined "insider" knowledge develops in particular social and historical circumstances. On the other, especially as women move into the professional world—in effect, migrating from one epistemological community to another—their deference to its Enlightenment standards of knowing conforms their experience to the inadequate empirical mode. In theological language, we would say that the appeal to women's experience is susceptible to distortion by sin; women's being, speech, and action are not necessarily trustworthy simply because they are women's. [82]

Thus feminist epistemology requires a *critical* approach to women's experience. [83] The trick is to develop criteria that do not rely on a "neutral," "objective" foundationalism of the sort feminist epistemologists want to overturn. [84] Far and away the most important is a criterion that analyzes and evaluates the modes of reasoning that epistemological privilege puts on the table: a *preferential option for women*, a primary commitment to women's well-being. The preferential option examines knowledge claims against the background of social and institutional power: for instance, does the claim that women are naturally nurturing empower or limit women? But even more significantly the preferential option for women is a condition of knowledge itself. Authentic moral knowledge and modes of moral reasoning arise out of feminist praxis: activity in solidarity and friendship with women and in commitment to their genuine flourishing. Sliding toward theological language, we can say that knowledge of women's true good, here and now, and development of modes of moral reasoning that are consonant with it depend on authentic, active love for women.

Other conditions follow from the need to articulate these sharp distinctions in a way that respects cultural difference and historical change. These conditions hold, it is essential to notice, whether pluralism merely evolves from a variety of angles on the truth—like the case of the blind men who took isolated features of an elephant for the whole of it—or is a reflection of irreducible difference. [85] First, feminism cannot aspire to a new absolutism. The goal is not to seek "the truth of the one reality" [86] but to distinguish between "less or more partial and distorted accounts of nature and social life" in order to encourage "knowledge makers to be responsible." [87] Consensus positions are important candidates for moral truth, but they cannot be accepted without critical examination; for on the one hand a whole community can adhere to the same distorted view, and on the other differences in sex and in social location will always yield some genuine differences in experience. [88] Second, data radically underdetermine theory. For instance, "the sidewalk is wet" can support at least the conclusions "it rained," "lawn sprinklers were used recently," and "snow is melting," although only one is likely to be true. Nonetheless theory is not arbitrary; communities must be able to draw on their comprehensive critical experience to recognize "crackpots" and departures from their standards of good reasoning. [89] For example, barring new accounts of experience, "space aliens poured water on the sidewalk" does not stand up to critical examination. In the much weightier case of women's flourishing and its moral implications, the invitation of all viewpoints to the table does not imply that all or even most will in the end meet the standards of women's flourishing and its just promotion.

Finally, an adequate feminist epistemology must observe its own critical conditions: it must privilege the intellectual and moral practices of women, especially marginalized women, while being watchful for oppressive sources and uses of women's modes of knowing; and it must arise out of active commitment to women's genuine flourishing. It must be inclusive in procedure but critical in method. Women's ways of knowing are, of course, perfectly legitimate without the blessings of such a formal epistemology. But only under such a banner will they be able to challenge the hegemony of Enlightenment thought in the academy.

ANTHROPOLOGY.   Lurking behind all of these criteria is a common claim: that an epistemology that enfolds all dimensions of human experience is essential *to women's flourishing*. But this leads directly into the more comprehensive and difficult anthropological questions: How do we know this? What are the other criteria against which we can recognize not only crackpots—people who simply resist or misunderstand their communities' moral discourse—but also communal adherence to mistaken accounts of women's flourishing? Anthropologies that profess to describe the unchanging core of human nature have generally been used to oppress women, it is true. But the flaws lie in the anthropologies, not in the instinct that relies on them. We have already heard Martha Nussbaum's argument that public policy without "a normative account of the human being and human functioning" first and most grossly endangers the most vulnerable. [90] In other words, it is wiser to risk getting anthropology slightly wrong than to have no critical leverage at all. The key is to walk the line between tentativeness and absolutism: to develop descriptions credible and detailed enough to yield morally normative, prophetic claims yet flexible enough to accommodate a degree of cultural pluralism and historical change; and to do so inductively, developing and refining descriptions (as we have already begun to do here) in the midst of the cross-cultural struggle for concrete flourishing. [91] This does not mean, as Martha Nussbaum notes, that we are heading into undefined chaos; rather, we can expect—over millennia!— "progress toward greater correctness in our ethical conceptions." [92] The social constructionist contribution to this project is continual interrogation of apparently established claims of anthropology: do they still ring true, or are they baseless?

Like all feminist intellectual endeavors, feminist anthropology is critical and prescriptive rather than naïvely naturalist or merely phenomenological: it asks which aspects of persons-as-they-are indicators for persons-as-they-might-be, and which are pathological. For instance, her reflection on women's worldwide practical experience leads Cahill to insist that kinship—including sex and reproduction—is a permanent human good, or at least a permanent dimension of human life in which good must be pursued: for all of us come from others' bodies. [93] The feminist critical eye comes in here: is Cahill mistaking kinship's ancient *social and historical* limits on sexuality for *permanent* features of flourishing? Or has she discovered a truly universal, perduring dimension of human life? The distinction is both crucial and misleadingly simple. For feminist anthropology draws from both social constructionism and naturalism: the larger cultural context that forms and influences us is humanly constructed within certain limits. As Rebecca Chopp notes,

> the very condition of our action, our being in the world, is our shared environment and structure of life. Though naturalism has, of course, often been made universally absolute in terms of natural law, the themes of human experience in feminism forces [sic] its naturalism to be varied, open, and inclusive. Yet the very claim that the natural is open, plural, situated, and historical is a new ground for a *social* naturalism. A social naturalism connotes the complex web of evolution, biology, history, language, and so on. Yet this web of social factors is seen as "natural," that is, *given of all human flourishing.* [94]

We exist in the moral tension between these fixities and limits and our purposeful creativity, striving for fulfillment not only individually but communally. [95]

But these criteria are rather "thin," in the liberal sense—without content. What is needed is something more akin to Martha Nussbaum's "thick vague theory of the good," a strong but revisable account generated from within human practical experience of the goods that define human life. [96] Looking across cultures, what are the needs that must be fulfilled, the goods that must be pursued, the spheres in which human life must be lived, in order for life to continue humanely at all? Recent candidates from all three genres have included human life itself; bodily needs for food, shelter, mobility, and sexual fulfillment; knowledge; thought; perception; imagination; consciousness; existential freedom; reason; capacity for pain and pleasure; affiliation with others, including friendship and social and political organization; kinship, or family connections cemented by reproduction and marriage; interdependence; death; existential freedom; spirituality and religion; humor and play; early infant development; aesthetics; historicity; separateness from others; a sense of genuine connection with the rest of the natural world. [97] Authors reveal their biases in their disagreements over the precise formulation of the list. Cahill, for instance, takes Nussbaum to task for addressing sexuality as a need of the body rather than in the context of kinship and reproduction, and for leaving the life of the spirit to local specification. [98] As we will see below, natural law philosophers Germain Grisez and John Finnis put life at the top of their lists, creating a hierarchy in which biological existence trumps other goods; Nussbaum, on the other hand, tips her hand by privileging practical reason and social connection. [99] Yet, as Cahill's discussion reveals, these disagreements are less over the existence of basic human goods or even about their content than about the ways in which they should be grouped and ranked. [100] The degree of consensus of American and European scholars on content is clear in the deep overlaps among their categories. [101]

What territory do these overlaps cover? To begin with, human flourishing is integral. It encompasses bodily, relational, emotional, and spiritual health; existential, social, and political freedom; and intellectual and moral maturity. Each of these elements is irreducible to but interdependent with the others. Their conditions can be spun out: adequate nourishment, clothing, shelter, and medical care; safe working conditions; meaningful work; adequate income; relationships that are just, appropriately supportive and intimate, and either egalitarian or aimed at egalitarianism; opportunities for education, expression, participation, and creativity in religious community; access to education; full membership in a community of moral reflection and accountability; a general atmosphere of respect for all persons in all of these dimensions.

What is feminist about this? To begin with, feminists insist that women belong to the circle of persons for whom these goods are to be sought—a significant point, given that although that circle has grown since Aristotle's time, it still does not always include all men. Women's integral flourishing demands that these conditions be not just theoretically available to them but actively, communally promoted. And it especially requires that dimensions that concern women in particular receive emphasis: sexuality, procreation, women's health issues, and the like. Some of the goods that are currently most threatened in women, feminism articulates as "freedoms from": freedom from violence (physical, emotional, and political), in particular from all pressured or unwanted sexual contact; freedom from pressure to bear children; and freedom from oppression.

At least as urgent as expanding the circle is redefining the relationships among both people and the goods to be pursued. One essential, permanent feminist insight is that flourishing is interdependent. This is true first on a social scale: feminist criticisms reveal the invisible others and social institutions that support the illusion of individual integral flourishing, falsifying the Enlightenment ideal of the self-made, completely autonomous man. One person's flourishing depends on social support, both broad and narrow. In addition, each dimension of our flourishing influences others. A child cannot truly take advantage of education if she is ill or hungry; it is hard for a man to find time and energy for religious community if he must work twelve-hour days. All details of our moral lives are actually, and ideally consciously, lived out communally. We determine ourselves in community; we make moral choices in conversation with our community; we live daily life—raising children, for instance—in mutual dependence and responsibility with others. Flourishing is also a matter of the common good: the good of one individual depends upon the good of the other. Each is an end *in se*, but her genuine good both depends upon and promotes the good of each other person and of all collectively. So women are ends in themselves, and yet their individual and collective flourishing depends upon and promotes that of all people.

Feminism also takes a unique stand on the pursuit of these goods. Nussbaum and Cahill are important examples. Like utilitarians, they seek improvement in the overall lot of society. Unlike utilitarians, they argue that society is obligated to strive for the concrete, integral fulfillment of human goods in each person. That is to say, as Nussbaum does, that the point of social justice is to bring *every human being*, in her social context and with her special needs, across the threshold at which all the most basic, humane requirements of flourishing are met. [102] Like Finnis and Grisez, Nussbaum and Cahill hold that human goods are irreducible; nutritious food may help learning, but vegetables are no substitute for knowledge. Yet unlike Finnis and Grisez, who hold that because human goods are theoretically harmonious, they are morally incommensurable—no good may be directly harmed in pursuit of another—Nussbaum and Cahill hold that even in an ideal situation, human goods would often be incoherent and that in fact we may need consciously to sacrifice one to another *in concrete circumstances*. [103] The human project is not to discover and preserve their elusive natural harmony but to recognize the inevitable tensions among them and struggle continually to bring them into balance. [104] In addition, we must adhere to a systematic open-mindedness that considers no case closed but entertains new questions and unfamiliar points of view. [105] Not only do we increase and refine our knowledge of human goods, [106] but the connections among them and threats to them vary across history and culture, and we must be able to respond to these changes by illuminating their current connection and privileging the ones that are most vulnerable. Thus the categories under which we organize and describe flourishing must remain flexible. Systems like Finnis's and Grisez's, whose goods are permanently defined and rigidly arranged, react more awk-wardly to these sorts of changes.

But flexibility in feminist anthropology is not an end in itself. It is a means to the protection of goods. Nussbaum proposes that in cross-cultural conversation about human life in its social and political contexts, we can discover the basic outlines of the human good. Cahill adds that in the critical, pan-cultural, concrete pursuit of women's good, we will discover that most of what constitutes women's good is simply human good, adequately under-stood. But Cahill insists just as emphatically that women *as women* do have experiences and needs that differ from those of men *as men* and that to either ignore these or treat them as signs of women's natural subordination is a fatal error. Here we return to the very mundane example of the VWs. They were both cars: both carried passengers, had four wheels and a gearshift, had to be fueled, cooled, and adjusted. In retrospect, we have to admit that most of what we knew about the first *did* apply to the care and feeding of the second. And yet it was their tiny differences that preoccupied us and our ignorance of which destroyed one. And its not running could not legitimately have been interpreted as an alternative mode of flourishing; no one could have sensibly said, "Oh, well, most cars run, but Jettas are meant to sit motionless." Such a person really would not have understood what a car was.

By analogy, as Jean Porter points out, it is true both that women are mostly like men—women and men have basic human identities that precede and ground their gendered identities—and that in no social setting can they be exactly alike—in practice, differences in gender create morally significant differences in moral experiences and concrete needs. [107] Epistemologically and socially this difference may, as Cahill claims, be more opportunity than limit for each. But if it is not to be a limit, then the special requirements for flourishing that difference generates *for both women and men* must be understood and met. [108] Here we begin to enter the realm of ethics proper: my sex counts as a social justice claim when it generates needs that you must meet in order for me to cross the threshold of human flourishing. In other words, as Jean Porter suggests, a person's gender is one element of the context that any prudent moral decision should take into account. [109] Here we must begin with the gendered body, although we should not end there. Because only women bear children, if women are to flourish society needs to protect them from unwanted pregnancy and provide supports for motherhood. Society must also guarantee receipt of just funding for research and treatment of women's diseases (like breast cancer) and for comprehensive understanding of women's normal life stages (like menopause). [110] No legitimate definition or condition of women's flourishing articulates these protections as limits on women's status or sphere of activity.

Finally, it cannot be overemphasized that definitions of women's flourishing and understandings of its requirements must arise from the practical pursuit of women's good. Rarely do we need to dither over what the good is not. In the case of the car, to flourish was to run well, what thwarted flourishing became painfully obvious, and we acquired indelible practical knowledge: never put cold water in a warm radiator. Likewise, it is fairly easy to recognize health and deterioration for both women and men. They are measured in the same terms: integral bodily, social, political, spiritual, emotional, relational, and moral flourishing. And, as with the cars, it is possible, if slightly more difficult, to uncover the causes of suffering. [111] The question is not whether we can identify goods but whether it is right to force people to make choices among them. The criterion of justice is the possibility of integral flourishing: no one may ever be required to forego education in the interest of bodily health or moral freedom in favor of food. [112]

My decision to give Nussbaum's Aristotelian social democracy a significant place in these conclusions may seem disingenuous, given the goal of demonstrating a compatibility between the natural law—with its admittedly Aristotelian roots—and feminist ethical projects. Certainly we must not accept Nussbaum's reasoning unabridged; relentlessly critical methods and claims for individual and social ends play far weaker roles in her thought than do old-fashioned Enlightenment liberal arguments for autonomy and twentieth century arguments for equal opportunity. But her method still fulfills the demands of a feminist ethic better than the alternatives. She employs the critical standards of justice and integral, interdependent flourishing, enabling her to speak authoritatively across cultures; her method is practical, developing its descriptions of flourishing out of observation of the struggles of concrete human beings; and it is self-critical—allowing her to refine the content and priority of the list of basic human goods in response to broadened experience—and moderately flexible—open to the possibility that the content of "a good diet" or "a proper education" may vary, within limits, among cultures and across eras.

Our next task—complicated by natural law's development in a long tradition with many variations—is to demonstrate that the core of the natural law tradition contains similar emphases and strengths and that the genuine, significant counterforces in the tradition are unnecessary or even inauthentic. We will begin with Thomas Aquinas, whose *Summa Theologiae* is a foundational text for the subsequent natural law tradition. Readers not familiar with internal debates over the interpretation of Thomas may prefer to move directly to the concluding section of chapter 2.

NOTES

1. For example, on the misfit of white, academic, often racist feminism to African American women's desires to correct the much broader affronts to flourishing that they suffer, see Delores S. Williams, "The Color of Feminism: Or Speaking the Black Women's Tongue," in *Feminist Theological Ethics: A Reader*, ed. Lois K. Daly (Louisville, KY: Westminster/John Knox Press, 1994), 42–58.

2. See the essays in Marianne Hirsch and Evelyn Fox Keller, eds., *Conflicts in Feminism* (New York and London: Routledge, 1990), especially Ann Snitow, "A Gender Diary," 19.

3. What Susan Parsons says of nature proves true for reason as well: "we are involved in creating what is real" (Parsons, "Intersection," 264). See also Ruether, *Sexism and God-Talk*, 86: "It becomes evident that one can no longer make the dichotomy between nature and history. Nature itself is historical."

4. Some exploit this ambivalence by proposing it as a methodological center, rather than a liability, for feminist theory. See Sandra Harding, "The Instability of the Analytical Categories of Feminist Theory," *Signs: Journal of Women in Culture and Society* 11 (Summer 1986): 645–64.

5. Parsons, *Feminism*, 14–65; idem, "Intersection," 252–57; see also Kay, "Human Nature," passim. Every typology has its own bias. For other typologies of feminism see Jaggar, "Feminist Ethics," 361–65; Rosemarie Tong, *Feminist Thought: A Comprehensive Introduction* (Boulder and San Francisco: Westview Press, 1989); Ruether, *Sexism and God-Talk*, 41–44, 99–109, 216–34; John Charvet, *Feminism*, Modern Ideologies Series (London: J. M. Dent, 1982); Jean Bethke Elshtain, *Public Man, Private Woman: Women in Social and Political Thought* (Princeton, NJ: Princeton University

Press, 1981), 201–97; Kay, "Human Nature"; Farley, "Feminism and Universal Moral-
ity," 172–76; and Shulamith Firestone, "On American Feminism," in *Woman in Sexist
Society: Studies in Power and Powerlessness*, ed. Vivian Gornick and Barbara K. Moran
(New York: Basic Books, 1971), 495–501.

    6. See Parsons, "Intersection," 256–57.

    7. Beverly Wildung Harrison, *Making the Connections: Essays in Feminist Social
Ethics*, ed. Carol Robb (Boston: Beacon Press, 1985); see especially chapter 4. This
leveling impulse appears in Harrison's ethic of abortion, for example. Women's right
to moral autonomy depends upon women's absolute freedom to choose for or against
parenthood, as men in fact do.

    Harrison's position is by no means purely liberal feminism; her interest in the
reality-forming character of language (*Making the Connections*, 22–41) points up her
strong conviction that nature, language, and rationality are interdependent. In addition,
it is important to note that Harrison and other liberal feminists usually define "reason"
much more broadly than do either Lockean liberals or natural law traditionalists.
Finally, although Harrison declines to develop a normative anthropology or corresponding method, she describes her own method as "congenial" to some natural law
assumptions (ibid., 286, note 2; quoted in Kay, "Human Nature," 171). It is on the
basis of Harrison's preference for natural law's stress on rationality, rather than for
its emphasis on nature, and of her reasoning in *Our Right to Choose: Toward a New
Ethic of Abortion* (Boston: Beacon Press, 1983) that I characterize her as an order-of-
reason feminist.

    8. Kay, "Human Nature," 107–8; see also Harrison, *Making the Connections*,
90, 42–45, 224, 204.

    9. Kay, "Human Nature," 104.

    10. Parsons, "Intersection," 252–53. The language of discovery may be mislead-
ing; Parsons does not imply that liberalism uncovers independently existing values.

    11. Ibid., 254; Kay, "Human Nature," 114. Kay (37–43) points out that Enlight-
enment thinkers, unlike most feminists, also developed emotivist moral theories.

    12. See Kay, "Human Nature," 111.

    13. Mary C. Segers, "Feminism, Liberalism, and Catholicism," in *Feminist Ethics
and the Catholic Tradition*, Readings in Moral Theology No. 9, ed. Charles E. Curran,
Margaret A. Farley, and Richard A. McCormick, S.J. (New York: Paulist Press,
1996), 591.

    14. Parsons, *Feminism*, 64.

    15. Because dichotomies like "nature/culture," even if artificial, structure domi-
nant thought and practice, the tensions they describe must be kept in view (Harding,
"Instability," 662).

    16. Annette C. Baier, "Hume, the Reflective Women's Epistemologist?" in *Moral
Prejudices: Essays on Ethics* (Cambridge, MA: Harvard University Press, 1994), 76–94.

    17. Sandra Harding, *Whose Science? Whose Knowledge? Thinking from Women's
Lives* (Ithaca: Cornell University Press, 1991). My suspicion is that liberal *feminists*
believe that regnant scientific notions of "nature" and "fact" are not "value-free" but
actually are so irretrievably shaped by the *wrong* values—or are so susceptible to this
wrong shaping—that it is better to deny the connection between fact and value entirely.
There is no need to agree on an interpretation of nature if it is irrelevant to the
normative project.

    18. Kay, "Human Nature," 115; and Porter, "Limits," 318.

19. Baier, *Moral Prejudices*, 29.

20. Parsons, "Intersection," 258.

21. Baier, *Moral Prejudices*, 316.

22. Baier, *Moral Prejudices*, 323–24.

23. Some early socialist feminists betray liberal roots: substituting technological for experimental reasoning, they proposed not transcending biological difference but eradicating it. See for example Firestone, *The Dialectic of Sex*, 10.

24. Kay defines internalized oppression as "the behavioral and affective habits acquired from oppressive mistreatment in which oppressed peoples incorporate and accept the perspective of the oppressor toward themselves and their group." See Judith Webb Kay, "Getting Egypt out of the People: Aquinas's Contributions to Liberation," in *Aquinas and Empowerment: Classical Ethics for Ordinary Lives*, ed. G. Simon Harak, 1–46 (Washington, DC: Georgetown University Press, 1996); see also idem, "Human Nature," 76.

25. Ibid., 250–51. An uncoerced choice is still not necessarily free from the effects of internalized oppression, even when it is a choice for which one is morally responsible.

26. Ibid., 112, 115.

27. Parsons, *Feminism*, 42. See also Baier, *Moral Prejudices*, 28–30. Christina Hoff Sommers ignores this point; see Christina Hoff Sommers, *Who Stole Feminism: How Women Have Betrayed Women* (New York: Simon and Schuster, 1994).

28. Jules Law, "The Politics of Breastfeeding," *Signs: Journal of Women in Culture and Society*, forthcoming.

29. Harrison, *Making the Connections*, 230. See also Parsons, "Intersection," 264–65; Baier, *Moral Prejudices*, 326; and Rebecca Chopp, "Feminism's Theological Pragmatics: A Social Naturalism of Women's Experience," *Journal of Religion* 67 (April 1987): 239–56.

30. Baier, *Moral Prejudices*, 320.

31. Parsons, "Intersection," 260.

32. Parsons, *Feminism*, 128.

33. Ibid., 131–34.

34. Baier, *Moral Prejudices*, 323. See also Cynthia S. W. Crysdale, "Revisioning Natural Law: From the Classicist Paradigm to Emergent Probability," *Theological Studies* 56 (1995): 481.

35. Lorraine Code, "Taking Subjectivity into Account," in *Feminist Epistemologies*, ed. Linda Alcoff and Elizabeth Potter (New York: Routledge, 1993), 21. See also Sharon D. Welch, *A Feminist Ethic of Risk* (Minneapolis: Fortress, 1990), 159.

36. Parsons, *Feminism*, 160–61, and "Intersection," 261–63; see also Cahill, "Feminist Ethics," 53.

37. For an argument for separatism, see Hoagland, *Lesbian Ethics*, 1–23. Rosemary Radford Ruether has argued for temporary or partial separation but against male-female dualism; see Ruether, *Women-Church* and *Gaia and God*. See also Lauritzen, "A Feminist Ethic and the New Romanticism," 41.

38. Marabel Morgan, *The Total Woman* (Old Tappan, NJ: Revell, 1967). See for example Karol Wojtyla, *Love and Responsibility*, trans. H. T. Willetts (New York: Farrar, Straus, and Giroux, 1981), passim (first Polish ed., 1960); John Paul II, *Blessed Are the Pure of Heart: Catechesis on the Sermon on the Mount and the Writings of St. Paul* (Boston, MA: St. Paul Editions, 1983), 125–27.

39. See Williams, "The Color of Feminism," 45–46, for a discussion of criticisms of Mary Daly, Rosemary Ruether, and others; Toinette M. Eugene defends Ruether against such criticism in "Moral Values and Black Womanists," in *Feminist Ethics: A Reader*, ed. Lois Daly (Nashville: Westminster/John Knox, 1994), 168. See also Susan Brooks Thistlethwaite, *Sex, Race, and God: Christian Feminism in Black and White* (New York: Crossroad, 1989); and Fraser, "False Antitheses," 71.

40. See Judith Butler, *Gender Trouble: Feminism and the Subversion of Identity* (New York: Routledge, 1990), 140–42.

41. For a useful typology of postmodern philosophy, see Rita Marie Lester, "Ecofeminism in a Postmodern Landscape: The Body of God, Gaia, and the Cyborg," Ph.D. diss., Northwestern University/Garrett-Evangelical Theological Seminary, 1997.

42. See, e.g., Parsons, *Feminism*, 82.

43. Parsons, *Feminism*, 76; emphasis added.

44. Parsons, *Feminism*, 75.

45. Seyla Benhabib, "Autonomy, Modernity, and Community: Communitarianism and Critical Social Theory in Dialogue," in *Cultural-Political Interventions in the Unfinished Project of Enlightenment*, ed. Axel Honneth, Thomas McCarthy, Claus Offe, and Albrecht Wellmer (Cambridge: The MIT Press, 1992), 54–55; idem, "The Generalized and the Concrete Other: The Kohlberg-Gilligan Controversy and Feminist Theory," in *Feminism as Critique: On the Politics of Gender*, ed. Seyla Benhabib and Drucilla Cornell (Minneapolis: University of Minnesota Press, 1987), 93; idem, "Feminism and Postmodernism: An Uneasy Alliance," in *Feminist Contentions*, ed. Nicholson, 29–30.

46. Parsons, *Feminism*, 92.

47. Cahill, *Sex, Gender*, 19–33.

48. Parsons, *Feminism*, 102; see also 106–7, 112, 231; and Joan Tronto, *Moral Boundaries: A Political Argument for an Ethic of Care* (New York: Routledge, 1993), 12–13.

49. Butler, "Contingent Foundations," 50–54. See also Benhabib, "The Generalized and the Concrete Other," 80–81.

50. Butler, *Bodies That Matter*, 221–22.

51. Butler, *Bodies That Matter*, 221, 93, 6.

52. The rule seems to withstand the trial of the exception; sex is either anatomically ambiguous or physically malleable for only a small (and in the latter case, wealthy) proportion of the population.

53. See Hoagland, *Lesbian Ethics*, 37.

54. Parsons, *Feminism*, 115–16.

55. Parsons, *Feminism*, 108; see also 114.

56. Parsons, *Feminism*, 117–18.

57. On justice as the "offspring of family cooperativeness and inventive self-interested reason" in Hume, see Baier, *Moral Prejudices*, 57–58.

58. Cahill, *Sex, Gender*, 24–29.

59. Reeder, "Foundations," 199.

60. Parsons, "Intersection," 264; see also Cahill, *Sex, Gender*, 96.

61. C.f. Annette Baier's criticism of Gilligan: "We should not equate a person's moral stance with her intellectual version of it, nor suppose that a person necessarily knows the relative strength of her own motives and emotions" (Baier, *Moral Prejudices*, 66).

62. Cahill, *Sex, Gender*, 53–54.

63. Parsons, "Intersection," 260.

64. Parsons, *Feminism*, 124, 154–55.

65. Crysdale, "Revisioning," 479–84.

66. Parsons, *Feminism*, 159.

67. On these tensions see for instance Toinette M. Eugene, Ada María Isasi-Díaz, Kwok Pui-lan, Judith Plaskow, Mary E. Hunt, Emilie M. Townes, and Ellen M. Umansky, "Appropriation and Reciprocity in Womanist/Mujerista/Feminist Work," *Journal of Feminist Studies in Religion* 8 (Fall 1992): 91–122.

68. Ruether, *Sexism and God-Talk*, 216–22; Ruether draws upon Zillah Eisenstein, *The Radical Future of Liberal Feminism* (New York: Longman, 1981).

69. Oppression does not erase moral freedom: "Despite the numbing and paralyzing effects of conditioning a person's nature remains intact and anyone can take the initiative and exercise responsibility for themselves and their environment" (Kay, "Human Nature," 201).

70. Katie G. Cannon, *Black Womanist Ethics*, American Academy of Religion Academy Series, no. 60 (Atlanta: Scholars Press, 1988).

71. Welch, *Feminist Ethic*, makes a similar point but carefully distinguishes resistance to injustice from survival of social conflict and other sorts of limits.

72. See for instance Ada María Isasi-Díaz, "Solidarity: Love of Neighbor in the 1980s," in *Feminist Theological Ethics*, ed. Lois Daly, 77–87; and Eugene, "Moral Values and Black Womanists," 160–71.

73. Sandra Harding, "Rethinking Standpoint Epistemology: What Is 'Strong Objectivity'?" in *Feminist Epistemologies*, ed. Linda Alcoff and Elizabeth Potter (New York: Routledge, 1993), 49–82; Lynn Hankinson Nelson, "Epistemological Communities," in Alcoff and Potter, 121–59; Elizabeth Potter, "Gender and Epistemic Negotiation," in Alcoff and Potter, 161–86; Kathryn Pyne Addelson, "Knowers/Doers and Their Moral Problems," in Alcoff and Potter, 265–94; Lorraine Code, "Credibility: A Double Standard," in *Feminist Perspectives: Philosophical Essays on Method and Morals*, ed. Lorraine Code, Sheila Mullett, and Christine Overall (Toronto: University of Toronto Press, 1988), 64–88.

74. Proof of the division has been the difficulty of finding acceptance within the academy of work that draws only on female authors. See Emily Erwin Culpepper, "Philosophia: Feminist Methodology for Constructing a Female Train of Thought," *Journal of Feminist Studies in Religion* 3 (Fall 1987): 9–11.

75. Carol Gilligan catalyzed feminist discussion of epistemology. See Carol Gilligan, *In a Different Voice: Psychological Theory and Women's Development* (Cambridge: Harvard University Press, 1982); Mary Field Belenky, Blythe McVicker Clinchy, Nancy Rule Goldberger, and Jill Mattuck Tarule, *Women's Ways of Knowing: The Development of Self, Voice, and Mind* (n.p.: Basic Books, 1986); Allison M. Jaggar, "Love and Knowledge: Emotion in Western Epistemology," *Inquiry* 32 (June 1989): 151–76; Susan Bordo, "The Cultural Overseer and the Tragic Hero: Comedic and Feminist Perspectives on the Hubris of Philosophy," *Soundings* 65 (Summer 1982): 181–205; Vrinda Dalmiya and Linda Alcoff, "Are 'Old Wives' Tales Justified?", in *Feminist Epistemologies*, ed. Linda Alcoff and Elizabeth Potter (New York: Routledge, 1993), 217–44; Elizabeth Grosz, "Bodies and Knowledge: Feminism and the Crisis of Reason," in *Feminist Epistemologies*, ed. Alcoff and Potter, 187–215; Susan E. Babbitt,

"Feminism and Objective Interests: The Role of Transformation Experiences in Rational Debate," in *Feminist Epistemologies,* ed. Alcoff and Potter, 245–64; and Elizabeth Bettenhausen, "The Moral Landscapes of Embodiment," in *Feminist Theological Ethics,* ed. Lois Daly, 262–70. Sandra Harding, among others, has pointed out that women's ways are likely more the products of their social location than of their biological sex and that it is really the academic/scientific model of knowledge that is anomalous, restricted largely to an oppressive class of powerful white men. See Sandra Harding, "The Curious Coincidence of Feminine and African Moralities: Challenges for Feminist Theory," in *Women and Moral Theory,* ed. Eva Feder Kittay and Diana T. Meyers (n.p.: Rowman and Littlefield Publishers, 1987), 296–315.

76. Grosz, "Bodies and Knowledge," 187–215, 203–4; Dalmiya and Alcoff, "Old Wives' Tales," 217–44; Bordo, "Cultural Overseer," 181–205.

77. Tronto, *Moral Boundaries,* chapter 2.

78. I disagree here with Daniel Maguire, "The Feminization of God and Ethics," *Christianity and Crisis* (15 March 1982): 59–67.

79. The work of Carol Gilligan, discussed below, is an important contribution to the latter project. See Gilligan, *In a Different Voice.*

80. Helen E. Longino, "Subject, Power, and Knowledge: Description and Prescription in Feminist Philosophies of Science," in *Feminist Epistemologies,* ed. Alcoff and Potter, 118.

81. Jaggar, "Love and Knowledge," 156–58; Christine Overall, "Feminism, Ontology, and 'Other Minds,'" in *Feminist Perspectives: Philosophical Essays on Method and Morals,* ed. Lorraine Code, Sheila Mullett, and Christine Overall (Toronto: University of Toronto Press, 1988), 102.

82. Bat-Ami Bar On points out that, for Marx, the epistemological privilege of the proletariat arose not from its inherent dignity but from its paradoxical indispensability to the bourgeois system and powerlessness within it. See Bat-Ami Bar On, "Marginality and Epistemic Privilege," in Alcoff and Potter, 83–100, 85–87.

83. Harding, "Rethinking Standpoint Epistemology," 71–72; Harding, *Whose Science?,* 286; Bar On, "Marginality."

84. Sheila Greeve Davaney, "Problems with Feminist Theory: Historicity and the Search for Sure Foundations," in *Embodied Love: Sensuality and Relationship as Feminist Values,* ed. Paula M. Cooey, Sharon A. Farmer, and Mary Ellen Ross (San Francisco: Harper and Row, 1987), 79–95. Davaney argues that an appeal to experience must not camouflage an illegitimate attempt at "ontological validation" (93–94), but it is not clear that the advantages of the pragmatic alternative she proposed there outweigh its indeterminacy.

85. See Cynthia Crysdale, "Horizons That Differ: Women and Men and the Flight from Understanding," *Cross Currents* 44 (Fall 1994): 345–61.

86. Addelson, "Knowers/Doers," 288.

87. Harding, "Rethinking Standpoint Epistemology," 72; italics removed.

88. Grosz, "Bodies and Knowledge," 202; Overall, "Feminism," 102.

89. Longino, "Subject, Power, and Knowledge," 118; Nelson, "Epistemological Communities," 134, 150; Code, "Taking Subjectivity into Account," 15–48, 21.

90. Nussbaum, "Human Functioning," 212.

91. See Nussbaum, "Human Functioning"; idem, "Non-Relative Virtues."

92. Nussbaum, "Non-Relative Virtues," 38.

93. Lisa Sowle Cahill, "Feminist Ethics, Differences, and Common Ground: A Catholic Perspective," in *Feminist Ethics and the Catholic Moral Tradition,* Readings in Moral Theology 9, ed. Charles E. Curran, Margaret A. Farley, and Richard A. McCormick, S.J. (New York: Paulist Press, 1996), 196–97.

94. Chopp, "Pragmatics," 253; latter emphasis added. Note that Chopp uses "natural law" in a different sense than it has been used in this book: to signify an inflexible system of moral codes. See also Margaret Farley, *Personal Commitments: Beginning, Keeping, Changing* (San Francisco: Harper and Row, 1986); and Carol Gilligan, *In a Different Voice,* below. For one explication of the link between sociality and epistemology see Mary Field Belenky et al., "Procedural Knowledge: Separate and Connected Knowing," chap. in *Women's Ways of Knowing,* 100–30.

95. Nonreligious feminism may be less insistent about the eschatological meaning of this social dynamism than Latin American liberation theologians, for instance, are. Even for religious feminists, social dynamism is a moral imperative and human choice but not always a means of channeling grace into the formation of the Kingdom.

96. Nussbaum, "Human Functioning," 214; also idem, "Aristotelian Social Democracy," in *Liberalism and the Good,* ed. R. Bruce Douglass, Gerald M. Mara, and Henry S. Richardson (NY: Routledge, 1990), 203–52.

97. See Nussbaum, "Human Functioning," 216–20; John Finnis, *Fundamentals of Ethics* (Washington, DC: Georgetown University Press, 1983), 50–53; John Finnis, *Natural Law and Natural Rights* (Oxford: Clarendon Press; New York: Oxford University Press, 1980), 86–92; Germaine Grisez, *The Way of the Lord Jesus,* vol. 1, *Christian Moral Principles* (Chicago: Franciscan Herald Press, 1983), 124; Louis Janssens, "Artificial Insemination: Ethical Considerations," *Louvain Studies* 8 (1980): 3–29.

98. Cahill, "Feminist Ethics, Differences, and Common Ground," 196. Nussbaum argues that she is merely following Aristotle in noting that religion is not something that should be provided for specifically by the polity; see "Aristotelian Social Democracy," 235. Yet she could as easily have included it as a realm of flourishing whose details must be filled out locally. Note that religion seems to be moving into a more prominent position on the list.

When society is secularized, religion and spirituality go underground or arise in new forms. Examples of the former are the survival of Christianity and Buddhism in communist countries and their resurgence under more lax controls on religion; an example of the latter is the American phenomenon of New Age spirituality.

99. Nussbaum, "Human Functioning," 222–23.

100. See Cahill, *Sex, Gender,* 46–61; and Nussbaum, "Human Functioning," 215, 223.

101. Martha C. Nussbaum, "In Defense of Universal Values," "Adaptive Preferences and Women's Options," and "The Role of Religion," lectures at Northwestern University, November 5–19, 1998. Nussbaum's list has been confirmed in the recent analyses of women's activism in India presented in these lectures.

102. Nussbaum, "Human Functioning," 231. In "Aristotelian Social Democracy," Nussbaum makes plain that the Aristotelian provisions are not remedial but universal: it is the responsibility of the polity to make available to each person what is necessary to lift him or her across the threshold (228). Note that Nussbaum makes a liberal argument here: not that all should flourish, but that all should be provided with the requirements of flourishing. Whether they take advantage of them is a matter of free choice.

103. Cahill, *Sex, Gender,* 97, citing Nussbaum, "Aristotelian Social Democracy," 225–26; see also Nussbaum, "Aristotelian Social Democracy," 212.

104. Cahill, *Sex, Gender,* 97.

105. Crysdale, "Horizons," 355.

106. Nussbaum, "Human Functioning," 216.

107. Porter, "Limits," 320–21.

108. Cahill, *Sex, Gender,* 89–90.

109. Porter, "Limits," 322.

110. The thinking behind this thought-experiment is indebted to Cahill, *Sex, Gender,* 73–107.

111. Nussbaum emphasizes that polling people about their desires and satisfactions is not an accurate measure of need. We need to know not only whether people report themselves to be healthy but whether they are in fact diseased; not only whether they report themselves as needy but whether they in fact have the resources to meet all their own basic needs in their community. See "Aristotelian Social Democracy," 213–15.

112. Saints may choose to sacrifice one dimension of their own good to another person, but this cannot be required. See Traina, "Oh, Susanna."

2

Thomas and the Natural Law

The "cafeteria-style" ethics and spirituality of the late twentieth century encourage us to construct our religious and moral identities the way we might construct lunch at a shopping mall food court: a little Buddhist detachment, a healthy serving of mainline liberal Protestant sexual ethics, a double portion of Mennonite roll-up-the-sleeves social action, and a dollop of Roman Catholic liturgical aesthetics. But (as any food court diner knows) if tacos, egg rolls, and granita taste good together, it is because all are barely recognizable shadows of their former selves; they no longer represent authentically distinct Mexican, Chinese, and Italian cuisines. Gustatory multiculturalism ends up as non- or even anticulturalism. Likewise, self-service moral formation often excises principles and methods from a variety of sources, ignoring their practical and theoretical roots, with the same result: cut off from their contexts, their rich, distinctive, and often disharmonious flavors quickly fade.

This should by no means imply that unselfcritical commitments to moral stances or theories are benign. They place strictures on individual lives and can even exert political genocidal power. But, as we have seen, *lack* of moral vision—lack of a significant, communicable moral center—is equally intolerable to any tradition that, like feminism, defines itself by prophecy and social action. Thus when a cafeteria-style approach to moral formation is combined with the otherwise healthy assumption that all moral outlooks have flaws and with the equally appropriate reluctance to exclude unfamiliar voices, the result can be an inability to commit to any single, coherent moral vision, or even to comprehend the importance of having such a vision.

The need for a coherent vision becomes clear when "the dictates of reason" fail to solve really thorny issues. For example, in the United States both pro-choice and pro-life forces, at their best, can legitimately claim to have had the weight of reason on their sides. What divides them is not their good or ill use of reason but their opposing anthropologies, which generate different "self-evident" facts about human nature, and so in turn yield divergent understandings of human ends, human reason, and law. [1]

Therefore a responsible, critical analysis does not approach theological or moral traditions as if they were random collections of individually tasty tidbits that could be chosen and developed in isolation from each other. Rather, it treats each as a cuisine with its own internal consistency and comprehensive vision. A theological moral tradition must be interpreted as a fully articulated moral theory and criticized—in Christine Korsgaard's terms—for its development of moral concepts like "goodness, duty, obligation, virtue, and justice" and explanations of "what [these] moral concepts mean or contain, what they apply to, and where they come from." [2] Thus the project of the current chapter is twofold. The first task is to argue that the ethic of Thomas Aquinas, the thirteenth-century founder and contemporary benchmark for the Roman Catholic natural law tradition, establishes just such a comprehensive moral theory within a rich theological anthropology. The second task is to lay the groundwork for a claim that a critically retrieved version of this theory, along with its most substantive and consistent conclusions, provides not just discrete, illuminating bits of insight but the superstructure of the sort of moral vision that contemporary feminism requires. [3]

Accomplishing the second task entails pointing to some more recent extensions of Thomistic ethics and adjudicating some debates over interpretation. But it does not, it must be emphasized, rest on any illusion that returning to origins will settle all the disputes that plague natural law ethics. Natural law's foundations, methods, and content have been debated for centuries. Many of these disputes were bequeathed to us by Thomas, who himself adopted somewhat inchoate ideas traceable to early Christianity and earlier classical philosophy without harmonizing all the conflicting elements, and it would be foolish to expect to resolve all of them now. [4] Nor does it rest on his official, de jure authority, established by Leo XIII's encyclical *Aeterni Patris* and confirmed in the title "Angelic Doctor." Rather, it takes a cue from his de facto authority, [5] from the insights of recent Vatican Council II–era theologians and philosophers, who have approached Thomas less with an air of duty than with a reformist's attitude of conviction and renewed appreciation.

The first part of this project must begin with the observation that for Thomas natural law is not simply an ethic in the stripped down sense: a system for evaluating acts. Rather it is a dimension of his systematic theology. Like any good theological ethic, it explains the significance of behavior in the world and against the ultimate aims of human life. It combines coherent accounts of God and God's relation to the world; of human beings, their circumstances, their experiences, their relationship to their surroundings, and the meaning of their action in the world; and of human capacities as moral agents, especially the capacity of and procedures for moral discrimination. [6] As Anthony Lisska has argued, what distinguishes Thomas's natural law importantly from most contemporary ethics is that its systematic complex of theological and anthropological claims converge in a telic or "dispositional" anthropology. [7] This anthropology depends upon an Aristotelian metaphysics: the essence of a thing is to be on a trajectory toward an end that fulfills or completes it. Our first task is to identify these ends. For plants and animals, these ends are concrete and earthly: for example, the ultimate end of a pear tree is to bear fruit, and the ultimate end of a bear is to raise and educate cubs. Human beings likewise have a natural, earthly end: flourishing of body, mind, and soul in human community, with all that this entails. But human beings hold a special place in this plan. According to Thomas's *exitus-reditus* scheme, they are created by—sent out from—God not only to accomplish natural, earthly ends but also to participate posthumously in the beatific vision, which is their true happiness or fulfillment. [8] Our second task, then, is to specify the relationships between these ends so that we can discern what moral obligations they entail. It is at this level—the coordination of claims about human ends and obligations—that Thomas's synthetic vision excels: it ensures the coherence of the human end in God with moral virtue and concrete social flourishing and affirms the perspicuity of moral principles in general.

THEOLOGICAL ANTHROPOLOGY AND THE NATURAL LAW

Contemporary scholars of Thomas disagree vehemently over the proper status of law in his theology generally and over the proper role of law in his ethics in particular. In the language of theological anthropology, this is the question, whether human conformity to divinely established ends involves adherence to principle or development of habits or character. Virtue theorists insist that reducing Thomas's ethics to law ignores his emphases upon growth in the virtues and upon the flexibility of practical reason in pursuit of the good; others counter that it is impossible to ignore the treatise on law or the important role law plays in the extensive ethical discussions in part II–II of the *Summa Theologiae*. [9] A balanced view of Thomas proves this to be a false dichotomy; we must retain both but read one in the light of the other. We will begin with law's connection to anthropology and return to virtue below, but the artificiality of the separation will be clear in both discussions.

We have already seen that for Thomas an essence is not static; it contains a dynamism that carries it in specific directions, like "a tulip bulb developing during the spring," toward its innate goal or end. [10] So for a thing to have an essence is to be in a state of potentiality, to be on a trajectory *toward* its fulfillment, its end, its good. Thomas's universe is a complex of divinely created potentialities and ends that range from the cosmic to the microscopic. To the modes of functioning that cohere with these ends, Thomas gives the general name "law": "the proper effect of law is to lead its subjects to their proper virtue: and since virtue is that which makes its subject good, it follows that the proper effect of law is to make those to whom it is given, good, either simply or in some particular respect." [11] The different sorts of ends entail different kinds of laws, each of which implies a power proportionate to its own end. The eternal law, which holds God's plan for all creation, is the law from which all others are derived. It directs the universe toward its fulfillment in God, inclining all things "to their proper acts and ends." [12] Divine law is the dimension of eternal law that directs human beings to their supernatural fulfillment in God, which they have a natural inclination but not the supernatural capacity to accomplish. [13] Human law—discussed at greater length later in this chapter—governs public life, ensuring that individuals advance (or at least do not harm with impunity) the public, common good. [14]

But human beings participate in the eternal law in one further way: through the natural law. Unlike other creatures, Thomas says, we bear the image of God in our intellectual nature. [15] This likeness to God enables us to participate intellectually in God's plan for us, to recognize and adopt the "divine style." [16] So although like all creatures we tend toward the goods of survival and physical flourishing, we also tend and are intended to act consciously, deliberately, and reflectively, rather than merely automatically or instinctively. The possibility of choosing opens the possibility of pursuing myriad ends and so entails the need for "the imprint on us of the Divine Light" in the natural law, so that by "the light of natural reason . . . we [may] discern what is good and what is evil," what is consonant with our true end and what is not. [17] Thus the natural law is "the participation of the eternal law in the rational creature," a reflection of the constitution and goals of divinely created human nature. [18] Its end is the moral life, which, as F. C. Copleston pointed out in the mid-twentieth century, is then simply "a special case of the general principle that all finite things move toward their ends by the development of their potentialities." [19]

From this anthropological point of view, as twentieth-century interpreters have pointed out, natural law is thus neither a deterministic power, nor an arbitrarily imposed requirement, nor a guide generated exclusively by human creativity. Plainly, human rationality prevents Thomas's version of natural law from functioning anything like what we are accustomed to calling a law of nature, like the laws of gravity or the conservation of energy. In addition, as Karl Rahner quips, "the philosophical axiom *agere sequitur esse* comes into play. The 'ought' is founded on the 'is'. . . . The principle suggests that for man the demands of morality are not merely juridical but stem from the structure of his being, his nature. Hence natural law is not a heteronomous morality." [20] This may be clearer if we contrast it with the other contemporary analogues of "law," civil laws (either imposed or democratically generated). For natural law is not primarily a list of propositions; its purpose extends beyond the common good; it is not punitive, in the sense of being enforceable, although its transgression harms us; it is "engraved on the heart" but largely unwritten; there can be no gap between it and the ideal of justice, of which it is the criterion; although its source is divine, it is a universal, inbuilt inclination of human beings; and yet to fulfill or observe it completely is beyond natural human powers. Natural law is a rich, thick description of human being with a view to its ultimate end in God.

Thomas's connection between anthropology and the natural law is also where we find perhaps the most convincing confirmation of the coherence of natural human ends with the ultimate goal of union with God. The existence of natural law depends on human rationality, which is the capacity that grounds the unique human orientation toward the beatific vision. And yet natural law is also incapable of leading people to this level of perfection; its bailiwick is the pursuit of natural goods in everyday human life. [21] But, as we will see in somewhat more detail below, because the human person is an integral whole, if the natural goods to be pursued under the rational dictates of the natural law do not directly advance the good of beatitude, they must at least be consistent with it. In other words, the natural law directs people to a life of temporal justice consistent with their ultimate end.

If we put the ultimate human end in God together with the human capacity to act consciously for proximate ends that are consistent with that ultimate end, we get natural law in its most concrete manifestation: practical moral reason. For Thomas "to seek an appropriate end" is the definition of "to act rationally."

> The first principle in the practical reason is one founded on the notion of good, viz., that good is that which all things seek after. Hence this is the first precept of the law, that good is to be done and pursued, and evil is to be avoided. All other precepts of the natural law are based upon this; so that whatever the practical reason naturally apprehends as a human good (or evil) pertains to the precepts of the natural law in that it is something to be pursued (or avoided). [22]

This is still a formal claim; many of the contemporary storms in Roman Catholic ethics brew precisely around the questions of what sort of good or evil is meant and what sorts of actions and attitudes fall under each heading. But the larger meaning is indisputable: God intends human beings to be creatures who can grasp goods, reflect on them, and determine themselves to act for them; this behavior requires *practical* intelligence; and although it is a temporal project it is coherent with one's ultimate end. [23]

Here the terms "nature," "reason," "law," "good," "end," and "happiness" are all defined by mutual reference; their existence and value depend upon their relationship to the universal human inclination to beatitude. [24] Human nature corresponds to its ends, both ultimate and immediate, and reason pursues them. By beginning with theological anthropology, then, Thomas links good and value to the ultimate, divinely ordained ends of human life and connects epistemology and reason to the structures of human being that outfit it for these ultimate ends. The goods to be pursued, their rough ranking, the human capacity to discern them, and their ultimate human significance are tied up in an organic whole.

Thomas's profound integration of theological anthropology and ethics has several important corollaries that are crucial both for a comprehensive understanding of natural law's theological core and for establishing the connection between natural law and feminist ethics. First and most obviously, as Anthony Lisska points out, there is no need to construct extrinsic connections between fact and value because "the value is built right into the fact as end or perfection to the disposition or potency." [25] To have a nature is to be inclined to one's own perfection, which is one's good, and to pursue it appropriately leads to both moral and ontic fulfillment. Pamela Hall develops the sometimes overlooked obverse of this claim: to act against nature is to act against the good in the most practical and concrete sense—to impede fulfillment and therefore happiness, both natural and supernatural. Moral failure is its own punishment. [26] It is a short distance from here to the feminist claim that whatever advances genuine flourishing is also morally good.

Second, although human life under the divine and natural laws is experienced as an integral whole, human fulfillment occurs on two separate planes, one subordinate to the other. Natural goods are coherent with ultimate, posthumous happiness, but (outside the influence of grace) rational pursuit of genuine natural goods not only fails to contribute to this supernatural end but cannot accomplish even its supposedly proportionate end of temporal happiness. As we might expect, perfect or true happiness can be accomplished by divine power alone, [27] but oddly enough beatitude is also the only true fulfillment of all "simply human" goods. [28] Natural and supernatural goods remain distinct but related: the former are ordered to the latter, and the latter subsumes and completes the former. [29]

Feminist thinkers tend to reject this strict distinction of planes, even when they embrace some version of the supernatural. But they do concur with a third point. Thanks to the coherence between the human goods and virtues philosophers recommend and one's final end in God, even for the religious person the moral life is a matter of appropriate pursuit of concrete human goods. Religious ethics speaks in most cases about the same concrete capacities and virtues as secular ethics and even does so in the language of the marketplace rather than in an exclusive idiom. [30] Religion need not be folly; faith does not necessarily contradict general human reason and moral experience; and the Christian community need not be morally sectarian. [31] This has its theological dangers, of course. The possibility of discussing the workings of natural law completely apart from its metaphysical grounding has in the past isolated moral theology from systematics and biblical studies; more recently, it has led to controversial experiments in creating natural law from the ground up, without reference to metaphysics. [32] In order to remain faithful to the tradition, then, care must be taken not to develop natural law in a way that contradicts the theological premises of its undergirding anthropology.

Finally, as I show in greater detail below, by placing the whole created order under divine providence, Thomas integrates not only the natural and supernatural dimensions of individual flourishing but also the individual and the social. Individual virtue—both acquired and infused—is consistent with individual natural and supernatural ends. But in addition, individual natural and supernatural goods and virtues are perfectly consistent with and even advance the *common* good, which includes temporal goods that can be achieved only in cooperative community. The ontic, moral, and spiritual flourishing of individual and community are bound up in an organic whole. The connections to both feminist theory—echoed by the slogan "the personal is the political"—and savvy feminist politics is clear.

This brief journey through Thomas's anthropology also puts us in a better position to allay some contemporary fears—particularly strong among feminists—about natural law. The broad variety of approaches that claim to be or are accused of being natural law probably owes most to equally great variations in the understandings of the term "nature." [33] As we saw above and will be reminded in chapter 3, this variety is one of the main sources of misunderstanding and conflict within and between feminist and Roman Catholic ethics. Yet Thomas's anthropology considerably narrows the range of possibilities. Natural law is not natural in a necessary or scientific sense; if natural law were reducible to the "laws of nature," human freedom, without which the idea of morality is impossible, could not exist. [34] Neither is natural law natural in the sense of being automatic or effortless. Fulfillment of one's true being is possible only with the help of divine grace under the New Law; and even with grace development of the acts of moral virtue requires effort. [35] In addition, natural law is natural, in the sense of being universal, only in a qualified sense. Its first principles are *in se* available to all human beings, but thanks to both differences in understanding and differences in circumstances its conclusions vary. [36] As we will see, it builds on natural inclinations, but these are easily warped, magnified, stunted, or disordered, and so must be organized and tutored by reason. Even more important, thanks to sin and ignorance even its first principles guarantee little; unaided human reason is unreliable enough that God revealed many of the more basic, universal second-ary precepts of natural law in the Old Law—chiefly in the Ten Command-ments—and confirmed them in the New Law revealed in Christ. [37]

Thomistic natural law is natural rather in an Aristotelian sense; it is the motion or tendency that is essential and appropriate to human being. [38] What is universal is really only the sort of being a human person is—telic and therefore rational in the broad sense—and apprehension of the first principle of practical reason: "good is to be done and pursued, and evil is to be avoided." [39]

In order to move from this still formal theological anthropology toward a more substantive ethic, we must explore its implications for three equally vital elements of Thomas's thought: an understanding of moral reason as practical reason; a vision of individual moral integrity; and an emphasis upon human communities as moral communities engaged in the pursuit of a practical common good. [40] Not coincidentally, as we will see in chapter 4, feminist and natural law ethics have in common a fierce insistence that any adequate ethic pursues all three claims with equal vigor.

NATURAL LAW AND PRACTICAL MORAL REASON

In the contemporary academy, reason—moral and scientific—has fallen under particularly intense scrutiny. When we apply a hermeneutics of suspicion to scholarly reason, it is said, we find pretensions to neutral universality masking often obscene gender, race, class, and cultural biases. Systematically excluded from scholarly, reasoned conversations—or admitted only by painful and artificial circumlocution—are the experiences and insights of all who are not academic moral philosophers and theologians—that is to say, the overwhelm-ing majority. Missing particularly are discussions of how to operate (as nearly everyone must) in awkward and compromising situations one has not freely chosen—from family obligations to oppressive politics—and how to account for affection, emotion, and the evolving wisdom of one's own moral experience.

What must be remembered, however, is that most of these contemporary critiques have in mind the Enlightenment ideals of deductive reasoning from universal truths. Roman Catholic moral theology from the Enlightenment to the mid-twentieth century—somewhat detached from its systematic roots and heavily influenced by Enlightenment ideals—is infected with the same diseases. [41] But a medieval understanding of practical moral reason, if it does not satisfy the contemporary critique entirely, still approximates it more closely than the intervening Enlightenment model does. We can begin by showing how natural law's method differs from logical or deductive reasoning.

METHOD IN PRACTICAL MORAL REASON. In Thomas a method of reasoning must be suited to its object. Thomas made use of Aristotle's distinction between scientific (or speculative) and practical knowledge. [42] Aristotle's speculative knowledge, as Jonsen and Toulmin note, is knowledge for its own sake. It is mathematical, necessary, deductive, and syllogistic, "concerned . . . with theoretical relations *internal to* a system of concepts." [43] Certitude lies "in a grasp of [eternal] theoretical principles"; and "all the elements in its arguments are governed by the basic 'universal principles' to which they can be led back by way of explanation, and from which they can be derived by formal deduction." Practical knowledge, on the other hand, is the knowledge of a "how-to" manual, directed toward accomplishing something concrete. It involves "recognizing what combinations of actions are appropriate to complex or ambiguous situations." Thus it deals with both general rules and "particular things"; certitude "arises from knowledge of particulars." Its logic is inductive. Considerations of efficacy and faithfulness to constellations of other values influence its conclusions heavily. [44]

Thomas applied this distinction to theological reflection. Dogmatic theology, which elaborates a system of eternal and necessary truths, employs speculative reason; moral theology, which directs the practical pursuit of the good in complex, shifting circumstances, makes use of practical reason. The path a practical argument takes, though it is hardly haphazard, is wider-ranging and more varied than the pattern speculative reason follows. Although it draws upon a few a priori principles, it is not derived from them; it draws also and primarily upon human experience, through which alone it can gain the knowledge of particulars essential to the process of practical reason. [45] It relies upon human experience for information about circumstances, for a reserve of knowledge about similar situations, for a "feeling" or intuition or "eye" for finding the heart of the issue and concentrating on the relevant facts. [46]

For Thomas these qualities fall under the virtue of prudence, modeled on Aristotle's *phronesis*: "right reason about things to be done." [47] Prudence is an intellectual virtue with a practical purpose: it tells us what pertains to the accomplishment of ends. Without it one cannot be moral:

> Prudence is a virtue most necessary for humans. For a good life consists in good deeds. Now in order to do good deeds, it matters not only what a man does, but also how he does it; to wit, that he do it from right choice and not merely from impulse or passion. [48]

Presented with an end, prudence "perfect[s] the reason and make[s] it suitably affected towards things ordained to the end." [49] This is not simply a matter of identifying moral principles—which is the task of conscience—or applying them to action—though Thomas occasionally uses that language—or choosing means. [50] Nor is it, as Thomas himself reminds us, a matter of over-cautious or self-protective calculation (the latter being prudence of the flesh rather than the genuine prudence that pursues all goods for the sake of the ultimate end). [51] Rather, as Daniel Westberg and Jean Porter argue, prudence properly understood not merely makes wise decisions about the pursuit of goods but also—by engaging the appetite, especially the will—harnesses desire and yields action. [52]

Prudence accomplishes all of this by installing flexible, multivalent, but rigorous reasoning at the center of practical moral reflection. As Thomas's recitation of the "integral parts" of prudence shows plainly, prudence is a broad-ranging, practical wisdom, an umbrella under which fall many habits and virtues, all of which one must possess and employ in order to reason well. [53] Taken together, these qualities both demonstrate the scope of practical reason and comprise formidable criteria for contemporary moral thought.

First and perhaps most important to us is memory of what is generally the case. Practical reason requires us to know not how one idea necessarily follows from another but, for example, what effect usually follows a particular sort of action, and this we can learn only by reflecting on the past. Thomas's preference for the term "memory" probably reflects a desire to use Aristotle's language, but the term "experience" links Thomas to the contemporary ethical debate without altering his insight; for "we need experience to discover what is [contingently] true in the majority of cases," and that "experience is the result of many memories." [54] Memory's residence in the sensitive part of the soul ties experiential knowledge securely to the body.

Thorough treatment of Thomas's theory of cognition would take us far afield. But with an eye to the contemporary discussion it is enough to notice the breadth of the knowledge that depends on experience and the contingency of the channels through which we receive it. For instance, Thomas does not claim that any sort of knowledge—even knowledge of basic moral principles or human nature itself—is available to the intellect by direct illumination. [55] As Armand Maurer confirms, there is for Thomas no "a priori knowledge or direct intuition of human nature that would tell us what it means to be fully human. . . . As we observe [man's] achievements we grow in our understanding of his nature." [56] Pamela Hall argues that for Thomas even the natural law is available to us only "by reflection upon our own and our predecessors' desires, choices, mistakes, and successes." [57] For not only contingents but the "what-ness"—the nature—of things are available only in our cumulative, sensible experiences of concrete, individual objects. Certainly sense does not constitute knowledge. But because for earthly human beings loss of senses impairs practical judgment by cutting off the channels through which we gain the knowledge out of which we form memory, [58] it is clear that the *body* is the sole conduit for the knowledge that practical reason manipulates. [59] In short, experiential knowledge is bodily knowledge. As a corollary, moral knowledge of human nature is social. Thus the contemporary catchwords "experience," "embodiment," and "relationship" are indispensable to Thomas's moral epistemology and ethical method. Finally, as Josef Pieper has pointed out, Thomas's memory is what we would now call critical memory: "honest" or "true-to-being" recollections undistorted by vice. [60] Memory is less like a random series of photos taken with variously colored lenses than like a watch-fully constructed, systematically labeled collection of reflections on events.

But prudence is not reducible to memory. The other parts of prudence help the practical reasoner decide which experiences to attend to and what use to make of them. Understanding—not awareness of the principles of practical reason, but the interior "right estimate of some particular end"—is essential to moral judgment. [61] Since "human knowledge begins with the outside of things as it were" and penetrates inward, [62] only a person in whom this capacity is well-developed can interpret sense data carefully and transform them into meaningful material for judgment. For us, the third part of prudence, docility, may call up an image of passive, unquestioning obedience. But Thomas defines docility rather as a readiness to be taught by others. The prudent person listens to cumulative communal wisdom. Thomas recommends as teachers "old folk who have acquired a sane understanding of the ends in practical matters." [63] But clearly it is their wisdom, not their age simply, that privileges them, which suggests that docility may amount to willingness to be taught by all whom experience has made wise. [64] Next is shrewdness, "an apt disposition to acquire a right estimate by oneself"; in other words, docility should be a companion and help to, not a substitute for, one's own capacity and resolve to arrive at a proper program of action. Fifth is reason in the narrow sense: good counsel, "research proceeding from certain things to others," the ability to understand whether in fact an action is likely to produce the desired end. Sixth is foresight, which has to do with "future contingents, insofar as they can be directed by man to the end of human life"; this capacity seems to be less the human ability to predict concrete consequences—which seems to fall under memory and good counsel—than the capacity of human providence to envision the future and shape it through the means by which it pursues divinely given ends. [65] Next is circumspection, the capacity to choose means that will be effective in accomplishing an end in given circumstances. For example,

> to show signs of love to someone seems, considered in itself, to be a fitting way to arouse love in his heart, yet if pride or suspicion of flattery arise in his heart, it will no longer be a means suitable to the end. Hence the need of circumspection in prudence. [66]

Finally comes caution, a firm grasp of the good; this last habit is indispensable because in "contingent matters of action . . . even as false is found with true, so is evil mingled with good" and "has the appearance of good." Thomas's extensive discussions of vices resembling virtues illustrate the necessity of a sharp and vigilant eye to protect one from the lure of attractive evils. [67]

Clearly, for Thomas good moral reasoning is a subtle and complex process. Taken together the parts of prudence present a picture of moral reasoning that is experiential, embodied, consultative, creative, calculating, inductive, flexible, and principled. Prudence requires a firm grasp of ends and principles, astute knowledge of circumstances, attention to both one's own experience and that of others. And, as Hall shows, prudence not only attends to principles but generates them as well, so that prudence and *synderesis*—knowledge of the first principles of practical reason—are related dialectically rather than deductively. [68] If moral reasoning does not display all these characteristics of prudence—if for example it styles itself as deduction from principles—it ceases to be properly practical.

CONCLUSIONS OF PRACTICAL MORAL REASON. Speculative reason's conclusions are necessary, singular, and univocal. The particularities of circumstance do not alter the relationships between its elements. In any weather, in any era, in any part of the universe, the only correct solution to the equation $2 + 2 = x$ is $x = 4$. But ethics, because it deals in contingency rather than necessity, is a matter of practical reason. [69] As we have seen, because practical reason accomplishes ends in concrete circumstances whose particulars vary with time and place, it must account for sensible, human, embodied experience. Thomas considers it obvious that the objective conclusions of practical moral reasoning vary as well. Thus once practical reason leaves very general first principles like "do good and avoid evil," which are ostensibly universal, it "descends" to secondary precepts that are less certainly universal.

> Accordingly then in speculative matters truth is the same in all men, both as to principles and as to conclusions: although the truth is not known to all as regards the conclusions, but only as regards the principles which are called common notions. But in matters of action, truth or practical rectitude is not the same for all, as to matters of detail, but only as to the general principles: and where there is the same rectitude in matters of detail, it is not equally known by all. . . .
>
> . . . As to the proper conclusions of the speculative reason, the truth is the same for all, but is not equally known to all: thus it is true for all that the three angles of a triangle are together equal to two right angles, although it is not known to all. But as to the proper conclusions of the practical reason, neither is the truth or rectitude the same for all, nor, where it is the same, is it equally known by all. [70]

Even without the complication of sin, perceptions would differ; for "the human act ought to vary according to diverse conditions of persons, time, and other circumstances: this is the entire matter of morality." [71] Yet oddly Thomas's comfort with the idea of variation in natural law's conclusions with place and other circumstances did not extend to similar variation across time—for instance, to significant subtraction or replacement of moral principles. He allowed only that secondary precepts of the natural law—"certain detailed proximate conclusions drawn from the first principles"—might sometimes shift slightly to accommodate involuntary impediments to virtuous behavior. [72]

If Thomas's practical reasoning was inductive and at least moderately flexible, why are he and his successors so often labeled as rigid and oblivious to circumstances? The first difficulty is that although Thomas's description of prudence clearly fits the practical mold, in other places his use of language often obscures the distinction between speculative and practical reason. Use of characteristically speculative terms like "descent" and "derivation" and logical connectors like "it follows that" to explain how concrete norms are related to general moral principles distract from the fact that the first principles of practical reason are heuristic rather than speculative: "not axioms but things aimed at." [73] In addition, although Thomas clearly allows in theory for variation and change in practical moral conclusions, he just as clearly does not expect that the amplitude of their oscillations will be very large. Although his own culture was hardly ossified or ignorant of other societies—and his own theology was initially intellectually disruptive rather than pacific—his ideal was relative homogeneity. Making peace with the panoply of functioning sets of norms coexisting in the contemporary dynamic, plural global culture was a task he certainly did not envision. Nor did he anticipate the historicism that makes casuistry continuously necessary. [74] Finally, during the Enlightenment love affair with "geometrical clarity," speculative knowledge became not just the ideal but the sole proper mode of knowing across all disciplines, even practical ones. [75] Applying speculative models to the dialectical project of moral reflection both warped the process and removed the humility and contingency of the result. For if an ethical analysis yields not just the best solution here and now, but the universal answer to a repeatable moral dilemma, it also produces a new axiom for future reasoning; it fills in a blank on a huge flowchart of independently and eternally valid moral principles. Moral thought loses its practical and dialectical edge.

The bounds and conclusions of Thomas's own use of prudence—and even those of his successors—are thus very narrow. But because they leave small openings for innovation, they do not permanently mark the limits of prudence's range. And the wider the variation one admits in time and circumstances, the more "the great commandments of love of God and of neighbor, the great principles of justice and charity"—rather than any specific set of concrete precepts—appear as the primary criteria of natural law's conclusions. [76]

HUMAN GOODS AND HOW WE KNOW THEM. We have seen how prudence judges the means to ends, and we have seen how concrete circumstances affect the conclusions of practical moral reflection, but we have sidestepped the element without which practical moral reason is meaningless: the goods, or ends, for whose realization practical moral reason strives and by which prudence judges means. For Thomas, "if we know what something *is*, we know what it *ought* to be." [77] Quite simply, our good is our own perfection. Our ultimate good is the perfect happiness of the beatific vision, for the sake of which we necessarily, even if unconsciously, will everything else—health, education, financial security, virtue—whether we understand what perfect happiness actually entails or not. [78] From this perspective the appropriateness of our choices is measured by their coherence with our final end. The prudent person must ask, are these proximate ends coherent with the beatific vision? Am I choosing them with that end in mind rather than as ends in themselves?

Seen from this angle, the question of the goods we are to pursue is the question of the shape of a life aimed at beatitude. The final, supernatural end's constancy and its coherence with the more immediate, familiar dimensions of natural perfection allows Thomas to indicate a number of perduring proximate human ends. [79] For example—as we already know—prudence proper judges means with respect to the last end. But one prerequisite for the virtue of prudence is a degree of bodily integrity. We "can be hindered, by indisposition of the body, from every operation of virtue," [80] for bodily imperfection "hinder[s] the mind from being lifted up" [81] and tricks the senses. So although "happiness does not consist in bodily good as its object," [82] still bodily health—as a condition of prudence—is in turn a condition of happiness.

Here Thomas is in part making a metaphysical point: the perfect happiness of beatitude, in which the soul remains united to the resurrected body, necessitates perfection of the body—otherwise cognition and prudence would be faulty, which is impossible. [83] This absolute perfection of the body belongs only to the next life. Yet it is also clear that one of the perduring, proximate goods of *this* life is a degree of bodily health that allows for the sharpness of mind and sense that prudence requires, and in this sense temporal health may be pursued for the sake of the ultimate end. Goods like wealth, communal cooperation, and friendship are not necessary to ultimate happiness even in the circumscribed and necessary way that the body is, for in the beatific vision, delight in God, "the supreme Fount of Goodness," exceeds the delight we might have received from any of them in this life. But these goods *are* necessary in the same way as the natural body to the proximate happiness of a human life oriented virtuously to its ultimate end. The virtuous person seeks them not purely in order to delight in them but because of what she can do with them. Her life is a social and material life, a life that requires friends on whom, and the bodily health and the tools with which, to practice virtue. [84]

My aim here has not been to exhaust the list of concrete goods that Thomas believes we may seek virtuously. There is no once-for-all list of these goods, for even though many of them—like friendship, a "natural" degree of wealth, and health—are clearly universal helps to a life in concert with beatitude, action in accord with any end varies somewhat with circumstances; particular situations may demand different emphases in the articulation of these goods or even the addition of less clearly universal goals. Rather, I have wanted to show that when Thomas begins from the perspective of the ultimate end—perfect happiness, repose, and fulfillment in God—he justifies proximate human goods as goods that can be subordinated to and aimed toward this end.

Yet the metaphysical justification of proximate ends is not a satisfying explanation of how living persons, who have little to no understanding of true happiness, actually identify natural goods and pursue them well. Inductive or experimental knowledge, indispensable for determining whether a particular means advances a concrete good, is just not decisive when the end is beyond view. Thomas's writings suggest that we often in fact come to know these proximate goods by examining our potentiality and our inclinations, which even when distorted are more reliably at hand than the clear understanding of our final end that we receive only through faith. For Thomas the inclinations are undeniably important: they function as divinely implanted impulses toward human goods, reminders of proper human ends, clues to the content of the natural law. [85] Yet subtle differences in the interpretation of their significance leads moral reason in two entirely different directions and toward two completely different sets of questions. In the contemporary conversation, the attempt to solve this puzzle turns out to be the attempt to answer the following questions. Does morality entail *rationally pursuing ends* inherent in human nature or *following rules* inscribed in that same nature? Does it involve discerning the requirements of virtue or conforming to objective moral truths? Do inclinations point to goods upon whose fulfillment progress toward the human end depends, or are they, thanks to their divine origins, adequate bases for moral reasoning in themselves? [86]

Some contemporary rehabilitators of Thomas—like John Finnis, Germain Grisez, and (in a slightly different way) authors of recent papal encyclicals—argue for the latter of each of these pairs of options. They derive human goods not directly from the ultimate end (specified in light of anthropology and situation) but from inclinations (to goods inherently oriented to the ultimate end). They begin with the fact that for Thomas, each thing inclines toward its own perfection; animals do so automatically and humans, rationally. Immediately questions arise: what to do with the fact that Thomas seems to recognize three diverse sorts of human inclinations, including apparently automatic elemental and animal inclinations as well as rational ones?

> Wherefore according to the order of natural inclinations, is the order of the precepts of the natural law. Because in man there is first of all an inclination to good in accordance with the nature which he has in common with all substances ... whatever is a means of preserving human life, and of warding off its obstacles, belongs to the natural law.

> Secondly, there is in man an inclination to things that pertain to him
> more specially, according to that nature which he has in common with
> other animals: and in virtue of this inclination, those things are said to
> belong to the natural law, *which nature has taught to all animals,* such
> as sexual intercourse, education of offspring and so forth. Thirdly, there
> is in man an inclination to good, according to the nature of his reason,
> which nature is proper to him: thus man has a natural inclination to
> know the truth about God, and to live in society: and in this respect,
> whatever pertains to this inclination belongs to the natural law. [87]

Thomas assumes that these three levels cohere; human nature—created as
substantial, animal, and rational—is directed *as a whole* to God. Practical
reason steps in to acknowledge and advance each level's particular goods. [88]
But he sometimes hints that each sort of inclination has independent moral
authority. Despite the fact that we are capable of submitting all our behavior
to a rational prudential calculus, some actions are still perfectly upright even
when we perform them without reflection. For instance, when my life is
threatened, the elemental and animal response of *physical* self-preservation is
perfectly appropriate, even if self-defense is fatal to my attacker. [89] While it is
true that self-preservation may be merely a matter of acting on goods I have
already ordered rationally, Thomas bases its reasonableness in experienced
inclination; it cannot be justified on the basis of the ultimate end alone. Other
actions that have animal or elemental purposes not only need not, but may
not, be detoured to other ends. The hackneyed example is sexual intercourse:
the central purpose of the sexual organs is generation. [90] Other goods may
arise from sexual activity, but these are side effects, not ends that by themselves
justify it. Occasionally the division between elemental inclination and reason
yields unexpected moral freedoms as well: the obligation to obey superiors
does not extend to decisions about "the nature of the body, for instance in
those relating to the support of [the] body or the begetting of . . . children.
. . . [and] the question of contracting marriage or remaining in the state of
virginity." [91] These examples can suggest that human rationality, and with it
peculiarly human forms of sociality, float above the elemental and animal
inclinations like oil on water, immiscible, without disturbing or qualifying
them. Only on the level of the peculiarly human does the "something natural,
to which we should conform ourselves" entail "right reason, human intelligence, prudent and thoughtful action directed to humane ends." [92] Rigid
maintenance of this distinction results in an ethic that treats human beings
as instinctively driven animals, except in transactions of which animals are
incapable. [93] Recent Roman Catholic ecclesiastical thought and the ecclesiasti-

cal natural law tradition on which it is based follow this line of thinking in Thomas, defining "natural" actions as those coinciding with "animal or biological processes" and declaring that their purposes and tendencies are not altered by the rational nature that guides higher human functioning. As a result, issues having to do with the "animal" body have been governed primarily by the order-of-nature ethic, an approach still discernible in official Roman Catholic ecclesiastical documents on sexual and reproductive ethics. [94]

John Finnis's and Germain Grisez's reliance on the inclinations is slightly different but has equally profound significance for ethics. They draw up lists of inclinations from across the categories. One such list includes

> living, in health and some security; the acquisition of arts and skills to be cultivated for their own sake; the relishing of beauty; the seeking of knowledge and understanding; the cultivation of friendships, immediate, communal and political; effective and intelligent freedom; a right relation in this passing life to the lasting principles of reality, "the gods"; the procreation of children and their education so that they can attain for themselves, and in their own mode, the foregoing values. . . . [95]

According to Finnis and Grisez, the fact that these inclinations happen to coincide with the conditions of concrete human flourishing—concrete proximate goods-for-us—yields no direct *logical* connection between "what constitutes flourishing" and "what constitutes a basic good." [96] The authority of the inclinations lies in their self-evidence. And these inclinations are not only irreducible but equally basic; no good they recommend may be directly harmed for the sake of another. With these two claims, Finnis and Grisez disengage moral knowledge from knowledge of the final end. First, basic goods are known speculatively, through introspection, not practically, through reflection on means to the ultimate good; and lacking any ultimate referent they by default become absolute rather than proximate goods. Second, although putting all the goods on even footing makes for much needed flexibility, it ignores differences not only in kind but in degree among them; all are ends in themselves, but arts and skills do not have quite the morally binding power of right relation to God. [97] Third, their theory is driven by logical necessity to contradict itself by declaring one good "first among equals." Because temporal life is a prerequisite for all the other goods, it takes de facto priority, contradicting Thomas's establishment of beatitude as the ultimate good. [98] Finally, as we have seen, in Thomas inclinations are secondary, imperfect paths to knowledge of ontic goods, subject to the will rather than in control of it. As Russell Hittinger, Anthony Lisska, Pauline Westerman, and Ralph

McInerny have all pointed out, by relying on the inclinations, Finnis and Grisez not only choose the inferior source of knowledge but cut their arguments about value off from any sort of discussion about the facts of concrete human existence and the practical conditions of human flourishing. Not only do they reject most of Thomas's method, but they discard the anthropology that justifies even the portion they retain. [99]

While the ecclesiastical and the Finnis/Grisez accounts of the inclinations may have a certain internal integrity, both fail as interpretations of Thomas. The first permits practical reason to make adjustments only in human goods that do not overlap with animal and elemental goods, but it trips over goods—like sexuality and work—whose human social and rational meanings may at times eclipse their sociobiological ends. The second reaches conclusions about basic goods independently of considering not only the final end but even the proximate end of integral, concrete flourishing; the inclinations indicate goods that are true abstractly and independently, like Platonic forms, rather than concretely, like Aristotelian essences. [100] Each account, in its own way, relies upon the inclinations and passions more heavily and limits the operations of practical reason more severely than Thomas does.

For despite his occasional, sometimes insistent, theoretical shortcuts through the inclinations, Thomas repeatedly warns that in practice the inclinations and natural and sensitive appetites are inadequate guides for action. As Stephen Pope argues, Thomas holds that the inclinations are indicators of true goods-for-us and so must be taken seriously and yet that they do not dictate which of these goods is to be pursued here and now; we cannot simply "read off" virtuous action from raw natural urges. [101] For our passions and sensibilities may be dampened, overdeveloped, or warped by vice, illness, sorrow, or physical pain, or they may simply be in competition with equally basic contradictory impulses. [102] Rather, inclinations must be tutored by human reason, prudently checked and corrected against our goal of beatitude and our experience of what leads to the sort of concrete flourishing that is coherent with beatitude, and trained by new habits of right action: [103] "for many things are done virtuously, to which nature does not incline at first; but which, through the inquiry of reason, have been found by men to be conducive to well-living." [104] Reason reflecting upon experience and human ends—ideally under the auspices of the theological virtues of faith, hope, and charity—determines what good is to take precedence here and now and how it is to be accomplished.

Thus proper readings of the inclinations and "lower" loves appreciatively but critically integrate them in the larger tasks of the rational life. For instance, Pope argues that for Thomas the perfect (and therefore rational and virtuous) love, charity, assumes and perfects rather than contradicts the innate natural and sensitive appetites. [105] Jean Porter argues that Thomas's tripartite division of the inclinations into elemental, animal, and rational is simply a distinction in "an inclusive life plan," "an outline of what a human life should properly look like" that includes "a number of different sorts of goods, pursued and enjoyed in an orderly and harmonious way." [106] In either case the inclinations are indispensable but not determinative. So, as Thomas insists, it is true both that inclinations indicate genuine goods and that these goods, once identified, must be analyzed and ordered before they can rightly be pursued. His occasional neglect of this last step does not narrow the gaping theoretical opening he leaves for the inclinations' qualification by practical wisdom and charity. [107]

Thus in Thomas practical moral reason employs embodied, experiential knowledge, but it also attends to natural but malleable inclinations towards goods. [108] The important interpretive question for the contemporary debate is whether it is the inclination or the good that is to be emphasized in this formula. As we have seen, Thomas's anthropology logically demands the inclinations, but Thomas's warning about their indeterminacy and unreliability indicates a need for other sorts of arguments—based in the *ordo caritatis*, or other guides to discernment—in concrete situations. So Thomas does not envision the inclinations as simple givens to be obeyed or natural law primarily as a strategy for the abstract, deductive derivation of permanent moral rules. Rather he claims that we can discern, through a variety of channels, that certain concrete human ends persist, can be described, and need to be accounted for in practical moral thought; and this discernment and activity are coherent with our final end in God.

This return to ends reminds us why a reading of Thomas that impoverishes his anthropology by tying concrete moral dictates merely to internal impulses or the shape of the body is simply inaccurate. Thomas bears part of the blame for this sort of reading, as the confidence and succinctness of his answers to objections often makes such details appear to be determinative. But in fact all of these intermediate reasons are subordinate to the final end of union with God and therefore contingent on one's interpretation of this end.

VIRTUE AND INTEGRITY

For centuries, in Roman Catholic moral theology, detailed applications of moral rules to dilemmas in practical moral reason eclipsed reflection on the virtues that practical reason presupposes. [109] In the past two decades, philosopher Alasdair MacIntyre and theologian Stanley Hauerwas have returned virtue to the center of the ethical stage; thinkers like Jean Porter and

James Keenan have contributed importantly to the task of critically recovering Thomas's theory of virtue; and both they and Anne Patrick have suggested reformulations of virtue in keeping with the pressures of contemporary life. [110] Their revival of virtue has been an important reminder of the distinction between Thomas's teleological ethic of natural and supernatural fulfillment on one hand and a strict utilitarianism—an ethic focused completely on advancing concrete goods—on the other. [111]

For Thomas the activity of the moral life is the pursuit of the ultimate good under the implicit or explicit guise of proximate goods. But this does not exhaust the meaning of the moral life, for as we have seen, capturing goods also requires well-ordered appetites and sharp powers of discernment—in short, the perfection of the moral agent. [112] In Jean Porter's words,

> precisely because she is a rational creature, capable of determining her own actions on the basis of rational knowledge, the human person's capacity to act well will be a component, and not merely a disposable means, of her attainment of perfection as a human being. [113]

Not just the immediate good pursued but also the habitual good pursuit of it, developed *in* well-doing of right acts, is a human good. Thomas articulates this conviction in his virtue theory, where he links consideration of an act's reasonableness—its appropriateness to the actor's current circumstances and proximate ends—with its significance to her own growth in moral perfection. [114]

As we have learned to expect, virtues come in two flavors, corresponding to the two sorts of human ends: supernatural and ultimate on one hand, natural and proximate on the other. [115] Supernatural or infused virtue, proportioned to the ultimate end and so bestowed by God, is "a good [habit] of the mind, by which one lives righteously, of which no one can make bad use, which God works in us, without us." [116] Natural virtues, on the other hand—intellectual and moral virtues proportioned to the end of natural happiness—are typically labeled acquired virtues, because they are built up by human effort. As in all other departments of Thomas's systematic, the natural and the supernatural are analogous, not continuous; they are distinguished by kind—literally, by end—rather than only by degree. [117] But they are still related in the sense that acquired virtues—each formed with natural ends in mind—are unable to perfect themselves even with respect to these ends without the aid of divine charity and its coterie of supernatural virtues. Charity, the keystone of the supernatural virtues, lifts prudence's sights, uniting and redirecting pursuit of all natural ends toward the singular love and pursuit of God. It does not oppose the acquired virtues but supersedes them, providing what is necessary for their genuine fulfillment even while exposing their inadequacy to the final end. [118]

The deeper details of Thomas's virtue theory—the further divisions within the virtues, their acts and contraries, their operations within actors, their connection to law, the precise methods of acquiring or losing them— deserve and have received careful attention from authors like James Keenan, Daniel Mark Nelson, and Jean Porter, to name only a few. But the point of this discussion is to reiterate features of virtue theory that sometimes seem too obvious to merit much comment. To begin with, the point of the moral life—natural or graced—is not just to pursue good ends through appropriate means but to become a person who does this wisely and habitually. The goal of becoming a competent, reasonable moral actor—emphasized by the dependence of both acquired and infused virtue upon their respective sorts of prudence, and the myriad considerations that prudence entails—is front and center, and it is a goal whose habits I am to cultivate in myself through thoughtful, rational, intentional action. [119] By extrapolation—taking a cue from the doctrine of the common good, discussed below—it is a goal whose habits should be encouraged in everyone.

Second, full development of every virtue, acquired or infused, requires time and practice. This is clearly the case for acquired virtues, which are discrete habits formed through the intentional repetition of acts over a long period. [120] Acquired virtues build up gradually; for example, through intention- ally telling the truth consistently over time one becomes increasingly disposed to tell the truth and so participates more and more fully in the virtue of honesty. [121] But it is equally true, if in a slightly different sense, for infused virtues. This would not seem to be the case, for unlike natural virtues, infused virtues are either present in one package or entirely absent. Infused virtues arrive instantaneously, remaining in full force unless a person sins mortally (in contradiction of charity and therefore of the final end); then they depart completely, as a group, and can be restored only by grace. [122] How then can there be any growth? Again unlike natural virtues, which are discrete habits that follow on or develop in acts, the infused virtues are habits only; and lacking acts, they do not create instant moral exemplars. For instance, supernatural prudence is infused *as a habit* at baptism but is realized *in act* only gradually by a healthy person, and sometimes never by a mentally retarded one. [123] In fact the process of instantiating infused virtues in acts is daunting because infused virtues do not erase lingering "contrary dispositions" or simplify difficult circumstances. [124] Even under charity's influence, we must contend with concupiscence (and therefore the capacity for mortal sin), patterns of past action that run contrary to the perfected forms of the infused virtues, and moral immaturity that owes to age or intellectual weakness. So the infused virtues come to fruition in the acts of daily life only through disciplined cooperation with grace. [125] In short, the moral life, in both its natural and its supernatural dimensions, is a process of maturation in virtue requiring diligence and practice. This fact warns us to keep on our toes. But it also forbids us to expect all the acts of the virtues even from a person who has their infused habits and so invites conversation with contemporary theories of moral development that might help us chart and evaluate progress in moral virtue. [126]

A third point confirms this hunch. As the foregoing discussion has implied, the entire matrix of virtues—moral and intellectual, infused and acquired—is interdependent. Moral virtue—right doing—depends on the knowledge acquired in the exercise of intellectual virtue, both practical and speculative, especially prudence. Prudence in turn cannot operate when the passions are in chaos, obscuring its ends, so it depends on moral virtue. [127] Likewise, the only power that can orient moral virtue to its proper, supernatural end is charity, and yet charity is helpless without the habits of the moral virtues that make action possible. [128] These interdependencies reinforce and extend what we already know. First, perfect virtue—virtue directed to the last end—requires charity. But, second, prudence depends not only on bodily integrity for its interpretation of information but also on moral virtue for its orientation to the end. In other words, it entails a moral hermeneutic. In fact Eugene Rogers argues that for Thomas speculative as well as practical knowledge depends upon the virtue of justice, leaving "ample structural room" for the liberationist claim "that injustice can hinder right knowledge of God." [129] Further, without prudence, which expresses virtue as adherence to the natural law, the virtues themselves are indeterminate. [130] As Thomas's extended discussion of the moral virtues makes clear, we need rules for judging what counts as adherence or contradiction to a virtue or vice. Finally—and easily forgotten given Thomas's habit of making divisions within the virtues, among the stages of acts, and within the psyche—growth in virtue, natural or supernatural, entails development across the virtues, not piecemeal cultivation of isolated habits. It involves, in other words, what we would call growth in character. [131]

Virtue theory also helps us to understand Thomas's teaching on conscience, crucial for its reinforcement of the priority of practical reason—especially the virtue of prudence—in moral judgment. [132] The doctrine of conscience enables us to distinguish the generic advisability of an act from an actor's moral culpability in performing it. In the language of contemporary moral theology, this is the distinction between a person's rightness (the objective conformity of her acts to the rational moral order) and her goodness (her intention and good-faith rationality). [133] One might think that for Thomas an act's significance for the actor's state of virtue depended ultimately on whether she adhered to a list of objective moral rules or even whether a panel of wise judges would agree that she reasonably pursued an appropriate good by fitting means. In perfect circumstances these measures might hold. But in practice, misinformation or inadvertent missteps often cause reason erroneously to propose actions as right (for instance) that it would judge forbidden had it not erred. [134] As a rational pursuer of the good, the prudent reasoner is obligated not to a hypothetical, perfect, omniscient judgment—which is in any case inaccessible to her through no fault of her own—but to her own best lights. [135] The brilliance of this argument is that the actor's moral uprightness—her accord with her ultimate ends—depends not primarily upon the objective trustworthiness of her reason or the objective rightness of her action but on her responsible exercise of practical reason and the coherence of her will with its conclusions. [136] And there is a good test for this uprightness: a rightly-oriented person whose behavior is wrong-headed responds favorably to information that helps her correct her error. In Thomas's argument for conscience, then, the actor's rationality, taken in the fullest sense, is the root criterion of what Thomas calls virtue or what we might call moral integrity. [137]

Finally, Thomas's virtue theory resists the Reformation complaint about work-righteousness, reconciling the Pauline admonition about the meaninglessness of actions uninformed by love—Thomas would say, charity—and James's insistence that faith without works is dead. On one hand, apparently fitting actions may not be informed by an interior orientation to an appropriate good and so may be performed for thoroughly sinful reasons; if so, they may do no outward harm, but then neither is the actor a virtuous person, someone from whom one could expect fitting actions in the future. On the other hand, faith without action cannot be true faith, for true grace and virtue—turning toward one's true end—issue in striving for good works. [138] True virtue is love in action. [139]

Progress in moral virtue, then, occurs through the union of well-intended ends with care in reasoning about and acting on them. Infused and acquired virtue are both entirely consistent with reason and the moral law, for natural prudence directs all proximate ends and actions to the goal of the good life, and infused prudence, under the guidance of charity, directs all ends and actions to God, who is the source of both charity and the good life.

But in the end, virtue does not exist without deed. The moral life is the growth of a moral character that issues in action—hence virtue's connection to social ethics.

NATURAL LAW AND SOCIAL THOUGHT

If Thomas's theory of virtue languished in relative obscurity until recently, over the past century his social and political ethics have been heavily exploited in the social encyclicals (papal and episcopal letters on questions of politics, economics, war, and human rights) and through them have influenced public debates on war, capital punishment, and other questions. [140] But what interests us here is the legacy of Thomas's account of the relationship between the person and the society as part to whole, particularly the rudiments of a theory of society's obligations to individuals. In order to articulate this vision, we must describe Thomas's understandings of the common good, justice, and human law.

Because these three are faces of an interdependent whole, separate treatment does some violence to their unity. Still, the distinctions among them also highlight the connection between social flourishing and individual virtue. We begin with the common good, and a welcome simplification: although of course particular temporal social acts can and should be referred to God, temporal society's proper concern is *natural, this-worldly* flourishing, an end we should pursue within reason. [141] Our whole discussion of Thomas up to this point provides a number of criteria for this end: life, and all that supports it materially; health; access to the information we need to reason well; social interaction and friendship; the freedom and resources to marry, procreate, and raise children; opportunity to exercise our rationality, especially in seeking God; well-developed acquired virtues, especially the virtue of prudence, and whatever education we may need in order to develop them; amusements (perhaps even of the politically satirical sort), games, and play. [142] Some of these goods—many material and cultural advantages, as well as security and peace—either are shared, social goods that a person cannot produce at all by herself or are goods that she can create more successfully in cooperation with others. A classic example is a system of education: a family cannot reproduce the richness or range of learning—or the social experience—available in schools and universities. Nor can any single educational institution remain vibrant and creative if it is isolated. But if people communicate, cooperate, and diversify, the good of an advanced, varied network of mutually supportive institutions is within reach—and, Thomas would say, will profit the whole society. In fact it is this sort of corporate benefit for which people unite in society. [143] So in Thomas and the engendered tradition the common good consists of goods that are generated cooperatively and that benefit everyone collectively. They are commonly owned but should be distributed proportionately, for, Thomas implies, as the parts that make up the whole, individuals "in a way" have claims on them. [144]

The theory of the common good reinforces the coherence of goods that we have learned to expect from Thomas. First, we have the coherence of nature and grace. It goes without saying that infused virtues encourage acts that are perfectly in keeping with the natural good. But participation in the common good that promotes the individual's natural good at least coheres with the individual's final end in God, even though it cannot, as a natural good, advance the final end directly. A top-notch education, for instance, might supply a breadth of knowledge and a refinement of reasoning that encourage the habit of infused prudence to blossom into act. The only claim this interconnection will not allow us is the claim that the common, natural good contributes to anyone's ultimate good. [145] Then we have the coherence of the individual good—material or spiritual—and the social good. What harms one, harms the other, and what advances one, advances the other. For instance, to protect one's own physical health (in appropriate balance with other goods) is also to protect one's ability to contribute to the common good through work, and to be infused with the theological virtue of charity is to be able to perfect one's contribution to the whole. Individual and common goods are organically interdependent. [146] There is no trade-off between the individual's *true* good and the *proper* goals of the social whole; it would not make sense to say that the common good trumps the individual good, or vice versa. [147]

The point is theoretical but has thoroughly practical implications: human beings *by nature* are social and *by nature* have practical needs that only a well-functioning society can fulfill, and only if these needs are being met is the society fulfilling its purposes. Jean Porter finds in Thomas a compelling account of some of these obligations. [148] For instance, a government should not execute, maim, or imprison the innocent or take property arbitrarily, and it should also forbid private individuals to do these things even to apparently guilty people. [149] In addition, individuals have obligations to each other in general and also specifically; for instance, one person's claim to property must give way when another is in extreme need. [150] But except that, as we will see, human law by definition should promote the common good, Thomas's dicta are more negative (forbidding harm) than positive (guaranteeing goods); government is not enjoined explicitly to ensure that all the natural goods listed above are provided to all citizens, for instance. [151] Thomas also focuses on duties—the obligations of individuals and governments to others concretely or to the common good in general—rather than on the incontrovertible claims of those others on society. These protections lay the groundwork for a modern theory of positive rights, but they do not provide one. [152]

In contrast, the natural law thought of this century shifts the emphasis of the common good doctrine from individuals' duties toward the common good to their claims on it. Here we begin to see what happens when the superstructure of Thomas's anthropology encounters modern political thought. The 1891 encyclical *Rerum Novarum* launched an emphasis on individual human dignity so overpowering that by mid-century Jacques Maritain could say that "the adage of the superiority of the common good is understood in its true sense only in the measure that the common good itself implies a reference to the human person." [153] Through Vatican Council II and into the current decade, ecclesiastical documents have emphasized society's duty to protect the rights and freedoms of individuals—albeit in social interdependence—"to attain their full flowering." [154] Concerned that the fruits of the common good are not often distributed evenly, they insist upon society's duty to honor the transcendent dignity of individuals by guaranteeing that they receive just wages and work in safe conditions. Besides, they remind their readers, people can best contribute to the common good when their basic needs are met: [155] "Consider a living organism: the good of the whole is not properly secured unless arrangements are made for every single member to receive all that it needs to fulfil its own function. Exactly the same is true of the constitution and government of a community." [156]

The early social encyclicals defined the social problem as unequal participation in the common good; but by the hundredth anniversary of the first social encyclical, the common good was seen not as a natural product of human sociality but as an end to be identified and pursued consciously, in opposition to other false ends. According to *Centesimus Annus,* de facto personal and social interests do not cohere automatically; they must be coordinated through a proper anthropology, one that brings "personal interest and the interests of society as a whole . . . into fruitful harmony." [157] For the common good "is not simply the sum total of particular interests; rather it involves an assessment and integration of those interests on the basis of a balanced hierarchy of values; ultimately, it demands a correct understanding of the dignity and the rights of the person." [158] Anthropology remains at the center of the doctrine, but—given more pessimistic and pluralist circumstances—less to explain the existing relation between the person and the common good than to justify an argument that the relation ought to be structured in a particular way. [159] Thus the normative power of the image of the common good has, if anything, increased over the centuries.

The second tradition, the justice tradition, is in current parlance inseparable from discussions of the first. Justice language too has undergone change since the time of Thomas, but that change has involved more a renewal of lapsed attention to the details of Thomas's theory of justice than, as in the common good, a new use of it. [160] New appreciation has arisen for the fact that justice differs from the other virtues in two crucial ways. The first is the fact that justice not only tends to but includes action. Like all the virtues, justice has a subjective reference: "the constant and perpetual will to render to each one his right." [161] But Thomas (in subtle, intentional contradiction of Aristotle) refines this definition in the following way: "justice is a habit whereby a man *renders* to each one his due by a constant and perpetual will." [162] Second, and consequently, it is wholly and uniquely concerned with the relationships between people—that is, with human social existence. [163] Thomas's justice requires a certain equality (or proportionality) of exchange with others, as well as restraint from harming or coercing them. [164] Most to be respected are the goods that correspond to our most fundamental inclinations to life and its necessities. [165] Nowhere in Thomas is it clearer that a proper orientation to God—or even to the temporal end of a naturally virtuous life—cannot exist outside consistently fair and respectful relations with others. [166] There is no habit without act here.

Of Thomas's divisions of justice we are concerned with the justice that directs people to the general, common good. Thomas labels this legal justice, "since it belongs to the law to direct to the common good." [167] But modern, narrow uses of the term—for instance, to describe simply the exercise of any positive law or to regulate existing contractual relationships or distribution systems—have sometimes obscured its original meaning. Thus when nineteenth- and twentieth-century writers wanted to resurrect Thomas's comprehensive ideal of a justice directed to the common good, they invented the term "social justice." [168] In the encyclical tradition, social justice became "the supreme objective norm of all social and economic activity," including "the institutions which form the frame within which these relations are realized." [169] It is this strand of the justice tradition—justice not as a procedural standard but as an objective social norm—that since Vatican Council II has played a prominent role in the thought of political, liberation, and feminist theologians. [170]

The specifically social dimension of justice pushes us toward the third category, human or positive law. Alasdair MacIntyre points out that Thomas's context—his experience of concrete abuses of civil law by Emperor Frederick II and Louis IX of France—reveals the radical intent of his doctrine on human law. [171] In brief, because human law is properly a specification of natural law, the legitimacy and bindingness of the human law depend not on the rank of the lawmaker but on the law's adherence to the natural law: "every human law has just so much of the nature of law, as it is derived from the law of nature. But if in any point it deflects from the law of nature, it is no longer a law but a perversion of law." [172] Given the perspicuity of the natural law, "plain persons" (not just university professors) at least in theory have the capacity to judge a law's legitimacy. [173]

To complete our circle, we must extend these points a bit. To begin with, human law is Thomas's analogue for all law, even natural law: "an ordinance of reason for the common good, made by him who has care of the community, and promulgated." [174] Thus measuring the legitimacy of a human law, generally or in a particular situation, entails measuring it against the concrete common good: "if a case arise wherein the observance of [a human] law would be hurtful to the general welfare, it should not be observed." [175] Even more radically, he declares that in extreme cases of tyrannical injustice—that is, complete disregard for the common good that it is their mandate to uphold—rulers lose their claim to govern and may be deposed. [176]

Second, as an ordinance of practical reason, law requires the careful use of prudence. Consequences and changing circumstances figure prominently. For example, human law can and must be improved progressively to correct newly apparent deficiencies in its efficacy toward the common good; altered to reflect "the changed condition of man"; and—particularly significant in the light of Louis IX's overriding of local authority—take a back seat to (rational) custom. [177]

The power of the ordinary person to discern and dissent is heavily qualified, of course. Thomas sets the threshold of the intellectual virtues high enough that, although most of us can recognize good arguments for exception and change in law, few of us can produce them. [178] He also presumes heavily in favor of obedience. [179] Likewise, he cautions that laws should be ignored or changed only when great harm would otherwise follow, for dispensations and alterations generally harm the common good more by lowering esteem for the law than they benefit it. [180] Finally, he assumes that revolution almost always causes more disorder than the injustice it sets out to correct. [181] But even these arguments for stasis are rooted largely in the criterion of the common good. If it could be shown that people are better educated—and that obedience and stasis are less important to the common good—than

Thomas thought, the answers to questions about popular criticism and legislative change would work out differently.

Thomas bequeaths social ethics a compelling account of relations and mutual obligations between the individual and the society. He provides a concrete criterion, the common good, by which to judge the legitimacy of laws and rulers and to abrogate or depose them if necessary; a claim that natural and supernatural obligations hold everyone to the pursuit of this larger good, as well as to the actual fair treatment of particular persons; and a belief that people not in positions of political authority can come to and act on some meaningful judgment about whether obligations to justice and the common good are being fulfilled. Although there are obligations of non-maleficence and even mutual aid, there is no explicit theory of individual positive rights—that individuals have a right to demand that these responsibilities toward them be fulfilled. But the foundations are clearly there.

HUMAN NATURE AND HUMAN ENDS

Chapter 1's discussion of feminist ethics generated preliminary criteria for an adequate ethic. Among these were a grounding in an anthropology in which persons have ends, at least in the formal sense, and in which any legitimate concrete end comprehends holistic flourishing; a belief that "plain persons" can make some judgments about what constitutes and threatens flourishing; a critical epistemology; and a strong connection between moral commitment and intellectual honesty.

Thomas is plainly not a feminist. His systematic translation of all differences into hierarchies is an enormous obstacle to feminist appropriation of his thought, as is the cumulative effect of his myriad apparently biologically deterministic judgments. Yet he meets or suggests ways of meeting all of these criteria and a few more. Thomas grounds natural law—as well as practical reason, virtue theory, and social ethics—in human nature. But the nature that serves as its basis is neither the disembodied autonomous mind of the Enlightenment nor the cultural- or self-creation of postmodernity. Rather, it is the nature of Thomas's *exitus-reditus* theology, the person created for fulfillment in God. On this view, natural law is the innate rational inclination to the good, both temporal and eternal. This-worldly good must not eclipse the ultimate end, but both natural and infused virtue entail the pursuit of temporal flourishing. In fact people are naturally social in part because their well-being entails cooperation. Contribution to communal well-being is both obligatory and in a person's self-interest. Just as individuals have natural responsibilities to their communities, communities have inherent responsibilities toward their members through the common good. Laws and policies draw their validity from their ability to promote and justly distribute the common good.

From this standpoint virtue is not merely a matter of attitude, nor is discernment of the good solely a matter of querying the inclinations; immanent ends are morally significant, and consequences matter. The example of Ward Connerly in chapter 1 reminds us of this need to complete intentions with prudent, effective actions. Intending fairness, Connerly reinforced or magnified inequity, and therefore fell short of justice. The need to seek concrete flourishing and temporal justice amid cultural difference and historical change mandates that the practical dictates of natural law be both flexible and staunchly mindful of the goods that integral flourishing entails. Bodily health, social justice, and natural virtue—particularly prudence—compatible with charity are constants in this formula. All of these goods and supports fall under the simultaneously descriptive and prescriptive standard of the final end.

In addition, careful attention to Thomas defuses many feminist objections to natural law reasoning by revealing them as responses to the later inventions of neoscholastic theology. For example, by situating ethics firmly in practical reason, Thomas signals the need for conclusions to vary with circumstances. By giving prudence such a prominent role in practical reason, he insures embodied experience and just plain common sense important influence in ethical deliberation. And by insisting both upon a theory of acquired virtue and a gradual actualization of infused virtues, he sets himself up for conversation with contemporary theories of moral development, both feminist and otherwise.

Thomas thus ties reason, revelation, law, creation, redemption, individual, and society up into one organic, telic whole. But this whole is neither peaceful nor static; as the relations among the parts become more complex, coherence among them becomes a project to be accomplished rather than a foundation on which to build. The shape that this task has taken in the centuries since Thomas is our next concern.

NOTES

1. For this reason I believe that Jonsen and Toulmin are a bit premature in discounting "the general truth and relevance of universal principles" in the moral discourse of the National Commission for the Protection of Human Subjects of Biomedical and Behavioral Research (*Abuse*, 18–19). They argue that the Commission's ability to reach consensus on practical issues—despite the members' giving very different ultimate warrants for the common position—is evidence that these ultimate warrants really do not make a significant difference in practical moral reasoning. I suspect

rather that despite theological and scientific differences of opinion, enough of an implicit, common, culturally ingrained anthropology and worldview remained among the Commission's members to ground a consensus. That such an anthropology and worldview did not function explicitly or deductively does not mean that they did not function at all.

2. Korsgaard, *The Sources of Normativity*, 10–11.

3. See Porter, "Limits," for the distinction between piecemeal retrieval and retrieval that remains within the bounds of Thomas's system. Pauline Westerman's argument against retrieving natural law is primarily a judgment of its usefulness for legal theory; she does not pass judgment on its ability to illuminate the moral life or moral norms. See Pauline C. Westerman, *The Disintegration of Natural Law Theory: Aquinas to Finnis,* Brill's Studies in Intellectual History 84 (New York: Brill, 1998), 13–17, 73, and 290, as well as part I on Thomas generally.

4. See Battaglia, *Reformulation,* 96; and Michael Bertram Crowe, *The Changing Profile of the Natural Law* (The Hague: Nijhoff, 1977) chapters 1–5, but especially 165. For more recent efforts to interpret Thomas in light of his theological and political context, see Alasdair MacIntyre, "Natural Law as Subversive," *Journal of Medieval and Early Modern Studies* 26 (Winter 1996): 61–83; Jean Porter, "Contested Categories: Reason, Nature, and Natural Order in Medieval Accounts of the Natural Law," *Journal of Religious Ethics* 24 (1996): 207–32; and Jean Porter's forthcoming book on medieval natural law.

5. See J. Romelt's review of *Natur als Grundlage der Moral: Die personale Struktur des Naturgesetzes bei Thomas von Aquin: Ein Auseinandersetzung mit autonomer und teleologischer Ethik,* by Martin Rhonheimer, *Zeitschrift für Katholische Theologie* 3 (1989): 213.

6. For further elaboration of these criteria, see James Gustafson, *Protestant and Roman Catholic Ethics: Prospects for Rapprochement* (Chicago and London: University of Chicago Press, 1978), 140.

7. Lisska, *Aquinas's Theory.* Lisska defines disposition as "a property which has a fundamental 'tending towards' built into its very nature" (ibid., 303).

8. See *ST* I-II 2.7 or 3.1. See also Josef Hofer and Karl Rahner, eds., *Lexikon für Theologie und Kirche,* 2nd rev. ed. (Freiburg: Verlag-Herder, 1962), s.v. "Naturrecht—Geschichte" and "Naturrecht—Systematik," by Phillip Delhaye.

9. Recent texts that have addressed virtue theory in general or in Thomas particularly include MacIntyre, *After Virtue;* Stanley Hauerwas, *A Community of Character: Toward a Constructive Christian Social Ethic* (Notre Dame: University of Notre Dame Press, 1981); James F. Keenan, S.J., *Goodness and Rightness in Thomas Aquinas's Summa Theologiae* (Washington, DC: Georgetown University Press, 1992); Daniel Mark Nelson, *The Priority of Prudence: Virtue and Natural Law in Thomas Aquinas and the Implications for Modern Ethics* (University Park, PA: Penn State University Press, 1992); Daniel Westberg, *Right Practical Reason: Aristotle, Action, and Prudence in Aquinas* (Oxford: Clarendon Press, 1994); Jean Porter, *Moral Action and Christian Ethics* (Cambridge: Cambridge University Press, 1995); and idem, *Recovery.*

10. Lisska, *Aquinas's Theory,* 97. See also Westberg, *Right Practical Reason,* 46–47. In traditional language, the goal is the final cause, and the natural capacities are the formal cause (see Lisska, *Aquinas's Theory,* 102).

11. *ST* I-II 92.1. See also Crowe, *Changing Profile,* 156.

12. *ST* I-II 93.3, 91.1–2.

13. *ST* I-II 91.4.

14. *ST* I-II 96.1.

15. *ST* I 93. See also Gustafson, *Protestant and Roman Catholic Ethics,* 6–7.

16. Westerman, *Disintegration,* 33–34, 50; *ST* I-II 93; ibid., 91.1.

17. *ST* I-II 91.2.

18. *ST* I-II 91.2; see also Richard Bruch, "Das sittliche Naturgesetz als Gottes- und Menschenwerk bei Thomas von Aquin," *Zeitschrift für Katholische Theologie* 109 (1987): 310–11.

19. F. C. Copleston, *Thomas Aquinas* (Harmondsworth, Middlesex: Penguin Books, 1955; reprint, London: Search Press; New York: Barnes and Noble, 1976) [original title: *Aquinas*; page references are to reprint edition], 219–20).

20. *Sacramentum Mundi: An Encyclopedia of Theology,* s.v. "Natural Law (Moral)," by Grundel.

21. In some sense the purpose of the natural law in the divine economy is beatitude (*ST* I-II 90.2). Beatitude is however "improportionate" to the human "natural faculty" (ibid., 5.5, 91.4); the natural law is necessary but not sufficient to gain the true human end in God. See also Battaglia, *Reformulation,* 118–19.

22. *ST* I-II 94.2. The translation of the last sentence is from lecture notes, Victor Preller, Princeton University, 1983.

23. In *ST* I-II.9.6 Thomas makes clear that God, ultimately, moves the will toward the universal good, but we decide under which guise to pursue it.

24. Pamela M. Hall, *Narrative and the Natural Law: An Interpretation of Thomistic Ethics* (Notre Dame: University of Notre Dame Press, 1994), 19–22, 38.

25. Lisska, *Aquinas's Theory,* 163.

26. Hall, *Narrative,* 96–100.

27. *ST* I-II.5.5. See also Hall, *Narrative,* 66–67.

28. In twentieth-century expression, "Only that which is Christian is truly and completely human. And that which is anti-Christian is inhuman." Pius XI, Speech to the Sacred College, 24 December 1938, in Jean Yves Calvez and Jacques Perrin, *The Church and Social Justice,* trans. J. R. Kirwan (London: Burns and Oates, 1961), 35.

29. Likewise, moral theology—the study of humanity "in the supernatural order, possessed of a supernatural destiny"—transcends and absorbs ethics—a consideration of humanity "in the natural order, possessed of a natural destiny" (Davis, *Moral and Pastoral Theology,* 1:3).

30. Natural law generally assumes that under ideal circumstances, when the conscience is well-informed, the action that best contributes to or reflects moral goodness is also the action that realizes an ontic good in the best or most appropriate way. The link between the two is not causal, however (realizing an ontic good does not make one morally good), but ontological (human material ends and ultimate ends are by and large harmonious). On first- and second-order moral questions see Alan Donagan, *The Theory of Morality* (Chicago and London: University of Chicago Press, 1979), 54–57.

31. A. P. d'Entreves, *Natural Law: An Introduction to Legal Philosophy,* 2nd ed., Hutchinson University Library Series in Philosophy, ed. S. Korner (London: Hutchinson, 1970), 40, 48.

32. See, e.g., Lisska, *Aquinas's Theory,* 237.

33. For more extensive treatment of this problem, see Crowe, *Changing Profile,* 255–67; Raimundo Panikkar, *El Concepto de la Naturaleza—Análisis Histórico y Metafí-*

sico de un Concepto (Madrid: Consejo Superior de Investigaciones Científicas, Instituto "Luis Vives" de Filosofia, 1951); G. J. Marshall, "Human Nature Changes," *New Scholasticism* 54 (1980): 168–81; Rahner et al., ed., *Sacramentum Mundi*, s.v. "Nature: The Theological Concept," by Juan Alfaro; Franz Böckle, "Einfuhrung," in *Das Naturrecht im Disput*, ed. Böckle, 7–14; G. W. Kaufman, "A Problem of Theology: The Concept of Nature," *Harvard Theological Review* 65 (1972): 337–66; and Christine Pierce, "Natural Law Language and Women," in *Woman in Sexist Society: Studies in Power and Powerlessness*, ed. Vivian Gornick and Barbara K. Moran (New York: Basic Books, 1971), 160–72. James Gustafson argues that natural law ethics is most susceptible to the probable impossibility of agreement upon the nature and purpose of human persons (James M. Gustafson, "Nature: Its Status in Theological Ethics," *Logos* 3 [1982]: 5–23).

34. T. H. Milby makes this mistake; see T. H. Milby, "Natural Law, Evolution, and the Question of Personhood," *Quarterly Review: A Scholarly Journal for Reflection on Ministry* 6 (Summer 1986): 39–47. On the laws of nature, inclinations, freedom, and their roles in ethics, see L. Thiry, "Ethical Theory of St. Thomas Aquinas: Interpretations and Misinterpretations," *Journal of Religion* 50 (April 1970): 174; Sperry, "Changed Concepts"; Crowe, *Changing Profile*, 276–77; and Lloyd L. Weinreb, *Natural Law and Justice* (Cambridge, MA: Harvard University Press, 1987), 264–65. On the connection between nature and natural law in Thomas specifically see Porter, "Contested Categories," 223, 228–29.

35. Fulfillment of the letter of the law would in theory be possible to uncorrupted human nature, but fulfillment of the spirit of the law—acting out of perfect charity— is impossible without grace (*ST* I-II 109.4; see also 107). See also John Langan, "Beatitude and the Moral Law in St. Thomas," *Journal of Religious Ethics* 5 (Fall 1977): 187.

36. *ST* I-II 94.2. First principles are self-evident, for they speak of what is universally familiar; others are evident only "to the wise."

37. E.g., *ST* I-II 91.4, 98.6.

38. *ST* I-II 2.1: "nature is the principle of motion in that in which it is essentially and not accidentally."

39. *ST* I-II 94.2. Thomas thinks as well that "as regards the general principles whether of speculative or of practical reason, truth or rectitude is the same for all, and is equally known by all" (*ST* I-II 94.4).

40. Some commentators argue that the way in which natural law theory has functioned—either in the protection of certain values or in the definition of acceptable methods of reasoning—is at least as important as its prescriptive content. Natural law reasoning is for them first a method of "getting at," not an ever-lengthening list of what has been "gotten to." See d'Entreves, *Natural Law*; Jonsen and Toulmin, *Abuse*; Battaglia, *Reformulation*; and Crowe, *Changing Profile*.

41. For this argument see Lisska, *Aquinas's Theory*, 161–63, and Thomas R. Kopfensteiner, "Science, Metaphor, and Moral Casuistry," in *The Context of Casuistry*, Moral Traditions and Moral Arguments, ed. James F. Keenan and Thomas A. Shannon (Washington, DC: Georgetown University Press, 1995), 207–20. This is not to say that the manuals of this period did not deal with compromised situations; but they dealt with them in such a way that they gave the impression that all scenarios had definite and scientifically discoverable solutions. The Enlightenment alternatives for moral reason were speculative reason and emotivism.

42. Copleston, *Thomas Aquinas*, 224; Westberg, *Right Practical Reason*, chapter 2; and *ST* I 79.11. The liberation hermeneutic, discussed in chapters 3 and 7 of this book, challenges this strict division.

43. Jonsen and Toulmin, *Abuse*, 327.

44. Jonsen and Toulmin, *Abuse*, 64–66.

45. Jonsen and Toulmin, *Abuse*, 19, 34, 64, 297.

46. For the latter see John Mahoney, *The Making of Moral Theology: A Study of the Roman Catholic Tradition*, The Martin D'Arcy Memorial Lectures 1981–82 (Oxford: Clarendon Press, 1987), 208; and Jonsen and Toulmin, *Abuse*, 67–68.

47. *ST* I-II 57.4. See Westberg, *Right Practical Reason*, 26.

48. *ST* I-II 57.5. Prudence, an intellectual virtue, is "something of a moral virtue" (*ST* I-II 61.1) because of its necessity to the moral virtues.

49. *ST* I-II 57.5.

50. For an example of the second, see *ST* II-II 47.36. Jonsen and Toulmin tend to describe practical reason as "relating and applying . . . concepts *outwardly*, to the world of concrete objects and actual states of affairs" (Jonsen and Toulmin, *Abuse*, 327); this description does not quite catch the flavor of the Thomistic pursuit of the good, in which principle or rule does not stand over against the actor or the context as something external to them but articulates pursuit of the good. See Westberg's *Right Practical Reason*, chapters 2 and 3. On the first point see ibid., 6–7, 10–11. On the last point see Westberg, *Right Practical Reason*, 165; Porter, *Recovery*, 157; and Porter, *Moral Action*, 154.

51. *ST* II-II 55.1–2.

52. Westberg, *Right Practical Reason*, 7–9, 218; and Porter, *Recovery*, 163. Porter, *Recovery*, 159, uses the language of instantiating the virtues rather than of pursuing goods. This difference in emphasis is just that, for virtue itself is a human good; the first emphasizes things to be accomplished outside oneself, but rationally, and the second, self-development through action.

53. *ST* II-II 49.

54. *ST* II-II 49.1.

55. Westberg, *Right Practical Reason*, chapter 7; Hall, *Narrative*, points out the way in which culture can bias knowledge.

56. Armand Maurer, *St. Thomas and Historicity*, the Aquinas Lecture, 1979 (Milwaukee: Marquette University Press, 1979), 18; italics added. See also Battaglia, *Reformulation*, 131.

57. Hall, *Narrative*, 94.

58. Ibid., I, 84. See also Battaglia, *Reformulation*, 37–38.

59. See Westberg, *Right Practical Reason*, 98, 113–15.

60. Josef Pieper, *The Four Cardinal Virtues*, various translators (Notre Dame: University of Notre Dame Press, 1966), 14–15.

61. *ST* II-II 49.2.

62. *ST* II-II 8.1.

63. *ST* II-II 49.3.

64. In the contemporary context one might, for example, emphasize accountability to oppressed or marginalized persons; see chapters 3 and 7.

65. Foresight is also "the principal of the parts of prudence, since whatever is required for prudence, is necessary precisely that some particular thing may be rightly directed to its end" (*ST* II-II 49.6.1).

66. *ST* II-II 49.7.

67. *ST* II-II 55, but see parallel treatments of other virtues throughout II-II.

68. Hall, *Narrative*, 39–40; on dialectic in medieval natural law thought in general see Porter, "Contested Categories," 212.

69. See Mahoney, *Making*, 206: "objectivity in morals . . . means deriving moral standards from things as they are."

70. *ST* I-II 94.4.

71. Saint Thomas Aquinas *IV Sententiarum* 33.1.1; quoted in Jonsen and Toulmin, *Abuse*, 135. Westerman notes that for Thomas human relations, and therefore the norms that govern them, follow "no standard recipes" (*Disintegration*, 60).

72. *ST* 94.5. See also Battaglia, *Reformulation*, 89–92, 99–100. Thomas did believe that the judicial and ceremonial precepts of the old law had changed with the advent of Christ, but these are not features of natural law proper (see *ST* I-II, 101–105).

73. Michael Novak, "Traditional Pragmatism: An Ethic Both Practical and Wise," *Journal of Ecumenical Studies* 5 (Spring 1968): 300–2; Thiry, "Ethical Theory," 183, note 41. See also Battaglia, *Reformulation*, 133.

74. Jonsen and Toulmin, *Abuse*, 183–93.

75. Kopfensteiner, "Science," 212.

76. John T. Noonan, Jr., "Development in Moral Doctrine," in Keenan and Shannon, 188–204, at 200. Noonan proposes a four-step historicity gauge. At one end it is claimed that natural law merely improves in expression over time, and at the other it is said that moral doctrine is merely "the projection of human needs"; intermediate claims, that reason employs Scripture and tradition to reach logically necessary but nonscriptural propositions, or that conclusions were maturations or developments of earlier insights, fall between. Noonan chooses the fourth; Thomas falls somewhere between the first and third (ibid., 194–95). See also Crowe, *Changing Profile*, 186–91.

77. Porter, *Recovery*, 44.

78. *ST* I-II 1.6, 3.8. For a more extended discussion see Porter, *Recovery*, chapter 2, and page 73.

79. On the connection between supernatural and natural ends, see Porter, *Recovery*, 67. On the ordering of ends, see Westerman, *Disintegration*, 40.

80. *ST* I-II 4.6.

81. *ST* I-II 4.6.3. Thomas is talking about the completeness of the sense faculties and therefore of a degree of bodily health that keeps the mind sharp and clear. He is not addressing perfection in appearance.

82. *ST* I-II 4.6.1

83. In this sense the goods of the body seem to have pride of place. In beatitude the soul's perfection fulfills the body "to which it is natural to the soul to be united" as nature perfects grace: "from the Happiness of the soul there will be an overflow on to the body, so that this too will obtain its perfection," adding "a certain charm and perfection to Happiness" of the soul (*ST* I-II 4.6 and 4.6.1). So although the body's perfection does not comprise happiness (*ST* I-II 2.5) but is consequent to the soul's perfection, still bodily perfection is a necessary result of beatitude.

84. On the common good, see below. On friendship, see *ST* I-II 4.8. On wealth and external goods, see *ST* I-II 2.1 and 4.7.

85. Westberg, *Right Practical Reason*, 47.

86. For opposing responses to the question, see Finnis, *Natural Law*, 34; and

Russell Hittinger, *A Critique of the New Natural Law Theory* (Notre Dame: University of Notre Dame Press, 1987), 193–98. On the latter see also Lisska, *Aquinas's Theory,* 107–15.

87. *ST* I-II 94.2; emphasis in translation. Whether this particular vision of human being is true to contemporary moral experience will be taken up in chapter 3.

88. Crowe, *Changing Profile,* 178–79. Thomas's attempt to strike a balance which integrates reason and other, seemingly animal inclinations was certainly not isolated. Numerous other canonists and theologians of the twelfth and thirteenth centuries attempted to sort these elements out, with quite disparate results. For the history of this issue, see ibid., 72–135.

89. *ST* II-II 64.7.

90. Sexual intercourse is excused only within marriage and then only for procreation or to discourage a spouse's fornication (*ST* Suppl. 49.4–5).

91. *ST* II-II 104.5.

92. Timothy E. O'Connell, *Principles for a Catholic Morality,* with a foreword by Charles E. Curran (San Francisco: Harper and Row, 1978), 135. O'Connell traces this view to Cicero.

93. An even more extreme reading—that biology governs all levels of human activity—finds resonance among some sociobiologists. See Stephen J. Pope, *The Evolution of Altruism and the Ordering of Love,* Moral Traditions and Moral Arguments (Washington, DC: Georgetown University Press, 1994). Nuancing the question requires a foray into the earlier history of natural law. Contemporary historians trace Thomas's ambivalence about the prescriptive power of the body back to the writings of the Roman lawyer Domitius Ulpianus. See Crowe, *Changing Profile,* 143–51. See Charles E. Curran, *Directions in Catholic Social Ethics* (Notre Dame: University of Notre Dame Press, 1985), 125–58; Charles E. Curran, *Ongoing Revision in Moral Theology* (Notre Dame: Fides/Claretian, 1975), 131; Crowe, *Changing Profile,* 43–51, 41–155; and Michael B. Crowe, "The Pursuit of the Natural Law," *Irish Theological Quarterly* 44 (1977): 3–29. See also Josef Th. C. Arntz, "Die Entwicklung des naturrechlichen Denkens innerhalb des Thomismus," in *Das Naturrecht im Disput,* ed. Franz Böckle (Düsseldorf: Patmos-Verlag, 1966), 87–120.

94. See for example Curran, *Directions,* 125–32, 156–57, and Pope Paul VI, *Humanae Vitae,* in *Humanae Vitae and the Bishops: The Encyclical and the Statements of the National Hierarchies,* comp. by John Horgan (Shannon: Irish University Press, [1972]), 33–56.

95. John Finnis, "Natural Law and Unnatural Acts," *Heythrop Journal* 11 (1970): 367; ellipsis in original. This list closely resembles those drawn up by Finnis and Germain Grisez elsewhere. See Finnis, *Natural Law,* 86–90; and Germain Grisez, *Abortion: The Myths, the Realities, and the Arguments* (New York and Cleveland: Corpus Books, 1970), 312–13.

96. John Finnis, *Natural Law and Natural Rights* (Oxford: Clarendon Press; New York: Oxford University Press, 1980), 33–34; also Finnis and Grisez, "The Basic Principles of Natural Law: A Reply to Ralph McInerny," 159, 161.

97. Finnis and Grisez disallow a *predetermined* hierarchy of basic values; establishment of a universal hierarchy of values curtails human freedom by limiting human self-determination. But a personal hierarchy—special stress, dictated by one's skills or vocation, on one or a few values—is not only permissible but virtually necessary.

See Finnis, *Natural Law*, 92–93; and Grisez, *Abortion*, 318. See also Finnis, *Fundamentals*, 136–42; Grisez, *Abortion*, 311; Germain Grisez, "Against Consequentialism," *American Journal of Jurisprudence* 23 (1978): 50; and William E. May, *Moral Absolutes: Catholic Tradition, Current Trends, and the Truth* (Milwaukee: Marquette University Press, 1989), 53–54. On mixing moral and premoral goods, see Lisa Sowle Cahill, "Teleology, Utilitarianism, and Christian Ethics," *Theological Studies* 42 (1981): 622–23.

98. According to Grisez one may subordinate one good to another if one has "reasonable basis" (Grisez, *Way of the Lord Jesus*, vol. 1, 216)—that is, if one good is "postponable," if its fulfillment will not be permanently cut off or significantly retarded by the accomplishment of another good. But *unique* human life is never a "postponable" good; a unique human life cannot be fulfilled in the future if it is ended—or even prevented from beginning—now (Grisez, *Abortion*, 319–20; Grisez, *Contraception and the Natural Law* [Milwaukee: Bruce Publishing Company, 1964], 94, 159). Therefore one may never choose directly to end a unique life.

99. Russell Hittinger replies that one cannot take the method and run; a natural law ethic that bypasses the issue of human nature is only a "trope on conventions" (Hittinger, *A Critique of the New Natural Law Theory*, 197–98). Hittinger adds, "But what strains credibility is that one could purport to have a coherent theory of practical rationality, even while disclaiming to know (in the strong sense of the term *to know*) what it is to be human, whether human beings have ends, and how the overall setting of nature either orients or distorts human action. Credibility is further strained by one who would insist that the latter type of knowledge is unnecessary, even if one should have it" (ibid., 193). For Lisska, the point of Thomas's ethics is "reaching an end as determined by the dispositional properties central to human nature"; to take Thomas Aquinas's ethic without its ontology is mistakenly to remove the end that makes inclination meaningful in the first place (Lisska, *Aquinas's Theory*, 100). Ralph McInerny argues that Finnis's version of basic values—and that of Germain Grisez, who argues similarly—separates fact from value in the development of moral norms. See Ralph McInerny, "The Principles of Natural Law," in *Natural Law and Theology*, Readings in Moral Theology, ed. Charles E. Curran and Richard A. McCormick, no. 7 (New York/Mahwah: Paulist Press, 1991), 146–48; and Westerman, *Disintegration*, 22, 45.

100. Lisska, *Aquinas's Theory*, 161–63; Hall, *Narrative*, 18. See also Porter, *Recovery*, 18–21. Stephen Pope implies something similar when he criticizes pre-Vatican II thinkers for retaining Thomas's ordering of love but ignoring his anthropology (Pope, *Evolution*, 68).

101. "What is biologically natural is not always normatively good, notwithstanding that it constitutes one important basis for human flourishing and indicates certain goods that will be included in lives lived well" (Pope, *Evolution*, 155).

102. See *ST* I-II 31.7, 33.3, 37.1, 38.3. On the latter see Pope, *Evolution*.

103. See Mahoney, *Making*, 79; Maurer, *St. Thomas*, 1, 8; *Sacramentum Mundi*, s.v. "Natural Law (Moral)," by Grundel; and *ST* I-II 51.3. The inclinations, whether divided or holistic, cannot be employed properly without prudence (*ST* I-II 65.1.1). See also Westberg, *Right Practical Reason*, 93–94; and Porter, *Recovery*, 71.

104. *ST* I-II 94.3; see also I-II 50.3.

105. Pope, *Evolution*, 55–58, 156. See *ST* I-II 26.1–2.

106. Porter, *Recovery of Virtue*, 79, 89–90. See also Pope, *Evolution*, 52, 156; see also Lisska, *Aquinas's Theory*, 100. In contrast, see for instance Finnis, for example, *Natural Law*, 94.

107. "Reason . . . directs *all* things regarding man; so that whatever can be ruled by reason, is contained under the law of reason" (*ST* I-II 94.2.3, italics added).

108. On "individual moral feeling" and identification of goods, see also Copleston, *Thomas Aquinas*, 233–34. Thomas's equation of the truly reasonable and the truly good—that which is to be loved and sought—infuses even practical knowledge with affectivity. See Daniel C. Maguire, "*Ratio Practica* and the Intellectualistic Fallacy," *Journal of Religious Ethics* 10 (1982): 22–39.

109. Mahoney, *Making*, 252–58; see also James F. Keenan, "Catholic Moral Theology, Ignatian Spirituality, and Virtue Ethics: Strange(r Than They Should Be) Bedfellows," *The Way Supplement* 88 (Spring 1997): 36–45. This is not to say that the manuals of moral theology ignored it altogether. For example, Henry Davis gives a good, concise account of Thomas's virtue theory in volume 1 of his *Moral and Pastoral Theology*; see especially 253–68. But whereas in the *Summa* Thomas *begins* his discussion of the moral life with virtue, continues with sin as the vitiation of virtue, and *ends* with a discussion of law, which specifies the shape of virtuous action, Davis does the opposite: he treats law first, then sin as the transgression of law, and mentions virtue almost as an afterthought. Just after mid-century, Ford and Kelly resurrected the idea of growth in moral perfection, yet the word "virtue" does not appear even in the index of their introductory volume; see John C. Ford and Gerald Kelly, *Contemporary Moral Theology*, vol. 1, *Questions in Fundamental Moral Theology* (Westminster, MD: Newman Press, 1958). The writers discussed in chapters 5, 6, and 7 of this book likewise avoid the term.

110. See James F. Keenan, "Proposing Cardinal Virtues," *Theological Studies* 56 (1995): 709–29; Anne E. Patrick, *Liberating Conscience: Feminist Explorations in Catholic Moral Theology* (New York: Continuum, 1996), 90–101; and Porter, *Moral Action*, chapter 5.

111. See Lisska, *Aquinas's Theory*, 100.

112. This link is expressed in Richard Gula's choice of subtitles for part 2 of his book on Catholic morality: "The Nature of the Human Person—Character of the Moral Agent," not "Content of Moral Norms" (Richard M. Gula, *Reason Informed by Faith: Foundations of Catholic Morality* [New York/Mahwah: Paulist Press, 1989], 61). Even in the manuals—one of the least self-consciously theological, most norm-driven genres of moral writing in the natural law tradition that followed Thomas—"the moral order was constituted by a set of goods ordered to the ultimate end of human persons and to their proximate welfare" (John A. Gallagher, *Time Past, Time Future: An Historical Study of Catholic Moral Theology* (New York and New Jersey: Paulist Press, 1990), 71; see also ibid., 78). Yet it is telling that one important transitional work, recognized for its insistence that moral theology take account of changes in historical circumstance, skips over the purpose of the moral law and goes directly to a chapter on "The Church and The Moral Law." See Ford and Kelly, *Contemporary Moral Theology*.

113. Porter, *Moral Action*, 140.

114. But one cannot reduce virtue to the principle of narrative unity of life; see Porter, *Recovery*, 83; Porter, *Moral Action*, 142; and *ST* I-II 58.4–5, 65.1.

115. *ST* I-II 62.1–2.

116. *ST* I-II 55.4. The definition, set out in the first objection, reads "quality of the mind"; Thomas argues for substituting "habit" in his response.

117. Porter, *Moral Action,* 148.

118. A power must be appropriate to its end. Therefore the virtue appropriate to the human last end must be supernatural. At the same time, no moral virtue can exist in its fullest sense without charity, which guarantees that prudence has the right end in mind; conversely, all moral virtues are infused with charity (*ST* I-II 65.2–3). See also Keenan, *Goodness and Rightness,* x, 99.

119. In this sense—made explicit in MacIntyre's description of the actor as author—by design or default I create myself morally. See MacIntyre, *After Virtue,* 213. MacIntyre notes that actually an actor is a co-author; she creates her end and "story" in the context of her community and its ends and stories.

120. See Keenan, *Goodness and Rightness,* 13; also *ST* I-II 51.2–3 on acquisition of habits.

121. *ST* I-II 51–53. In Thomas a virtue must be appropriate to its end. Human natural goods all have their own virtues. It is almost impossible to ruin an acquired virtue through one contrary act, even if that act is a mortal sin. One lie rarely obliterates a habit of acquired honesty; except in very unusual circumstances, a person who has told one lie can still be thought of as honest.

122. *ST* I-II 65.3. A single, calculated, serious lie might mar acquired honesty slightly, but it would destroy infused virtue altogether (63.2.2). But a less serious sin, one that did not reject the charity of God, could coexist with the theological virtues. James Keenan notes that Thomas contradicts himself on whether a lie can be compatible with charity. In Thomas's discussions of sin, he implies that it cannot; in his discussions of charity, he implies that it can. See Keenan, *Goodness and Rightness,* chapter 7, especially 164–75.

123. *ST,* II-II 47.14; see also III 69.4–5. This possibility—having efficacious but incompletely realized infused virtue—allows for a senile, incompetent, or young person to be united with God; she is already directed toward God and would, if she could, behave accordingly. It also parallels liberation theology's focus on the moral obligation to realize the previous gift of salvation; see chapter 7 of this book.

124. Ibid., I-II 65.3.2–3. This is never a problem with acquired virtue, as one must overcome contrary dispositions in order to acquire the virtue in the first place. Thus people striving for a well-ordered life and genuinely motivated by charity may still be in a state of relative moral disorganization and even—in extreme cases—exhibit fewer of the acts of the virtues than some diligent people who possess some level of acquired virtue without charity. See also Porter, *Moral Action,* 163. This implies that acquired virtue may be an indirect help in developing the acts of the infused virtues, by reducing the force of the contrary dispositions.

125. Keenan draws on Thomas to elaborate his own distinction between goodness and rightness: a "good" person—a person infused with charity—strives out of love for God to act "rightly," that is, according to reason (Keenan, *Goodness and Rightness,* 8). In order to preserve the balance of Thomas's position, one must preserve both the *distinction* and the *connection* between act and habit.

126. Hauerwas is concerned to find theoretical ways of affirming both a person's present moral integrity and her potential for moral maturation (*Community,* 133). Richard McCormick proposes that standards for moral integrity should be realistic—

i.e., should account for *incomplete* moral development—and therefore should not establish norms that assume moral perfection. See chapter 6. Porter (*Moral Action,* 163) rightly points out that the infused virtues are hardly intuitive but depend on Thomas's doctrine of grace. This is true, but their analogue—for instance, in a person widely thought "good at heart" who nonetheless constantly falls short of true virtue in action—is common. See ibid., chapter 5, for other ways in which maturation or development might modernize or corroborate Thomas's conception of the virtues.

127. *ST* I-II 58.4–5, 59.2.

128. *ST* I-II 65.2–3.

129. Eugene F. Rogers, Jr., "The Narrative of Natural Law in Aquinas's Commentary on Romans 1," *Theological Studies* 59 (1998): 254–76, at 272.

130. See Porter, *Moral Action,* chapter 4. Keenan points to the same connection when he argues that the (acquired) moral virtues—acts of adherence to the law—are merely "steps on the way to the perfection of prudence" (Keenan, *Goodness and Rightness,* 105).

131. On the connection of the virtues, see Jean Porter, "The Unity of the Virtues and the Ambiguity of Goodness: A Reappraisal of Aquinas's Theory of the Virtues," *The Journal of Religious Ethics* 21 (Spring 1993): 137–63.

132. For a revival of the conscience tradition in light of contemporary psychology, see Sidney Callahan, *In Good Conscience: Reason and Emotion in Decision Making* (San Francisco: Harper and Row, 1991); for a feminist interpretation, see Patrick, *Liberating Conscience.*

133. This connection is the burden of Keenan, *Goodness and Rightness,* which argues that Thomas needs such a distinction but develops it only inadequately.

134. *ST* I-II 19.5–6. Of course, if the error is willful or negligent, reason is not to be honored.

135. Thomas insists that "absolutely speaking, every will *at variance* with reason, whether right or erring, is always evil," even though "the will that *abides* by human reason, is not always right, nor is it always in accord with the eternal law" (*ST* I-II 19.5, 19.6.2; italics added). This distinction is especially important for Josef Fuchs; see chapter 5 of this book. See Mahoney on Thomas, *Making,* 184–93. As Keenan notes, the explanation for these claims is not wholly satisfying, but they capture something true to the human moral experience (Keenan, *Goodness and Rightness,* 106–7).

136. As Keenan notes, Thomas is oddly unable to assign a bad fruit to a good tree and so stops short of calling the act or the erring actor good; the innocent error is simply "excused." Still, the only alternative—disobeying faulty judgment—is outright evil because it contradicts rationality. The nonculpably erring reason binds (*ST* I-II 19.6 and Keenan, *Goodness and Rightness,* 106–7).

137. See Finnis, *Natural Law,* 126.

138. In Thomas this distinction is expressed also as the difference between the Old Law, an external, written law which consisted primarily of commands to perform outward deeds, and the New Law, an internal, unwritten law of love implanted by grace which consists only secondarily in deeds. See *ST* I-II 106–7.

139. Virtue calls forth "the works of reason proper to man" (*ST* I-II 55.2); that is, as noted above, works appropriate to humans as beings created with their end in God and fitted with natural inclinations that indicate something to reason about how to behave in conformity with this end.

140. See especially the papal encyclicals *Rerum Novarum, Quadragesimo Anno, Octogesima Adveniens,* and *Centesimo Annus,* as well as the Vatican II document *Populorum Progressio.*

141. See Keenan, *Goodness and Rightness,* 99, quotes *ST* II-II 17.1: "Every human act is good, which attains reason or God." In the context the emphasis is on attaining God in hope, but reason points us toward temporal ends as well.

142. *ST* II-II 94.2 is the source for a number of these. Most of the elements in this list come from Porter, "Limits," 321; see also Porter, *Recovery,* 177. The latter three come from *ST* II-II 168. MacIntyre argues that Thomas likely has in mind the *jongleurs,* who were often quite critical of both government and the Dominicans. See "Natural Law," 74–75.

143. "Society is obviously nothing else than the unification of men for the purpose of performing some one thing in common." Saint Thomas Aquinas, *Contra impugnantes Dei cultum et religionem,* iii, in *The Political Ideas of St. Thomas Aquinas: Representative Selections,* ed. Dino Bigongiari (New York: Hafner Press, 1953), x-xi.

144. On distributive justice, common goods, and ownership, see *ST* II-II 61.1.2. See also David Hollenbach, *Claims in Conflict: Retrieving and Renewing the Catholic Human Rights Tradition* (New York: Paulist Press, 1979), 147–48.

145. *ST* II-II 57.2, 58.5–6, 63; ibid., I-II 96.3–4. Hence the tendency of the early social encyclicals to focus on religious conversion as the true prerequisite to the common good.

146. See Porter, *Recovery,* 127.

147. In fact Thomas points out that we may pursue our own goods in an orderly way (*ST* II-II 26.4); see Porter, *Recovery,* 126–27. The key condition here is "truly." For Thomas, not just anything I happen to like is a genuine good. A benefit may not be considered in isolation. Living a life of crime may be to my material benefit, but it harms my victims, and it reduces the peace and security of the society at large, indirectly harming me as well. It also conflicts with my end in God. Thus generating the common good does require common effort and the stilling of individual impulses, and to that end, it also requires cultivation of social virtue: behavior that leads to the common good (*ST* I-II, 92.1.3).

148. Porter, "Limits," 321–22.

149. *ST* II-II 64.6; II-II 65.1, 3; II-II 68.8; II-II 64.3.

150. On the former, *ST* II-II 31.3 and II-II 32.9; on the latter, II-II 66.7.

151. Porter adds that "there is certainly nothing in his account of justice that rules out [positive promotion of the well-being of its individual members]. ("Limits," 322).

152. See also Lisska, *Aquinas's Theory,* chapter 9, especially 228–32.

153. Jacques Maritain, *The Person and the Common Good,* trans. John J. Fitzgerald (New York: Charles Scribner's Sons, 1947), 5–6. See also Calvez and Perrin, *Church,* 132.

154. Pope Paul VI, *Populorum Progressio,* in *Renewing the Earth: Catholic Documents on Peace, Justice and Liberation,* ed. David J. O'Brien and Thomas A. Shannon (Garden City, NY: Doubleday, Image Books, 1977), 317, par. 13; see also 318–19, par. 15–17. Par. 17 speaks of "humanity advancing along the path of history" and of its historical achievements as cumulative but prescinds from any discussion of the theological significance of this advance. In *Centesimo Annus* John Paul II is particularly

interested in protecting individual freedom from social tyranny justified by false anthro-pologies.

155. According to Pius XI, "the common good of a society cannot be provided for unless each individual member, a human being endowed with the dignity of personality, receives all that he needs to discharge his social function" (Pope Pius XI, *Divini Redemptoris*, par. 71; quoted in Calvez and Perrin, 152). Pius XI first reunited justice and the common good in the 1931 encyclical *Quadragesimo Anno*, in *Five Great Encyclicals: Labor, Education, Marriage, Reconstructing the Social Order, Atheistic Communism*, ed. Gerald C. Treacy (New York: Paulist Press, 1939), e.g., 146–47, par. 74–76. See also Pope John Paul II, *Centesimus Annus*, in *Origins* 21, no. 1 (16 May 1991): 17, par. 43.

156. Pius XI, *Divini Redemptoris*, par. 71. See also Lisska, *Aquinas's Theory*, 234–36, on the derivation of rights from duties.

157. *Centesimus Annus*, 10, par. 25. On the importance of anthropology for defining the common good, see for example Lisa Sowle Cahill, "The Catholic Tradition: Religion, Morality, and the Common Good," *Journal of Law and Religion* 5 (1987): 76. Hollenbach also discusses the post-*Rerum Novarum* era in Roman Catholic social thought (see *Claims*).

158. Pope John Paul II, *Centesimus Annus*, 19, par. 49. This claim is anticipated in Calvez and Perrin, *Church*, 103.

159. Alasdair MacIntyre points out that Thomas could not imagine "a political common good shared by individuals and groups of differing religious belief." These arguments, he says, always stem from theology rather than natural law and so should perhaps be discounted in considerations of the latter. See MacIntyre, "Natural Law," 80. But Thomas's theological and philosophical commitments, as I have been arguing, are so closely intertwined that no strict separation can be made between them.

160. Calvez and Perrin, *Church*, chapter 6.

161. *ST* II-II 58.1.1.

162. *ST* II-II 58.1; see also Keenan, *Goodness and Rightness*, 105.

163. *ST* II-II 58.2, 11. Thomas expressly argues that our dealings with ourselves fall under the other moral virtues (*ST* II-II 58.2.4).

164. See the discussion of the common good, above, and *ST* II-II 61.1–3.

165. Porter, *Recovery*, 144; see also idem, "Limits," 321; and Keenan, "Propos-ing," 719–21.

166. Porter argues that intrinsic evil has specifically to do with the violation of justice. (Porter, *Recovery*, 141–43). Here again the argument has the flavor of an obligation to treat others well, not of a right to be treated well by them.

167. *ST* I-II 58.5; see also 58.6–7.

168. Calvez and Perrin, *Church*, 144–47.

169. Calvez and Perrin, *Church*, 152, 151. See also the introductory essays in *The Gospel of Peace and Justice*, ed. Joseph Gremillion (Maryknoll, NY: Orbis Books, 1976).

170. This does not mean that justice-as-norm can be theoretically separated from justice-as-virtue. The link between the two is their subsumption under infused charity, which—thanks to the natural law link between human proximate and ultimate ends—perfects both human social relations and individual virtue. See Calvez and Perrin, *Church*, chapter 7.

171. MacIntyre, "Natural Law as Subversive."

172. *ST* I-II 95.2; see also 96.4. See also Calvez and Perrin, *Church,* 133; the common good is the "concrete norm" of human society.

173. MacIntyre, "Natural Law," 68; but see caveats on 76–77.

174. *ST* I-II 90.4. Novak even argues that Thomas does not intend this definition to apply, even analogically, to natural law, which is primarily a power or principle rather than a collection of rules (Novak, "Pragmatism," 301).

175. *ST* I-II 96.6.

176. *ST* II-II 42.2.3.

177. On the first two points, see *ST* I-II 97.1. Human law, unlike natural law, "compels through fear of punishment," for its purpose is to make individuals virtuous not with respect to their end in God but merely with respect to the common good (*ST* I-II 95.1, 3, and 96.1). Also unlike natural law, human law prescribes only acts, not virtues, and among these only those that are "ordainable to the common good"; it proscribes mainly acts "without the prohibition of which human society could not be maintained" (ibid., 96.2–3). On the latter point, see *ST* I-II 97.3 and the discussion in MacIntyre, "Natural Law," 70–71.

178. MacIntyre, "Natural Law," 76–77. For MacIntyre the capacity to recognize still preserves the revolutionary tint.

179. *ST* II-II 104.

180. *ST* I-II, 96.6, 97.1–2.

181. *ST* II-II 42.2.3.

3

Natural Law Since Thomas

A close look at Thomas's theological anthropology and its implications for ethics reveals much more that is friendly to feminism than most feminist ethicists likely expect. For revealing Thomas's sometimes offensive conclusions as practical rather than speculative truths uncovers a structure of reasoning that can yield more liberative conclusions in new circumstances. Is the solution to all methodological problems in ethics then a return to Thomas's method? Perhaps, one might argue, the more than seven intervening centuries of moral thought have done nothing to improve on Thomas's wisdom and in fact have done much to obscure it. If we simply went back to his texts, and especially if we read them in tandem with Aristotle's, we would find a brilliant, insightful, up-to-date moral theory.

Like most simple solutions, this sort of nostalgic revivalism is misleading. Certainly it is true that feminists, as well as many other natural law thinkers who might not label themselves feminists, have in common a distaste for the post-Thomistic scholastic and neoscholastic traditions of moral theology. But in fact cultural change has brought with it more or less permanent modifications in the sorts of answers that will satisfy the question "what must I do, and why?" For example, as Christine Korsgaard points out, today a satisfactory moral theory must address itself to each of us as particular agents, not to a hypothetical or uninvolved third party; it must appeal to our fundamental sense of our identities; and it must allow "us to act in the full light of knowledge of what morality is and why we are susceptible to its influences, and at the same time to believe that our actions are justified and make sense." [1] Today a satisfactory moral theory cannot tell us merely how moral obligations come to exist, how we know them, and how we come to be moral actors; it must also convince each of us that these obligations are deeply binding on us in particular, here and now. Post-Thomistic scholastic and neoscholastic theology—along with transcendental Thomism—cannot lightly be dismissed, because they represent the responses the natural law tradition has made to profound, cumulative changes in our senses of ourselves and our surroundings, changes of which any viable contemporary ethic must also take account.

The metamorphoses that we need to consider are cumulative rather than successive. For example, from the eighteenth century forward, any convincing moral theory must either have a place for—or find a good reason to reject—the autonomous agent; indeed, Korsgaard's criteria of adequacy for moral theories themselves reflect the permanent heritage of the Enlightenment vision. Natural law thinkers in this century responded to this challenge by pointing out that the rational, self-legislating agent is quite compatible with a vision of natural law as active participation in divine reason. [2] Similar cultural changes have elicited more complex and, usually, more ambiguous responses from natural law ethics. Among history's other bequests to natural law is the tradition of casuistic reasoning, inspired—with unhappy as well as salutary results—by new demands made on ethics and law by the sudden expansion of ecclesiastical power (in the eleventh century) and of trade, global travel, and colonization (especially in the sixteenth and seventeenth centuries). [3] Natural law has also been illumined and transformed by the twentieth-century turn to the subject, the Marxist critiques of dominant moral discourses, and Enlightenment claims about inherent human dignity. Likewise, the apparent danger that Vatican Council II's *aggiornamento* would slip into undifferentiated relativism has inspired disputes over magisterial authority and over the peculiarly Christian character of natural law claims, both of which have raised questions about the ethical implications of the conduct of moral deliberation itself.

The influences of these cultural forces are incontrovertible, but outlining and evaluating their effects is a more delicate task. We must guard against two sorts of oversimplification. On the one hand, to reduce post-Thomistic natural law reasoning to its grossest misuses or its most awkward attempts to respond to change and then dismiss it as corrupt is to discard much that is of value to the contemporary moral discussion. On the other hand, to imply that the natural law tradition—or some pure core of it—is absolutely benign and unproblematic is to fail to consider the possibility that some accommodations have been either unfaithful to natural law's key claims or inadequate to the real challenges history poses. The question at each stage is whether the natural law tradition's response to cultural pressure is both adequate to the challenge at hand and faithful to the theological anthropology laid out in chapter 2.

CASUISTRY

The earliest of the permanent changes in natural law moral theology was the flowering of casuistry, or the case method of solving moral dilemmas, in the early fourteenth to mid-seventeenth centuries. Casuistical method evolved to deal with the disjunction between moral principles that had been refined gradually during a period of relative cultural stability and new questions that had been generated by sudden, dramatic changes in cultural circumstances. The commonly cited example is the misfit between prohibitions of usury (developed in a period in which barter was the most common form of exchange) and the pressure to raise capital to meet the financial needs of rapidly growing money economies. Casuists generally rejected the obviously available principle—in this case, "do not charge interest on money lent"—as inadequate to the apparently new place of money in the economy. Instead, they searched for other familiar cases whose solutions seemed better to comprehend the new circumstances. Over the course of time, they developed systems of these analogous cases out of which new principles evolved—for instance, "charge no more interest than you might reasonably expect to earn if you invested your money in another way." [4] Roman Catholic high casuistry fell into disrepute in the mid-seventeenth century—just as deductive, speculative moral reasoning was ascendant—when Blaise Pascal lampooned Jesuit casuists for frivolous and far-fetched choices of analogous cases. [5] But interest in and use of the method have revived significantly over the past two decades. [6]

Historians of casuistry differ slightly over whether periods in which casuistry is used heavily are aberrational periods of adjustment in the human moral framework or permanent models for moral deliberation in all periods. Some, for example, hold that wide use of casuistry is necessary and appropriate only during cultural transitions, and others imply that it is the normal, healthy mode of moral reasoning; for the latter, the proclivity of some Enlightenment rationalists to model moral reasoning on deductive, speculative models was a temporary and misguided deviation from the casuistical norm. [7] They also disagree over whether casuistry is ultimately about solving immediate cases or—more broadly—about proposing, testing, and confirming new moral principles. [8] Yet all imply that contemporary thinkers would have been justified in consigning casuistry to the historical dust bin if it did not seem to be a peculiarly fruitful approach to contemporary moral conundrums. Questions like, "What are our obligations to the dying, when we can keep their bodies alive indefinitely?" that lack clear precedents or fit only awkwardly under existing principles beg for casuistical treatment. Whether or not every age is an age of casuistry, they declare, this age surely is.

The advantages of casuistical reasoning are many. It is useful—and perhaps unavoidable—when the principles at hand do not seem to comprehend the subtleties of an historical period or a particular case. When it is carried out in a community of critical discourse it generates new paradigmatic cases and eventually new principles. At its best, it is an instrument of continuity in change, transplanting guiding insights like organs from a cadaver into a new, living system of principles in which they will have a vital function. Thus the challenge of Christian casuistry is not, as Jonsen and Toulmin imply, to compromise by "linking a faith that includes moral imperatives of paradoxical sublimity with the incessant demands of a rough and mean world." [9] What is paradoxical about Christianity's "sublime moral imperatives" is the belief that ways to perform them can be found, even and indeed only in this "rough and mean world." Incarnating the virtues is the true point of casuistry.

Casuistry also fits the inductive model of scientific learning with which we have become comfortable: we learn by formulating hypotheses about the present or future based on our experience of the past, and then testing them. Up for grabs with the hypotheses is our whole body of cumulative wisdom. There is always the possibility that this case will burst open our old ideas of the world and send us looking for new rules. If it does, we will need to be casuists.

All of these qualities give casuistry a peculiar advantage against the contemporary fad of condemning all foundational principles that seem to produce practical failures or questionable norms. Deconstructionist feminists and political conservatives—many of whom adhere to classical models of liberalism—both are particularly adept at this game. For instance, some feminists blame the core doctrines of Christianity or religion in general for women's oppression, and some conservatives in return blame women's assertions of their rights for the dissolution of two-parent families. As we will see in chapter 7, Michael Novak argues from the failure of liberation theology to produce economic health to the corruptness of its grounding beliefs. Casuistry allows us to explore the possibility that an apparently unjust principle may instead simply be a never or no longer valid conclusion of a still credible and coherent view of the moral universe.

For instance, Thomas thought of the cosmos as an intrinsically harmonious, divinely created system to which we must conform. Natural and transcendent ends were compatible; the Christian and the universal were identical; the body and reason were not in conflict; virtue and concrete flourishing were coherent; and individual and social goods were not at odds. In moments of doubt about what was truly good at one level, the good of another provided a quick check on judgment. The disruptions of sin and the confusion generated by apparent conflicts between these levels gave the lie to any easy assumptions about the possibility of temporal harmony, but they did not jeopardize the belief in coherent origins or the hope in eschatological harmony. Casuists managed to preserve this cosmology precisely by showing that a fixed origin and end did not entail inflexibility in the concrete terms of its moral requirements for temporal life. Their eventual acceptance of lending at interest is a good example. That some of these machinations perverted rather than preserved the moral insights of the tradition is beyond dispute. The point is that casuistry permits us to raise the question whether in a particular case a moral norm reflects or compromises the life of virtue a Thomistic metaphysics requires, and it therefore forbids anyone to discard the whole metaphysics on the basis of the mere observation that some of its moral norms seem misguided.

Responsible casuistry can demonstrate that it is not the metaphysics that is at fault but the norms that need critical reformulation in light of charity, justice, and the requirements of integral flourishing. But casuistry's critics are also correct that it can be and has often been misused to cover up discordances between experience and theory. Thus our assessment of casuistry must encompass not just its methodological appropriateness to the periods in which it has been popular but the concrete details of its use. Here disturbing problems arise. The received casuistical tradition is hobbled by its narrow focus on the avoidance of sin, the limited perspectives of its small, homogeneous band of practitioners, and its lack of interest in developing the powers of moral reasoning in ordinary people. The purpose of Roman Catholic high casuistry was narrow: to guide parish priests in hearing confessions and assigning penances. Casuistry was also the purview of a few highly trained, male, academic clerics. [10] Certainly they did not act alone, for they were members of a privileged community of discourse with its own limits and rules; the principles of probabilism and probabiliorism, which required people to evaluate the relative soundness of competing arguments, in theory forbid them merely to follow the advise of "experts" without questioning their reasoning; and the fact that their conclusions would be applied widely in the confessional mitigated, theoretically, against ill-considered or idiosyncratic reasoning. [11] Yet they were also not about the business of teaching the ordinary person how to apply principles, evaluate cases, or in general to become a wise and prudent moral reasoner. [12] In addition, they typically began their training for the priesthood very young, and, despite the aspirations to comprehensiveness they may have had, this narrowness of their experience colored strongly their perception and phrasing of issues and therefore their choice of paradigmatic cases. It is unlikely that, laboring under these limits, these clerics either understood all the pertinent details of the problems they discussed or provided those whom the problems directly involved with tools for analysis. These factors combine to call into question both the success of their conclusions and the efficacy of their hard work for encouraging growth in moral virtue.

A contemporary case illustrates the distortion that "objective" distance sometimes produces. Contemporary advertising ethics rely on a Rawlsian understanding of free speech generated by a pluralistic liberal "overlapping consensus." In Chicago, the Reverend Michael Pfleger and his parishioners have argued that, on the contrary, the analogy by which the practice of targeting alcohol and cigarette advertising at poor urban neighborhoods should be judged is not "free" speech among equals but the exploitation of geographically confined poor people by powerful corporations. Proximity to the situation alters Pfleger's choice of paradigmatic cases; it also inspires the communal reflection that can lead to widespread moral wisdom and moral agency. Thus before we can decide which interpretation, analogical case, and conclusion to accept, we must identify the casuists and their purposes.

Care is especially necessary because casuistry's viability depends on wide knowledge of cases that have clear solutions. An individual without a well-developed habit of prudence—or even a society whose moral tradition is in chaos—does unreliable casuistry. [13] In a plural, heterogeneous culture, then, casuistry cannot rest on the possibility of finding a single perfect, analogical case. It must become "an eclectic, interdisciplinary inquiry" in which analysis of multiple cases generated by different disciplines or in different social locations is simply the first step in the corporate struggle to make moral sense of a tough issue. [14]

Finally, as in the moral literature of the manuals and the penitentials, the limits within which academic and seminary casuistry were practiced distorted the image of the moral life. If the inspiration for casuistic reflection is avoidance of individual sins rather than pursuit of the virtuous life, it is easy to forget casuistry's true purpose: to discern what is good, both existentially and concretely, in a given situation and for particular actors. [15] Casuistry must not be cut off from the virtue tradition or especially from a lively, participatory understanding of practical moral reason.

Casuistry thus can mediate marvelously between the metaphysical and moral tradition and the exigencies of both everyday and not-so-everyday life. It seems friendly in theory—if not in its historical clerical practice—to feminist descriptions of "webbed" decision making. If it grates against Thomas's intimations that practical moral reason's descent to particulars is consistent and predictable, it is perfectly coherent with a reading of Thomas that focuses on method: his flexible use of practical syllogisms and his insistence that the details of natural law will be worked out differently in diverse persons and circumstances. [16] It can protect a principle or a metaphysics from premature demise. But it also is only as good as its choice of paradigmatic case and therefore is only as good as the chooser, the casuist. A strong self-critical—or even a critical—principle is lacking in most of the Roman Catholic casuistical tradition.

PERSONALISM

If casuistry's contemporary merits are still under debate, personalism is so firmly established in the natural law landscape that it is difficult to find a nonpersonalist contemporary interpretation of natural law. If casuistry asks the question "what or whose good is at stake in this moral norm?" personalism evaluates the answer: a legitimate norm advances the integral good of particular persons. What is now known as Roman Catholic personalism grew largely out of the moral reflections of Jacques Maritain, Emmanuel Mounier, Gabriel Marcel, and others in pre–World War II France, as well as Nikolai Berdiaev. Their achievement was their synthesis of the natural law tradition with the Enlightenment respect for human dignity and human rights, a twentieth century turn to the subject, and a special concern to preserve the integrity of intimate relationships among people from destruction by the state. They rejected rationalist Enlightenment individualism (evidenced in the dehumanizing conditions of capitalist industrial labor), fascist and Stalinist totalitarian subordination of the individual to the state, and Marxist reduction of human beings to pawns of historical forces. [17] But wanting to preserve the Enlightenment's esteem for the dignity and rights of individuals and socialism's penchant for economic justice and interdependence, they insisted that the subject and criterion of moral philosophy should be the person, considered as "an indissoluble whole": [18] not only reason and will, but body, emotions, and concrete social connections. Likewise, Christian personalist ethics threads its way between a self-absorbed, entirely self-determining individualism and a reduction of salvation to historical social progress; historical social, political, and economic change is genuinely progressive when it promotes both the earthly flourishing of human beings and their ultimate end in God. The Vatican Council II Document on the Apostolate of Laypeople declared,

> All that goes to make up the temporal order: personal and family values, culture, economic interests, the trades and professions, institutions of the political community, international relations, and so on, as well as their gradual development—all these are not merely helps to man's last end; they possess a value of their own, placed in them by God, whether considered individually or as parts of the integral temporal structure.

... This natural goodness of theirs receives an added dignity from their relation with the human person, for whose use they have been created. And then, too, God has willed to gather together all that was supernatural, into a single whole in Christ. ... Far from depriving the temporal order of its autonomy, of its specific ends, of its own laws and resources, or its importance for human well-being, this design, on the contrary, increases its energy and excellence, raising it at the same time to the level of man's integral vocation here below. [19]

The early personalists rooted their critique of the social order in the holistically considered person. The Enlightenment priority of mind over body, reason over emotion, and abstraction over experience all came under fire, as did individualism and the liberal capitalist fiction of the free contract. Likewise there was a fundamental suspicion of the powerful and a commitment to empowering all whom contemporary political and economic systems dehumanized. Personalism also condemned any institution that treated human beings like animals or pieces of machinery; its counteremphasis on "repersonalizing" social relations, though intended to break down hierarchy, has sometimes eclipsed tough-minded social analysis.

Also central to the critique was a fundamentally antisystematic proclivity for diversity. Personalist philosophy, Mounier insisted, must never be a system, for a system is "an apparatus of thought and action functioning like an automatic distributor of solutions and instructions; a barrier to research; an insurance against disquiet, ordeal and risk." Philosophical systems, not unlike totalitarian governments and impersonal corporations, are tyrannical; a premium falsely placed on internal coherence takes precedence over the "unpredictability" of "the existence of free and creative persons" who should occupy the position of supreme value. [20] Personalism had to be plural and flexible, as created human beings were plural and historical. [21] And indeed personalism has inspired most Roman Catholic moral thinkers of this century, with very different results. For instance, both Karol Wojtyla and the Lublin personalists and their adversaries, Louis Janssens and German and American revisionist originators of proportionalism, all spring from personalist roots. [22] Peter Maurin and Dorothy Day popularized personalism in the United States in the *Catholic Worker*'s "gentle personalism"; it also left its mark on Vatican Council II documents like *Gaudium et Spes* and *Dignitatis Humanae*, [23] on the controversial encyclical *Humanae Vitae*, [24] and on the germination of Latin American liberation theology. [25]

Personalism is then less a unified philosophy than a presupposition, for the precise shape of a personalist ethics depends upon how the person is described. But personalists have tended to center their ethics on one or both of the following: the person as integral moral actor and as holistic source of moral norms. Thus personalism demands a more narrative understanding of moral activity than the manual tradition assumed. [26] First, acts must be evaluated not as isolated, generic events but as expressions of a person's life or self. [27] Here concern for moral purity is nuanced by attention to what would earlier have been called virtue's fruits: individually, the integration of body, mind, and spirit, and of reason and affectivity; and socially, the development of a just and peaceful society.

This shift from private worry about "acting rightly" to public concern about living a full and humane life reveals persons and their ends as the true criteria of moral norms, shifting the focus of moral reflection from acts—as in casuistical reflection—to the shape and conditions of human flourishing. Norms make sense only if they serve human ends. *Gaudium et Spes* begins with "man considered whole and entire, with body and soul, heart and conscience, mind and will." [28] The good of the whole person encompasses and transcends these dimensions. [29] For example, personalists use the larger criterion of the integral human good to argue that sexual ethics—traditionally measured by the short-hand, biological standard of openness to procreation—must not subordinate relational, psychological, and spiritual goods to reproduction. Language about the "ordination" of marriage to procreation is still present, but the basis of this ordination is not a "natural" animal urge but a love that deeply respects the dignity of the spouse. [30] Mutual, embodied, self-giving love overflows into the (thoughtful) procreation and education of children; pleasure and self-fulfillment are part of this integral whole, but they occur only through total self-gift. [31]

This commitment to holism runs across the personalist spectrum. Yet the diversity of conclusions—and therefore the indeterminacy of the approach—is spectacular, especially in sexual ethics. The variety owes to disagreements over whether conflicts among the many dimensions of the integral human good in concrete situations are real or apparent and whether relational or physical criteria provide the surest safeguard to other, interdependent dimensions of the human good. On one hand lies Pope John Paul II's approach, materially identical to traditional manualist ethics in its unbending censure of all nonmarital and nonprocreative sex. In his view (shared by Paul VI and supporters of *Humanae Vitae*) contraception not only prevents reproduction but also—because it encourages or even entails a shift of focus from procreative relationship to sheer selfish pleasure—damages the emotional and moral bonds of marriage. [32] On the other hand lie arguments that entertain contraception, nonmarital intercourse, and homosexual lovemaking. [33] Revisionist personalists, for instance, argue that human rationality and attachment transform or at least qualify biological sexual function; not only does sexual affection bestow goods beyond reproduction, but these goods are so basic to human flourishing that the good of reproduction can often legitimately be sacrificed for them. [34]

But variability in personalist conclusions comes not only from diversity in contemporaneous anthropologies and mediating principles but also from disagreement over the possibility of genuine historical change in human nature and therefore in the concrete normative implications of natural law. Transcendental theology holds that not only do persons create themselves morally, and not only is humanity as a whole historical and dynamic, but humanity even freely determines history and ultimately, within limits, human nature. [35] Because the eternal natural law is "the nature of [humanity] as [it] plans and acts rationally, that is, a nature which founds history," [36] natural law's concrete conclusions are dynamic and humanly generated to the same degree that humanity itself is. Moral theology is not the progressive refinement of the "descent to particulars" but the answer to the question, "in which direction should human potential be developed?" [37] Consequently

> much of what was long regarded as the unalterable order of nature is now seen to be a historical form, and sometimes a specifically Western form of human self-fulfillment. . . . The personal nature of man, his call to shape the world, his social character, are undoubtedly basic postulates founded on the nature of man and always recognizable by man. But in each age he has to learn and decide anew how far he can claim mastery over the infraspiritual reality and over "nature" within man himself. . . . Hence the actual actions of man cannot be determined merely in the light of an abstract metaphysical nature. His historical nature as it has come to be in the present, and his situation, must also be envisaged. [38]

Even so, variations in estimates of the limits of self-determination yield corresponding variations in estimates of the limits within which natural law's conclusions can change. In short, countless anthropological and ethical decisions intercede between a personalist starting point and concrete judgments.

The profusion of contradictory approaches that therefore crowd under the personalist umbrella mitigate against crisp, comprehensive assessments of its implications for Thomistic ontology and ethical method. Still, like Thomas, personalists treat the person as an embodied whole and insist that the variety of human experience must lead to variety in moral conclusions. A Thomistic understanding of prudence is operative here, as is a belief in the coherence of the immediate and ultimate individual ends; a confidence in the interdependence of individual and social flourishing; an appreciation, if not theoretical development, of moral virtue; and a general trust in the good will and moral perceptiveness of the average person.

Yet there are elements of more recent origin as well. With the encouragement of Enlightenment individualism, personalists center moral reflection upon a modern doctrine of rights: human dignity grounds the right to appropriate self-development and flourishing. [39] As we have seen, the degree of overlap between personalist norms and Thomas's system of moral conclusions depends upon the degree to which variations of time and context are thought to affect moral rules. For John Paul II, these oscillations alter material norms almost not at all; personalism is simply a richer, more contemporary rationale for absolute standards set long ago. For proportionalist revisionists, who embrace more radical versions of pluralism and historicism, personalism's new criterion for ethics alters some traditional norms substantially. Personalist ideals of moral reflection also vary, but in practice personalist deliberations have surely been more open and public than those of Thomas or the high casuists, implying a concern to move ethical reflection out into the world at large and to cultivate moral wisdom in ordinary individuals. These are small but significant changes. For example, though nearly all widely known personalist thinkers have been men, not all of these have been clerics. Personalist ideas also engendered a journal, *Esprit*; have been popularized (if for a limited audience) in the *Catholic Worker*, and have been spread to lay and clerical intellectuals in papal encyclicals, pastoral letters, newspapers, other journals, and scholarly monographs. John Paul II has promoted the more traditionalist strand not only in encyclicals but also in published sermons and popular books. [40] This development owes partly to higher literacy rates and greater ease of printing, but it also reveals an earnest desire to inspire a utopianism, a habit of serious moral reflection, and a political activism robust enough to challenge the insidious alternatives that threatened the theoretical evisceration of Thomism and the actual destruction of Europe in this century.

Personalism's greatest contribution has been its reintroduction of holism into a moral theology that had become paralyzed by its own compartmentalization. Its decision to start over with the question, what is the good that is the end and criterion of the moral life? gave moral theology the prophetic energy both to press for the holistic fulfillment of natural human ends in interdependent community and to resist mistaking these ends for the entire human good. Notwithstanding the antifeminism of John Paul II's Lublin personalism, the first part of this impulse in fact has much in common with the twentieth century feminist critique of systematic ethics.

Yet although the old system of moral theology was certainly Ptolemaic in its complexity, the personalist insight has not shown itself to be fully Copernican. It is theoretically inadequate to deal with some of the challenges of contemporary culture. In at least some of its versions, it simply uses new formulae to explain the same motion of the largely unchanged person around the eternal norm rather than accepting the double reorientation that motion of the dynamic norm around the historical person would demand. The personalist criterion itself is not specific enough to make clear whether the latter description is really more adequate than the former. For example, influential German and Lublin phenomenological personalists' tendency to make sweeping claims based on their immediate consciousness of experience exposes them "to the dangerous propensity of claiming a false 'obviousness', not guarded against by hermeneutic or systematic principles." [41] This is especially true of John Paul II's sexual ethics, in which the necessity of the connection between self-gift and openness to conception is never made clear. [42] Even the French thinkers Marcel and Mounier have been criticized for making claims characterized by a "lack of argumentative support" inspired by an "unseemly haste" and "an urge to leap straight from insights and positions which are true and even valuable in themselves to conclusions which are certainly not entailed by these insights." [43] In short, personalism like casuistry lacks a critical theory of experience.

Personalism also fails to resolve the Enlightenment tension between transformative, transcending reason and the physical givenness of the body. Again, sexual ethics are paradigmatic. Absolutist personalists have forestalled conflict among the normative dimensions of the person by limiting reason's range to the possibilities indicated by their interpretation of human physical nature: biological boundaries provide the templates for moral action. Revisionists have followed the opposite path, rejecting "the obligation (perceived by reason) to conform to nature" in favor of "the obligation (built into nature) to use reason in moral judgment." [44] We act creatively upon our bodies; our essential rationality guides and directs the totality of our beings, [45] outfitting us for the ongoing, creative transformation of the world, of moral norms, and of ourselves. [46] Not only does this heavy reliance on transformative reason tend to obscure the body's constraints, but it simply reverses the problematic hierarchy of "nature" over reason. The risk here is rarefication of the body. As Charles Curran has recognized,

> a word of caution is in order. In the last few years the ecological crisis has made us aware of the danger of not giving enough importance and value to the physical aspects of worldly existence. We are not free to

> interfere with nature any way we see fit. Just as it is wrong to absolutize the natural and the physical, so too it is wrong to give no meaning or significance to the natural and the physical. [47]

Both ends of the personalist spectrum resolve the tension between normative reason and physical "nature" by subordinating one to the other. Neither fully adopts the integral Thomistic vision of nature as the embodied, social, particular rational human being with a supernatural end, [48] and yet neither produces a completely satisfactory alternative account of this connection. This failure should give feminists pause.

Personalist descriptions of history are similarly inadequate to contemporary philosophical standards. Personalist ethics often speak of the progress of "man" as if humanity were a single subject with a discernible, unified trajectory and common historical goal. Change is tidily unanimous, and variations are chalked up to developmental differences among cultures: deviation, backwardness, or anticipation. [49] Yet in the contemporary view, history is not so single-minded. We do not have to go so far as to deny that history can have a common, this-worldly end to see that "grand narrative" interpretations of history turn out eventually to be not only naïve but also self-serving. Some early personalist claims about the historical, corporate progress of humanity toward temporal justice and peace tend to overlook both the contributions of non-Western cultures and the havoc wreaked by the Christian West. They tended to ignore the facts that the determining group has been small; its advantages, narrowly distributed; and the majority, nearly powerless to make contributions or draw benefits. Post–World War II personalists, especially John Paul II, are less sanguine about historical progress, but their systematic tendency to emphasize the ethics of personal relationships even in their treatment of social justice issues has meant that their recent contributions to policy debates have been more exhortatory and prophetic than concrete and constructive.

In addition, personalist egalitarian moral discourse remains largely theoretical. According to traditionalist personalists, promoting widespread moral reflection amounts to cultivating genuine acceptance of detailed, established norms. Even for revisionist personalists, expanding the moral conversation means fostering discussion among theologians and other high-ranking professionals: doctors, lawyers, and politicians. For example, Paulinus Odozor faults Richard McCormick for presuming to tutor a doctor who might need to decide whether to perform an operation, especially for doing so without mentioning the need either to consult with or to educate the patient whose life the operation—or lack of it—will affect. [50] Clearly the openness of personalist inquiry is determined by the degree of variety in insights and norms the practitioners expect to entertain. When revisionists draw the circle of conversation only wide enough to include medical professionals, they signal a belief that this variety is quite limited: ordinary patients have no relevant insights that cannot be discerned, articulated, evaluated, and defended by their doctors. The operative epistemology is still a theory of self-evidence; context has no serious influence on our experiences or the analysis we bring to them. Personalism's populist methodological aspirations are in fact not radical at all if they rest on an assumption that wide consultation is unlikely to turn up new insights. Personalism's credibility depends upon its trying out its proposals in a wider conversation.

In the end, the twentieth century personalist movement has succeeded brilliantly at retaining the humane insights of modern political philosophies, integrating them into a renewed Thomistic theology, and—as we will see—inspiring liberation theology. But the anthropology that it developed is insufficiently critical to meet the challenges of either contemporary feminist ethics or Thomistic revival. For instance, personalism's overriding focus upon integrity within particular relationships can obscure the larger social and institutional inequities in whose shadow they exist. The effects of structural injustice can be invisible when seen through the lens of a relationship between ostensible equals.

For example, in *Veritatis Splendor* John Paul II recounts the story of Susanna, surprised in her garden by two powerful and scheming judges who threaten to accuse her publicly of adultery unless she agrees to have sex with them. When she refuses, she is brought to trial, narrowly escaping death when Daniel comes forward and catches the judges in their lie. On John Paul's personalist interpretation, the point of the incident is Susanna's sexual fidelity. He portrays the judges as having tempted Susanna by promising immunity from specious persecution in exchange for sex; he depicts Susanna's possible submission as selfishly seeking her own benefit, "using" the blackmailing judges immorally, and therefore violating their dignity. Such an analysis is possible only if one maintains the fiction that the story of Susanna is a story of illicit sexual relations between equals rather than of rape, which carries no stigma for the victim. A true telling of the tale puts at the center not sex, but the judges' calculated abuse of power, Susanna's near helplessness, and her therefore supererogatory refusal. [51] Not all whom personalism has inspired neglect the political dimensions of personal relationships. But personalism itself—despite its admirable success in combining natural law's anthropological holism with the best insights of modern political philosophy—has no internal mechanism that protects against such misreadings. Discernment of what constitutes justice in a concrete situation requires social justice analysis. [52]

In sum, personalism steadfastly directs ethics toward supporting the integral goods of individuals, comprehensively considered. Yet in other ways personalism lacks even the critical capacity of Thomas's version of natural law, in which a carefully described virtue of prudence is a condition of valid concrete choices, in which the body mediates sense knowledge but theoretically (if not always practically) prescinds from determining moral norms, and in which what people owe to one another, if at times unjustly prescribed, at least depends partly on their social and political relationships and is sometimes mitigated by powerlessness or other sorts of poverty.

SOCIAL JUSTICE AND LIBERATION

The third crucial development in Roman Catholic ethics enfolds two movements: the turn-of-the-century genesis of the social justice tradition, discussed in chapter 2, and its later transformation into liberation thought. Both have close connections to personalism; the early social encyclicals helped to inspire it, and the later social justice and liberationist traditions have developed it by asking what sorts of social, political, and economic relationships honor human dignity and promote interdependent human flourishing. And both respond to the nineteenth century epiphany that rights encompass material as well as political freedoms, that industrial, economic, and social oppression can be as indomitable as governmental power.

The early social encyclicals *Rerum Novarum* and *Quadragesimo Anno* appealed to governments and corporations to treat workers humanely. Initially they gave laborers no leverage to demand humane conditions, forbidding them to strike and advising them instead merely to form Christian fraternal organizations to ease the financial uncertainties of a life of wage labor. [53] The central worry was the impact of inhumane conditions on the workers' spiritual and moral life. [54] But by mid-century the rhetoric had shifted perceptibly from their early primary emphasis on individual conversion and future salvation to an emphasis on the concrete fruits of integral human fulfillment as criteria for the transformation of human society. By 1959 Jean Yves Calvez and Jacques Perrin even hinted confidently at a connection between salvation and the human right to a share in the common good: "Society and social activity appear to be the natural requirements for the realization of the person." [55] Not only that, but the common good, the locus of collective movement toward human material fulfillment, was now the manifestation of the already present

Christ, a prerequisite and foretaste of integral human fulfillment in the not-yet-present Kingdom of God. Maritain chimed in: the common good "is *intended* to favor the higher ends of the human person." [56] Thus both the most radical and most delicate development in Catholic social ethics in this century has been to redirect Thomas's integral person from a single to a two-pronged goal: her natural fulfillment in interdependent society is integrated, if not identified, with her individual, spiritual end rather than being subordinate to it.

Vatican Council II documents continued this trend, supporting it with an explicitly incarnational Christology. Christ's embodiment in Jesus is the salvific entrance of God into the changeable and imperfect human world, granting human actions and institutions salvific significance: [57] "To the extent that [earthly progress] can contribute to the better ordering of human society, it is of vital concern to the kingdom of God." [58] When statements like this are yoked with claims that human beings have a common "human and divine" destiny and are admonished by God to work together "to build up the world in genuine peace," the sense of being called to cooperate in something more than human is clear, even when claims about kingdom-building are intentionally avoided. [59] Similarly, in Pope John Paul II's interpretation, the paschal fruition of the eschatological in the temporal "constitutes the integral dimension of man's development and all that which is human"; the historical resurrection both gives a foretaste of eschatological fulfillment and unleashes for the faithful the love that makes possible true human, concrete, earthly development. The compelling logic of the incarnation and resurrection thus knits together divine eschatology and worldly progress, transcendence and historicity, individual and community. [60]

Social justice concerns transformed ecclesiology as well. Like Thomas, the authors of Vatican Council II documents reiterate the church's central purpose of spiritual salvation; the independent value of the material, temporal order; widespread spiritual conversion as the prerequisite for truly just social structures; and the distinction between earthly progress and the increase of the Kingdom of God. [61] Yet the church's interest in the salvation of historic, concrete humanity entails the individual and ecclesiastical responsibility to improve human society. [62] Here the traditional call to contribute to the common good is transformed from a civic into a religious and ecclesiastical vocation requiring not only works of mercy but attention to and elimination of the causes of injustice. [63] Christian corporate life acquires an irrevocably and self-consciously political dimension.

Latin American liberation theology was the fruit of this gradual shift toward social justice, fertilized by the complex influences of new Latin

American evangelization, European political theology, Marxism, a tradition of prophetic Latin American theological criticism stretching back to early colonial times, Vatican Council II, and the 1968 CELAM II conference at Medellín. Liberation theology distinguished itself by applying the Roman Catholic social justice critique to theology itself. Vatican Council II documents applied accepted principles—social justice teachings—to concrete contexts—"signs of the times" interpreted sociologically and economically. Social analysis simply organized the context in order to make the identification of applicable moral principles easier. The bishops at Medellín, coopting the "see-judge-act" method of pre–Vatican II Catholic Action, stepped up the emphases upon social analysis and upon the overwhelming claims posed by the urgent needs of the poor. [64]

Contemporary liberationism—discussed in more detail in chapter 7—takes this critique a step further, extending it to the institutional church and even to the practice of theology. The question for liberation thinkers is not "What do moral norms rooted in traditional theology teach the world today?" but "How do I continue to believe in God when the institutional church and its friends support gross economic and political injustice in the name of benevolence and order?" Hence Gustavo Gutiérrez, like other liberationists, reorders the process of theological and ethical reflection. He begins with a crisis or a contradiction in the lives of poor people of faith; uses social sciences to identify the problem's roots, implications, and solutions; reflects theologically, with the aid of Scripture, on the results of the analysis; and proposes a new model for the praxis of theological reflection or of active faith. [65] His insight is that the relationship between theology and social behaviors and systems is not unilateral. Social activities are not the automatic and predictable products of fixed theoretical origins. Rather, theology and practice influence each other dialectically. For this reason a consistent, solid, prophetic ethic demands a theology equally transformed by the search for genuine justice. And not only philosophy but also evangelism requires this, for how can one believe in the love of a God whose church practices and condones oppression? Hence liberationism, unlike casuistry or even most of personalism, aspires not only to social justice but also to theological reflection from the point of view of the victims of injustice. [66]

For liberation theology, questions of method (the approach to moral reason) and procedure (the institutional execution of method) are indivisible because the trustworthiness of moral reflection depends greatly on the social location of its author. This was true for Thomas too; that the general principles of the natural law were universally accessible did not imply that just anyone could reason well. Nor did it mean that just anyone could be a moral theologian. To begin with, not just anyone could write, or read. Solid moral reasoning depended upon a well-developed habit of prudence, including familiarity with the moral tradition, advantages only highly educated, vowed religious men in universities could expect to cultivate. Sin, in the shape of a disordered appetite or culpable ignorance, could distort reason, but development of the moral and intellectual virtues provided resistance, and the circle of scholars seemed large enough to protect their ruminations from gross error.

Liberationists concur that ignorance and ill-chosen ends obstruct moral reasoning. In this spirit, they add—as I did in the discussion of casuistry above—that a responsible hermeneutic approach to traditional social ethics must ask in what ways the homogeneity of its unwitting authors' experiences and interests may have biased their collective thinking. [67] Gutiérrez and others realize that all parallax produces perspectival vision; the question is which perspective is most revelatory. The person most likely to see clearly the causes of injustice is not the comfortable "ivory tower" academic (who benefits from the social systems that perpetuate poverty and so habituates herself to almost unconscious participation in moral vice), but the victim of injustice (who is likely to inquire more deeply into the causes of her own suffering) or her genuine advocate. [68] Liberationism exposes these perspectives as choices rather than "natural" starting points. It is not that ethicians and theologians never before privileged particular interests or experiences. They were simply not conscious of this choice and of its implications.

The liberationist transformation of social ethics is thus quite traditional in its insistence that moral and intellectual virtue united in charity are prerequisites for genuine truth-seeking; in its claim that a particular sort of background promotes moral and intellectual virtues; and in its demands for social justice. But it replaces traditional practitioners (altering procedure and shifting the locus of authority), traditional starting points (transforming foundations), [69] traditional standards of prudence (transforming method), and traditional criteria of social justice (altering content). Scholars are not completely displaced, but they must yoke their learning to an active, sympathetic commitment to the poor. [70]

Thus liberation theologians in Africa, Asia, and Central and South America have striven to move the moral debate's center of gravity and authority out of the academy and into the field. Early use of Paolo Freire's pedagogy and the development of *comunidades de base* confirm liberation theologians' intent not just to think on behalf of the oppressed, but to recognize the oppressed as authentic moralists and theologians in their own right. In local practice the impulse is inclusive, is accountable to ordinary people, and even anticipates surprising results. Yet the international apologetic face of liberation

theology remains largely academic, shaped by the European university educa-
tions of its scholarly practitioners. This owes partly to the need to phrase
method in language acceptable to Americans and Europeans, but it also reflects
the doubts of some that closeness to a situation always affords a clear view
of it. [71] Thus for liberationists as for feminists the temptation to distill a pure
theory or method from a concrete communal practice is ever present and
must constantly be resisted.

Liberationism's methodological and procedural overlap with feminism
is unsurprising given that Christian feminism often goes by the name "feminist
liberationism" and that liberationists and feminists operate with a similar set
of critical and dialectical tools. The question here is how liberationism reflects
and augments the evolution of natural law. To begin with, it grows out of
serious efforts to incarnate natural law, social justice, and personalist visions
of flourishing in societies in which the church has tolerated gross injustice.
Exposing the myth of the "objective" scholars' "neutral" standpoint that has
so often legitimated this injustice, it insists that *all* perspectives are limited.
The search for truth entails discovering the perspective from which self-
interest is unarguably legitimate: the perspective of the oppressed. There are
two important and very traditional insights here. First, self-preservation—
both bodily and spiritual—is an appropriate end. Second, thanks to the
interdependence of moral and intellectual virtue, a person not possessing the
virtue of justice cannot truly possess the virtue of prudence. Powerful, self-
interested people are likely to end up writing the rules in their own favor,
and their opinions should therefore be treated skeptically. But neither does
a serious liberationism founder on a theologically untenable naïveté about
the omnipresent power of sin. It does have a self-critical side, for it recognizes
that social powerlessness does not entail moral and intellectual virtue. Because
the oppressed also oppress, [72] a mature liberation theology must not naïvely
transfer authority and epistemological privilege from one flawed band of
"experts" to another. [73] Reflective responses to immediate experiences of oppression must be criticized, combined, and kneaded into communicable standards of justice in a process that closely resembles natural law casuistry.

The nagging systematic ambiguity in liberation theology is the precise
connection between individual salvation from sin and communal salvation
from oppression: is a theology based in a moral hermeneutic a new, more
faithful rendition of the gospel, or does it put the political and economic cart
before the spiritual horse? From the Thomistic natural law perspective, in
which society's ends are purely temporal and salvation is entirely otherworldly,
liberation theology's double insistence that social analysis not only precede
but ground theological reflection, and that social justice and temporal flour-

ishing not only cohere with but advance the kingdom, seems to reduce salvation to social transformation. [74] On top of this, liberation theology exchanges an assurance that contemporary society is a perfectible, well-functioning mechanism in an orderly world for a vision of "disharmony, disorder, suffering, oppression. . . . an 'already damaged *humanum*' in an already damaged cosmos." [75] Liberationist social justice requires radical transformation of the existing order, not conformity to it.

In the end, liberation theology does draw upon central methodological and normative insights of Thomas's thought. It depends upon the integration of moral and intellectual virtue and ultimately—as we will see in chapter 7—upon the completion of both by charity; it also puts society to the test of justice. Liberationists extrapolate the Thomistic criterion of law (because justice is the measure of law, an unjust law is no law) to institutions: an unjust system is illegitimate. They also make strong ecclesiological and epistemological claims, arguing that the poorest of the laity are not the passive recipients of doctrines that originate in the church hierarchy but the authoritative, active shapers of theology, ethics, and politics. But traditional ethics never dreamed of an objectivity or an egalitarianism of quite the liberationist sort.

THE MAGISTERIUM AND CHRISTIAN ABSOLUTISM

While liberationists have been developing one set of Thomistic insights on justice, knowledge, and the connection among the virtues, contemporary ecclesiastical authors have been refining the somewhat contradictory implications of equally traditional claims about ecclesiastical charism for the content, procedure, and method of theological reflection. Thus unlike the first two influences, casuistry and personalism, liberationism and contemporary magisterial theology represent conflicting alternatives, and it remains to be seen which, if either, will become an indelible part of the church tradition.

Both liberationism and personalism draw upon the ambiguous legacy of Vatican Council II. From one point of view, the Council was a break with the medieval past. It was arguably the Roman Catholic hierarchy's first systematic sympathetic response to Enlightenment social optimism and to democratic political movements, ending over a century of ecclesiastical suppression of theological responses to modern developments in scriptural study, philosophy, science, and politics. [76] Accordingly, the Council documents' incarnational language flattens traditional hierarchical relations, softening rigid neoscholastic distinctions between (for example) nature and grace, church and world, or government and citizen, so that the members of the pairs are no longer unequal opposites but interdependent, interpenetrating dimensions of a unified whole. [77]

Evidence of this holism was *Lumen Gentium*'s shift toward a vision of a cooperative, egalitarian church. First, within its reaffirmation of ecclesiastical hierarchy, the document advances the principle of collegiality. The ministry of each member of the clerical hierarchy is independently authentic, not derivative; yet it draws meaning and support from his organic interdependent connection to the larger church. [78] Second, *Lumen Gentium* elevates the laity by stressing the equal importance of the different ministries within the church: "all the faithful are invited and obliged to holiness and the perfection of their own state of life," and despite differences in calling "there remains, nevertheless, a true equality between all with regard to the dignity and to the activity which is common to all the faithful in the building up of the Body of Christ." [79] On one level the "separate but equal" principle of ministry is even revoked; laypeople are encouraged to join the ranks of theologians, and clerical and lay theologians alike are to enjoy freedom of inquiry and equal status. [80] The potential significance of this theoretical equality and freedom cannot be overstated: the charism of ordination, despite setting a man apart for a sacramental vocation, does not bestow epistemological privilege. The varied perspectives of male and female lay theologians in theory carry as much weight as the potentially more homogeneous views of their male, ordained colleagues, despite the fact that de facto magisterial authority resides in a subset of the latter group.

Yet in addition to these messages of egalitarianism, the Council documents faithfully bring forward conflicts that are implicit in the historical natural law tradition, and indeed they magnify the conflicts by—for example— emphasizing the democratic implications of natural law epistemology and the collegial basis for a theology of hierarchical charismatic power. The result is an unresolved tension between the ultimately democratic implications of ethics' reliance on universal human reason and the hierarchical structure of the charismatic institution that purports to guard both dogmatic and moral truth. Openings are left for both egalitarian and hierarchical ecclesiologies, both univocal and pluralist epistemologies, both charism- and reason-dependent doctrines of authority. [81]

During the pontificate of John Paul II, magisterial theology has subsumed the more modern, egalitarian "people of God" imagery of the Vatican Council II documents under a more traditionalist interpretation of magisterial authority. [82] John Paul II, who interprets Vatican Council II's accomplishment as simply a personalist reintegration of traditional themes in modern terms, not surprisingly adopts a nuptial ecclesiology of intimate union. The church hierarchy represents the "active" bridegroom, Christ, and the laity represents the "receptive" bride. [83] Natural law thought's alliance with ecclesiology is inherently uneasy at this point, for hierarchical exercise of ecclesiastical charism—the divine guarantee that the official church will not err in formal doctrinal or moral teaching—potentially circumvents cooperative and critical reasoning among laypeople, both cutting off new sources of insight and discouraging mature moral reflection. Truth—in the Enlightenment scientific paradigm—is univocal, and the vocation of the theologian is to explain and confirm the truths the hierarchy identifies.

This recent trend has two systematic repercussions for ethics. First, it identifies reason with juridical authority. Second, the juridical authority establishes absolute, context-independent norms. The possibly pluralist implications of egalitarian reason are dissolved by declaring only those who agree with the absolute, charismatically guaranteed position to be competent reasoners. [84] Anyone may ponder moral questions, but the church hierarchy is the authoritative critic.

In the past, the priority of hierarchical charism over broad consultation may have been justified partly by the fact that competence in moral reasoning was thought to require virtue, plus education in Scripture, theology, or moral thought. All who were theologically well-equipped reasoners in this way were clerics. The institutional church has had much less experience with either alternative definitions of competence or contemporary lay scholars, who fall outside the juridical authority of its clerical structure and draw upon a wider range of experience than traditional scholars. Whether they (or thoughtful laypeople in general) possess or contribute to ecclesiastical charismatic authority is a question that the magisterium has so far answered mainly in the negative—for instance, in Pope Paul VI's rejection of the report of the papal commission on birth control and in the Congregation for the Doctrine of the Faith's later instruction on the vocation of the theologian. [85]

The new magisterial absolutism intends to preserve concrete traditional moral norms, as well as the scholarly method and institutional procedure by which they are produced. But it clearly privileges traditional content and procedure over traditional method because in place of the broad Thomistic approach—with its potential to introduce morally significant new information from disciplines outside moral theology—it has slipped in an uncritical clerical personalism whose purpose is to generate new justifications for old authoritative structures and moral norms. But, as I have argued, personalism is an insufficient foundation for ethics. No ethic that employs reason merely to justify conclusions received independently qualifies as Thomistic, either. [86] Thus the authority of the moral norms and of the proposing hierarchy itself—

formerly solidly supported by a complex, sophisticated epistemology and ecclesiology—now rests on a vulnerable phenomenological foundation. As a result, although the new absolutism wards off postmodern relativism, it is no more traditional—and is epistemologically much weaker—than the more egalitarian liberationist model that it also purports to defeat.

The effects of this new absolutism upon ethics and ethical discourse are manifold: it fractures the ecclesiastical community by disenfranchising the ordinary moral reasoner, it cuts off all new insight that seems to contradict its conclusions, and—despite its personalist overtones—it preserves norms without adequate personalist, liberationist, or casuist criticism. Above all, it discourages mature moral reflection by valuing obedience to established moral truths, regardless of hardship, over continual discovery of truth through responsible engagement of norms and context. "Liberal" theologies inspired by Vatican II's openness to the wisdom of the world may avoid some of these pitfalls, but their focus on the moral deliberations of individuals in concrete situations leaves them struggling to explain what theological and methodological protections stand between the flexibility and pluralism they advocate and the utter relativism absolutists rightly fear.

Thus magisterial teaching of the past thirty-five years presents natural law theology with the same puzzle feminism faces: how to make claims both for the existence of prophetically binding truths and for the legitimacy of diverse, prudent, experientially inspired insights. The difficulty is that neither ecclesiological and epistemological combination—the charismatically inspired hierarchy illuminating the church with the single truth, or each member of the community acting as the rational and spirit-filled child of God—entirely fulfills the methodological and metaphysical commitments of traditional natural law or a liberatory theology. Yet as we have seen, the traditionalist ecclesiology is less successful than the democratic one. By accepting the conclusions of traditional natural law reasoning but refusing to permit natural law's methods to operate freely, hierarchical personalism rejects the rich and complex Thomistic understanding of prudence and thus implicitly also denies the holistic anthropology upon which prudence rests.

THE CHRISTIAN AND THE HUMAN

The final important historical challenge to natural law is the postmodern debunking of pretensions to universal, objective, or neutral moral argument. Theologians are struggling to redefine natural law's Christian and rational character just as rules for establishing one's identity in a moral conversation have changed. Taken to extremes, the deconstruction of moral positions can easily destroy natural law's anthropology, its epistemology, and even its capacity to engage in a pluralistic conversation, and it is to this danger that contemporary magisterial documents have responded with alarm. But as we will see, any version of the deconstructive impulse mild enough to permit any sort of ethical dialogue actually aids rather than endangers the project of combining a Christian identity with claims to address universal factors of anthropology and perspicuous reason. Both dangers and benefits, however, appear in relief only when we describe the shift and its implications.

One of natural law's purported advantages—especially in the post-Enlightenment era—has been its ability to speak the language of the world, unburdened by privileged revelation or divine directives. For centuries Roman Catholics saw natural law as human reason, simply: a universal, neutral language of morals, functionally independent of theological claims, intended to guide human action in the world. Indeed, neoscholastic natural law thinkers historically saw little distinction between "doing moral theology" and "arguing from universally self-evident principles." [87] In its most truly scholastic moods, natural law ethics has made use and sense of exactly the same sources of information about humanity that guide secular moral thought: the hard and social sciences, history, philosophy, psychology, and anthropology. To this degree it has rightly been able to claim to converse with secular thinkers on their own terms; hence the traditional unhesitating entrance of Roman Catholic natural law thinkers into legal, political, and economic theory.

But this modern celebration of natural law's useful detachability from theology has met the postmodern claim that ideas ethical and theological are not self-generative but evolve from the history and practice of living communities. [88] From this perspective natural law *is* a thoroughly Christian ethic, even when it is not using Christian language. Thomas himself was a scholar of the Scriptures, and a quick look through the *Summa Theologiae* confirms that, even if Thomas preferred allusion and proof-texting to meditative exegesis, his theology relied upon the unique authority of biblical revelation. [89] His moral norms did as well. Although they, unlike doctrines, were accessible to reason, in case of reason's incapacitation by sin, revealed "back-up copies" of these norms stood ready in Scripture. [90] In addition, the scholastic doctrine of natural law occupied a place carved out by theology, relying on the universal divine origin and end of humanity; and it was of no ultimate use without divine law, revealed by God to direct humanity toward its final end. [91] Because natural human moral knowledge was actually participation in God's eternal law, secular thinkers were thought simply to employ reason in ignorance of its divine origins.

More recently, Vatican Council II documents (with a prescience for which they are rarely credited) raised the need to reemphasize the specifically Christian character of Catholic moral thought. After a long period in which moral theology and biblical study had been treated as independent fields, Vatican II reunited them: "the study of the sacred page" became "the very soul of sacred theology," including moral thought. [92] This conviction has before and since been reflected in the revival of interest at all levels—from the popular through the highest reaches of the hierarchy—in the use of Scripture in Catholic ethics. [93] What these ambitions will mean for moral theological method is still not clear; for instance, the documents do not make clear whether Scripture is to be a source of specific directives, of themes, of alternative rationales for "human" behavior, of examples, or merely of proof texts for independently valid "scientific presentations." [94] Yet they plainly agree that natural law ethics is only apparently detachable from systematic theology; natural law ethics cannot function without at least implicit reference to criteria that fall outside both unaided human reason and the observable features of nature. Natural law thinkers, in other words, must rely on additional philosophical or theological commitments if they wish to transform observations about human nature (including human rationality and apparent ends) into rational, ordered guides for human behavior. [95] The context in which natural law ethics is "natural" is not presuppositionless. Merely leaving the underlying *exitus-reditus* theology out of the discussion does not protect natural law ethics from the impress of religious beliefs, not to mention religious experience. Therefore *Roman Catholic* natural law theory, taken as a whole, is a religious interpretation of human reality, and secular critics of activists who base their political arguments upon Roman Catholic natural law theory are correct to call it so.

But postmodernism's deconstruction of natural law's neutrality hardly disarms natural law. At the same time that the postmodern proclivity to uncover the interests and convictions behind all positions reveals natural law ethics as religious ethics, it also reveals the impracticability of the Enlightenment ideal of ideological neutrality in public speech; as a consequence, it dissolves any justification for the tacit twentieth-century banishment of religious moral argument from public discourse. [96] Natural law ethics may rely on idiosyncratic claims, but no more than do other purportedly "public" arguments. The postmodern turn actually enables natural law to retain the double claim of universal perspicuity and Christian identity that the Enlightenment view ultimately forbids. For the postmodern question is not whether natural law can don the mask of neutral rationality but whether it can, with all of its commitments revealed, make sense of human experience. Natural law cannot credibly merely assert its relevance, but it *can* test its claim to "universal validity. . . . in conversation with rival traditions." [97]

Yet Catholic natural law has not made this postmodern turn comfortably, tending to opt instead for either self-evident universal principles or evangelical claims about categorical Christian uniqueness. [98] On one hand, as we will see in chapters 5 and 6, contemporary Roman Catholic revisionists tout universality of norms: all people operate under the same general principles, and Christians simply have unique motivations and refer their actions to transcendent ends. Similarly, Vatican II–era documents like *Populorum Progressio* and *Pacem in Terris* call upon all people of good will to apply human political and economic wisdom in protection of human dignity. No special theological presuppositions are necessary to this task. Accordingly, later documents like the National Council of Catholic Bishops' *A Challenge to Peace* have been shaped heavily by consultation with secular experts, an influence that extends beyond a description of the signs of the times to practical recommendations.

On the other hand, liberationist and recent magisterial writings emphasize the uniqueness of Christian principles and the exclusivity of their source in Christian revelation—in short, the necessity of self-consciously Christian starting points. The liberation approach is discussed above and in chapter 7, but the magisterium's position can briefly be addressed here. Increasingly, magisterial documents portray Christian moral principles as running *against* the conventional moral wisdom of the world. Pope John Paul II makes clear in *Centesimus Annus* that his concern is "to discern the new requirements of evangelization" and to put *Christian* anthropology forward as the correct basis for social and economic organization everywhere. [99] Similarly, *Veritatis Splendor* often speaks of the evangelical counsels—traditionally believed to be accessible to the mind only through revelation and to the will only through divine charity—as basic moral requirements. [100] Certainly infused charity was always a prerequisite for intricate application and fulfillment of the demands of the natural law, but in *Veritatis Splendor* natural reason does not supply even knowledge of minimal requirements. This is, in essence, a reversion from the Vatican Council II emphasis upon the mutual education of church and world to the turn-of-the-century emphasis upon social change through religious conversion. The intent of this contemporary magisterial reassertion of the peculiarly Christian character of moral obligation seems to be to beat back the relativism that has infected secular moral discourse. But the effect is to give up on the traditional natural law doctrine of the universal perspicuity of reason: now moral truth comes through revelation and communal religious reflection alone.

It would be wrong to suggest that the church should not stand against the world when the world is wrong; as Cynthia Crysdale has pointed out, to accept as valid a claim that is radically contradictory to one's own is to disembowel one position or the other. [101] But the conviction behind recent Vatican documents cuts beyond claims about intellectual honesty, all the way down to epistemology. If we do not in fact naturally desire our own good and so, implicitly if imperfectly, love God—if basic knowledge of moral truth is completely impossible outside of a connection to the Christian moral tradition—there can be no universal, rational participation in the eternal providence of God. Natural law does not exist. We then stand entirely in need of illumination by revelation.

Thanks to postmodernism, it is no longer possible for natural law thinkers to assume that they share the same, basic, de facto moral convictions as other thoughtful people. The alternatives appear to be a theology of revelatory illumination with univocal norms and a conviction that rationality is the ability to measure the capacity of moral claims to make sense of contextual experience. If the first is true, then it no longer makes sense to speak of natural law. If the second is true, then we can have natural law, but not precisely on Thomas's terms: the sources of its insights will be more scattered and the range within which its conclusions will fall will be wider than he envisioned. On this view, the particular, exclusive contribution of Christianity may have universal significance. But rather than being assumed, it must be tested publicly.

THE MARKS OF CONTEMPORARY NATURAL LAW

The Renaissance, the Enlightenment, and postmodernity have left characteristic marks on natural law and natural law scholarship. Casuistic reasoning, personalism, and social justice analysis are now permanent elements of its legacy. Method, epistemological privilege, and the precise Christian character of natural law are still under debate, but the diversity of solutions under discussion ensures that each will also have a lasting significance for the tradition's development. What have been the cumulative effects of these transformations and debates upon natural law? Where has it adjusted coherently to new demands? Where has it failed? Where has it modernized by giving up core commitments?

First, thanks to these transformations, commitments to holism and historicity, as well as acknowledgment of the need to deal constructively with pluralism, now characterize the natural law landscape. [102] For instance, the concrete holism of the social justice criterion of integral flourishing has an analogue in the integrative methodological tendencies of Vatican Council II documents. *Gaudium et Spes* recognizes the church's reliance on the historical, scientific, and philosophical disciplines and calls for even greater reference to them not just in the generation of moral norms but in proclamation and theological reflection. [103] The efforts of Karl Rahner, Bernard Häring, and others—including the writers discussed in the following chapters—to reconnect ethics to theology reflect a similar concern for holism within theology. The same impulse lies behind Joseph Cardinal Bernardin's plea for consistent content—a consistent ethic of life—and Christine Gudorf's call for a consistent method across discussions of "public" and "private" morality. [104]

Second, if the practice of casuistry accommodates historical change implicitly, Vatican Council II documents deal directly with its challenges and requirements: to substitute "a dynamic and more evolutionary concept of nature for a static one" is to take on the difficult task of "recognizing permanent values and applying them to recent discoveries." [105] Faithfulness to truth—and ultimately, to God—must take different forms in new generations. [106] Further, implied in the responsibility to "work toward the establishment of a world that is more human" is the human ability consciously to *construct* a world in history, and not merely to *adapt* to an existing dynamic context. [107]

In addition to embracing global interdependence and human historicity, church documents and theologians have described cultural pluralism as a fact to be acknowledged and a value to be pursued rather than a fad to be withstood. [108] *Gaudium et Spes* insisted that "increased exchanges between cultures" must be kept from "overthrowing traditional wisdom" and "endangering the character proper to each people." [109] Karl Rahner went further, concluding that cultural pluralism entails ecclesiastical adoption of multiple proclamations, canon law codes, and ecclesiastical practices—in short, relinquishment of Western hegemony over belief and practice. Whereas universality and uniformity were synonyms, they are now mutually exclusive options. [110] Although neither Rahner nor the official documents of Vatican Council II anticipated fully the additional challenges of pluralism within cultures, they did open the door to variety in theological expression. [111]

Yet pluralism raises serious questions about truth, unity, and objectivity that are not easily dismissed. [112] If traditional doctrines and norms hold only for the culture from which they emerged and even within that culture are open to criticism, whence comes the unity that binds the diverse communities? Is natural law method universally applicable? Would its point be lost if it were not? [113] How can we distinguish perspectives that are simply different from our own from perspectives that are in error? Would we recognize our own error? [114]

It is these irreversible changes and their dangers that generate the fears to which magisterial absolutism is, for some, a comforting response. But the other developments in natural law thought described in this chapter offer alternatives to a defensive Christian absolutism and to utter relativism. The imaginative and analogical structures of thought that have outfitted casuistry to bridge historical periods also equip it to bridge cultures. By working out the details of the claim that similar goods may demand different sorts of protection in different circumstances, casuistry identifies and articulates areas of agreement. Personalism—if an inadequate foundation for moral reasoning—is an indispensable criterion for moral thought and action. Especially when we are tempted to remain at the level of systematic analysis, personalism forbids us to forget that the point of ethics is to advance the dignity of concrete human beings. Liberationism reminds us that part of that project is to cultivate moral reason and integral flourishing in everyone and especially to privilege the needs and insights of people who suffer under the current state of affairs. Moral absolutism, despite its methodological weaknesses, reminds us that moral evil exists, that not only cross-cultural methods of inquiry and discussion but some cross-cultural moral norms must be articulated, and that it is possible to tell good from faulty moral argument. Finally, the postmodernist unmasking of "universal" claims and "neutral" starting points has removed metaphysical agnosticism from the list of requirements for participation in civil discourse, leaving natural law free to bring its renewed connection to theology into the public conversation.

Together these developments suggest two larger questions, the answers to which are now more firmly in our grasp than they were a chapter ago. First, does this litany of pressures absorbed and resisted teach us anything new about the character of the natural law? For instance, we have seen clearly that it early became impossible to hold on to all the elements of Thomas's ethic—biology, cosmology, method, conclusions, detailed anthropology—simultaneously. To try to preserve the whole unchanged would actually be to transgress prudence by refusing to reflect on new experience. But we have also acquired an eye for authenticity, for determining which elements of this whole may be altered without grave consequences and which may not. For instance, if conclusions are held constant, the project of generating compelling new explanations for them often requires a change of method, epistemology, and thus ultimately theological anthropology; the "plain person's" capacity to reason and her natural inclination to the good may thus fall under suspicion. On the other hand, choosing method over content by holding fast to Thomistic prudence may entail replacing Thomas's biology, and therefore reconsidering the indications of the "natural" for human behavior, and therefore altering the concrete implications of biology for ethics.

In order to rank these and other options for the transformation of the tradition, we must seize the medieval and postmodern claim that natural law is a theological ethic. That is, it involves an anthropology with a divinely devised end that, even if we do not always grasp it firmly, inspires us to seek the good and often enables us to recognize it. More specifically, the end encompasses social and physical flourishing and integral growth in virtue, including practical moral reason. Thus the basic structure of the anthropology, the goal of integral fulfillment, and the main outlines of moral reason are nonnegotiable. The alternatives—rigid visions of ecclesiastical charism or of moral claims immune from reconsideration—implicitly disavow these fundamental claims and so deny the capacity to develop moral judgments. If we choose against these alternatives, we must live with the fact that our new version of Thomas's synthesis—just given the complexity of contemporary cosmology and biology, never mind political and cultural variety—will be flexible, subject to further criticism, and lacking permanent and automatic connections. [115]

The second issue, less widely discussed, is the practical and institutional use of natural law theory. This question is related to the debate over institutional charism and magisterial authority, covered at greater length in chapter 6, but is not identical to it. It is the question of where—in whom—what we think of as "the moral tradition" unfolds. For instance, within Roman Catholicism, natural law method has been generated and applied within small, highly specifically trained groups of male clergy. In Roman Catholic practice, then, natural law methods have only rarely been methods of discernment (to be employed by any reflective person). They have more often been methods for derivation of moral norms (to be developed by a few but followed by everyone). In Korsgaard's terms, we might say that Roman Catholic moral theology has assumed that ordinary clerics and lay people would automatically accept scholars' *explanations* of moral norms as existentially gripping *justifications* of them.

The universal perspicuity of natural law has thus been interpreted to imply the neutrality and self-evidence of moral reason and consequently the interchangeability of moral reasoners. One scholar can reason on behalf of all because, given his good will, training, and leisure to reflect, all others would arrive at conclusions identical to his. This position is even easier to support when Thomas's rather complex epistemology is traded for a theory of knowledge as illumination—as information passed directly, as if by electronic transfer, from God to the mind of the charismatically privileged knower. [116] If the phrase "the experts say" is merely shorthand for a universally reproducible process of coming to a given conclusion, it becomes an existentially gripping justification for a norm or even for its application to a fairly concrete circumstance. Explanation and justification cohere. A few scholars can do the intellectual work on behalf of all.

The institutional use of natural law never worked this smoothly, of course; the history of cases and manuals is a history of debate and disagreement. Even so, this debate has been conducted among small numbers of recognized authorities who, despite differences in contexts and opinions, have been homogeneous in several respects: they have been male, with few exceptions clerics, and normally intellectuals or educators trained in natural law methods. And they have been assumed to be neither biased by self-interest nor ignorant of pertinent facts and experiences.

Yet the traditional claims about the universal perspicuity of the natural law and the—to Thomas, unfortunate—increase in variation in conclusions in the descent to particulars need not lead to this sort of narrowing and hierarchical privilege. It can as easily team up with contemporary pluralism and hermeneutic theory to point out that "the experts say" is a poor justification for either norms or actions. Thinkers are not interchangeable. Each person is a potentially competent moral reasoner with some privileged insight and yet inevitably interprets the world through the lens of her own interests and experience; so the companion to privileged insight must be humility before the possibly different and likewise privileged experiences of others. One good and responsible scholar cannot do the work of a thousand, because he can neither contain their collective breadth of insight nor be trusted not to abuse power. Instead, moral thought must be communal and mutually critical.

Thus the argument for broadening the moral conversation is not merely the argument that previously excluded communities must be heard and engaged; nor does it rest on a claim that the approach of a particular group—women, the poor, or the Roman Catholic hierarchy, for example—is inherently flawless. It is, more properly and radically, an argument for acknowledging that "the moral tradition" is as broad as the existing authentic moral conversation; and it rests on the very traditional claim that moral reason is practical reason, involving prudence, which in turn involves wisdom gleaned from experience. The narrower the experience and interest, the less virtuous the exercise of prudence, the less sure the conclusions of moral reason. What Thomas assumed to be harmonious under ideal conditions—the insights of the intellectual elite and the moral wisdom of varied "common" people—are in fact inherently diverse; their common ground must be negotiated; their positions are open to mutual scrutiny. Thus contemporary faithfulness to natural law anthropology and method demands not just flexibility in conclusions but alterations in the whole culture of moral reflection. Contemporary revisers of casuistry, for instance, illustrate one form this new flexibility may take. As we will see in chapter six, they agree with historical casuists that the flawed norms they correct do not implicate the core of theological tradition as essentially evil and erroneous. But, like liberationists, they also recognize that appropriate changes in moral norms that come about through casuistry often in fact imply a need for important revisions in traditional theology.

It goes without saying that contemporary natural law and feminist ethics must respond, even if differently, to the same cultural forces. But, as I will show, an authentic contemporary version of natural law ethics and a viable feminist ethics are linked by much more than the fact of their contemporaneity.

NOTES

1. Korsgaard, *Sources*, 17.

2. Bruno Schüller, *Wholly Human: Essays on the Theory and Language of Morality*, trans. Peter Heinegg (Dublin: Gill and Macmillan; Washington, DC: Georgetown University Press, 1986), part I.

3. On the history of casuistry in the West, see Jonsen and Toulmin, *Abuse*.

4. For a discussion of casuistry's role in altering the moral estimate of usury, see Jonsen and Toulmin, *Abuse*, 181–94.

5. Blaise Pascal, *The Provincial Letters*, trans. A. J. Krailsheimer (New York: Penguin Books, 1967). The *Letters* were written in 1656–1657.

6. See especially Jonsen and Toulmin, *Abuse;* Keenan and Shannon, *The Context of Casuistry;* and Richard B. Miller, *Casuistry and Modern Ethics: A Poetics of Practical Reasoning* (Chicago: University of Chicago Press, 1996). Westberg points out that even in Thomas the need for self-conscious moral deliberation arises only when normally unproblematic principles do not generate a clear answer to a moral question (*Right Practical Reason*, 165).

7. See Jonsen and Toulmin, *Abuse*, 20; and Kopfensteiner, "Science."

8. In *Abuse*, Jonsen and Toulmin seem to embrace a casuistry without need for common grounding convictions and therefore with reliance only on intermediate, consensus principles; see 16–19, 330–31. Yet it is likely that their exemplary casuistic community—a community designed to develop guidelines within a particular culture—did tacitly share many grounding principles. In support of a casuistry designed to serve principle, see James F. Childress, "Ethical Theories, Principles, and Casuistry in Bioethics: An Interpretation and Defense of Principlism," in *Religious Methods and Resources in Bioethics, Theology and Medicine*, vol. 2, ed. Paul F. Camenisch, 181–201 (Boston: Kluwer Academic Publishers, 1994), 190. See also the following essays in Keenan and Shannon, *The Context of Casuistry:* James F. Keenan, "The Casuistry of John Mair, Nominalist Professor of Paris," 85–102; idem, "William Perkins (1558–1602) and the Birth of British Casuistry," 105–30; James F. Keenan and Thomas Shannon, "Contexts of Casuistry: Historical and Contemporary," 221–31.

More recently, Albert Jonsen has spoken of "oscillation between fact and theory" with cases providing "a middle ground between principles and conscience," suggesting that principles in fact anchor one side of a casuistic dialectic (Albert R. Jonsen, "Casuistry, Situationism, and Laxism," in *Joseph Fletcher: Memoir of an Ex-Radical: Reminiscence and Reappraisal*, ed. Kenneth L. Vaux [Louisville: Westminster/John Knox, 1993], 18; Jonsen, foreword to Keenan and Shannon, *Context*, xiii).

9. Jonsen and Toulmin, *Abuse*, 239.

10. See Mahoney, *Making;* and Gallagher, *Time Past.*

11. See, e.g., Jonsen, "Casuistry," 22. For a more extensive discussion of probabiliorism, probabilism, and related terms, see Mahoney, *Making,* 135–43.

12. Keenan, "Mair," 96–97; idem, "Perkins," 108.

13. Thanks to William P. George for this observation.

14. Miller, *Casuistry,* 245. Keenan and Shannon argue that the rhetorics of virtue and of the case simply have more power to exhort—and therefore to inspire genuine, healthy moral reflection—than the rhetoric of principles. Wide use of casuistic reasoning would overcome its weaknesses without undermining its strengths or its connection to principle (Keenan and Shannon, "Contexts," 225–30).

15. On this problem in moral theology or the manuals, see Mahoney, *Making,* 27–32; and Gallagher, *Time Past,* 60–62. Brief treatment of sin as general orientation away from one's end in God usually was overshadowed by the lengthy treatment of individual sins.

16. On the former, see Westberg, *Right Practical Reason.* On the latter, see *ST* I-II 94.4–5.

17. Emmanuel Mounier, *Personalism,* trans. Philip Mairet (London: Routledge and Kegan Paul, 1952), xvii; Joseph A. Selling, "Introduction," *Personalist Morals: Essays in Honor of Professor Louis Janssens,* ed. Joseph A. Selling (Leuven: Leuven University Press, 1988), 2–3; and Gabriel Gersh, "Emmanuel Mounier and Christian Personalism," *Religion in Life* 31 (Summer 1963): 436–37.

18. Mounier, *Personalism,* xiii.

19. *Apostolicam actuositatem,* in *Vatican Council II: The Conciliar and Post Conciliar Documents,* ed. Austin Flannery (Northport, NY: Costello Publishing Company, 1975), 773–74, par. 7.

20. Mounier, *Personalism,* vii–viii.

21. Mounier, *Personalism,* xii, viii. This position can be found in writers as different as John Paul II and Janssens.

22. European Catholic personalism should not be confused with American Methodist personalism, which was inspired by the somewhat different philosophical personalism developed at Boston University. See Frederick Ferré, "Boston Personalism," in *Religion and Philosophy in the United States of America: Proceedings of the German-American Conference at Paderborn, July 29–August 1, 1986,* vol. 1, ed. Peter Freese (Essen: Die Blaue Eule, 1987), 197–211.

23. Selling, "Introduction," 3. Christopher Butler finds in some Vatican Council II descriptions of faith and truth a subtle shift in diction from strictly objective, propositional language to subjective, experiential language. This shift may be read as a new official appreciation for the indispensability of the formerly devalued side of the "horizontal" distinction between objectivity and subjectivity and is consonant with perceptible post-Vatican Council II shifts toward personalism in morality (Christopher Butler, *The Theology of Vatican II* [London: Darton, Longman and Todd, 1967], 143–69).

24. This influence came through John Paul II, *Love and Responsibility;* see Leo D. Lefebure, "John Paul II: The Philosopher Pope," *Christian Century* 112, no. 5 (15 February 1995): 171.

25. Juan Luís Segundo, *Berdiaeff: Une Reflexion Chrétienne sur la Personne* (Paris: Aubier, 1963).

26. See Mahoney, *Making*, on the personalistic implications of the drive to totality (309–21). Roman Catholic personalism since Vatican Council II is not precisely the same as philosophical personalism.

27. James F. Bresnahan, "Rahner's Ethics: Critical Natural Law in Relation to Contemporary Ethical Methodology," *Journal of Religion* 56 (January 1976): 53. See also Norbert J. Rigali, "Toward a Moral Theology of Social Consciousness," *Horizons* 4 (Fall 1977): 178; Norbert J. Rigali, "The Moral Act," *Horizons* 10 (Fall 1983): 252–66; John Paul II, "Thomistic Personalism," in *Person and Community: Selected Essays*, trans. Teresa Sandok, OSM, Catholic Thought from Lublin, vol. 4 (New York: Peter Lang, 1993), 172; and Karol Wojtyla [Pope John Paul II], *The Acting Person*, trans. Andrezj Potocki (Dordrecht; Boston: D. Reidel, 1979).

28. *Gaudium et Spes*, in *Vatican Council II*, ed. Flannery, 904, par. 3. On the implications for moral reasoning see Norbert J. Rigali, "Artificial Birth Control: The Impasse Revisited," *Theological Studies* 47 (December 1986): 681–90, and chapter 6 of this book.

29. Anton Charles Pegis, *At the Origins of the Thomistic Notion of Man*, The St. Augustine Lecture, 1962 (New York: Macmillan, 1963), 34, 38–40; see also Thiry, "Ethical Theory," 170. Van Melsen therefore argues that it is impossible to act "against nature" in the biological sense; one can act "against human nature" only in the integral sense, which includes the dynamic power of rationality (A. G. M. van Melsen, "Natur und Moral," in *Das Naturrecht im Disput*, ed. Böckle, 85).

30. *Gaudium et Spes*, 949–57, par. 47–52.

31. *Gaudium et Spes*, 924, par. 23, and 925, par. 24.

32. See *Humanae Vitae*, par. 17, italics added; quoted and interpreted in John Paul II, *Blessed Are the Pure*, 266.

33. On contraception in particular see the notes in chapter 6 on Richard McCormick.

34. The "animal," procreative rationale for sexuality is inadequate because it does not account for peculiarities of human bonding or for the human ability of reasonable persons to turn sexuality to (good) ends other than procreation. See Crowe, *Changing Profile*, chapter 10.

35. According to Grundel "man does not merely have a history; he *is* history"; "man remains ultimately the personal subject who is capable of history and is historical" (*Sacramentum Mundi*, s.v. "Natural Law [Moral]," by Grundel).

36. Rahner et al., eds., *Sacramentum Mundi*, s.v. "Thomism," by Paulus Engelhardt.

37. Van Melsen, "Natur," 80–83.

38. *Sacramentum Mundi*, s.v. "Natural Law (Moral)," by Grundel. On implications for moral reasoning, see Charles E. Curran, "How My Mind Has Changed, 1960–1975," *Horizons* 2 (Fall 1975): 196–201; Edward A. Malloy, "Problem of Methodology in Contemporary Roman Catholic Ethics," *St. Luke's Journal of Theology* 22 (December 1978): 24; and Edward A. Malloy, "Natural Law Theory and Catholic Moral Theology," *American Ecclesiastical Review* 169 (1975): 465–69.

39. In the process they have often romanticized the medieval guild system and its "personal," hands-on labor, projecting their modern notion of rights back into the often (to the modern mind) dehumanizing and limiting conditions of medieval life and work. See for example Nikolai Berdiaev, *Christianity and Class War*, trans. Donald Attwater (London: Sheed and Ward, 1933).

40. Pope John Paul II, *Original Unity of Man and Woman: Catechesis on the Book of Genesis* (Boston: Daughters of St. Paul, 1981); idem, *Blessed Are the Pure.*

41. See *Sacramentum Mundi: An Encyclopedia of Theology*, s.v. "Personalism," by Eberhard Simons (New York: Herder and Herder, 1969), 421; Although Simons does not address Lublin and French personalism here, his comment applies to them as well.

42. See Traina, "Oh, Susanna."

43. Eric Matthews, *Twentieth Century French Philosophy* (Oxford; New York: Oxford University Press, 1996), 45–46, 56.

44. The terminology is from O'Connell, *Principles*, 137.

45. Paraphrase of Curran, *Directions*, 130–31.

46. See O'Connell, *Principles*, 150; see also Curran, *Directions*, 133–34; Karl Rahner, "The Experiment with Man: Theological Observations on Man's Self-Manipulation" and "The Problem of Genetic Manipulation" in *Theological Investigations: Writings of 1965–67*, trans. Graham Harrison (New York: Herder and Herder, 1972), 9:205–24 and 225–52; and Crowe, *Changing Profile*, 262–63.

47. Curran, *Directions*, 134; see also Curran, "How My Mind Has Changed," 200; and O'Connell, *Principles*, 142–43. For examples of the revisionist elevation of reason, see Richard M. Gula, *What Are They Saying About Moral Norms?* (New York: Paulist Press, 1982), 41; and Richard J. Regan, *American Pluralism and the Catholic Conscience*, with a Foreword by John Courtney Murray (New York: Macmillan Company; London: Collier-Macmillan Limited, 1963), 189. Crowe hints that anxiety over the ill effects of pushing the body too far into the background was what prevented Thomas from discarding Ulpian's awkward order-of-nature reasoning entirely (Crowe, *Changing Profile*, 151).

48. See for instance O'Connell, *Principles*, 144–54.

49. See for example Crysdale, "Horizons That Differ," 347.

50. Paulinus Ikechukwu Odozor, *Richard A. McCormick and the Renewal of Moral Theology* (Notre Dame: University of Notre Dame Press, 1995), 22.

51. Traina, "Oh, Susanna." Similarly, in recent years the lay and clerical obligation to obey authoritatively defined teaching receives much greater attention than the hierarchy's obligation to take care in its articulation.

52. Despite its origins in practical social movements—Mounier wrote *Personalism* only at the end of a life of activism, for instance—in its philosophical form it is easily susceptible to individualism; see Selling, "Introduction," 4; and Simons, "Personalism," 421–22.

53. Pope Leo XIII, *Rerum Novarum*, in *Five Great Encyclicals: Labor, Education, Marriage, Reconstructing the Social Order, Atheistic Communism*, ed. Gerald C. Treacy (New York: Paulist Press, 1939), 1–30; and Pope Pius XI, *Quadragesimo Anno*, in *Five Great Encyclicals*, ed. Treacy, 125–68.

54. Mahoney, *Making*, 34; see also Pope Pius XI, *Quadragesimo Anno*, 161, par. 43; and McCool, *Catholic Theology*, 32–34. The early social encyclicals made no recommendations for societies in which powerful persons refuse to participate in the "reform of manners" that is the prerequisite for an equitable economic order (e.g., Pius XI, *Quadragesimo Anno*, 152, par. 97).

55. Calvez and Perrin, *Church*, 118.

56. Maritain, *Person*, 54.

57. "As the assumed nature, inseparably united to [Christ], serves the divine Word as a living organ of salvation, so, in a somewhat similar way, does the social structure of the Church serve the Spirit of Christ who vivifies it, in the building up of the body" (*Lumen Gentium*, in *Vatican Council II*, ed. Flannery, 357, par. 8).

58. *Gaudium et Spes*, 938, par. 39; see also ibid., 946–47, par. 44; and ibid., 934, par. 34.

59. Ibid., 938, par. 39; and 1000–1, par. 92–93.

60. Pope John Paul II [Karol Wojtyla], "The Perspectives of Man—Integral Development and Eschatology," trans. A. N. Woznicki, *Center Journal* 3 (Spring 1984): 135–38. For him Christ is "the goal of human history" and "the fulfillment of all aspirations" in whose Spirit "we press onwards on our journey towards the consummation of history which fully corresponds to the plan of his love" (c.f. *Gaudium et Spes*, 947, par. 45). See also *Gaudium et Spes*, 937–38, par. 38–39.

61. See *Gaudium et Spes*, 927, par. 26; 935, par. 36; 938, par. 39; and 942, par. 42; and *Apostolicam Actuositatem*, 773–74, par. 7. See also the later *Centesimus Annus*, 20, par. 53.

62. See *Centesimus Annus*, 20–21, par. 53–55.

63. On this transformation, see *Lumen Gentium*, 350, par. 1; ibid., 351, par. 3; *Gaudium et Spes*, 904, par. 2; and ibid., 940, par. 40. On the requirement to focus on systematic ills see *Apostolicam Actuositatem*, 775–76, par. 8. For a more liberationist reading see *Centesimus Annus*: redress of injustice and elimination of poverty require "above all a change of lifestyles, of models of production and consumption, and of the established structures of power which today govern societies" (21, par. 58; see also ibid., 15, par. 36).

64. Thomas L. Schubeck, S.J., *Liberation Ethics: Sources, Models, and Norms* (Minneapolis: Fortress Press, 1993), 48–49. On liberation ethics see also Arthur McGovern, *Liberation Theology and Its Critics: Toward an Assessment* (Maryknoll, NY: Orbis Books, 1989); Patricia McAuliffe, *Fundamental Ethics: A Liberationist Approach* (Washington, DC: Georgetown University Press, 1993).

65. Schubeck, *Liberation Ethics*, 154; after Clodovis Boff, *Theology and Praxis: Epistemological Considerations*, trans. Robert R. Barr (Maryknoll, NY: Orbis Books, 1988), 133; see also chapter 7 of this volume.

66. Schubeck, *Liberation Ethics*, 24. See also chapter 7 of this volume.

67. See Crysdale, "Horizons," on culpable group bias.

68. To hew studiously to the rules of an unjust system, to choose the interests of the powerful, is sinful and disordered (Schubeck, *Liberation Ethics*, 24).

69. See McAuliffe, *Fundamental Ethics*, chapter 1.

70. Schubeck, *Liberation Ethics*, 191–93, and Juan Luís Segundo, "The Shift Within Latin American Theology," *Journal of Theology for Southern Africa* 52 (September 1985): 17–29.

71. Segundo, "Shift."
72. See Kay, "Getting Egypt out of the People."
73. See McGovern, *Liberation Theology*. Questions have been raised about whether it is marginality per se—or the combined centrality and powerlessness of workers in a capitalist society—that produces epistemic privilege. See Bar On, "Marginality and Epistemic Privilege."
74. For the arguments and their roots in the ambiguous messages of ecclesiastical writings, see Gregory Baum, "Faith and Liberation: Development Since Vatican II," in *Vatican II: Open Questions and New Horizons*, Theology and Life Series, no. 8, ed. Gerald M. Fagin, 75–104 (Wilmington, DE: M. Glazier, 1984), 95–101; Avery Dulles, *The Reshaping of Catholicism: Current Challenges in the Theology of Church* (San Francisco: Harper and Row, 1988), especially 147–48, 151; and Charles E. Curran, "Moral Theology: The Present State of the Discipline," *Theological Studies* 34 (September 1973): 462–63.
75. McAuliffe, *Fundamental Ethics*, ix.
76. See Stephen Duffy, "Catholicism's Search for a New Self-Understanding," in *Vatican II: Open Questions*, ed. Fagin, 9–10, 19; Gabriel Daly, "Catholicism and Modernity," *Journal of the American Academy of Religion* 53 (December 1985): 774–76; and John W. O'Malley, "Developments, Reforms, and Two Great Reformations: Towards a Historical Assessment of Vatican II," *Theological Studies* 44 (September 1983): 405.
77. See, e.g., *Lumen Gentium*, 360, par. 9; and *Gaudium et Spes*, 939–42, par. 40–42.
78. See *Lumen Gentium*, chapter 3, "The Church is Hierarchical," 369–87. The principle of collegiality extends to the hierarchy only; hence my use of the male pronoun.
79. *Lumen Gentium*, 402, par. 42; ibid., 389, par. 31. The essential, ecclesiastical ministry of uniting "in one conscience" the secular and sacred orders belongs to laypeople. See ibid., 390–91, par. 33, and 393–94, par. 36; *Gaudium et Spes*, 944, par. 43; *Apostolicam Actuositatem*, 772, par. 5. Francine Cardman argues that Vatican Council II's limitation of lay ministry primarily to the upbuilding of secular society actually reflects a medieval worldview (Francine Cardman, "The Church Would Look Foolish without Them: Women and Laity Since Vatican II," in *Vatican II: Open Questions*, ed. Fagin, 109–19).
80. *Gaudium et Spes*, 968, par. 62.
81. Hierarchical promulgation and postconciliar application of new ideas—even the convening of the Council itself—have run counter to their apparently collegial, participatory message (see Duffy, "Search," 22–24; and O'Malley, "Developments," 398). A recent example is the isolation potentially imposed on theologians by the *Instruction on the Ecclesial Vocation of the Theologian* (Congregation for the Doctrine of the Faith, *Instruction on the Ecclesial Vocation of the Theologian*, in *Origins* 20 [5 July 1990]: 117–26). The promulgation of *Humanae Vitae* first focused these questions, for here the collegial method set up to explore the issue of contraception was circumvented at the last moment in favor of a unilaterally written document whose logic and biology many have called weak. See Mahoney, *Making*, chapter 7, especially 259–71, 292–94; Margaret A. Farley, "Moral Discourse in the Public Arena," in *Vatican Authority and American Catholic Dissent: The Curran Case and Its Consequences*, ed. William W. May (New York: Crossroad, 1987), 174; Joseph Komonchak, "Authority and Magiste-

rium," in *Vatican Authority*, 103–14; Richard A. McCormick, "Loyalty and Dissent: The Magisterium—A New Model," *America* 122 (27 June 1970): 674–76; and Richard A. McCormick, "What the Silence Means: Richard A. McCormick Answers His Critics," *America* 129 (20 October 1973): 289. Behind this issue is the tension between Vatican Council II's images of church as people of God and as hierarchy (see Albert Ottenweller, "Clergy-Laity Tension Cited as Critical," *The New World* [5 April 1991]).

For the debate over reasoned dissent and magisterial prerogative, see Curran, "Moral Theology: The Present State," 460; Daniel C. Maguire, "Moral Inquiry and Religious Assent," in *Contraception: Authority and Dissent*, ed. Charles E. Curran (New York: Herder and Herder, 1969), 127–48; and *Sacramentum Mundi*, s.v. "Natural Law (Moral)," by Grundel.

82. For differing assessments of this fact, see Dulles, *Reshaping*, especially 155 and 205–6; and Daly, "Catholicism," 778–96.

83. On nuptial imagery, see Susan A. Ross, "The Bride of Christ and the Body Politic: Body and Gender in Pre-Vatican II Marriage Theology," *Journal of Religion* 71 (July 1991): 345–61; William C. Spohn, "Notes on Moral Theology: 1992, The Magisterium and Morality," *Theological Studies* 54 (1993): 95–111. This language may be found in Pope John Paul II, *Veritatis Splendor*, in *Origins* 23 (14 October 1993): 297, 299–334; see also Congregation for the Doctrine of the Faith, *Instruction on the Ecclesial Vocation of the Theologian*, in *Origins* 20, no. 8 (5 July 1990): 117, 119–26.

84. See, for example, Ronald D. Lawler, OFM, Cap., *The Christian Personalism of Pope John Paul II*, The John Paul Synthesis: The Trinity College Symposium I (Chicago: Franciscan Herald Press, 1982).

85. Pope Paul VI did in fact weigh the commission's report carefully, but the encyclical obscures rather than highlights its influence on his thought. Its rhetoric might easily have been conversational rather than declarative.

86. Westberg, *Right Practical Reason*, 7.

87. For Davis, "the existence of God, the fact of a supernatural destiny," and other items of Christian faith are issues for systematic theologians, not moralists (*Moral and Pastoral Theology*, vol. 1, p. 1).

88. See for example George A. Lindbeck, *The Nature of Doctrine: Religion and Theology in a Post-liberal Age* (Philadelphia: Westminster Press, 1984); Hauerwas, *A Community of Character;* or MacIntyre, *After Virtue*.

89. See *ST* I 1.8.2.

90. *ST* I-II 91.4.

91. *ST* I-II 99.3.

92. *Dei verbum*, in *Vatican Council II*, ed. Flannery, 763–64, par. 24; see also ibid., 753, par. 7; and *Optatam Totius*, in *Vatican Council II*, ed. Flannery, 719–20, par. 16.

93. See Mahoney, *Making*, 78–80. In mid-century Bernard Häring, and before him the modernists, agitated for more scholarly scriptural study and its wider application in theology.

94. On the use of Scripture in Roman Catholic ethics, see *The Use of Scripture in Moral Theology*, Readings in Moral Theology, no. 4, ed. Charles E. Curran and Richard A. McCormick (New York/Ramsey: Paulist Press, 1984); William C. Spohn, "The Use of Scripture in Moral Theology," *Theological Studies* 47 (March 1986): 88–102; and William C. Spohn, *What Are They Saying about Scripture and Ethics?*

(New York: Paulist Press, 1984). On the hermeneutical problem in ethics, see Malloy, "Problems of Methodology," 25–27.

95. Crowe, *Changing Profile*, 269–70; the "something more" includes an awareness that the nature described is conditioned by time and culture. See also William Luijpen, *Phenomenology of Natural Law*, trans. Henry J. Koran (Pittsburgh: Duquesne University Press, 1967).

96. See for instance Ronald Thiemann, *Religion in Public Life: A Dilemma for Democracy*, A Twentieth Century Fund Book (Washington, DC: Georgetown University Press, 1996); Kent Greenawalt, *Private Consciences and Public Reasons* (New York: Oxford University Press, 1995); idem, *Religious Convictions and Political Choice* (New York: Oxford University Press, 1988); Stephen L. Carter, *The Culture of Disbelief: How American Law and Politics Trivialize Religious Devotion* (New York: Basic Books, 1993); Michael Perry, *Religion in Politics: Constitutional and Moral Perspectives* (New York: Oxford University Press, 1997); idem, *Love and Power: The Role of Religion and Morality in American Politics* (New York: Oxford University Press, 1991); and forthcoming work by Jean Bethke Elshtain.

97. Porter, *Recovery*, 175.

98. At times both stances appear in the same document, but awkwardly connected. A good example is the 1983 National Council of Catholic Bishops' pastoral letter "The Challenge of Peace: God's Promise and Our Response" (Washington, DC: United States Catholic Conference, 1983).

99. Pope John Paul II, *Centesimus Annus*, 3, par. 3.

100. *Veritatis Splendor*, chapter 1.

101. Crysdale, "Horizons."

102. See Gerald A. Arbuckle, "Inculturation Not Adaptation: Time to Change Terminology," *Worship* 60 (1986): 516; also see Dulles, *Reshaping*, 19–33.

103. *Gaudium et spes*, 946–47, par. 44. This is true as well of the church's interaction with cultures (ibid., 962–63, par. 58). The first chapter discusses the global changes that have precipitated a reevaluation of the church's relationship to the world. In addition, the first paragraph in chapter 4, "The Role of the Church in the Modern World," is entitled "*Mutual* Relationship of Church and World" (ibid., 939, par. 40; emphasis added). Despite John Paul II's attention to "the signs of the times," docility— a willingness to be *taught by* the world—is much less evident in *Centesimus Annus* than in many Vatican Council II documents.

104. Joseph Cardinal Bernardin, "The Consistent Ethic of Life: An American-Catholic Dialogue," in *Consistent Ethic of Life*, ed. Thomas G. Fuechtmann (Kansas City, MO: Sheed and Ward, 1988), 1–11; Christine Gudorf, "To Make a Seamless Garment, Use a Single Piece of Cloth: The Abortion Debate," in *The Public Vocation of Christian Ethics*, ed. Beverly W. Harrison, Robert L. Stivers, and Ronald H. Stone (New York: Pilgrim Press, 1986), 275; and Christine Gudorf, "Renewal or Repatriarchalization? Responses of the Roman Catholic Church to the Feminization of Religion," *Horizons* 10 (Fall 1983): 231–51. Gudorf argues for carrying over "public," proportional consequentialism into traditionally "private" areas such as abortion and sexuality, but this choice is not logically entailed by her main insight. Other "unified ethics" could be proposed. For applications of "private" caring to social ethics, see Joan Tronto, *Moral Boundaries.* James Gustafson argues for the recognition of several interdependent modes of moral discourse with overlapping or complementary competencies. See James

M. Gustafson, *Varieties of Moral Discourse: Prophetic, Narrative, Ethical, and Policy*, The Stob Lectures of Calvin College and Seminary, 1987–88 (Grand Rapids, MI: Calvin College and Seminary, 1988).

105. *Gaudium et spes*, 906–7, par. 4 and 5.

106. See Daly, "Catholicism," 781; and John W. O'Malley, "Reform, Historical Consciousness, and Vatican II's Aggiornamento," *Theological Studies* 32 (December 1971): 597.

107. *Gaudium et Spes*, 959, 961, par. 55, 57. The authors are concerned here to commend construction of a world consistent with human nature. Although post-Vatican II ecclesiastical reluctance to make specific economic and political recommendations may be intended as a criticism of liberationist dogmatism, it too respects human historical creativity: "models that are real and truly effective can only arise within the framework of different historical situations through the efforts of all those who responsibly confront concrete problems in all their social, economic, political and cultural aspects as these interact with each other" (*Centesimus annus*, 17, par. 43; see also ibid., 18, par. 46).

108. For a dissenting view, see Louis C. Midgeley, *Beyond Human Nature: The Contemporary Debate over Moral Natural Law*, Charles E. Merrill Monograph Series in the Humanities and Social Sciences, vol. 1, no. 4 (Provo, UT: Brigham Young University Press, 1968), 64–67, 77.

109. *Gaudium et spes*, 960, par. 56.

110. Karl Rahner, "Toward a Fundamental Theological Interpretation of Vatican II," trans. Leo J. O'Donovan, *Theological Studies* 40 (December 1979): 718–26. "This, then, is the issue: either the Church sees and recognizes these essential differences of other cultures for which she should become a world Church and with a Pauline boldness draws the necessary consequences from this recognition, or she remains a Western Church and so in the final analysis betrays the meaning of Vatican II" (Rahner, "Interpretation," 724). See also Arbuckle, "Inculturation," 517; Dulles, *Reshaping*, 43–46; *Lumen Gentium*, 77–78, par. 23; and *Gaudium et Spes*, 1000, par. 92.

111. Rahner recognizes that individual cultures are also in the process of unprecedented, rapid change and that this fact complicates the application of principles of pluralism ("Interpretation," 718).

112. On these questions see Philip S. Keane, "The Objective Moral Order: Reflections on Recent Research," *Theological Studies* 43 (1982): 260–78; Charles E. Curran, *Faithful Dissent* (Kansas City, MO: Sheed and Ward, 1986), 61–62; and Bresnahan, "Rahner's Ethics."

113. See Porter, *Recovery*, 54–55 and 174–76.

114. See Crysdale, "Horizons."

115. Patrick Byrne, "The Thomistic Sources of Lonergan's Dynamic World View," *The Thomist* 46 (1982).

116. Westberg, *Right Practical Reason*, chapter 7. For a contemporary example, see Lawler, *The Christian Personalism of Pope John Paul II*, especially 77–99. For Lawler, confident agreement with defined doctrines can be had only through the experience of coming to existential faith. Rejection of church teachings is a category error—either one does not really have faith, or one is rejecting something that cannot consistently be rejected.

4

Critical Principles for Feminist Ethics

Chapter 1 argued for a particular approach to feminist ethics and listed some of the goods it should pursue. Thanks to our intervening discussion of the natural law tradition, we can extend these observations in two directions. First, we can articulate these general feminist claims as precise criteria of adequacy for ethics with a much clearer sense of the ways in which they confirm or contradict natural law criteria. Second, we can confirm the suspicion that arose at the end of chapter 1: any feminist ethic that makes a strong and meaningful contribution to the project of women's welfare inherently makes important claims in common with natural law ethics. That is, the demand that natural law reflection live up to feminist standards is not philosophically or theologically arbitrary. Feminist ethics criticizes natural law from the inside.

Narrow enough to be prophetic but broad enough to allow for flexibility, the "thick, vague" anthropology and criteria of flourishing developed in chapter 1 provide a constructive point of departure for firm but revisable, common feminist guidelines for moral life and moral thought. Here we can begin to specify feminism's critical leverage against natural law. Feminism affects ethics at three levels: method (the theoretical structure of ethical argument), procedure (the practical structure of ethical conversation), and content (the norms or guides the method develops). These levels are interdependent: wide methodological attention to women's experience both alters norms and enlarges the "official" moral conversation; expansion of the vision of women's good to include a communally informed moral autonomy demands changes in procedure; a method that claims to have broad regard for experience derails if it is applied by a small group of thinkers—even feminist thinkers—to the reported or projected experiences of a larger group. [1] Because natural law ethics tends not to observe the distinction between method and procedure, we must treat it with special care.

METHOD

Typically, method in ethics is the series of rational steps through which a thinker develops or applies a moral norm. It dictates what authorities she will consult, in what order; it tells her what is permitted as evidence and when and how deeply she can consider the particularity of circumstances. It is generally thought that responsible and right-minded thinkers using the same method will resolve the same moral problems similarly; in other words, method corrects the parallax a thinker inevitably brings to a moral question. Feminist ethics does not make quite such sweeping claims for method, taken in this narrow sense. But its commitment to advancing women's integral well-being means, among other things, that its method must be faithful to women's *critically examined* experiences and thought. This starting point yields three important methodological criteria, each of which is implicit in the anthropological and epistemological claims made so far.

UNIFIED METHOD. First, ethical method must honor the deep connections among the apparently disparate dimensions of the moral life. Liberalism has differentiated matters of individual, relational, or "private" ethics—most notably sexual ethics, but also all other ethics that treat our relationships with other individuals, things, and God—from issues of social or "public" ethics—political and economic policy, as well as war and peace. For instance, although the *Roe v. Wade* decision may have been intended to balance state and individual interests, it is now a popular symbol of the right to privacy. According to this popular understanding, reproductive ethics are matters for individuals' decisions and have no bearing on the social good; or more precisely, and even more in keeping with the liberal tradition, the common good is best served by absolute autonomy and free choice in all decisions that do not directly infringe on the freedom of fully enfranchised others to pursue their chosen ends. [2]

On the other hand, feminists have argued—at first rooting their claims in their own or other women's experiences, but later backing up these reports with critical analyses of social relationships—that the personal is the political. All "personal" moral decisions both are constricted by social structures and mores and have social repercussions; likewise, social policy decisions—welfare cuts and tax breaks, for instance—reverberate through the intimate lives of individuals. For instance, a woman's reluctance to repel a man's sexual advances may have to do with her economic dependence upon him; their sexual relationship is not merely a private matter but likely reflects an uneven distribution of social and economic power between men and women in the society at large. [3] Outrage on the part of some over President Bill Clinton's admitted sexual infidelity and habitual dishonesty about it reflects both this anxiety about power and the accompanying conviction that the moral subject is an integral whole. A habit of infidelity and dishonesty is just that. If private and public are continuous, then a vice that so grossly betrays private commitments must infect public responsibilities as well. [4]

Failure to account systematically for the continuity between what are often thought to be two separate spheres leads to a schizophrenic theory in which the choice of method depends upon the sphere into which an issue appears to fall, a premature classification that in turn limits the sorts of critical questions that can be brought to bear on the problem. For example, Christine Gudorf points out that the Roman Catholic natural law tradition's prohibition of abortive killing employs the same sort of reasoning as its treatment of "private" sexual ethics, which are governed by inflexible moral absolutes; yet it has assigned killing in war to the sphere of "public" policy, where flexible proportional consequentialism aided by social analysis selectively permits killing. Gudorf argues that this dual method ignores both the social complexity of the abortion issue—for instance, its link to sexual violence against women— and the direct consequences of armament for the "private" lives of the poor, whose further deprivation is one of the costs of maintaining a strong military force. The separation of private from public ethics thus overlooks both the grave contingencies and the social ramifications of "private" acts and the ease with which basic moral principles can be pushed aside in a "public" teleological calculus. Worse, when yoked with the assignment of women to private, familial roles and men to public, social roles, this division supports a double standard: because "private" moral dilemmas have pat answers, women need not and may not deliberate over them; because "public" dilemmas must be solved by a teleological calculus, men can slide into committing moral outrages in the name of apparently good ends. Pregnant women are flat out forbidden to abort, but male military leaders are gently requested to weigh matters carefully and follow their consciences. If the same, comprehensive moral calculus were applied to both questions, she intimates, two effects would follow: first, abortion would seem less proscribable, and war less permissible, than in the old dual system; and second, men would have to recognize women as competent moral reasoners. [5]

Gudorf's argument yields the first methodological criterion: because human beings are inherently particular and social beings, an adequate ethical method must be a unified method, considering both the social dimensions and particular implications of *all* moral stances and behaviors. The distinction between public and private need not be erased—the family need not be reduced to a subsidiary social institution, for instance, and obligations to friends or siblings need not be determined in exactly the same way as obligations to strangers—but neither should the intrinsic connection between public and private affairs ever be obscured. [6]

RESPECT FOR MODES OF REASONING UNRECOGNIZED IN THE ACADEMY. Critical attention to the de facto practice of women's moral reason results in a second criterion: a feminist ethical method must employ the actual practice of moral deliberation as a critical lever against the theories of moral development that have become so popular as "scientific" justifications for the elevation of classical scholarly ethics. For instance, Carol Gilligan's groundbreaking study *In a Different Voice* insisted that classical schemes of moral development—based almost exclusively on studies of well-educated, white, Western men and boys—systematically miss or devalue an alternative moral logic prevalent among women (and, as others have argued since, among African and African-American men and the poor in general). [7] The women whom she studied tended to replace or supplement the logic of impartial justice with the logic of care, in which subjects see themselves not as isolated and independent but as attached to others in interdependence. [8] In a way that recalls casuistry, care reasoning tends to preserve relationships by altering principles and descriptions rather than to ensure mathematical equality by adhering to these principles and descriptions, and it often refuses to limit itself to a simple yes or no response when faced with a dilemma. [9] It is narrative, contextual, and "webbed" rather than abstract or linear. [10]

By attending to *women's* practices of care, Gilligan has transformed the norm of *human* moral logic; she has argued that care reasoning, empirically discovered and carefully described, ought to receive a greater share of attention not just from feminists and students of "personal" ethics, but from all moral theorists. [11] For instance, care reasoning raises profound questions about the expansiveness and uniformity of traditional natural law accounts of both human nature and human reason. It points especially to the need to recognize that the selfless maternal affection off-handedly mentioned in Roman Catholic social documents is not a bounteous, homogeneous natural instinct but a complex moral discipline that bears ethical analysis and—keeping in mind Judith Butler's warnings about ways in which individuals' desires and practices can be bent by cultural expectations—sharp-eyed critique as well.

Gilligan has been condemned—often unfairly—for proposing a "feminine" logic that not only ignores the probable influence of internalized oppression on the development of women's patterns of moral thought but also borders on romantic essentialism. [12] An uncritical use of Gilligan's work would be guilty of these trespasses. But the ultimate significance of Gilligan's theory is not her addition of care to the feminist moral vocabulary but her ability to see what had previously been considered a deficiency as a worthy moral logic. She has demonstrated how to go about accounting for and accommodating widely used structures of moral reasoning previously unrecognized by the academy. If women—and others who are underrepresented in or absent from the academy—employ logics of reasoning that run counter to the dominant models of ideal moral thought, their methods must be described, evaluated for systematic integrity, and critically related to dominant scholarly approaches. [13] An adequate method must not only accomplish this in the present but also leave openings for future additions and adjustments from presently unexpected quarters.

WOMEN'S FLOURISHING.   Finally and most importantly, this chapter has argued that an adequate ethic (and an adequate ethicist) must adhere to feminist criteria of truth. Feminism, like other liberationist approaches, applies a moral hermeneutic to truth claims: no ethical system that does not promote women's good can be true; nor can it be authentically holy. [14] Given that I have praised casuistry for its ability to recognize that even a good systematic tree, poorly cared for, generally bears fruit in substandard judgments, this feminist claim needs to be explained carefully. The casuist assumes that the tree is healthy; a little careful attention will correct the problem, and the tree will again bear well. Feminism appends an addendum to the casuist's optimism: it is the caretaker's job to discern whether a tree that bears bad fruit simply needs fertilizer and careful pruning or ought to be chopped down and replaced. Consistently poor fruit that does not inspire notice and dismay in the caretaker of the tree may well be the sign of a bad tree, but it is certainly proof of a caretaker with poor judgment. For instance, a widely accepted, internally consistent method that privileges men and their styles of moral thinking, or that either disrespects or stunts women and their moral and intellectual development, is almost certainly false. But, more to the point, its practitioners are sinful.

PROCEDURE

OPEN AND PARTICIPATORY DISCOURSE.   History makes clear that there can be vast discrepancies between method—the guidelines that direct an individual's moral reflection—and the actual practices of individual and institutional moral reasoning. For example, when an institution like the Roman Catholic

Church installs itself as guardian of a method, institutional claims—like the assertion of magisterial infallibility in morals—can run at cross-purposes to the methodological caution that abstract moral judgments become less certain as one descends to particulars. Similarly, we have seen that institutional self-authorization—including a judgment that those educated in the institution's ways are those who can be trusted to identify and apply natural law principles properly—and centuries of concentration on the confessional, penitential applications of ethics combined to undercut the methodological claim that the principles of natural law are universally accessible. As a result, judgments of knotty problems were reserved to the clergy and even to the upper echelons of the hierarchy. This division of labor—hardly unique to Roman Catholicism—usurps power, placing ordinary men and all women (to whom natural law is also in theory perspicuous) "out of the loop" of authoritative moral deliberation. [15] The failure of this majority to influence the official Roman Catholic ethical conversation is due less to incompatibility of their ideas with natural law theory—which is *methodologically* open to all new evidence about the human—than to this *procedural* exclusion from the community that makes normative moral judgments. The procedure of exclusion, backed up by an epistemology of privilege, in turn enforced by an ecclesiology of limited charism, thus incapacitates natural law's methodological openness to new information and eventually profoundly distorts both its content and its conduct. This contradiction yields the first procedural criterion: the concrete procedures of moral discourse must be genuinely open and participatory. [16]

ADVANCING WOMEN'S MORAL AGENCY. Participation in meaningful moral discourse is essential to women's welfare in a second, more direct way. Because communal moral discourse is of value *in itself,* the cloistering of an influential group harms the common good by stunting the moral development of the excluded majority. For, as Gudorf suggests, broad, self-conscious participation in public moral discourse promotes the moral maturity and autonomy of the participants. Feminist criteria for procedure insist that it matters not only who thinks and how but with whom they think and to what end. Sarah Lucia Hoagland concurs: women's exclusion from the process in which publicly binding communal norms are developed has limited their deliberation to the narrow question of whether to obey rules set by others. As a result, women are morally "de-skilled." [17] Hoagland therefore shifts the focus of ethics away from the limited project of finding "right" answers to moral problems and toward creation of a community in which, and a protocol by which, the moral life can be lived and discussed by all. Hoagland's vision of the moral life recalls natural law conceptions of virtue and conscience: [18] "The function of ethics . . . is enabling and developing individual integrity and agency within community. I have always regarded morality, ideally, as a system whose aim is, not to control individuals, but to *make possible*, to encourage and enable, individual development." [19] Inclusive, communal moral discourse is not merely a matter of standard-setting; its primary goal is building up the participants' individual and collective moral integrity, self-knowledge, and moral power. Before a community can even pose moral questions, let alone discern and arrange values to guide their solution, it must ensure that the procedure to be employed promotes rather than undermines or short-circuits moral development: producing a skilled moral reasoner is no less important than generating a good answer.

Here our discussion of method registers one caveat. Oddly, an initiative to increase women's moral agency can subtly privilege public or "male" discourse, implying that the latter is the field of "real," normative, politically significant ethics and that women are left standing around dejectedly, like the starless Sneetches in the Dr. Seuss story, without a meaningful moral language. [20] Rather, as Gilligan shows, unless they are completely isolated, women and men who are cut out of this authoritative public moral discourse still engage in significant communal moral reflection *with each other*. It is more the case, then, that the moral skills of women (and many men) are invisible to or dismissed by academic moral thinkers than that they are non-existent. Therefore we need to edit our demand for moral development a bit: if moral truth is sought in a way that thwarts or ignores anyone's individual moral development, it is, in the sense of being antimoral, immoral; it compromises everyone's well-being. Thus an ethic that aspires to public consensus must actively advance *and engage* women's moral agency, both in theory and in practice.

Solidarity. Finally, legitimate moral reflection requires solidarity with women—not just sympathy but active identification and promotion of women's good. [21] Feminist reflection is liberationist reflection. [22] As we have seen, not only is women's flourishing an objective (moral) criterion of (speculative) truth, but the practical, experimental commitment to identify and accomplish women's good—a moral preferential option for women—is an epistemological criterion for the development and application of ethical method. [23] Feminist ethics, in other words, is practical reason in the fullest sense of the term. It serves the goal of the good-for-humanity, in the specific guise of the good-for-women. This is a matter not only of attitudes and ends but of the practical wisdom that comes from committed efforts in women's behalf. [24]

Admittedly, the criterion will lead to exclusivism and elitism if this involvement is not very broadly drawn; few have the luxury of making pursuit of women's good an explicit vocational or professional focus. Letty Russell's recommendations for members of oppressing groups still fairly characterize what solidarity requires of them. According to Russell, solidarity entails trusting the oppressed to work for liberation and to declare when empowerment has been accomplished; taking supporting, not leading, roles in the process of liberation; using political and social leverage to push for liberation; and deepening their consciousness of their own histories and experiences of oppressing or suffering oppression. [25] Kay, as we have seen, adds that members of oppressed groups must adhere to similar guidelines in order to avoid reproducing oppression.

CONTENT

NORMS ROOTED IN A THICK, VAGUE ANTHROPOLOGY. My premise has been that a just, broad discussion rooted in active commitment to women's welfare will yield what is more commonly thought of as the content of ethics: norms, rules, or guidelines, and the rubrics for their application. [26] But we must be able to judge these by substantive as well as procedural criteria. First, the meaning and content of moral norms must be adequate to women's critically interpreted moral experience. I have argued that a liberal, "thin" good obsessed with the maximization of individual freedom is ultimately androcentric and antifeminist; [27] for many women who theoretically are free moral agents and so are fulfilled in the "thin" sense do not in fact have resources at hand that enable them to flourish as fully as men who have an equal degree of freedom. Substantive feminist moral norms therefore depend upon a thick, vague understanding of women's good, as Nussbaum advocates, and a clear understanding of the practical conditions for its fulfillment. This is a question not merely of abstract metaphysics but of practical inquiry into the requirements of women's flourishing in a particular time and place. Neither an abstract liberal criterion of freedom of choice nor a technical measure of the organic functioning of the body is expansive enough to do the job here. A "thick" description of women's contemporary flourishing includes not just the theoretical freedom to do as we please but the prerequisites for truly free choices: healthy bodies, healthy relationships, and a degree of economic and political security. Sexual and reproductive self-possession, as well as a social position secure enough to enable women truly to choose intercourse, childbirth, or parenting, are thus among the prerequisites for women's flourishing. Feminist ethicists are particularly adamant that no legitimate moral arguments can be based in a pretense to encounter "pure," transparent, self-interpreting bodies; as Lisa Cahill illustrates, the body cannot be abstracted from the person, and therefore "the individual body is always interpreted and ordered to reflect social relationships." [28] We must apply social critiques to all normative descriptions of the body, for, as Paul Lauritzen notes, the normative and descriptive claim "women are their bodies" means something entirely different when it comes from within a tradition that promotes women's equality and integral flourishing than it does when it is spoken from within a tradition that does the opposite. [29]

Although the anthropology that underlies these criteria is agnostic about ultimate ends, it is telic in a more restricted sense: it sets out parallel prerequisites for flourishing for men and women, implying that men and women are similarly fulfilled.

PRINCIPLES THAT SERVE ENDS. Especially in a plural, changing world, no less important to feminists than the content and development of norms is their role in moral discernment. This is not, as it was in the discussion of method above, a matter of the approach to moral reasoning within the moral life but of the status of the guides or criteria that reason develops. What sort of hold a moral guideline has is not obvious. Margaret Urban Walker argues against what she labels the "universalist/impersonalist tradition," in which "moral responsibility is envisioned as responsiveness to the impersonal truths in which morality resides." [30] That tradition, Walker argues, tends—in practice if not ultimately in theory—to place responsibilities to principles above those to persons, to hide behind general principles when faced by a particular and personal demand. [31] Walker outlines an alternative moral epistemology based in attention to particular others, narrative and contextual appreciation of the self and "the others I need to understand," and communication and dialogue as means of working out competing claims. [32] The point of such an epistemology is to move beyond the mere confrontation of actor and principle to many sorts of encounters of "direct mutual response." [33]

Does Walker then jettison principles? This would be a dangerous move, for exclusive reliance on a fresh process of communal discernment in every particular case can undermine the protections provided by basic rights and cause paralysis when quick decisions are imperative. In language somewhat reminiscent of traditional casuistical theory, Walker instead urges the adoption of criteria that ensure that responsibility to principle serves rather than obscures one's primary responsibilities to concrete persons, especially in impersonal settings. [34] So the shape of one's accountability to both persons and principles is something to be hammered out with an eye to the interests of those who will be affected, normally in conversation with them. Principles serve people.

Thus despite Nussbaum's cautions that desires can be stunted or bloated, so that they measure human needs inaccurately, we must resist the temptation always to take refuge in principles when others' desires seem off-target. The line between a sensitive, critical eye and a principled, paternalist hand is a thin one. Ann Hope tells the story of a Ugandan village that lacked clean water, adequate schools, health facilities, and many other basics. At a meeting with community organizers, village leaders reached a consensus: their greatest need was a soccer field. The incredulous organizers barely resisted their urge to veto the choice, and the field was built. Out of that act, a soccer league developed, creating a network among neighboring villages; the local community, inspired by their success at organizing soccer tournaments, united to correct the more obviously basic problems that had drawn the organizers' attention originally; and—as a completely unexpected side effect—underage drinking decreased. The door to integral flourishing, in this case, opened only after an apparently frivolous initiative unleashed creativity, autonomy, and legitimate pride in the community. [35]

Thus a simple criterion—the full being and welfare of women—generates substantive guidelines for ethics. First, the ethical enterprise must adhere to women's critically evaluated experiences of the structures of moral reasoning: "public" and "private" issues should be resolved according to the same criteria; openings must be left for previously—and currently—unrecognized structures of moral reasoning; and ethical method must not be derived from its companion philosophy or theology but be connected to it through a moral hermeneutic. No intellectual system that fails these tests—that does not seek women's good—can be valid. Second, the procedure by which the community applies the method must be just and consistent: the structure of the moral conversation coheres with the method of moral reasoning; legitimate moral discourse arises as part of the larger pursuit of the good-for-humanity, here expressed as active solidarity with women; and it advances women's moral agency, both in theory and in practice. Third, the content and use of norms draws from feminist anthropology and bears up under feminist claims: specifically, advancement of women's good requires a thick, telic description of the person's good; and principles are derived corporately and applied flexibly and cooperatively, by "actor" and "patient," with the good of concrete persons in mind.

These criteria coalesce in a practical and inductive ethic with substantial critical leverage against the natural law tradition, both early and developed. The crux of the feminist critique is that neglected viewpoints and methods cannot simply be grafted into the existing plant. In order to be taken seriously, they must be seen not as exceptions to the human norm but as counting among the criteria of that norm. And because natural law's content and method also depend on an anthropology built inductively upon practical experiences of oppression and flourishing, it is susceptible to the whole of this critique. Some might counter that basic inclinations, not practical experience, generate descriptions of genuine human goods, but this does not alter the claim: inclinations are never abstract; they are of very different kinds (some capable of being overridden by reason or will, others not); and they are also subject to bias or distortion. Whether natural law reasoning develops from concrete experience or an analysis of inclinations, then, the feminist critique of natural law is truly an inside critique.

BASES FOR CONVERSATION WITH NATURAL LAW

Some connections between feminist and natural law ethics—especially contemporary natural law—can be traced to the fact that they evolved within the same Western intellectual atmosphere. Both feminist and contemporary natural law ethics embrace the turn to the subject, personalist criteria for moral norms, a creed of individual dignity, a commitment to improving concrete, practical human welfare through systematic change, a strategy for dealing with pluralism, and a mechanism for adapting and transforming principles. The claim that method, norms, and procedures of moral reasoning have some connection to anthropology is so obvious as to be banal. Yet we can point to subtleties within these more self-evident links, as well as to other more specific connections, that support a case for a closer alliance.

LEGITIMATE SELF-INTEREST. The most significant connection between feminist and traditional natural law arguments in ethics would be easy to overlook were it not absent or awkwardly handled in Protestant ethics: the legitimacy of protecting one's own genuine good even before seeking the good for others. Thomistic telic anthropology entails this claim theologically, for only I can pray, participate in the sacraments, cooperate with grace, and do all the other things that keep me on the path to beatitude. But it is true of both natural law and feminist ethics in the more immediate sense: my good is worth pursuing, and I am not required to sacrifice it for lesser or similar benefits to others. If I do sacrifice my own good in such a case, this is an act of heroism rather than an obligation. The self-regard that resides at the core of natural law and feminist anthropologies is absent from traditional Protestant theologies and from the liberal "angel in the house" rendition of women. [36]

ANTHROPOLOGY. Prudence advises dealing with the obvious anthropological disagreements before the common affirmations. As we saw in chapter 1, social constructionist feminism is not only antiteleological but antianthropological, in the sense that it sees anthropology itself as a cultural artifact rather than as a reflection of inexorably given structures. At most, social constructionists can agree that the person is a social, creative, self-interpreting being. This is not, I have argued, a description on which we can build an ethic. Yet these three factors are indispensable elements of an adequate anthropology, just as social constructionism's relentless critiques are indispensable to the development and maintenance of a responsible constructive ethic.

Thus a critical, constructive, political feminist ethic of the sort that I have outlined generates, like natural law, a rich, holistic anthropology and insists that the method and the matter of moral thought must be consonant with it. A feminism of this kind thus argues with natural law anthropology over its content—e.g., over claims that men are inherently more capable of rational reflection than women—rather than over the importance of anthropology to ethics generally. Their agreement here is hardly trivial. Yet it does not exhaust their common claims. As in the early natural law tradition, the contemporary feminist judgment about women's flourishing is a practical, commonsense judgment, based in experience of the conditions and contours of flourishing. And as in natural law, feminist accounts of women's flourishing embrace not only individual physical health, but also intellectual, psychological, and spiritual flourishing in interdependent community. [37] In practice, the feminist moral critique ultimately depends also upon the perspicuity of common *human* criteria of flourishing. Most feminists argue that whatever dominant, woman-oppressing system they wish to replace is, although ostensibly designed with men's interests in mind, ultimately antithetical to men's integral flourishing as well, and that a feminist ethic would better promote men's integral welfare. [38] Finally, although wariness of oppressive essentialism steers some feminists toward exclusive concentration on self-creativity, the feminist anthropological conversation as a whole balances the fixities, dynamisms, and ends of human existence. [39] Human physical givenness sets conditions for human flourishing, but it does not dictate moral restrictions on ends or roles any more than social status at birth morally dictates one's adult role in society. [40] The goals of feminist ethics and revisionist natural law theology coincide: to express adequately the tension between the limitations of being-as-given and the transformative possibilities of the transcending visions that paradoxically are grounded in that finitude.

Precisely these anthropological affinities position the broader feminist moral conversation to make an inside critique of natural law ethics. [41] If by definition natural law ethics must be faithful to the structure of human being and moral reasoning, then it must account for any apparently perduring conditions and features of human life. But "women's ways" of seeing, knowing, thinking, acting, and flourishing are *human* ways, and on that basis natural law anthropology is answerable, according to its own criteria, to feminist visions of human being. [42] It has fallen short in this respect. Rooted in Stoicism and refashioned in the Middle Ages, natural law anthropology has consistently been the product of male intellectual elites; it has reflected their experiences, their ways of knowing, and their projections of women's experience. Women's (and other men's) understandings of human being, insofar as they differ, are absent or undervalued.

To the extent that medieval anthropology remains normative, natural law ethics is impoverished and inadequate to its own standards. A perduring problem is the conflict between Thomas's habit of seeing gender difference— like all other differences—hierarchically and his insistence "that the sexes are equal with respect to their fundamental humanity." [43] Thomas could sustain this conflict only by assuming that male experience (more accurately, his own experience as a clerical academic trained in Aristotelian thought) was normative human experience and thus was a reliable resource for his anthropology. A good contemporary example of this gap between supposedly gender-neutral definitions of normative humanity and women's experience is the tradition's continuing nearly exclusive preoccupation with genital sexuality. As Niles Newton pointed out, women she studied tended to experience their sexuality as encompassing pregnancy, childbirth, nursing, and menstruation as well as genital pleasure; interpreted against this larger background, genital pleasure may not exhaust sexual pleasure for women in the way that it defines sexual pleasure for men. As Mary Pellauer has pointed out, even women's genital pleasure bears careful analysis; unlike ejaculation, it is not and has never been a procreative good, and so describing exactly what sort of good it is is an important ethical exercise. [44] Feminist analyses of sexuality demonstrate that natural law's continuing focus on the ethics of genital pleasure and intercourse not only inflates their importance but fails to provide any sort of moral context for the larger proportion of women's sexual experience. [45]

Can this gap be closed by an "add women and stir" strategy, in which (like the other experts whom Vatican Council II documents urge the church of *aggiornamento* to consult) women simply supply data—in this case, data about themselves? Such a strategy assumes that new data affect the conclusions and applications of traditional moral reason without threatening the structure of that reasoning process, just as substitution of new values for the variables in a formula can alter its result without calling the formula itself in question. [46]

But just as further experiments in physics eventually demonstrated the old Newtonian mechanics to have been simply a crude, narrowly applicable instance of Einsteinian relativity, so feminist expansion of medieval natural law anthropology reveals the latter to have been only one—inadequate—take on humanity. For in natural law, ethical method is tailored to fit the human being not only as object—with ends that must be protected or fulfilled—but also as subject—with certain experiences and patterns of moral thinking. When the description of reasoners changes, so does the description of reasoning. [47] Thus Vatican Council II's invitation to experts to contribute additional grist for the existing mill—"still more information about the human"—opened the door to unanticipated radical change in method.

Yet feminism's anthropologically grounded moral hermeneutic challenges natural law method on an even deeper level. As we have seen, the inherited natural law tradition's methodological distinction between speculative and practical reflection—undergirded by an anthropological distinction between intellect and will [48]—was not a strict theoretical separation; knowledge of the truth was dependent upon the virtue of justice. But in practice it yielded a division of intellectual labor that excluded theology from any direct role in the process of practical moral reason; even more important, the findings of practical moral reason did not and might not influence purely theological reflection on divinely revealed truth. In its most exaggerated neoscholastic presentation, the natural law tradition embraced an intellectual concept of faith: deep assent to revealed truth. [49] This assent, in harmony with the demands of human reason, entailed as well a commitment to the pursuit of the good, a good that was assumed to have been captured and held permanently motionless in revelation. In this view, ethics was an unfolding of moral truth, each new conclusion permanently valid. Because the content of the human telos required no critical reexamination, practical moral reason could in theory accomplish this unfolding without much further attention to the content of revelation and without any effect on speculative theology. In fact, as the following chapters will show, one of contemporary natural law ethics' greatest challenges is reuniting faith and moral reason credibly.

In contrast, the dialectical, self-critical character of feminist moral reflection requires that feminist theory and practice inform each other so thoroughly that they cannot be considered separately; theology and ethics are distinguishable but indivisible. In addition, especially because much of the content of revelation is troubling to them, feminist theologians reverse the terms set out in natural law's description of faith. Faith is a moral stance as well as an intellectual assent; an intellectually honest faith cannot survive outside an activism inspired by a self-conscious moral commitment to women's flourishing. [50] Thus commitment to women's flourishing is the condition not only for ethics but also for theological reflection upon revelation. That is to say, the shape of the human telos may be generally known, but its details are under constant critical review by practical experience. This is not to imply that feminist theologians either discount or fail to find scriptural and traditional support for this telos and their commitment to it; in fact they have found much. It is simply to say that faith in a God who loves women, accomplishes their salvation, and intends a fulfilling life for them must be skeptical of doctrines, creeds, and written records of revelation that, susceptible to human foibles, contradict this faith. [51]

Feminist anthropology's stress upon the interdependence of the elements of the dimensions of human being and thought makes feminists wary of hierarchizing these elements so strictly as natural law theory sometimes has: for instance, as we have seen, for many feminists the indispensability of emotion to responsible moral reasoning forbids either ranking reason over emotion or juxtaposing the two. Here feminists forge a connection with both Thomas's and Vatican Council II's anthropological holism, but they also point out the Council's radical implications.

Finally, feminists also show that the historicism and pluralism that underlie Vatican Council II's more novel teachings have much broader and more radical consequences for ethics than the Council or most of its interpreters seem to recognize. For instance, not only is the Council's accommodation of cultural pluralism limited, but it misses the possibility of pluralism *within* cultures, the most universal—and universally overlooked—example of which is gender pluralism. [52] Laying the groundwork for a pluralism that reduces neither to a new, more integrative universal moral theory nor to an absolutely atomized relativism is difficult. [53] Here, as we have seen, negotiations among the feminist schools can yield solid and fruitful results if they deal openly with deep philosophical differences within feminism. [54]

EMBODIMENT.   Natural law's and feminism's common concern with anthropology is substantive as well as formal. One of the most important areas of substantive agreement is their emphasis upon embodiment. First, moral thought is embodied thought. As chapter 2 shows clearly, Thomas builds his epistemology on sense knowledge. In this life the body and the soul are an indivisible unit, and all events of the sort that create memory, sustain prudence, and relay knowledge of context are experienced through the bodily senses— so much so that defects in the senses can cause errors in judgment. Likewise, as the example of women's sexual experience above shows, feminist ethics relies systematically upon reflection upon embodied experience in both its critical and its constructive work; frequently women's experiences of physical maternity—and of bodily suffering, health, pleasure, and pain, generally— are the first truth tests to which feminists subject any ethical theory or concrete judgment.

Second, emphasis on embodied, social flourishing is at the center of both the feminist and the Thomistic natural law traditions. Chapters 1 through 3 have returned again and again to the claim that temporal flourishing is a good that we are to pursue for ourselves (although self-critically) and for our communities. Jean Porter, for example, has pointed out that in Thomas justice begins with bodily goods: the most basic inclinations for physical, temporal survival generate the strongest obligations of nonmaleficence. [55] Similarly, the heavy concentration in feminist ethics on issues of women's health care, reproduction, violence, and images of the female body generally reveals its preoccupation with embodied flourishing and especially with the connection between flourishing and public respect for women's embodiment.

VIRTUE. The second bridge between the feminist and natural law traditions is the concept of individual moral integrity: virtue. For feminists as for the natural law tradition, virtue is a habit of right discernment and action, not merely the ability to make isolated "good decisions." Contemporary feminist theologians and popular authors alike point out that women have been dishonest moral thinkers, frequently shirking responsibility for their own moral decisions, describing themselves as victims rather than actors, or at least permitting others to define the issues at stake. [56] As Hoagland argues, the discipline of ethics itself must aid them in becoming virtuous, autonomous-yet-interdependent moral reasoners. The point of moral thought is not simply to reach a "correct" conclusion but to strengthen one's ability to carry out honest and thorough moral discernment in dialogue with others and to act upon it. A habit of prudent and courageous reasoning is detectable here, as are—if in a new key—connections among prudence, a habit of well-ordered behavior, and good results.

A second question that feminists ask but to which natural law thinkers since Thomas have rarely felt the need to respond is the query, "Who defines virtue?" Judith Webb Kay and Diana Fritz Cates both insist that habits publicly held to be virtues, promoting the integral good of the actor and others, are often in fact vices, stunting and restricting the moral actor for the benefit of more powerful people. Examples are the ideals of passivity in women, or of uncomplaining diligence among blue-collar workers. Only if the oppressed undertake a practical, critical investigation of these ends, fueled by a degree of self-love great enough to inspire resistance to these false virtues, can they hope to overthrow this sort of oppression. [57] At even greater risk and urgency, we must admit that in an unjust world virtue is not always defined by the ideal of comprehensive flourishing; for instance, womanists insist that habits that allow oppressed women to survive with some degree of self-respect are virtuous for them but vicious when exercised by people with nearly unlimited social power. [58] On this interpretation true virtue may not always resemble the stereotypical examples of the acts of the classical virtues; how honesty, for example, should bear fruit in action depends upon the context. Thomas's understanding of virtue leaves many theoretical but few procedural openings for these adjustments.

REASON. Although they share liberationists' reluctance to divide practical from speculative reason, feminist thinkers support the traditional natural law position that moral reason is practical in two senses: it seeks knowledge about goods-for-humanity, their concrete shapes, and means of pursuing them, and it relies not just upon an innate or a priori sense of the moral but upon experimental familiarity with human beings and the conditions of their flourishing. [59] Feminists concur that conclusions of practical reason vary with circumstance; they also echo evidence from the history of casuistry that historicism and pluralism require fluidity of both norms and their applications. And, having resurrected human experience as an indispensable source of moral knowledge, feminist moral thinkers have begun the task of specifying what sorts of experience are morally significant in which ways. [60] For instance, feminism's emphasis upon the affective dimensions of moral experience is an important bridge to natural law theology's understanding of practical moral reason as a tool for pursuit of the good, not in the abstract, but as an object of love. [61] The feminist complaint that Roman Catholic natural law moral reasoning ignores emotions and affections does aptly fit an Enlightenment interpretation of natural law, which sees reason as dispassionate, neutral, objective, and disembodied. But Thomas understood reason to function (for better or worse) under the influence of the passions, which incorporate affections and emotions. [62] Thus a *Thomistic* version of natural law is, if not adequate to contemporary feminist concerns about attachment, at least resonant with them.

In addition, the feminist ethics insists that moral guidelines evolve from engagement with practical experience. As Hall shows, in Thomas's opinion knowledge of the natural law develops gradually and often imperfectly; depends on astute observation of the correspondence between certain sorts of behavior and the advance or erosion of the integral good toward which we naturally tend; and refines its general principles only through constant, prudent wrestling with the concrete details of daily life. [63] It may also revive casuistry by expanding or shifting the available set of principles and analogous cases, as in Patricia Beattie Jung's experimental analogy between pregnancy and organ donation. [64] In other words, a natural law method faithful to its Thomistic roots contains means of avoiding the sort of deductivisim that feminist moral thinkers rue.

COMMON GOOD. Both the natural law and feminist traditions not only value and work toward the perfection of the social order but do so under the rubric of the common good. As we have seen, even separatist feminism is implicitly or potentially committed to the betterment of society at large. In addition, feminist thinkers consistently draw connections between individual integrity and participation in social structures. The oft-quoted feminist assertion that the personal is political is not hyperbole. It is a recognition that common welfare—with the institutions, philosophies, and economies that support it—and individual welfare are mutually dependent. [65] Natural law's traditional insistence that charity informs and infuses all moral acts—that grace brings about a heightened mode of being that automatically rather than under coercion acts for others' and society's good—connects individual moral and spiritual development with the good of society in a way that parallels feminist thinking on the same issues. The feminist insistence on the political character of the personal may be seen, therefore, as an extrapolation of the theory of the common good; for when the definition of the common good expands to include more dimensions of human life, so must the list of human activities that affect it.

ETHICAL REFLECTION AS A COMMUNAL ENDEAVOR. Feminists and natural law thinkers concur that moral reflection is inevitably shaped by our social connections, even when we try to carry it out in isolation; and both, rather than regarding this as a compromise of pure reflection, exploit it methodologically. On the natural law side, the scholastic theory of probabiliorism recognizes that a change in norms proposed by a number of responsible, independent thinkers is more likely to be reliable than a competing proposal supported by a single source. [66] Thus communal reflection sometimes reveals the subtle influence of inappropriate self-interest on an individual's moral reasoning. Finally, the natural law tradition has a healthy, if not always self-critical, respect for the role of custom in moral reasoning. [67] This is not to say that natural law thinkers have recognized the degree to which sin may—for an extended period or in a given segment of society—bias discourse, even when many voices are involved in the moral discussion. Certainly the circle of mutually critical conversation has often been ridiculously intimate.

Feminists concur that human interrelatedness, human moral development, and the need for a critical theory of experience combine to make moral reasoning an ideally communal, participatory project. Abandonment of the neoscholastic model of virtue-as-obedience-to-established-norms for the feminist model of virtue-as-capacity-to-reason-and-act-morally would correct natural law's false sense of comprehensiveness by shifting moral authority out of the academy and into the wider community, a larger public in which biases based on class, race, or gender would be less likely to survive. In fact only if natural law adopts such procedures can it remain true to the democratic, egalitarian implications of its anthropology and method. Such a move will never protect any ethic from de facto group bias because it does not guarantee that anyone exercises appropriate self-criticism; but it does guarantee that any dissenting, critical arguments will be widely known and therefore accessible to any responsible reasoner who wishes to make use of them. [68]

FEMINISM AS INTERNAL CRITIQUE

These shared commitments and assumptions outfit the Thomistic natural law tradition and the feminist tradition to mount mutual, incisive internal critiques. From one perspective, as Lisa Cahill has argued, Roman Catholicism's "characteristic confidence in moral objectivity and universal values *opens onto* the sort of inductive and communal model of reasoned moral insight needed to reestablish public discourse after the postmodern critique"—and thus also to save feminism from morally debilitating relativism. [69] Likewise, as Jean Porter argues, Thomas may be no "proto-feminist," yet liberative, feminist arguments that may go beyond and even contradict some of Thomas's concrete conclusions nonetheless fall within the space carved out by his most basic theological claims. [70]

Among natural law's most important reminders to feminist ethics is that a "thick, vague" description of goods *is* vague: it accommodates and even anticipates a telic anthropology but—in Nussbaum's case, intentionally—provides no telos. This is as it should be. Feminism as I have presented it is a coherent set of critical and constructive tools, not a comprehensive moral theory; and a feminist politics in a society governed by Enlightenment liberal assumptions must leave room for a variety of ways of organizing goods and ends. But if concrete, everyday moral reason is practical reason it must be able to organize its ends; therefore it needs to adopt a thick telic anthropology and with it guidelines for organizing and choosing among goods. One credible telos is a version of natural law's final end, union with God. In its Thomistic version, this union seems to some people ethereal, but in fact its combination of moral and intellectual virtues—with all of its implications for social justice and critical vision—and its coherence with a life of genuine physical flourishing hold great promise for a Christian feminist ethic.

We can see the constructive potential for the natural law tradition of an overhaul by feminism. I have argued that two claims are especially potent. First, exercises in feminist anthropology lead to richer, more self-critical descriptions of human flourishing and moral reasoning, taking the moral practices and embodied experiences of both men and women into account but attending first to the accounts of those whose views have been sidelined. In any concrete situation, the content, procedure, and method of ethics must aim toward protecting, nurturing, and revisiting the working definition of integral flourishing. The universal moral truth is that what stunts or devalues any dimension of that full human being is wrong, and what promotes it is right. What it means to specify this norm—to protect and nurture concrete human beings in particular situations—depends upon infinitely many particulars, among which gender always figures.

Second, feminist writers argue forcefully that honest integration of gender differences into ethics calls not only for consideration of new facts in the process of moral reasoning but also and more radically for changes in the way moral reasoning is understood to function for individuals, for communities, and in ethical method itself. If who we are determines how we should reason morally, methods of ethical reflection must now be redesigned to reflect feminist anthropology's more holistic image of us. The feminists discussed above therefore argue variously for moral reflection that is thoroughly communal (in procedure), webbed (in structure and logic), affective, concrete, and embodied. [71] Feminists especially see moral reasoning as a matter of communal and interpersonal honesty, receptivity, and charity, leading them to the demand—underlined by Hoagland—for a social ethic of moral discourse. Improving the quality of human relationships strengthens individual moral integrity, but it also protects moral reflection; for a concern for rigorous reasoning entails and must not eclipse insistence upon open and fair discussion.

In sum, then, feminist thought draws upon and reinforces the historicity, holism, and pluralism that Vatican Council II documents accept as features of contemporary life. It also depends upon "thick" and telic descriptions of women's good of the sort upon which natural law method and norms also rely. But feminism challenges theology and ethics to accept the more radical implications of pluralism and thick description. First, pluralism demands deep-rooted change in both methods and norms. In addition, moral reflection and discourse are themselves social and moral acts: the way in which moral discourse is structured and institutionalized is a matter of social ethics, for an exclusive or uncaring conversation not only produces questionable results but excludes, disrespects, and possibly stunts some moral subjects. Therefore genuine individual integrity, true social justice, and legitimate structures of practical moral reason are interdependent; none can exist in the absence of the others.

Thus if "reason reflecting on human nature" is to return to the center of moral reflection, we must understand both reason and human nature differently than have philosophers and theologians during most of the past six centuries. Over the past decade, feminist theological ethicists have articulated just such a replacement. Rebecca Chopp's pragmatic social naturalism proposes that we draw on experience to lay out "working models of the natural in human flourishing." "Nature" still founds norms, but it is susceptible to revision. [72] Following Nussbaum, Lisa Sowle Cahill—drawing more self-consciously than Chopp on the natural law tradition—points out that Chopp's apparent "constants" of human existence need not be arrayed in permanent and strictly observed hierarchies: "Ethicists, Christian and humanistic, may need to acknowledge ambiguity and a certain 'incoherence' to human life as embodied. Tension among the constitutive components of our nature gives morality and culture the character of a *project of integration*, rather than of a *call to authenticity* to our 'real' or 'true' nature." [73] There is no single ideal of flourishing, no final and authoritative set of moral principles, no unique path to moral wisdom. The task is rather to discern, in each place and age, which ways of life, guidelines, and ways of moral discernment seem best to respect and promote the integral good of particular people. Cynthia Crysdale adds that we are composed both of "schemes of recurrence beyond the reach of human agency" ("physical, chemical, organic, and psychic processes" understood through both classical causality and statistical probability) and of "intelligent consciousness," with its ability to interpret these schemes and, within limits, to create and transform. [74] Crysdale concludes,

> A revised natural law is both possible and imperative. It will recognize the conditioned nature of all of existence, and in particular the statistical laws that contribute to world process. It must further locate itself in an analysis of history that is critical and normative, but that grounds its critical stance in the norms constitutive of human intelligence. It will attend to chemical, biological, and zoological schemes of recurrence as conditioning factors in human existence, both within the human subject

and between that subject and her environment, without seeking to derive moral norms directly from these natural processes. It will take as an important task, not defining ways in which persons should conform to nature, but clarifying the values implicit in interventions in nature, and stipulating which transformations are ultimately conducive to human flourishing and which are not. [75]

Even Chopp and Crysdale use the Enlightenment language of nature as "the chaos out there" or "the biological system down here"; yet successful articulations of the nature/reason distinction, as both natural law and feminist ethics tell us, must insist that "nature" is not simply matter that occupies a space outside or below our true, spiritual, "rational" selves, for "reason" and "nature" are not mutually exclusive quantities. Human reason is neither subject to nature, merely adhering to unchanging organic processes; nor opposed to nature, seeking release from it; nor queen over nature, molding it to her arbitrary will. Rather reason is part of nature, the source of nature's dynamism and the tester of its plasticity. It pursues the human good within a range of possibilities for integral flourishing defined by our intellect, psychology, embodiment, sociality, place in the ecosystem and—for theologians—the relationship of all of this to the divine. [76]

APPLYING THE CRITERIA

The distinction between moral theology and feminist ethics that was so clear even a decade ago has softened to the point at which it is almost unthinkable that a comprehensive treatment of natural law ethics written today would exclude Cahill, Crysdale, Gudorf, Porter, Farley, and other feminists who are both appreciative and critical of the tradition. Still, it is the work of contemporary male Roman Catholic moral theologians that has had the most profound effect—paradoxically evident in recent pointed papal warnings [77]—within the Roman Catholic Church and, especially through treatments of political and medical ethics, on Western society at large. The coming chapters explore the work of three such influential, representative thinkers to learn to what degree their approaches to ethics succeed in fulfilling the criteria that natural law foundations, natural law history, and feminism have set out. They will entail a return to intramural moral theological debates, but with the purpose of evaluating the authors' success at meeting the criteria of a genuinely feminist rendition of natural law ethics.

My choice of authors corresponds to the criteria set up in the chapters on natural law. The authors discussed in chapters 4 and 5, Josef Fuchs and

Richard McCormick, both fall into the group of American and Continental natural law revisionists known as proportionalists and are often mentioned in the same breath by both adherents and critics of the latter group. [78] Why two such closely allied thinkers should be treated separately, rather than together in juxtaposition to one or a group of their critics, deserves explanation. Josef Fuchs is to Richard McCormick as theologian is to ethicist. Fuchs is concerned above all with a person's basic orientation toward God, or personal moral goodness, and with the formal rightness of actions in the abstract—for instance, whether or not in theory one might be right to tell an untruth and what it might mean for a lie to entail turning against or remaining open to the Absolute. McCormick is preoccupied with questions of orderly action in the world, or material moral rightness in the concrete—for instance, whether a desire to protect one's spouse and lover from embarrassment is a legitimate excuse for publicly denying an extramarital affair. To the extent that these categories impinge upon each other—and the ways in which they do are discussed below—so do the writings of Fuchs and McCormick.

The third author, Gustavo Gutiérrez, presses rightness as the prophetic criterion of goodness. He argues that the justice with which concrete human goods are pursued and distributed within society is, in large scale, an indicator of the general degree of personal moral goodness of the controllers of that society. Thus although Gutiérrez is not a natural lawyer or even a social ethicist per se, he insists that social systems are the fields upon which the good-right relationship is laid bare and in which prophetic discourse can press for the coincidence of good and right. In describing that right, he implicitly falls back on natural law's link between anthropology and moral norms, revealing Catholic liberation theology's deep reliance on natural law anthropology.

The question, in all cases, is whether the adaptation is adequate: do these influential moral thinkers in fact serve as good models for a critically reconstructed natural law ethic?

NOTES

1. This interdependence is not peculiar to feminist thought but ought to characterize any consistent approach to ethics. Susan Secker has aptly demonstrated these connections in contemporary American Catholic moral thought. See Susan Secker, "The Crisis within Official Catholic Sexual and Biomedical Ethics and American Revisionist Moral Theology: The Relationship between Selected Methodological and Ecclesiological Aspects" (Ph.D. diss., University of Chicago, 1989), 40–42, 89–90. See also Virginia L. Warren, "Feminist Directions in Medical Ethics," *Hypatia* 4 (Summer

1989): 85. Warren argues that legitimate feminist *theory* must be constructed from women's experiences—i.e., it must employ a "bottom up," not a "top down," *procedure*.

2. It also assumes, obviously, that the life destroyed in abortion is not the life of a being who has an equal claim to this pursuit.

3. On the relationships among sex, sexuality, and power, see Beverly Wildung Harrison, "Human Sexuality and Mutuality: A Fresh Paradigm," *Journal of Presbyterian History* 61 (Spring 1983): 154–57.

4. That some feminist groups—most prominently, the National Organization of Women—interpreted the Clinton-Paula Jones case on liberal lines (their relationship had no ill effects on Jones's employment or career and so therefore was "private" and beyond the reach of the law) simply demonstrates the degree to which political expedience can affect the choice of critical perspective.

5. Gudorf, "Seamless Garment," 271–86.

6. See Jean Bethke Elshtain, *Public Man, Private Woman*, 318–37; and Stephen J. Pope, "Christian Love for the Poor: Almsgiving and the 'Preferential Option,'" *Horizons* 21 (1994): 288–312.

7. Sandra Harding, "The Curious Coincidence of Feminine and African Moralities: Challenges for Feminist Theory," in *Women and Moral Theory*, ed. Eva Feder Kittay and Diana T. Meyers (n.p.: Rowman and Littlefield Publishers, 1987), 296–315. See also Tronto, *Moral Boundaries*, 77–85.

8. Gilligan, *In a Different Voice*, 63. Gilligan slides back and forth rather easily between describing care as an independent ethic and describing it as a moral orientation. The two are not synonymous. The former implies a comprehensive structure of moral reasoning guided by moral principles and the latter, an outlook or perspective that may not be capable of grounding such a comprehensive structure.

9. Ibid., 44, 101; Carol Gilligan, "Moral Orientation and Moral Development," in *Women and Moral Theory*, 22.

10. Gilligan, *In a Different Voice*, 19, 62.

11. Gilligan, *In a Different Voice*, 164–65; Gilligan, "Moral Orientation," 31–32. In the latter pages Gilligan proposes that, despite this interdependence and complementarity, *at this point in history* the ethic of care should perhaps be ascendant. Care logic's influence already extends beyond the bounds of "personal" ethics; Joan Tronto has shown how it might affect public policy (see Tronto, *Moral Boundaries*).

12. The work of Sarah Ruddick and Nel Noddings, which binds a logic of care to maternal experience, has come under similar fire. For a critical discussion of Gilligan, Noddings, Ruddick, and their detractors' arguments, see Rosemarie Tong, *Feminine and Feminist Ethics* (Belmont, CA: Wadsworth, 1993), chapters 5–7. See also Susan Sherwin, *No Longer Patient: Feminist Ethics and Health Care* (Philadelphia: Temple University Press, 1992). It is, however, worth asking whether women who are paralyzed over the decision whether to have an abortion—as Gilligan's subjects were—are exercising a de facto, revolutionary moral theory or are experiencing the breakdown of their own resources for moral reasoning. As was argued in chapter 1, we rarely examine or replace our moral assumptions except when they fail us. Pathology is of limited value when one is out to describe healthy function.

13. Several relationships are possible: for instance, a "new" ethic may supersede, complement, supplement, or reinterpret the "old" one. However, simple complementarity—assignment of the ethic of care to "private" life and the ethic of justice to

"public" affairs—can violate the criterion that forbids development of different systems of moral reasoning for different spheres of life. Hence feminists should be wary of complementarity. Joan Tronto points out that Gilligan's and Kohlberg's analysis of reports of moral reason is still not analysis of moral reason in practice; see Tronto, *Moral Boundaries*, chapter 3.

14. Ruether, *Sexism and God-Talk*, 19.

15. Gudorf is concerned particularly about the misogynist implications of (male) Church theologians and (male) public officials effectively removing women's freedom to make significant moral decisions. See Gudorf, "Seamless Garment." It could be argued that ethics in general is so specialized that in most instances highly technical problems should be turned over to moral thinkers who are expert in narrow areas, as only they know, for example, exactly how chlorine affects wildlife. Individuals cannot all read stacks of environmental impact reports before deciding which cleanser to buy! See Richard A. McCormick, *Moral Theology in the Year 2000: Reverie or Reality?*, The Nash Lecture (Regina: Campion College, University of Regina, 1988), 16. The general public is not "disempowered" unless the experts dictate, and/or the public believes, that moral goodness and rightness depend on its following their recommendations *merely on the basis of their expertise*. In most cases *the public* does the *final* weighing, even when *experts* set up the issues.

16. See Benhabib, "Autonomy, Modernity, and Community," 51, 54–55.

17. See Hoagland, *Lesbian Ethics*, 33–34.

18. See Hoagland, *Lesbian Ethics*, chapter 1 and Finnis, *Natural Law*, 126.

19. Hoagland, *Lesbian Ethics*, 285.

20. Dr. Seuss [Theodore Seuss Geisel], "The Sneetches," in *The Sneetches and Other Stories* (Random House, 1953), 2–25. The starless Sneetches in the tale, excluded from all "starred Sneetch" events, ruminate on their exclusion but do not form a "community of resistance."

21. Letty Russell observes that cooperation upon a common project is frequently the most effective means to build unity among members of oppressing and oppressed groups. See Letty M. Russell, *Human Liberation in a Feminist Perspective: A Theology* (Philadelphia: Westminster Press, 1974), 165–66.

22. See Rosemary Radford Ruether, *Liberation Theology: Human Hope Confronts Christian History and American Power* (New York: Paulist Press, 1972).

23. Hence Daniel Maguire's observation that one cannot properly *learn about* feminism without first being *converted to* it; feminist commitment is the prerequisite for feminist knowledge, for the latter requires a certain point of view. See Daniel C. Maguire, "The Feminist Turn in Ethics," *Horizons* 10 (1983): 341–42.

24. Russell, *Human Liberation*, 32, 169–70.

25. Ibid.

26. For example, Parsons puts them to work on a new, hermeneutical understanding of universals, a novel humanism, and a fresh understanding of redemptive community (Parsons, *Feminism*, 180–242).

27. Parsons, "Intersection," 252–57; and Kay, "Human Nature," 101–16.

28. Lisa Sowle Cahill, "'Embodiment' and Moral Critique: A Christian Social Perspective," in *Embodiment, Morality, and Medicine*, ed. Lisa Sowle Cahill and Margaret A. Farley (Boston: Kluwer Academic Publishers, 1995), 206. For a particularly instructive illustration of this critique at work, see Emily Martin, *The Woman in the Body: A Cultural Analysis of Reproduction* (Boston: Beacon Press, 1987).

29. Paul Lauritzen, "Whose Bodies? Which Selves? Appeals to Embodiment in Assessments of Reproductive Technology," in *Embodiment, Morality, and Medicine*, 121.

30. Margaret Urban Walker, "Moral Understandings: Alternative 'Epistemology' for a Feminist Ethics," *Hypatia* 4 (Summer 1989): 20. Although Immanuel Kant seems the most obvious exemplar of this approach, Walker takes for her model Henry Sidgwick, *The Methods of Ethics* (1907; reprint, Indianapolis, IN: Hackett Publishing, 1981), 199, 214, 228, 262, 425. To a degree Walker attacks a straw argument. Ultimately few moral systems recommend service to the impersonal truth for truth's sake or obedience for obedience's sake.

31. Walker, "Moral Understandings," 21. See also Hoagland, *Lesbian Ethics*, 9–13.

32. Walker, "Moral Understandings," 17–19.

33. Ibid., 24.

34. Ibid.

35. Ann Hope and Sally Timmel, *Training for Transformation: A Handbook for Community Workers*, Book 1 (Gweru: Mambo Press, 1984), 71.

36. Valerie Saiving, "The Human Situation: A Feminine View," *Journal of Religion* 40 (1960): 100–12.

37. On contemporary western European moral theologians' ideals of self-realization in relationship, see James F. Keenan, S.J. and Thomas R. Kopfensteiner, "Moral Theology Out of Western Europe," *Theological Studies* 59 (March 1998): 107–35.

38. Harrison argues that "advocacy for women is also finally advocacy for everyone's full humanity" (*Making the Connections*, 233). See also a popular author, Anne Wilson Schaef, *When Society Becomes an Addict* (San Francisco: Harper and Row, 1987). Even separatist feminists base their exile from the dominant social order on the premise that it is absolutely corrupt and therefore is to no one's ultimate benefit. For instance, Hoagland's explicit concern is building lesbian moral agency in voluntary community; the dominant moral culture's effects on the moral development of both *unsympathetic women and men* is irrelevant. But despite her reluctance to use the term, what is at stake for her is *human* moral agency: "lesbian," which she intentionally leaves undefined, stands in for transformed human being, freed from heterosexualist male and female identities (Hoagland, *Lesbian Ethics*, 7–15).

39. See Parsons, "Intersection," 265. See also Kay, "Human Nature," 252.

40. Parsons, "Intersection," 265. Judith Butler misses this distinction; see Butler, *Bodies that Matter*, 32.

41. Parsons, "Intersection," 263.

42. Jean Porter argues that for Thomas "the most basic morally relevant difference between the sexes is a difference of situation" (Porter, "Limits," 322).

43. Porter, "Limits," 327; see also Børreson, *Subordination and Equivalence*.

44. Mary D. Pellauer, "The Moral Significance of Female Orgasm: Toward Sexual Ethics That Celebrates Women's Sexuality," *Journal of Feminist Studies in Religion* 9 (Spring–Fall, 1993): 161–82.

45. Niles Newton, *Maternal Emotions* (New York: Hoeber, 1955); and Niles Newton, "Interrelationships between Sexual Responsiveness, Birth, and Breast Feeding," in *Contemporary Sexual Behavior: Critical Issues in the 1970s*, ed. Joseph Zubin and John Money (Baltimore: Johns Hopkins University Press, 1973), 77–98. See also

Alice S. Rossi, "Maternalism, Sexuality, and the New Feminism," in *Contemporary Sexual Behavior*, 145–73, especially 165–70; Sidney Callahan, "Abortion and the Sexual Agenda: A Case for Pro-Life Feminism," *Commonweal* 113 (25 April 1986): 236–37; Debra Evans, "The Price of the Pill," *Christianity Today* (11 November 1991): 40; and Cristina L. H. Traina, "Passionate Mothering: Toward an Ethic of Appropriate Mother-Child Intimacy," *Annual of the Society of Christian Ethics, 1998* (Washington, DC: Georgetown University Press, 1998), 177–96.

46. This view is not limited to Roman Catholic church functionaries. Russell writes that "the importance of women doing theology. . . . [is that] they make a contribution to the *unfinished dimension* of theology. Women want to add to the understanding of the Christian faith, not to replace the other insights that have been contributed in the past" (Russell, *Human Liberation*, 53); italics in original.

47. Sheryle Bergmann, "Feminist Epistemology," *Eidos* 6 (December 1987): 201–14.

48. This is not to deny the mutual dependence of the perfection of the moral and intellectual virtues in Thomas, for instance (see *ST* I-II 58.4–5), or the simultaneous intellectual and moral fulfillment associated with the vision of God.

49. See Battista Mondin, "Faith and Reason in Roman Catholic Thought from Clement of Alexandria to Vatican II," *Dialogue and Alliance* 1 (1987): 18.

50. See for example Ruether, *Sexism and God-Talk*, 18–19. Mondin notes that "in contemporary theology faith has become a dimension of the whole person, who through the gift of faith lives in confidence and obedience to God" (Mondin, "Faith and Reason," 18). This sort of holism leaves a significant opening for the feminist interpretation.

51. See Elisabeth Schüssler Fiorenza, *In Memory of Her: A Feminist Theological Reconstruction of Christian Origins* (New York: Crossroad, 1984); and Sandra M. Schneiders, *Women and the Word: The Gender of God in the New Testament and the Spirituality of Women*, the 1986 Madaleva Lecture in Spirituality (New York: Paulist Press, 1986). I thank James F. Keenan for pointing out a number of insights in the preceding two paragraphs. The worthwhile project of tracing the phenomenology of feminist faith remains; white feminists, especially, are skeptical of revelation and its traditional interpretations, making this a particularly difficult task.

52. See Mary Jo Weaver, *New Catholic Women: A Contemporary Challenge to Traditional Religious Authority* (San Francisco: Harper and Row, 1985), 145–54.

53. See Harding, "Instability," 649–50; Rosemary Radford Ruether, "The Future of Feminist Theology in the Academy," *Journal of the American Academy of Religion* 53 (December 1985): 704; Walker, "Moral Understandings," 21–24; and Kathy A. Thomas, "Creating a Womanist Theology: Why Feminist Theology Is Not Enough for the African-American Woman," *AME Zion Quarterly Review* 101 (October 1989): 26–34.

54. Crysdale, "Horizons." For example, feminist epistemologies uncover oppressive mechanisms missed by Marx, but womanist epistemology corrects feminist race and class biases. See Charles W. Mills, "Alternative Epistemologies," *Social Theory and Practice* 14 (Fall 1988): 258–59.

55. Porter, "Limits," 321.

56. See for example Schaef, *Society*; and Harriet Goldhor Lerner, *The Dance of Anger: A Woman's Guide to Changing the Patterns of Intimate Relationships* (New York:

Harper and Row, 1985); Susan Nelson Dunfee, *Beyond Servanthood: Christianity and the Liberation of Women* (Lanham, MD: University Press of America, 1989); and Saiving, "The Human Situation."

57. Kay, "Getting Egypt Out"; Diana Fritz Cates, "Taking Women's Experience Seriously: Thomas Aquinas and Audre Lorde on Anger," ed. Harak; *Aquinas and Empowerment: Classical Ethics for Ordinary Lives,* ed. G. Simon Harak (Washington, DC: Georgetown University Press, 1996), 47–88.

58. Cannon, *Black Womanist Ethics,* especially chapters 4 and 5; implied in Cates, "Women's Experience," 70–78. On reinventing the virtues to fit contemporary circumstances, see also Keenan, "Proposing Cardinal Virtues."

59. Thomas judges what is good for humans not deductively but by "observing inclinations" or making judgments "in the presence of" those inclinations (Kay, "Human Nature," 25, 28).

60. For instance, see Chopp, "Pragmatics," 242; and L. Shannon Jung, "Feminism and Spatiality: Ethics and the Recovery of a Hidden Dimension," *Journal of Feminist Studies in Religion* 4 (1988): 55.

61. As Daniel Maguire points out, practical reason can in this sense be seen as an ethic born of care. Daniel C. Maguire, "Service on the Common," *Religious Studies Review* 10 (January 1984): 11; Maguire, "*Ratio Practica,*" 22–39. Maguire's claim that "ethics rises from caring" ("Service," 11) suggests but does not, I believe, refer precisely to Gilligan's care ethic. Maguire means to point out that in early scholastic thought, "moral knowledge is born in awe" rather than in syllogistic reasoning ("*Ratio Practica,*" 32). See also Christine E. Gudorf, "Parenting, Mutual Love, and Sacrifice," in *Women's Consciousness, Women's Conscience: a Reader in Feminist Ethics,* ed. Barbara Hilkert Andolsen, Christine E. Gudorf, and Mary D. Pellauer (San Francisco: Harper and Row, 1985), 175–91.

For Thomas Aquinas affection and the multiplicity of connections to neighbors, family, and friends are justifications for loving them more intensely than others, even than more virtuous others. See *ST* II-II 26.7. See also Pope, *Evolution.*

62. Kay, "Getting Egypt Out," 14–15; Westberg, *Right Practical Reason,* 203–4, 209–10, 228. Kay points out that Thomas adopted Aristotle's account of the emotions: emotions are "judgments or beliefs that involve cognition" ("Human Nature," 225); likewise Westberg describes passions as impulses that influence the way in which we reason.

63. See Hall, *Narrative,* 39–40, 94–98, 111–12.

64. Patricia Beattie Jung, "Abortion and Organ Donation: Christian Reflections on Bodily Life Support," *Journal of Religious Ethics* 16 (Fall 1988): 273–305.

65. Traditional natural law extends this effect only to individual human or natural fulfillment. Some feminists and, as will be shown in chapter 7, other liberationist thinkers also draw a connection to spiritual fulfillment.

66. On probabilism and probabiliorism see Jonsen and Toulmin, *Abuse,* 260.

67. *ST* I-II 97.3. Thomas here refers to *human law,* a specification of natural law, not natural law per se. On the benefits and liabilities of this influence, see Hall, *Narrative,* 104, 111–12; and MacIntyre, "Natural Law," 67, 80–81.

68. I thank Cheryl Johnson Odim for this observation.

69. Cahill, *Sex, Gender,* 12; italics added.

70. Porter, "Limits," especially 327–28.

71. These notions, typically linked to an assessment of emotion as a women's "disability," would have to be examined critically (see Elshtain, *Public Man, Private Woman*, 75).

72. Chopp, "Feminism's Theological Pragmatics," 253–54.

73. Cahill, *Sex, Gender*, 97.

74. Crysdale, "Revisioning," 481.

75. Ibid., 484.

76. See Hall, *Narrative*, 32–35, on the plasticity of the shape that fulfillment of the inclinations can take.

77. See *Veritatis Splendor*, par. 110, where the theologians' role is described as developing explanations for changeless norms. Evidence of Roman Catholic ecclesiastical cognizance of the critical power of feminism (and of pluralism and social constructionism generally) is the recent reaction against it. For instance, in response to contemporary awareness of theological pluralism and of the relativity of all theological stances, Joseph Cardinal Ratzinger argues that "magisterial teaching, by virtue of divine assistance, has a validity beyond its argumentation, which may derive from a particular theology" (Congregation for the Doctrine of the Faith, *Instruction on the Ecclesial Vocation of the Theologian*, par. 34). This would imply, for instance, that theological narrowness or misogyny in authoritative magisterial arguments on morals does not compromise their conclusions, whose truth transcends the assumptions of the narrow theology or anthropology in which they are couched.

78. Revisionists hold that "acts, especially sexual acts, have to be evaluated in light of human relationships and circumstances within which those relationships take their actual texture." See Lisa Sowle Cahill, "The Instruction and Roman Catholic Moral Teaching," in Thomas A. Shannon and Lisa Sowle Cahill, *Religion and Artificial Reproduction: An Inquiry into the Vatican "Instruction on Respect for Human Life"* (New York: Crossroad, 1988), 109. On revisionism and proportionalism, see chapters 5 and 6 of this book.

5

Josef Fuchs and Individual Integrity

The writings of Josef Fuchs and his like-minded European and American contemporaries must be read as responses to the moral theology of the manuals. Their work is a reinterpretation of, not a replacement for, the long Roman Catholic tradition of analysis of acts and identification of universal norms. For instance, their spotlight on the free, integral subject as the condition for the possibility of moral action assumes a backdrop of continuing preoccupation with discrete acts and moral rules; it simply rebuts magisterial teaching that even now virtually restricts the blameless conscience to the moral judgments of the magisterium. [1] Yet it accomplishes this familiar task from within a new understanding of what constitutes moral objectivity. Josef Fuchs's version of this counterweight combines the personalist, casuistic, and egalitarian trends of twentieth-century natural law thought with transcendental theology to produce a moral theology rooted in the fundamental, existential option for the Absolute. [2] Rather than delineating the conditions for the possibility of human beings' receiving God's self-revelation, Fuchs explores the conditions of the possibility of their being moral, of their orienting themselves toward the God whom they receive in revelation. From this perspective it is of first importance not what one does but why one does it—that it is an expression of existential openness to God, or goodness. In addition, in transcendental theology revelation—both God's act of self-disclosure and the human experience and acceptance of it—is not vague or generic but concrete and particular. Similarly, in Fuchs, a person's basic commitment to the Absolute is made real only in concrete, categorial right action. This connection between *being good*—striving out of love to live a life ordered to God—which is not always the same as *doing right*—acting habitually and consistently according to practical reason—is the key to Fuchs's moral thought. [3] It also echoes the connection between the habits and the acts of the virtues in Thomas and the feminist insistence that to be good is to do good.

As Fuchs's case for grounding ethics in the individual's fundamental option for the Absolute has absorbed most of his scholarly energy, so will it absorb our attention here. But he conceived this argument as an aid to more open, more fitting ethical discernment. Although his personalist convictions prevent him from hazarding once-for-all norms, he has begun to engage practical issues more explicitly. Thus we can get a sense not only of his foundations but of the sorts of moral reasoning they can and cannot support. We begin where he begins, with theological anthropology: the person created in the image of God and destined for salvation.

GOOD PEOPLE AND RIGHT ACTS

Fuchs's transcendental approach to the moral subject makes for a subtle and difficult connection between personal moral goodness and worldly moral rightness, between the subject's relationship to the Absolute per se and the interactions with others that both express and define that primary relationship. This connection is pivotal for any ethician who intends, as Fuchs does, to make a meaningful turn to the subject without abandoning claims about the existence of an objective, universal morality. The salvation of persons governs this recasting: the human end of union with God is the first concern of the church and of moral theology. For Fuchs the moral, existential dimension of this union eclipses the intellectual dimension, and an interest in the mechanisms of individual salvation far outweighs a concern to describe soteriology generally. Individual salvation is about basic moral goodness, variously described as free acceptance of the divine offer of grace, "inner reshaping," or openness to the Absolute as the ultimate good. [4] Although either persons or acts can be thought of as right or wrong, only persons can be morally good or bad, and only this goodness and badness matter ultimately. Even a person's explicit attitude toward a given description of God is insignificant; the issue is her unconscious, unthematic "surrender or withholding of the self." [5] Moral theology in the first and proper sense is concerned with this fundamental option, not with the moral rightness of her acts. Therefore the "science" of deciding what actions would be right and wrong in a given concrete situation has no immediate bearing on salvation and has only a secondary place in moral theology.

So far, Fuchs's doctrine of salvation sounds a bit like Luther's most polemical statements of *sola fide:* right action does not make a person good, and salvation does not depend on works. Luther, of course, not only refused to equate moral goodness and salvation—he considered moral goodness beyond the reach of even the justified—but also implied that God's offers of salvific grace were limited. Fuchs, on the other hand, assumes both a universal offer of grace and the human capacity to cooperate with or reject it. But what Fuchs takes away from moral theology with one hand he gives back with the other. He quickly inserts a Calvinist (and Thomistic) caveat. Habitual moral wrongness of action—or at least demonstrable lack of concern for moral rightness—could be a sign of rejection of the Absolute, a sign of personal moral evilness. For total disjunction of good (orientation) and right (action) would lead, if combined with Fuchs's emphasis on internal moral goodness, to antinomianism; and this is an impossible result for a Christian natural law thinker. Fuchs weaves a subtle connection: human life is a process of self-actualization and self-definition. [6] People make fundamental choices for or against the Absolute only in and through concrete actions in their daily lives. [7] As Garth Hallett argues, the *rightness* or *wrongness*—objective moral status— of a concrete action (and therefore, as James Keenan would say, of its agent) does not directly transfer moral *goodness or badness* to the agent in an immediate, mathematical sense. Nonetheless, over time a person's concrete actions both reveal and sculpt her basic moral orientation. [8] According to Fuchs,

> The basic, free self-realization of the subject always takes place *in particular acts related to an object distinct from the person as a whole.* The spiritual person can only attain basic, free self-realization when he emerges from his spiritual unity into the physically conditioned diversity of his development in space and time, to which his personal freedom of choice is directed. [9]

The obverse of this claim is that "if one is morally and personally good, one tends toward the good." [10] The "good" person—one who is saved, and therefore committed to true self-actualization—wants to do what is "right." The complex interdependence of these claims is unmistakable in Fuchs's own account of them:

> In the area of "categorial" life, the moral goodness of the person as a whole expresses itself as an inclination of mind, intention, goodwill, etc. The lack of such an intention would be a sign that the person is not "good" and does not live within the realm of "salvation." Personal moral goodness. . . . is therefore also the will for the "right" realization of the world of man, that is, a realization which is good precisely for man: of the individual, of interpersonal relationships, of society, and of the material world. More exactly, it is the intention to try to find this rightness and, inasmuch as it is found, to realize it. . . .

The person realizes himself and his goodness. . . . in and through the realization of the world. Because he is "good" and within the realm of "salvation," he. . . . is concerned with the "right" realization of his world—this means, as I said above, good for man.

. . . The "rightness" of the realization of the world is not directly and in itself concerned with personal moral goodness. Rightness is concerned, rather, with the question of which way of realizing the earthly data of the world of man is really human and therefore precisely right—both in the abstract and in general, and in the concrete here and now. [11]

Fuchs's "will for 'right' realization" is thus an attitude of *caring for and about* "the world of man" and its realization, among the most important elements of which is justice, sensitively and delicately applied.

Not surprisingly, God accomplishes salvation not through an external decree of moral goodness but through a graced conversion of the whole person, the person-in-the-world, to an attitude of concern for moral rightness that bears fruit in concrete action. [12] Moral reflection connects the attitude and the act. Thus although the rightness or wrongness of actions is of only secondary, derivative importance to salvation and to moral theology, acts that express the person's commitment to the Absolute do have ultimate importance, and the good person relies heavily upon moral reflection after all. [13]

From these distinctions flow several important corollaries. First, as in Thomas's accounts of virtue and conscience, there is frequently a disjunction between a person's basic moral innocence or culpability and the coherence of his external act with reason. Fuchs describes this as the disjunction between the moral goodness of a person's fundamental attitude toward the Absolute and the moral rightness of his external acts. "Good" people do "wrong" things out of either lapses or ignorance, and "bad" people do "right" things. For most acts are only analogously moral—that is, they are not full, conscious expressions of the actor's basic commitment to the Absolute. Many sorts of altruism, behavior inspired by a desire to meet social standards, and commitments motivated by the superego are simply reactive or automatic; they "do not call on the freedom of the human being." [14] This means not only that many "wrong" acts are not precisely sins but also that many "right" ones are not precisely either virtuous or charitable, as neither sort is a true self-expression. *Concrete, fully good or evil acts*—acts that fully express a commitment to or rejection of the Absolute—are extremely rare. [15] Second, to mean well is not enough, for simply caring about moral rightness does not solve any practical issue. Part of fundamental goodness is undertaking the analysis that indicates the morally right path and following it. Both applied moral theology and virtue theory are still very much in business. Third, the graced, basic commitment to the Absolute—"moral goodness" or "salvation"—may be *personal* in the sense of being individual, interior, and unconscious; but it is absolutely not *private*, because it engages the whole person in her particularity and sociality. Two quite different implications follow: one for reflection and the other for evaluation. The social dimension of commitment reminds us that all sorts of family, social, and political presumptions form our moral outlooks; they do not exist a priori, and we do not generate them in isolation. [16] But it also permits an inference (a very limited one, as we saw above) from a person's pattern of public, wrong action to her existential moral depravity. Fourth, all are free to choose the good. Even when a problem is so complex that it seems impossible to identify or realize the right, one is never forced to choose between several *sinful* options, for no concrete situation, no matter how badly compromised, ever forces anyone to reject the Absolute. If sin—turning against God—appears inevitable, then one's analysis of the options must be faulty. [17] In short, "personal moral goodness is always possible." [18] Finally, Fuchs's personalist, transcendental shift of focus from universal norms to the diverse experiences of the Absolute reopens the possibility of variety in moral norms and in their interpretation. As we will see below, for Fuchs, as for Thomas, to demand in every case complete correspondence among good, right, and norm—the moral state of the subject, the appropriateness of the action, and the formula that helps to define the latter—would fly in the face of human freedom. But more radically, neither nature nor culture holds still long enough for unambiguous, universally valid norms to be developed. Norms simply cannot keep up. Adherence to established norms is not always right, and transgression of them is not always wrong. Everything turns on the procedure for discovering the right in concrete situations.

TRANSCENDENTAL PERSONALISM

For Fuchs as for Thomas, moral and intellectual perfection are mutually dependent, and both rely on grace. For Fuchs especially individual moral goodness—existential openness to the Absolute—is an epistemological condition of morality, an intellectual prerequisite for recognizing the right and just as good. Thus Fuchs implicitly embraces a moral hermeneutic: a correct moral commitment, whether explicitly religious or not, is a prerequisite for knowledge of the truth. Within this frame of reference, the only moral absolutes are the human capacity for free self-realization and the principle "do good and avoid evil." [19] Yet Fuchs's vision of historical dynamism and cultural pluralism guarantees that any genuine expression of these absolutes will also be dynamic and plural. Of what use and power are moral norms in this dynamic context? What then does it mean for a norm or a moral decision to be "objective"? For certainly if human beings and their experiences are plural and dynamic, so must moral norms be; not only this, but the norms must be flexibly interpreted. Moral hermeneutics is not just the art of interpretation of norms but also "the transcendental conditions of possibility for human subjects to establish the moral truth of concrete human situations by reference to moral norms" through "the mutual influencing of norm and subject." [20] A morally objective judgment is a judgment that corresponds not to a universal norm but to a concrete situation. For "right human behavior in this world—'morally right' in the sense of moral truth in the singular— can be understood only as what is right and appropriate *with regard to the acting person*" in her context. [21] Universal concrete or material norms could not be objective because they would of necessity be finite; they cannot correspond truthfully to all situations. As times change, so must concrete norms—for example, norms on sexuality in marriage; [22] and often norms that conflict when they converge may when investigated (a characteristic understatement) "possibly be in reality not incompatible at all." [23] Because of these conflicts and transformations of norms, the turn to the subject—to the concrete actor and that person's view of the situation and issues at hand—guarantees, rather than jeopardizes, objectivity. Thus Fuchs's insistence upon the existence of a single human morality—a universal structure of moral commitment—implies neither that a single, permanent, comprehensive set of norms guides concrete behavior nor that such common norms as may exist may be applied without regard to circumstances. Right reason—objective and impartial *because* concrete—is the ultimate moral hermeneutic. [24] Again, Fuchs's words prove the point.

> If norms of correct behavior in man's world are substantially "human" norms (i.e., from the natural moral law), their objectivity consists only in the necessity of man's right reason judging precisely what human behavior corresponds to the given human reality. Therefore, whether the *recta ratio* of acting is expressed in previously stated or accepted norms, or is first known in "knowing conscience," has nothing to do with the question of objectivity itself. [25]

Clearly objectivity not only permits but requires pluralism and historical dynamism in the application and interpretation of moral norms. But, as we have seen, Fuchs's case for the pluralism and dynamism of moral norms runs deeper than mere cultural pluralism and change: if with respect to the subject's salvation the primary issue is her commitment to the Absolute (or moral goodness), then both unanimity in moral norms and faithful adherence to them are of secondary importance. [26]

> The materiality of culturally and ethically right mastery of the concrete reality of life—education, economy, technology, sexuality, etc.—is not directly concerned with salvation, or union with God; only faith and love, together with the effort to incarnate this materiality in the "true" way in the reality of life are thus concerned.
>
> That the material mode of this incarnation can represent only a *secundarium*, already makes it reasonable that within certain limits moral pluralism might well be possible. [27]

So according to Fuchs the effort to specify moral norms once and for all not only ignores from the start human pluralism and dynamism but misleads people into believing that salvation—as moral goodness—can be gained or proven through particular sorts of external action.

Fuchs's twofold relativization of moral norms points up the need for criteria for the development, evaluation, and application of concrete norms: around what common concern is the dialectic or "mutual influencing of norm and subject" to be carried out? On what basis, if any, can it be criticized? To begin, the context judges the norm: concrete right action depends upon arriving at objective moral truth, "the moral judgment that actually corresponds to a given, concrete, real, personal situation." [28] Norms "can (and often do) indicate moral truth only inadequately" and so "cannot truly correspond to the concrete reality," [29] which may "contain morally relevant elements that have not yet been sufficiently taken into account in preformulated 'moral truths.'" [30] But an uncritical description of context provides no more moral guidance than a limited particular norm. What is the transcendental factor that underlies varied expressions of moral truth? Fuchs thinks it is "the *values that are in question* in various modes of conduct, rather than the formulated norms which seek in their fashion to bring recognition to such values." [31] Value is the formal, perduring aspect under which human concrete, ontic good is pursued. So values, and not specific norms or even virtues, are the all-important links between transcendental commitment and responsible, right action.

Fuchs's stance here is that of a reformer retrieving treasure from a too hastily discarded tradition. Value is its mechanism of casuistic continuity. For example, only reference to perduring, transcendent values explains apparent discontinuities in the moral teachings of the church. [32] Vatican Council II's

Declaration on Religious Freedom is, as material norm, a radical departure from earlier magisterial teaching on religious freedom, the expression of faith, and the proper use of political power. Despite this, Fuchs argues, the document is consistent with earlier, less tolerant Roman Catholic instructions on religious liberty in one important respect: all concur "in the unbroken teaching on the impermissibility of coercion and hindrance with regard to the acceptance of the Christian faith." Here Fuchs displays his trademark criterion: continuity in ethics is expressed formally, as *preservation of a value*—here, respect for moral subjects' freedom to commit themselves to the Absolute—not materially, as recurrence of a literal practical guideline—adherence to a creed or membership in a church. Discontinuities therefore occur in material norms "as the *various concrete expressions* of that continuity." [33]

These changing expressions, or norms, are not mere window dressing but are the concrete, authoritative mediations of transcendental truth at a given stage of history. Such "coping" with discontinuous expression is inherent to the moral theological task. Times change; the point is to find "the correct solution, in terms of natural law, for today under the circumstances and in the consciousness of today." [34] Fuchs believes that this position is faithful to scholastic natural law thought. Yet Fuchs does replace Thomas's bias toward stability—and its companion fear of change's destabilizing effects—with a bias toward dynamism—and its fear that stasis in moral norms compromises the incarnation of value in new, changed situations. He also seems uncritically to assume that every inherited norm was objective and fitting in its original situation, that it truly incarnated a perduring value, and that it is easy to tease this value away from other wrongheaded or less perduring purposes the norm may have served. Certainly the central issue for Fuchs is whether contemporary norms incarnate values *here and now;* but if these values are to be gleaned from old norms, the need for stiff criteria is pressing.

Thus the methodological implication of Fuchs's transcendental personalism is that moral reasoning is a matter of identifying perduring values and determining how they can best be incarnated in concrete goods. [35] Norms serve as concrete, limited, imperfect guides in this process, and moral reason is responsible for their development, adaptation, and application. But moral reason must not have a swelled head. Neither it nor the actions it recommends can save or damn, for it is merely a response of openness to God's already effective salvation. [36]

Does moral reflection then have any theological significance at all? Although both are categorial expressions of transcendent truth, theology articulates the all-important doctrines of salvation; ethics, like human behavior itself, is of secondary and derivative importance. Yet because the Christian vocation is expressed in the world but "is still not of the world but a true gift" of grace, ethics, *seen as moral theology, is* sacred doctrine and *is* about salvation: moral theology is "a scientific discipline which has as its subject-matter the sublime vocation of the believer in Christ." [37]

There is an inkling of a moral hermeneutic here. Although dogmatic and moral theology are not equal or mutually influential—moral theology is a subcategory of theology proper, and no judgment, as in feminism, of the adequacy of a theology by its moral implications comes into play explicitly—for Fuchs as for McCormick and Gutiérrez, the inspiration for developing a new theological approach is moral. Fuchs intends transcendental personalism, ultimately a doctrine of salvation, as a corrective to the theology that lies behind the inadequate, misleading, stunting approach to the moral life he finds in manual and magisterial theology. In addition, Fuchs clearly renders Thomas's claims about the interdependence of the moral and intellectual virtues in a transcendental key: a correct moral stance—existential openness to the Absolute—is a condition for the possibility of genuine moral knowledge. The implications of this choice for theological method are demonstrated rather than (as for moral reason) explained, but they are discernible.

Transcendental method has implications for the procedure of moral reasoning as well. Fuchs has little to say about the doers of moral theology, except that they had better apply reason to concrete reality; truth is the criterion of moral competence. This relative unconcern for establishing formal moral authorities is based in two assumptions. First, truths of faith and of morals are in separate classes. Unity in matters of faith, because it has directly to do with salvation, is the proper purview of the ecclesiastical magisterium; the issue of right and wrong behavior, while important, is secondary and derivative. [38] In addition, because moral objectivity is faithfulness to the minute details of the concrete situation, the search for moral truth prohibits strict unanimity of detailed moral norms. Because the latter logic can as easily multiply interpretations of revealed truth, it is unclear why Fuchs thinks unity in matters of doctrine is of any more importance to salvation than unity in moral norms. But in any case moral reasoning is to be carried out on the ground, not in the tower studies of church leaders and moral theologians.

Thus Fuchs has argued steadfastly that neither theologians nor bishops have inherent, superior competence to judge concrete moral issues. [39] Magisterial pronouncements on morals must stand up to reason; they jeopardize concrete moral objectivity when they dictate norms in too great detail. [40] Magisterial establishment of even limited universal concrete norms, especially when combined with a damper on dissent, entails other risks as well: the development of magisterial positivism (the belief that the source of a norm's validity is its endorsement by ecclesiastical authorities), the impression that God is encountered primarily in ecclesiastical directives, the smothering of theological creativity, the promotion of moral immaturity among laypeople and "superegos" among church officials, and a general loss of trust in leadership. [41] One might add to this list the deterioration and entrenchment that result from the limitation of moral argument to a small and homogeneous group. Fuchs's circumscription of institutional authority is by no means universally accepted; it puts Fuchs in clear contradiction to contemporary Vatican thinkers, especially Joseph Cardinal Ratzinger. [42]

Yet despite their theoretical clarity, Fuchs's treatments of history, freedom, values, objectivity, and their implications for method—all the elements of his fundamental moral theology—are of more help in determining whether in a particular case moral reasoning has been carried out in the right spirit than they are in judging the quality of its conclusions. For this we need more anthropological detail and a subtler sense of what Fuchs assumes—beyond the human capacity to recognize and pursue good and identify and avoid evil—when he speaks of natural law.

THEOLOGICAL ANTHROPOLOGY AND THE NATURAL LAW

In keeping with the Roman Catholic natural law tradition, Fuchs holds that the human capacity to be moral is grounded in the human end of communion with God. There is no really existing "*natura pura*"; all are graced and destined for fulfillment, and all are touched by original sin. [43] In addition, "the human person is constituted by the Creator as dialogical partner and thus as lord in the world." [44] This divine intention for universal salvation and dialogical lordship form the theological basis for the idea of a universal morality, for here the basic commitment of "openness to the Absolute" takes on the more definite character of love and responsibility for the world. Finally, thanks to Fuchs's personalism, anthropology and ethics must consider the whole person in all of her dimensions: "What matters is conformity to the person in his or her totality." [45] This criterion cuts both ways. Just as no feature or dimension of the human can be discarded as inessential, none is defining or determining; for instance, only rational beings are fully human, but rationality is not an adequate description of human being.

Human being is not only integral but dynamic. Like any author who embraces doctrines of both universal anthropology and genuine historical pluralism and dynamism, Fuchs searches for metaphors that express continuity in change. He settles on the images of development and maturation. Although in one sense the "facts" of our being never change—the core of human nature itself is constant—our vision of these facts metamorphoses as we learn more about ourselves and our place in the world around us. This gradual maturation of vision applies not only to individual human lives but to historical human culture in general. [46] Yet this mildly naturalist claim—that as individuals and cultures "grow up" their understandings of their unchanging selves and their constant world simply deepen—sits uncomfortably with Fuchs's recent, more nearly social constructionist argument that "nature" or the "given" (his quotation marks) is not a mythical "zero point" but the world and ourselves as we encounter them today, formed by generations of human creative action. [47]

What then is the relationship between human givenness and human creativity (rationality, in the natural law tradition)? Like other revisionists Fuchs cites reason and physical nature as equally constant and indispensable elements of anthropology but implies that reason—with its capacity for free self-realization and creative lordship—is the source of creative dynamism. [48] Physical nature-as-given is integral, morally significant, and worthy of respect. Yet it is not determinative: "a moral judgment about right ethical conduct cannot be deduced from what is given in nature, but can be found through human, rational, evaluative reflection within human reality as a whole." [49] Of course, nature is never "just nature"; reason always already interprets, shapes, and changes it. [50] But even interpreted nature decides nothing absolutely. For instance, nature presents us with a number of different kinds of potentially meaningful sexual expression but lacks an instrument for determining which are fitting here and now. [51]

The consequences of this tension for ethics are twofold. First, because "mutability belongs to man's immutable essence," it is impossible to pin down, once for all, the "basic, unchangeable nature of man"; our functioning description of human nature *in its totality* changes, even if reason and the body perdure. [52] Second, progress—an absolute duty, according to Fuchs [53]— must be appropriate to human dignity. Again Fuchs has a dynamic but "essential" humanity in mind: progress thus both alters and is measured by the idea of the human. [54]

Yet whether this account of dynamic human nature and reason yields sufficient criteria by which to judge human creative self-transformation is an important question. Respect for the totality of the human being would be a meaninglessly circular criterion unless it specified these quantities further, if still formally. Other dimensions of human being receive some treatment, but Fuchs's cursoriness is evidence of both preoccupation with a particular sort of reason and his wariness of sacrificing universality in the descent to particulars. For example, emotion is a permanent feature of human being, but in an early work Fuchs warns of its dangerous tendency to compromise reason. [55]

Desires, passions, and affections—except for the often misdiagnosed desire for God—are given no formal roles in Fuchs's ethic, despite their importance in traditional and contemporary descriptions of moral reason and conscience. [56] Similarly, historicity entails changes in human and environmental nature, but it is not clear that the means by which reason properly determines the fittingness of action also changes. Only if reason's methods may change are adequate paths left open for relating "new," formerly invisible dimensions of humanity to reason and physical being.

In sum, human persons are reasoning, growing, historically situated cocreators with God—hence the power for and possibility of change, and impossibility of defining intrinsically evil acts; and yet there is only one humanity—hence the possibility of formal "universal ethical statements" and carefully stated norms "to which we cannot conceive of any kind of exception." [57] Fuchs thus refuses to define once for all the essential humanity on which his whole system nonetheless relies.

NATURAL LAW. Fuchs's version of natural law bears the impress of his transcendental personalist theology. Over the course of his career, he has progressively lost interest in pinning down natural law's concrete content and enforcing conformity to it, for (as we have seen) rules are malleable, and natural law's legislative potential is of only secondary importance. He bypasses the temptation to legalism by returning to another classical natural law theme: the subject's participation in natural law.

Fuchs's natural law, like Thomas's, has existential, concrete, and cosmic dimensions. It is an internal orientation given to individuals through Christ's grace. [58] It is also a concrete guide to working out the "right" in one's relationship to the external world. But even when taken in the second sense, as a guide to right action, Fuchs's natural law is a *lex interna*: "the natural law is in itself not a written or given code of moral norms but is rather man himself insofar as he can understand and formulate normative moral propositions and judgments in a right way." [59] Natural law is also part of the one, universal law of Christ, which it serves and by whose salvific purpose it is judged: "there is a natural order of creation, a natural moral law, but it does not stand by itself; it is a part of the whole, the order and the law of Christ. Therefore, there is only one single law for all men, the law of Christ." [60]

This "natural order of creation" converges with the doctrines of the incarnation and of common humanity to guarantee that Christian and human moralities—the contents of the moral life—also coincide. Christian morality—and, implicitly, any truly human morality—is "the incarnation of God and of his wisdom through the creation of the human person who is partner in

God's own image." [61] This partnership is substantive; the creation of human beings in the image of God, as cocreators, signals that God intends them to work out the details of human morality among themselves. [62] A God who did not leave the (concrete, categorial) details to human reason would cease to be transcendent; human beings deprived of this task would cease to be human. The deliberations about right action that give form to their basic commitments would become superfluous, and therefore the meaning of their creative lordship in the world, which grounds their concern to do right, would be called in question. [63]

> If the human person is constituted by the Creator as dialogical and cooperative partner and thus as lord in the world, then neither such talk [of arbitrary authorization or delegation of authority over human life] nor the recurring reference to God's law and right has an adequately justifiable ground. Human authority does not become true authority because of the fact that God adds a genuinely binding character to human "authoritative" decrees; rather, in itself true categorial authority is created participation in God's transcendent authority. Similarly, the human search and discovery of morally right conduct and action in this world have the character of moral norms because of the fact that God has established the earthly lordship of human persons, certainly not only with regard to some universal laws, but also through their *insights* which go into detail and hence are very differentiated. [64]

Divine moral "decrees" would be fundamentally senseless because they would violate the Christian belief that God created human beings free and rational and intended that good people employ, and right behavior observe, human reason. [65] The natural moral law is both "voice of God"—because personal, reasoning human beings are "a created participation in the reality of God and of his wisdom"—and product of human reflection—because it is "fundamentally identical with the human person." [66]

As we saw above, Fuchs's anthropology struggles to balance continuity and stability with historicity and change, and his version of natural law inherits this challenge. [67] In his early writings he wavers between naturalism and dynamic rationalism. Reason reads natural law "in the nature of things" and then applies this law in the primary (but practically useless) sense to an abstract, nonhistorical "human nature in general." [68] Yet even so "nature is not the decisive element in the creation of man." [69] Fuchs's later work treats "natural givens" as part of saved human being; physical nature is morally relevant but not morally determinative. Moral categories are not deducible from physical being. [70]

The relationship between natural law and history had a similarly ambiguous beginning in Fuchs's thought. In his early work Fuchs postulates a changeless, "primary" natural law that must be applied and specified in each historical situation; for instance, natural law tells human beings that they need a government but does not dictate precisely what sort. [71] Concrete natural law precepts are secondary natural law. In his later writing Fuchs eliminates the language of "primary" and "secondary," arguing simply that as nature and human being change, "what is human" in given circumstances shifts too; therefore evolution and even discontinuity in natural law's concrete precepts must be expected: [72] "The natural moral law is rather to be understood in a dynamic sense; as the ever new and still to be solved problem of being a person of this world. This, however, implies development and progress." [73]

Similarly, although in both his early and his later writings Fuchs insists that flexibility in norms need not compromise objectivity and universality, the implications of this claim shift perceptibly over time. For instance, Fuchs consistently insists that, in all identical situations, the same norm holds. [74] Even in his early work this determination required an exhaustive investigation of the details of the external context of an act, but by 1991 context had grown to include actors' life-plans, psychological structures, and other internal factors imperceptible to the eye. [75] It becomes not only theoretically but practically impossible to develop any *detailed*, concrete norms from nature, in advance, or in abstraction from circumstances. Changeless, concrete absolute norms whose transgression constitutes moral wrongness, regardless of circumstance or intention, simply do not exist. [76] Thus Fuchs increasingly presents universal norms as formal and unspecified, dependent on cumulative historical experience, and subject to reevaluation. [77] He moves from belief in limited absolute moral prohibitions to a preference for the language of virtually exceptionless norms to the claim that the only moral absolute is "do good and avoid evil." Very recently he has charged that ecclesiastical support for detailed absolute norms is guilty not only of the naturalistic fallacy but also of thinly veiled, arbitrary designs on cultural hegemony. [78]

This judgment does not preclude the existence of norms prohibiting actions that could never conceivably either be morally right or be the products of a morally good disposition. Fuchs simply forbids the automatic inference from wrong action to personal evil. [79] But (virtually) exceptionless (often called absolute) concrete moral norms are acceptable *if* they account for circumstances and intention. [80] The unstated implication is not that violation of an exceptionless concrete norm transforms a good moral attitude into a bad one; it is that one is unlikely to find a reasonable justification for violating these norms and so could not normally transgress them in moral innocence. Hence, *in these cases,* moral wrongness of action entails moral wrongness of intention, which in turn suggests the possibility that the actor has turned against the Absolute.

In the end, Fuchs still subscribes to the traditional natural law assertion, "*agere sequitur esse.*" Yet he rejects the caricatured interpretation, "the structure of human nature as found dictates proper human behavior." Rather, he tries to consider human being *in its totality and changeability, with a view toward its destiny and fulfillment, in the concrete,* and above all, *as transcendent and rational.* [81] Fulfillment of the human telos—for Fuchs, complete existential openness to the Absolute rather than intellectual vision of it—occurs not only through but exclusively in concrete and active commitment in the world. In this way Fuchs retains the traditional telic structure of human moral life and the traditional natural law rootage of precepts in nature and yet responds to the contemporary sense of dynamism and pluralism and the renewed interest in the link between public action and private relationship with the divine. He does this, finally, in a way that responds to two concerns of Christians in a largely agnostic culture: he assures them that many of their companions are "right with God" despite lack of explicit Christian faith and that basic *human* reflection on *human* rightness, without explicit recognition of its foundation in the *imago dei,* leads to solutions—and even reflects attitudes—that are also and necessarily consonant with Christianity.

NATURAL LAW AND CONTEMPORARY PRESSURES.   Fuchs's place on the modern continuum is clear. Not Thomas's conclusions, but his methods and his confidence in human reason, attract Fuchs. He combines a Thomistic soteriology with contemporary personalism to lower the stakes for moral reflection: the task is no longer to avoid the eternal punishment that follows mortal sin but to put one's love for God into action. An historically conscious academic casuistry, which uncovers perduring values in past, often defunct decisions, supports the effort. But rather than exploring the tiniest conceivable permutations of every possible moral question himself, Fuchs lays the responsibility for moral reason at the feet of the free, rational, mature (and possibly not so ordinary) individual, for only "on the ground" can the pertinent details of a situation be teased out and the value at stake be identified. Conscience, integrity, and intimate knowledge of details, not continuity with past or present ecclesiastical interpretations of norms or with Fuchs's own analyses, guarantee objectivity.

First, Fuchs's moral theology turns upon the individual's ground in God and consequent potential for transcendental moral commitment (conscious or unconscious) to the Absolute. Integrity—complete openness to the Absolute—

originates in personal conversion. Yet not only are individual moral goodness and its conditions the primary concern of moral theology, they are also the criteria against which the practice, methods, and conclusions of all moral theology is measured. Whatever encroaches upon this primary individual openness to the Absolute is to be rejected. With this individual moral integrity comes genuine self-realization; one embodies or incarnates one's commitment in the world. Personal integrity is thus expressed primarily not in adherence to a body of norms but through pursuit of the concrete human good in openness to the Absolute.

Second, self-conscious awareness of this openness and its indispensability to genuine self-realization constitute for Fuchs the "mystery of conscience." This mystery guarantees the possibility of authentic, objective judgments by a concrete person in her minutely specific circumstances. The dictates of a person's conscience are "absolute demands" upon her: objectivity in utter particularity. This is not, as it was for Thomas, merely the informed judgment of moral reason, which might be erroneous, culpably or inculpably. Neither, as it was in the intervening moral tradition, is it the application of norms to circumstances. Rather, it is the opposite: the creative evaluation of received norms in light of the situation. Conscience is the authentic decision of the particular subject open to the Absolute. That is, attentive subjectivity is the criterion of genuine objectivity. There seems, however, to be only one true or good judgment in a given concrete situation. Thus the judgment of conscience resembles an elusive platonic ideal more than it does a conscientious Aristotelian judgment of experience and reason: properly speaking it is never wrong, even though it may be misread or ignored. [82]

This emphasis on individual authenticity helps to explain why social ethics, as a communal project of concrete, changeable moral decision making, falls outside Fuchs's fundamental theological concern. It smacks more of a negotiated settlement than of authentic individual openness to the Absolute in a completely unique circumstance. For

> the principal task of the church and her magisterium (just as for Jesus) is ... the salvation of mankind, of persons as such. From a moral viewpoint, this means that the church is not interested primarily in acts and their moral rightness but in the person and his moral goodness. To fail to see this is to misunderstand the true mission of the church and of its authority. The church must insist above all that people accept the grace that is offered of a continuous true personal conversion, that they not be so closed within themselves but that they be open to what is good, to their neighbor, to God. This personal opening, which is the

church's primary concern, includes a free interior opening to the search for right human behavior in mankind's world and a personal decision to realize such a world as far as is possible. [83]

In addition, issues of social rightness and wrongness are matters of practical reason, not faith; therefore they lie within the purview of "the new humanism," not of explicitly theological thought. [84] Then there is the matter of practical competence. The church hierarchy's ability to judge social questions is no greater, and is often less, than that of secular experts. [85] Finally, for Fuchs social questions are not ultimately pressing because the state of the world has no eschatological significance. In fact, for Fuchs, structural evils are only analogously immoral, because although they are clearly wrong and harmful, they have no clear current agents. [86] Fuchs's morally converted person is not *eradicating others' sin and bringing about the kingdom* but *loving or caring for the world*. He asks not whether she is contributing to the *world's* salvation but whether she is living out *her own* commitment to God faithfully in the world through an effort to act rightly.

Yet social ethics is not worthless in itself, and theology does make some appreciable contributions to it. Theologically generated moral criteria can be applied to humanly generated moral norms, for the public moral discussion is theoretically compatible with Christian criteria. And moral theology can develop Christian criteria for true human progress, which it is Christians' duty to pursue as "continuously converted" people. [87] There is room as well for Christian sociology, whose contribution is "to study society in its entirety, in all its dimensions," not only the natural ones. [88] More recently, Fuchs has shown how his theologically grounded conditions of objectivity affect the way in which questions of social ethics are phrased and analyzed.

Despite all of this, and despite the fact that thorny social issues are moral problems, *moral theology* is the wrong venue for their detailed solution; they are *human* moral issues. This is not to say that Fuchs thinks he has solved anything by making the human person the criterion of social ethics or by turning social issues over to "experts," for human historical and cultural existence precludes a "unique or universally binding Christian response" to Fuchs's "questions of humanity." [89] In fact a permanent, conclusive, concrete social ethic is not accessible to anyone, anywhere, no matter what her religious convictions or openness to the Absolute. Concrete, local wisdom is the key to objectivity.

This reorganization of responsibilities cleverly excludes social issues from the list of topics on which the church and theologians have privileged competence, leaving the individual, informed conscience to operate unfettered.

For the same reasons that ground Fuchs's simultaneous esteem for social ethics and his unwillingness for the church—or moral theology proper—to engage in it, he considers practical moral reasoning to be both indispensable to the "continuously converted" Christian life and outside the purview of his discipline. The descent to practical particulars that discovers what sort of behavior best incarnates value in given, unfamiliar concrete situations is impossible to him, for he believes that he lacks practical expertise generally and comprehension of the relevant factors of concrete situations particularly. [90] Moral theologians lay the groundwork for dealing with practical questions: they set up values, explore motivations, and erect minimal criteria for openness to the good. Ordinary people can, and must, carry out practical reason. For example, Fuchs begins his article on the disposing of life by saying that he does not really plan to address this issue at all; rather he wants it to serve as an example of "the basic question of the significance attached to the Christian faith in solving normative problems on the level of morally correct (right) behavior." Here Fuchs's understanding of the moral theological task prevents him from engaging in practical moral reason himself, as moral theologian. [91] This steadfast refusal to trespass on the territory of ordinary moral reasoners is admirable, but it is also unfortunate, for as a result Fuchs fails to provide any exemplary models of practical reason at work on a concrete, difficult problem.

In other cases, the line between theology and practical reason is not so sharp. Although Fuchs's treatments of concrete moral issues are generally still cautious, suggestive illustrations of his method, they have grown more pointed and detailed since the mid-1980s. His premise is often that moral theologians have interpreted core ecclesiastical teachings either too narrowly or downright wrongly. The first crucial step of the argument is fact-gathering. For example, for sexual and biomedical questions especially, Fuchs wants to know when individuated human life exists. [92] But he also asks about the presence of human consciousness; the position of the person on the continuum of human development; the likely effects of therapy; and, in the cases of lies and sexuality, the contemporary social meanings of language and sex. [93] To this, he adds personalist ruminations on personhood—the potential for conscious, social existence figuring prominently—and critical reflection on historical and contemporary theological opinions—especially the values they embrace and the technical information they assume. The next step is to ask what human value is at stake here and now. In the case of artificial nutrition for a patient in a persistent vegetative state, for example, is the crucial value continued biological function, or integral, conscious, relational existence? [94] Fuchs always leans in the direction of integral personhood: what attitudes and actions most clearly respect the life of the integral, mortal human being? The desires of the people involved are part of this formula. The Golden Rule sharpens the dictum "do good, avoid evil" to "do as you would have done to you": imagining myself in the shoes of another, what would the good be? [95] One must describe the context as fully as possible and lay out all one's philosophical and theological resources before hazarding a judgment; even then one must expect to be in respectful disagreement with others who see things differently and therefore to be willing to live with policies that may be more or less restrictive than one's own ethical conclusions.

These more concrete treatments clarify the implications of Fuchs's fundamental moral theology for ethics. He argues almost exclusively for the relaxation of strict, misguidedly naturalistic norms, leaving maximum freedom for the truth of conscience to rise to the surface. For instance, his recent reflections on biomedical ethics remind us especially that human life is never only present or absent; we need moral ways of describing its emergence and decline as well. Fuchs's own peculiar brand of *epikeia*—the interpretive principle that discerns how to fulfill the intent behind a norm when literal obedience to the norm seems to thwart that intent—takes a central role in these discussions. For Fuchs *epikeia* is not a way of getting around an inconvenient norm—say, through an arbitrary and unique dispensation—but a means of enacting it more fully and of mitigating the felt incongruity, objective harm, and other ill consequences of over-rigid interpretation. [96]

But his more pointed analyses also demonstrate clearly that an explanation of the objectivity and flexibility of conscience is no substitute for a communicable guide for moral reasoning or a credible mechanism for the prophetic condemnation of inhumane or irresponsibly lax behavior. Communal and political ethical life depend on some agreement about who or what dictates, in particular cases, which values are at stake and which of these should be pursued. The nurture of potentially social, conscious human life seems to be Fuchs's central criterion. [97] Yet without further specification even this value produces arbitrary results. For instance, he hints that abortion is appropriate when there is no chance that a child will be born alive or develop into a conscious, marginally functional person, or when a mother's life is endangered. But usually we have more than two human lives to consider, and their needs often conflict. If context is everything, why does Fuchs arbitrarily exclude from consideration the mother's economic situation, other children she may have, the medical care available to her, and her own wishes and feelings? [98] Further, simply to imagine oneself in others' shoes is an important exercise in compassion, and it may even suffice as a moral argument when those others are not yet or no longer able to communicate. But in other cases it invites unilateral, nonparticipatory reflection that excludes the important fact of the neighbor's *actual* wishes. Finally, a privileging of the capacity for social exchange and for consciousness, combined with Fuchs's sliding scale of human realization, becomes demonic if it alone determines which person's good is to be sought. Have those who are not and never will be fully social and rational less weight in Fuchs's calculus?

Fuchs's practical moral theology is not completely free-floating: the Absolute and human moral integrity are constants. Yet its success at connecting interior moral authenticity to objective states of affairs resists systematization of moral norms. This reluctance to develop even provisional moral guidelines may well reflect a desire to curb the Vatican's zeal for ratifying concrete universal norms; it may also indicate a preference for the German habit of positing good questions over the American proclivity to spin answers in excruciating and excessive detail. [99] But because Fuchs does not give examples of concrete moral reflection, his approach also does less than it might to advance public conversation about social ideals and norms. Thus we can say that Fuchs splendidly fulfills the twentieth-century mandate to reconstruct casuistry around the holism and integrity of the subject. But he is not as successful at demonstrating how we should connect these tasks to the prophetic, decisive, and even sometimes coercive mandate of social ethics.

CHRISTIANLY HUMAN AND HUMANELY CHRISTIAN

Fuchs insists that his ethic is both profoundly Christian and universally human. His is a believer's description from a Thomistic perspective. Everyone is grounded in the same Absolute and occupies the same moral universe; Christian and human moralities are materially synonymous; Christ adds no new commandments. For love appears in humanist ethics, and even sacrifice and the cross "are in accord with a truly human morality." [100] Then does Christianity have any special significance for the believer's moral reflection and life? Fuchs gives a three-layered answer. [101]

As we have seen, Fuchs draws primarily upon experience and practical reason rather than on metaphysics and theology to settle practical questions. [102] For because there is only one *humanum,* there is really only one human ethic, accessible to all. [103] The true Christian ethic is therefore a "genuine humanism." [104] But, second, Christians' conscious transcendental intentionality separates them from secular humanists. Christians understand and commit themselves to the Absolute in explicitly Christian terms, rather than athematically or anonymously. [105] In a system in which knowledge of the Absolute becomes fully significant only when it is conscious and concrete, those who "know" God better realize their humanity more completely. Finally, a believer's action is fortified by its self-conscious connection with "the religious realities" of faith: "the believing Christian finds that he must live in Christian love by realizing the whole reality of his Christianity in all the acts of his life, a reality to which belong also his human nature together with the whole human morality of a Christian." [106]

Clearly Fuchs intends that concrete faith—both proposition and commitment—motivate Christian morality and moral thought, but he is vague about the manner in which "the whole reality" of one's Christianity is to be realized. Faith simply puts a face on transcendental commitment and attaches ultimate meaning to human ends; it illumines the already "accessible moral truth that is comprehensible to the human moral self-understanding." [107] Human reasoning about human nature supplies the methods and materials for ethics: philosophical and practical approaches, information about human being, human ends, human flourishing, and evidence for a single human morality based in reason. It also describes the natural order, whose significance for ultimate human ends faith assigns. To have faith merely means that one does the human thing for religious reasons, and the doing has religious meaning. [108]

Thus for Fuchs as for Thomas the pertinent question is not "How does Christian ethics differ from secular ethics?" but "How does the Absolute ground of existence known thematically to Christians determine all human ethics?" Explanations mentioned above include the doctrines of vocation, conscience, and self-realization; the relative unimportance of acts for salvation; and the fundamental option for the Absolute. But Fuchs does not discard traditional belief in the completion of nature by grace. Without grace, human moral codes are unfulfillable and their assumptions, arbitrary. [109] Only grace— the infused virtue of traditional natural law theology—enables one both to meet the concrete demands of human ethics and to act entirely out of love, or—as Fuchs might say—out of openness to the Absolute. Fuchs's concern to preserve the gratuity of this openness is likely an additional source of his reluctance to deal with concrete cases: he wants to avoid the impression that salvation can be earned or grace, contained. But one could point out, as Fuchs does not, that grace not only empowers but forgives. If salvation—which in the Roman Catholic tradition implies sanctification or elevation—is synonymous with forgiveness—which implies a merciful attitude toward continuing morally wrong acts and past morally bad fundamental orientations—then reasoned discernment and execution of acts can remain gravely important without being a matter of salvation and condemnation. Errors in reasoning and lapses in acting, although they remain objectively wrong, are already forgiven.

In the end, Fuchs's transcendental perspective mutes and qualifies Christian Scripture and theological symbols until they are reduced to Christian grounds for a general admonition to reason well. Here the gulf yawns wide between Fuchs and thinkers who believe that content, and not vocation alone, divides Christian ethics from those of other communities. [110] From Fuchs's point of view, the aim of the Sermon on the Mount is the development of a new internal attitude rather than the exposition of external moral rules. [111] In addition, particular norms expressed in the Bible are of significance today only to the extent that they belong to practical reason. The Decalogue, for instance, remains morally authoritative because it expresses natural law, not because it was revealed. [112] Much biblical moral exhortation is paranesis, not ethics, and therefore is now only as binding as the historical moral code it reflects. For example, because in I Corinthians Paul accepts rather than critically examines the moral assumptions of the Corinthian church, his exhortations are normative today only if the Corinthian moral code stands up to contemporary practical reason. [113]

Fuchs's transcendental theology likewise informs and universalizes his Christology. Jesus is at the center of both the natural law and the moral life; he is the most concrete and most universal norm, and the imitation of him is the focus of the human vocation. Yet it is his attitude toward the Absolute, not his concrete behavior, that we are to imitate. [114] In Christ's life, Fuchs claims, there is no "genuine endeavor to teach us how to administer the human world rightly." Even "Jesus' preaching . . . aims at the moral and personal goodness of the human person; the question of the rightness of the realization of the reality of the human world does not directly interest him." Jesus only "admonishes us to be personally and morally good and consequently not to forget or rather, not to betray—the due rightness of human social, interpersonal and individual life." Christ's example and grace lead people only to an attitude of openness toward the Absolute and concern for the concrete that *entails and subsists in* the secondary right realization of the world and humanity. [115] Because the whole world rests in the hand of God, Christian symbols and Scriptures can open only onto the universal criteria of human salvation. Yet Fuchs's insistent return to our common theological ground is not reassuring in the face of his equal insistence that genuine objectivity requires standards carefully tailored by people immersed in the concrete details of particular situations. Whence comes any sort of practical unity?

CONTRIBUTIONS AND CRITICISMS

Fuchs's great contribution to the contemporary discussion of natural law is his renovation of Thomas's medieval theological anthropology according to the building codes issued by the twentieth-century turn to the subject. Over the course of his career he has also subtly delineated the ways in which modern understandings of pluralism and historicity multiply the conclusions of moral reason. His thought has been a fine demonstration of his own premises: that change is human, inevitable, and good, and that the constants in the flux are the human telos in God and the capacity of rational, graced human beings to discern the right. His concern for the actualization or erosion of the fundamental option in concrete acts preserves Thomas's complex connections among action, infused and acquired virtue, and grace. [116] Fuchs thus demonstrates the possibility of developing a moral theology that is consistent with Thomas's central claims and yet is more obviously responsive to the peculiar demands of the subject's commitments and context. Even more to the feminist point, this invitation spotlights the objectivity and moral authority of the thinking subject and the crucial moral relevance of concrete circumstances and experiences. He also packages a version of Thomistic virtue—character as the attitude and act of caring effectively for others—palatable to feminist ethicists for whom care is the pivotal organizing principle in both personal and social ethics. [117]

Fuchs's corpus is successful precisely as a fundamental moral theology, as a description of the conditions and goals of moral reflection. This purpose stands out clearly when his work is read alongside the technical handbooks of his manualist predecessors, with their abbreviated theologies; instead of parsing Mass obligations, he ruminates upon the powers of salvific grace and human reason, the preconditions for human morality. Intent on keeping the Absolute before us, he consistently prefers merely to stake out a place for the evaluation of concrete conditions and norms than to render judgments on particular cases. This demurral also amounts to a reassignment of the task of moral discernment from the ecclesiastical leadership and the theological academy to the whole human community, in deference to the objectivity of conscience. For the practical, concrete nature of moral discernment and the integrity of the individual conscience require that moral reasoning be carried out in and for concrete situations, by and for involved persons. Besides confirming Fuchs's continuing confidence in the perspicuity of the right, his invitation to his readers to work out ethical judgments for themselves clearly parallels the feminist insight that freedom in moral discernment is a condition of moral maturity and therefore of integral human flourishing.

Yet Fuchs's formal anthropology is both a blessing and a curse. Fuchs takes excruciating care to preserve the theoretical separations between the good and the right, between formal and concrete norms, [118] and between formal and concrete anthropology. Clearly Fuchs agrees, then, that concrete practical reason needs a concrete anthropology, one that consciously expresses and responds to the insights of a specific context and is open to its own reformulation and replacement. Just as plainly, Fuchs's formal anthropology is too general and permanent to provide this sort of definitive help in the identification and pursuit of concrete human goods. And he does not attempt a concrete anthropology.

This failure would be less significant if his formal anthropology were at least adequate to the formal needs of ethics. But it is not. Transcendence, historicity, and physical givenness do not exhaust the characteristics without which it is impossible to imagine a human being. [119] Other apparently permanent givens of human being—for example, emotion, of which he is somewhat distrustful—that are not precisely specifications of Fuchs's formal anthropology may not be "accidental" in the Aristotelian sense. Just how plastic are our psychological and physical qualities? Are there limits to their acceptable reinvention? This gray area—the status of apparently permanent but concrete characteristics of human nature—is one point of contention between Fuchs and those of his critics who argue for the existence of concrete absolute moral norms. [120] But Fuchs's vagueness about the degree of plasticity of human nature should also give pause to feminists, especially to those who would like to limit the use of reproductive technology.

Similarly, although Fuchs expresses an increasingly subtle sense of the malleability of concrete historical descriptions, he seems less aware of the degree to which "formal" descriptions too are historically and culturally relative. Theology can and must (continually) attempt a formal anthropology, but this anthropology must be seen as both authoritative and provisional; the "self-transcending free subject" will not be the last word. Thus we are caught between an insufficiently developed concrete anthropology and an insufficiently critical formal anthropology.

The same modern sensibility colors his understanding of the connection between Christian and secular ethics. From the modern viewpoint, his claim that Christian morality is simply the morality of human secular reason is generous and comforting. But from the pluralist perspective it is (at worst) disingenuous and surreptitiously hegemonic or (at best) mistaken. From a contemporary perspective, there is no basic set of "human" moral norms or methods to which a religious commitment can simply be added. Rather, all people bring all of their histories and commitments to their moral deliberations, including their religious ones. To be Christian is *a way of being* human. One may as well wear one's religion on one's sleeve. In order to be consistent, Norbert Rigali argues, Fuchs's treatment of the historical and cultural roots of moral pluralism should encompass the religious sources of that pluralism. [121] For if the norm of Christian, human morality is "the historical human person," that norm must always already include Christian faith, "one of many intrinsic modes of being a human person in history." [122] Fuchs—and other natural law moralists—must recognize that the vision of moral reason supported by their version of Christian faith (a humanity divinely created with the goal and capacity of recognizing and embodying divine love in concrete situations) is actually a partisan vision; that they will have to argue for their particular understanding of humanity and moral reason publicly; and that a stable, universally normative "secular reason" is nonexistent. In practice this may mean, for instance, that Christian thinkers not only can but must base many moral decisions on peculiarly Christian warrants, just as they inevitably adduce warrants rooted to their eras and cultures. For instance, a humanist who disagrees with the pacifism of a natural law Christian may quite properly trace the difference to the latter's explicit Christian commitment.

Fuchs's recent forays into bioethical questions do not protect him entirely from the charge that Roman Catholic moral theologians fail meaningfully to link what Kenneth Himes terms the "ethics of being" with the "ethics of doing": "the connection between theological belief and ethical justification." [123] Fuchs's centerpiece, his analysis of personal, fundamental moral commitment, has almost no definitive bearing on the resolution of concrete moral issues; it does not, as our earlier discussion of abortion showed, provide any strong indication of how large a circle of persons, how wide a range of values, or how extensive a list of goods we need to cover in order to discover the right. In that discussion Fuchs provides no definitive theological reasons why, if a healthy embryo is only a person-in-the-making, danger to its mother's life is the circumstance that justifies abortion. Why not more generous or more restrictive criteria? Without such indications Fuchs's revision of moral theology could easily end up merely replacing the theological foundations of existing moral theological positions or, on the other hand, justifying any moral conclusions at all. Such a theological revision does involve a change in the conception of practical moral reasoning; and in an historically conscious age, a change of perspective on moral reason is a change in moral reason itself. Yet it requires such a change in moral reason only implicitly, not explicitly. An explicit theological commitment ought to affect moral deliberations in some concrete way. The alternative is the now questionable religious commitment to remove explicitly religious language from ethical deliberation. If Fuchs's revision is to accomplish what it promises, he must—as he will not and cannot—be more specific about his theology's concrete impact on normative discourse. He must, in short, develop a credible theory of practical moral reason.

I have hinted throughout at the adequacy of Fuchs's ethic to the criteria of chapters 2 and 3. Fuchs bends over backward to retain the core of Thomas's theological anthropology and to articulate it in terms that account for the historical, self-conscious subject, for continuity of values through change, for an integral anthropology, and—most significantly for feminists—for a meaningful return of the power for moral reasoning to the individual conscience: the objectivity of the alert person in the concrete situation. Yet Fuchs's thorough and potent description of the moral subject is of little concrete help without a revised method of practical moral reasoning and a social ethic. The question is whether this lack inheres in his approach or merely results from intentional self-limitation. The answer is that both are true. Fuchs's decision to work out a *transcendental* moral theology automatically implies a relegation of *concrete* moral ruminations to other thinkers; even his recent treatments of practical issues are very general. And his focus on individual integrity makes development of concrete moral norms—and even of reliable approaches to determining them—very difficult. In fact one leaves Fuchs's most recent writing wondering whether even provisional moral norms have any useful role in practical reason; for what can necessarily generic norms mean in a world in which there are no generic situations? The "Christian sociology" he proposed early—a description and analysis of the state of human society from an integrative, comprehensive Christian viewpoint—could possibly have contributed to the development of a Christian social ethic; and in fact ecclesiastical documents on social justice employ something like it. But Fuchs himself has never practiced the discipline. Thus it is unclear how Fuchs imagines a Christianly human practical moral reason operating or what its peculiar results would be for concrete moral decisions.

Then there is the question of the relationship of human culture to salvation history. If Christianity is an historical religion, then structures and movements in history must have not only human but Christianly human or theological significance for Christian thinkers. Christians' moral responses to historical developments then have explicitly theological, and not just human, meaning. Fuchs's transcendental theology, with its emphasis upon personal salvation and fulfillment, leaves the *theological* significance of collective phenomena like human suffering, freedom, and oppression largely unexplored. It would be far easier for Fuchs to enjoin an attitude and activity of just compassion than it would be for him to describe suffering theologically.

In the end, then, Fuchs succeeds in renewing the theological credibility of the natural law project; he also scores a pastoral victory by making a strong theological case against an act-centered interpretation of morality. But he accomplishes both in a way that severely undercuts the possibility of concrete religious moral dialogue, and his limited generic demonstrations of natural law reasoning leave many practical questions unanswered. He seems caught between the natural law commitment to universally perspicuous argument and his own stipulation that moral reason be shaped by and respond to one's concrete situation. Fuchs thus provides a powerful and engaging *moral theology*, but he lacks an *ethic* in the concrete, practical sense. For this we turn to Richard McCormick.

NOTES

1. *Veritatis splendor*, especially pars. 62–64.

2. For the parallel see *Sacramentum Mundi*, s.v. "Transcendental Theology," by Rahner: "Systematic theology can be called transcendental when it a) uses the instruments of transcendental philosophy and b) takes as its themes, more explicitly than before and not just in general (as in traditional fundamental theology), the *a priori* conditions in the believer for the knowledge or important truths of faith, using genuinely theological methods of investigation."

3. This articulation of Fuchs's distinction is indebted to Keenan, *Goodness and Rightness*, chapter 1.

4. Josef Fuchs, *Christian Morality: The Word Becomes Flesh*, trans. Brian McNeil (Dublin: Gill and Macmillan; Washington, DC: Georgetown University Press, 1987), 19–21, 114.

5. Fuchs, *Christian Morality*, 106; see also 99. See also Josef Fuchs, "Good Acts and Good Persons," in *Considering Veritatis Splendor*, ed. John Wilkins (Cleveland: Pilgrim Press, 1994), 21–26 (22). Thus salvation is a fundamental orientation toward the Absolute, and sin, in the grave or mortal sense, is fundamental rejection of it. Josef Fuchs, *Christian Ethics in a Secular Arena*, trans. Bernard Hoose and Brian McNeil (Washington, DC: Georgetown University Press; Dublin: Gill and Macmillan, 1984), 49–53, 141–44.

6. Josef Fuchs, *Personal Responsibility and Christian Morality*, trans. William Cleves and others (Washington, DC: Georgetown University Press; Dublin: Gill and Macmillan, 1983), 12–13; and Josef Fuchs, *Natural Law: A Theological Investigation*, trans. Helmut Reckter and John A. Dowling (New York: Sheed and Ward, 1965), 179. Fuchs echoes Rahner: "Ultimately [the person] does not do *something*, but does *himself*" (Karl Rahner, *Foundations of Christian Faith: An Introduction to the Idea of Christianity*, trans. William V. Dych [New York: Seabury Press, 1978], 94). From this viewpoint sin is self-alienation: "the conscious non-realization of the self," a rejection of unselfish, genuinely open self-realization. See Fuchs, *Christian Morality*, 148; Fuchs, *Personal Responsibility*, 19–20, 33, 87, 121; Josef Fuchs, *Human Values and Christian Morality*, trans. M. H. Heelan, Maeve McRedmond, Erika Young, and Gerard Watson (Dublin: Gill and Macmillan, 1970), 33, 57–58; and Fuchs, *Christian Morality*, chapter 8.

7. Fuchs, *Natural Law*, 179–80; see also Fuchs, *Personal Responsibility*, 13. Fuchs does not seem to define self-realization precisely. Consistent with the Roman Catholic natural law tradition, the term emphasizes the continuity between the "old" and the "new man"; grace and its demands do not obliterate but illuminate and fulfill the "natural" dimensions of human being. One's goal is not to repudiate oneself but

to become more fully and genuinely oneself. See Fuchs, *Personal Responsibility*, 14–15.

8. Garth L. Hallett, *Greater Good: The Case for Proportionalism* (Washington, DC: Georgetown University Press, 1995), 155–57. The passage refers to proportionalism generally, a movement of which Fuchs is considered to be a founder.

9. Fuchs, *Human Values*, 98–99; italics added.

10. Fuchs, *Christian Morality*, 111.

11. Fuchs, *Christian Ethics*, 50–52. See also 108–9.

12. Fuchs, *Christian Morality*, 116–17.

13. This distinction is also clearly demonstrated in Fuchs's distinction between fundamental conscience (about goodness of being) and situational conscience (about rightness of acts); see Josef Fuchs, "Conscience and Conscientious Fidelity," in *Moral Theology: Challenges for the Future: Essays in Honor of Richard A. McCormick, S.J.*, ed. Charles E. Curran (New York/Mahwah: Paulist Press, 1990), 110–13.

14. Josef Fuchs, "The Phenomenon of Conscience: Subject-Orientation and Object-Orientation," in *Conscience: An Interdisciplinary View*, ed. Gerhard Zecha and Paul Weingartner, Theory and Decision Library Series A: Philosophy and Methodology of the Social Sciences, 27–56 (Boston: D. Reidel Publishing Company, 1987), 28. See also 29–30.

15. Fuchs, *Human Values*, 95–103. *Truly moral* acts "spring from a true commitment of the person" and "engage the person as a whole in basic freedom" (ibid., 98). See also ibid., 99; Fuchs, *Natural Law*, 179; Fuchs, *Christian Morality*, 117. More recently, Fuchs has argued that a person's "peripheral," analogously moral acts can gradually and cumulatively reverse his fundamental option (Fuchs, "Good Acts," 23).

16. Fuchs, "Phenomenon of Conscience," 40, and transcript of discussion on 47–56.

17. Josef Fuchs, "Christian Faith and the Disposing of Human Life," *Theological Studies* 46 (December 1985): 680–82.

18. Fuchs, *Christian Morality*, 109.

19. Fuchs, *Moral Demands*, 15–29.

20. Fuchs, *Christian Ethics*, 44–45.

21. Ibid., 40; italics added.

22. Josef Fuchs, "Married Love: Christian Pluralism in the Twelfth Century," chapter in *Christian Morality*, 173–88.

23. Fuchs, "Phenomenon of Conscience," 45.

24. Fuchs, *Moral Demands*, 1–11.

25. Fuchs, *Personal Responsibility*, 47.

26. For Fuchs theological pluralism is a slightly different issue than moral pluralism precisely because revelation impinges more closely on salvation; see, e.g., *Christian Ethics*, 134–35. Clearly Fuchs's point of view dictates some sort of theological pluralism, but it seems to be more carefully controlled.

27. Fuchs, *Personal Responsibility*, 121–22. This position depends greatly upon his transcendental anthropology, which will be described in greater detail below.

28. Fuchs, *Christian Ethics*, 29.

29. Ibid., 40.

30. Ibid., 29–30.

31. Fuchs, *Christian Morality*, 141–42; italics added.

32. See Josef Fuchs, "Continuity in the Church's Moral Teaching? Religious Liberty as an Example," chapter in *Christian Morality*, 157–72. Fuchs here deals "with

the question of how the Council coped with the problem of an apparently non-continuous tradition of moral theology; the decisive word here is 'coped'" (159).

33. Ibid., 170, italics added.

34. Ibid., 171. An analogy is Rahner's idea of the relationship between the deposit of faith and dogma; for Rahner dogma is "the *form* of the abiding validity of the tradition of the deposit of faith in the Church which itself remains always the same" (*Sacramentum Mundi*, s.v. "Dogma," by Karl Rahner). Fuchs's (formal) values are to concrete, historical norms as Rahner's deposit is to concrete statements of dogma. Yet dogma is of *primary* importance for salvation and norm (and ethics in general), of *secondary* importance.

35. Fuchs, *Human Values*, 196.

36. One does not *earn or forfeit* salvation through deeds as deeds; rather one *accepts or rejects* salvation through one's deeds as expressions of commitment to or rejection of the transcendent. A hint of Reformation sensibility is detectable here; concern for moral rectitude should be a product of faith (in Fuchs, openness to the Absolute). See Martin Luther, "Freedom of a Christian," in *Martin Luther: Selections from His Writings*, ed. John Dillenberger (Garden City, NY: Doubleday, Anchor Books, 1961), 70: "As works do not make a man a believer, so also they do not make him righteous. But as faith makes a man a believer and righteous, so faith does good works."

37. Fuchs, *Personal Responsibility*, 12–13. See also Josef Fuchs, *Für eine menschliche Moral: Grundfragen der Theologishen Ethik*, 2 vols., Studien zur theologischen Ethik; Études d'éthique chrétienne, 25–26 (Freiburg, Schweiz: Universitätsverlag; Freiburg, Wien: Verlag Herder, 1988–89), bd. II, 257–307.

38. Fuchs, *Christian Morality*, 143–44; 114. See also Fuchs, *Christian Ethics*, 131–53.

39. Fuchs, *Christian Morality*, 131–53.

40. For recent, especially clear, statements of this position see Fuchs, *Moral Demands*, chapters 9, 11, 13.

41. See Fuchs, *Christian Ethics*, 138; idem, *Moral Demands*, chapter 13.

42. See Joseph Ratzinger, "The Church's Teaching Authority—Faith—Morals," in *Principles of Christian Morality*, Heinz Schurmann, Joseph Cardinal Ratzinger, and Hans Urs von Balthasar, trans. Graham Harrison (San Francisco: Ignatius Press, 1986), 47–73. Ratzinger implicitly criticizes the position that norms that find a basis in human nonreligious reason or culture "can be separated off from the core of covenant faith" (58), a separation of which he thinks Fuchs and others guilty. Ratzinger argues that "Christian praxis is nourished by the core of the Christian faith, that is, the grace that appeared in Christ and that is appropriated in the sacrament of the Church" (70). Because "faith involves fundamental decisions (with definite content) in moral matters," and "the first obligation of the teaching office is to protect these fundamental decisions against reason's capitulation to the age, as well as reason's capitulation in the face of almighty praxis," the magisterium has, on the grounds of protecting faith, "competence to make detailed and practical decisions for or against an interpretation on the morality that springs from grace" (72–73). Ratzinger's quick move from the idea of faith to its protection by teaching authority puts more freight on the intellectual content of faith than Fuchs does; in addition, the possibility of reason's "capitulating" signals a very different understanding of reason—or of its reliability—than Fuchs's; for "right reason" by definition cannot capitulate. In sum, Ratzinger's cautious stance and his desire to guarantee the correctness of moral decisions suggest that his main

argument with Fuchs is over the importance of the rightness of moral acts to the life of salvation.

43. Fuchs, *Human Values*, 65; Fuchs, *Natural Law*, chapter 3. Fuchs is increasingly wary of the use of the doctrine of original sin to "explain away" social ills, however. See *Moral Demands*, 68.

44. Fuchs, *Christian Morality*, 47.

45. Hoose, *Proportionalism*, 19. Hoose refers to Fuchs, *Human Values*, 116: "Thus it is not the physical law that has to be considered as a moral law and invoked to regulate the free actions of mankind, but the '*recta ratio*' which understands the *person* in the *totality* of his reality."

46. Fuchs, *Moral Demands*, 22–24, 97–99, 161; Fuchs, *Human Values*, 184–85.

47. Fuchs, *Moral Demands*, 95. The unique perspectives of individuals and societies also influence human renderings of nature, and these perspectives too are mutable (ibid., 22–23, 36).

48. Fuchs, *Für eine menschliche Moral*, bd. I, 234–36. In Fuchs's earlier accounts, power or force must be exerted over physical nature. Human beings must take their proper places at the center of the world and force nature to serve their reasoned purposes (Fuchs, *Human Values*, 115–16, 185, 197). This is not a mere "seeing-as" but a materially forceful transformation of the environment in correspondence to human rational purposes. Fuchs gives insufficient attention here to the idea that nonhuman nature may be more than material for humanity to dispose of, more than pure means, even if this disposition is "human."

49. Fuchs, *Moral Demands*, 33. See also Fuchs, *Christian Ethics*, 9 and chapter 6; Fuchs, *Human Values*, 141–45; and Fuchs, *Natural Law*, 163.

50. See Fuchs, *Christian Ethics*, chapter 6; idem, *Moral Demands*, 36–37. For Fuchs "*culture*, in its moral dimension, is established by reason, distinct from nature but informed by it" (*Christian Ethics*, 97).

51. Fuchs, *Moral Demands*, 101.

52. Fuchs, *Personal Responsibility*, 126; Fuchs, *Natural Law*, 192; and Fuchs, *Christian Ethics*, 120–21.

53. Fuchs, *Human Values*, 201.

54. Fuchs, *Human Values*, 199.

55. See Fuchs, *Natural Law*, 160. Were Fuchs to fill out his description of human being, the elements likely would be arranged hierarchically.

56. For recent work on conscience that accounts for these factors, see Callahan, *In Good Conscience*, and Patrick, *Liberating Conscience*. The former attends to the significance of emotion, and the latter especially addresses the implications of the postmodern linguistic turn.

57. Fuchs, *Personal Responsibility*, 143, 141. The emphasis in the latter quote is on conception: not that we are sure no exception exists but that we cannot imagine one.

58. See, e.g., Fuchs, *Human Values*, chapter 6.

59. Fuchs, *Christian Ethics*, 120. Bernard Hoose describes Fuchs's *lex interna* as "man's possibility and duty of discerning what, in the concrete, human action is capable of being here and now, and what can be affirmed propositionally about behavioral norms" (see Hoose, *Proportionalism*, 36).

60. Fuchs, *Human Values*, 78.

61. Fuchs, *Christian Morality*, 60.

62. Ibid., 47–48; see also Fuchs, "Christian Faith," 675–76.
63. Fuchs, *Christian Morality*, 47, 57.
64. Ibid., 47–48.
65. See, e.g., Fuchs, "Christian Faith," 680–81.
66. Fuchs, *Christian Morality*, 53. See also Fuchs, "Conscience and Conscientious Fidelity," 119–20.
67. See for example Fuchs, *Human Values*, 185.
68. Fuchs, *Natural Law*, 8–11, 86–91.
69. Ibid., 163.
70. Fuchs, *Für eine menschliche Moral*, bd. I, 303. Volume I of this work contains little that has not already been published in English. See also Fuchs, *Christian Ethics*, 9, chapter 6; and Fuchs, *Human Values*, 141–45.
71. Fuchs, *Natural Law*, 86–101.
72. See for example Fuchs, *Christian Morality*, chapter 11.
73. Fuchs, *Human Values*, 184.
74. See Fuchs, *Natural Law*, 123; Fuchs, *Für eine menschliche Moral*, bd. 1, 303; Fuchs, *Personal Responsibility*, chapter 7; and Fuchs, *Moral Demands*, 5.
75. Fuchs, *Moral Demands*, 4–5.
76. See, e.g., Fuchs, *Personal Responsibility*, 140.
77. Fuchs, *Personal Responsibility*, 140–42.
78. Fuchs, *Moral Demands*, 28–29.
79. Fuchs, *Practical Reason and Christian Morality,* 141, 145–47.
80. See Hoose's discussion of Fuchs's "The Absoluteness of Moral Behavioral Norms" (chapter in Fuchs, *Personal Responsibility*, 115–52), in Hoose, *Proportionalism*, 34–37. See also Cahill, "Teleology," 601–29. Cahill concurs that the proportionalist position "does preserve absolute norms which are *specific* in their denotation of value relations" (617) and that violation of these norms is not only wrong but sinful, i.e., morally bad (611). The latter point refers to McCormick but holds for Fuchs as well.
81. Ibid., 213.
82. See especially Fuchs, *Practical Reason*, 218–25.
83. Fuchs, *Christian Morality*, 114.
84. See John Langan, "The Christian Difference in Ethics," *Theological Studies* 49 (March 1988): 138.
85. Fuchs, *Christian Morality*, 114–15.
86. Fuchs, *Moral Demands*, 63, 68. However, simply to accept a majority position uncritically is sinful; see Fuchs, *Practical Reason*, 227.
87. See Fuchs, *Human Values*, 200–3. Christians must be both worldly, or immanent, and world-renouncing, or transcendent, in their attitudes toward progress.
88. Fuchs, *Natural Law*, 203. This discussion emphasizes ways in which "natural" structures can contain or function for fuller, supernatural meanings.
89. Langan, "Christian Difference," 138.
90. Fuchs, *Human Values*, 175; idem, *Personal Responsibility*, chapter 7.
91. Fuchs, "Christian Faith," 664.
92. Fuchs, *Moral Demands*, 76–77.
93. Fuchs, *Moral Demands*, 178–79, 37–38.
94. Fuchs, *Moral Demands*, 176–79.
95. Fuchs, *Moral Demands*, 5–11.

96. Fuchs, *Practical Reason*, 185–99. *Epikeia* for Fuchs is not a pastoral exception but a judgment of objective moral truth, or conscience. On epikeia's history, see Mahoney, *Making*, 231–41.

97. See Fuchs, *Moral Demands*, 10–11.

98. Fuchs, *Moral Demands*, 10.

99. This is James F. Keenan's insight.

100. Fuchs, *Human Values*, 122–23, 127.

101. Fuchs, *Human Values*, chapter 5; see also *Für eine menschliche Moral*, bd. II, 257–307.

102. See Fuchs, "Christian Faith," 667–68, 672, 677; Fuchs, *Christian Ethics*, 11, 146–47; Fuchs, *Natural Law*, 162; Fuchs, *Personal Responsibility*, 147, 107–9; and Fuchs, *Christian Morality*, 203. See also Richard A. McCormick, "Human Significance and Christian Significance," in *Norm and Context in Christian Ethics*, ed. Gene H. Outka and Paul Ramsey (New York: Charles Scribner's Sons, 1968), 233–61; Charles E. Curran, "Is There a Distinctively Christian Ethic?" in *Metropolis: Christian Presence and Responsibility*, ed. Philip D. Morris (Notre Dame: Fides, 1970), 92–120; and Norbert J. Rigali, "The Uniqueness and the Distinctiveness of Christian Morality and Ethics," in *Moral Theology: Challenges for the Future: Essays in Honor of Richard A. McCormick, S.J.*, ed. Charles E. Curran (New York/Mahwah: Paulist Press, 1990), 74–93.

103. Fuchs, *Human Values*, 13–15; and Fuchs, *Personal Responsibility*, 71, 85–93.

104. Fuchs, "Christian Faith," 670–71.

105. Fuchs, *Human Values*, 123–25. See also Karl Rahner, "Anonymous Christians," in *Theological Investigations*, vol. 6, *Concerning Vatican Council II*, trans. Karl-H. and Boniface Kruger (Baltimore: Helicon Press; London: Darton, Longman and Todd, 1969), 390–98.

106. Fuchs, *Human Values*, 130. Keenan points out that this love is the concrete expression of the fundamental option: charity is a "thematic or categorical description" of acts. . . . Thus, charity rescues fundamental option from the recesses of the human person" (Keenan, *Goodness and Rightness*, 143).

107. Fuchs, "Christian Faith," 670–71; also ibid., *Christian Morality*, 54.

108. Norbert Rigali makes much of Fuchs's claim that there is "a distinctively Christian element in the concrete categorial conduct of Christians." In the quoted article Fuchs claims that Christianity provides a motivating power; an *ethos* that affects the concrete, categorical content of ethics; and a moral "religious and cultic relationship to God" (Fuchs, *Personal Responsibility*, 63–66). Yet the "obvious tendency to downplay the material content of morality determined by faith and . . . even to ignore it altogether" that Rigali notes in Fuchs's recent work, when joined with Fuchs's many other denials of uniquely Christian content for ethics, substantially undercuts the significance of this brief and very circumscribed claim for a uniquely Christian content in Fuchs (Rigali, "Uniqueness," 82).

109. Fuchs, *Personal Responsibility*, 62–63, 107.

110. Stanley Hauerwas, for example, agrees that "what it means to be Christian is but an intensification, not a denial, of what it means to be human," but he counters that beyond being a source of motivation for human behavior, Christianity—in the concrete form of Christian historical community—forms the character that recognizes and pursues these Christian-and-human ends. Christian-and-human norms are developed within the Christian community on Christian terms, not on secular common ground. See Stanley Hauerwas, "Nature, Reason, and the Task of Theological Ethics," in *Natural Law and Theology*, Readings in Moral Theology, ed. Charles Curran and Richard A. McCormick, no. 7 (New York/Mahwah: Paulist Press, 1991), 43, 51–53.

111. Fuchs, *Natural Law*, 35–37. See also Fuchs, *Christian Morality*, 5, 12, 93; Fuchs, *Human Values*, 26. See John Langan: "what Scripture provides is not a set of timeless norms but an orientation which is to be concretized in human persons. This new orientation requires and does not replace the human effort to understand and to evaluate" (Langan, "Christian Difference," 137).

112. Fuchs, *Human Values*, 30–31.

113. Fuchs, *Christian Morality*, 92.

114. See, e.g., Fuchs, *Human Values*, 3–8, 76–91.

115. Fuchs, *Christian Morality*, 109.

116. Fuchs leaves openings for conversation with Calvinist doctrines of sanctification: the salvific event of conversion does not instantly perfect one's behavior. The struggle against vice continues, and repentance is continually necessary. See John Calvin, *Institutes of the Christian Religion*, vol. 1, trans. Ford Lewis Battles, The Library of Christian Classics, ed. John T. McNeill, v. 20 (Philadelphia: Westminster Press, 1960), 600–9, III.iii.9–15. Luther too advised good works to "reduce the body to subjection and purify it of its evil lusts" (Luther, "Freedom," 68). Yet Fuchs would not agree with Calvin and Luther that one is *decreed* righteous; one is rather actually *made* righteous; and, Fuchs (like Augustine, whom Calvin chides) is reluctant to label the "smoldering cinder of evil" that "remains in a regenerate man" *sin*, unless it turns directly and intentionally against God (Calvin, *Institutes*, 602, III.iii.10).

117. Tronto, *Moral Boundaries*.

118. Fuchs, *Moral Demands*, 44–45.

119. Other objections—that Fuchs at times presents nonhuman nature as an object to be conquered, that he considers the body to be only the condition of human concrete existence, or that his understanding of reason is too narrow—could rightly be countered by the observation that these are oversights in concrete definitions, not formal assumptions, and therefore do not threaten his formal anthropology. Yet it is not clear that new, more adequate definitions would be consistent with Fuchs's transcendental theology.

120. See for instance May, *Moral Absolutes*. Joseph Ratzinger argues against Fuchs that to describe "intrinsic evil" as failure "to do justice to concrete human reality" is "clearly inadequate"; even if given "definite content" such formulas remain "only formal and ultimately say nothing." Ratzinger suggests that there may be rather "an indispensable bedrock of 'deontological' norms." For Ratzinger, then, absolute norms are concrete, not formal. A chief part of Ratzinger's complaint is that Fuchs and others assume too abstract and neutral a concept of reason, but he neither elaborates this criticism nor suggests a more adequate understanding (Ratzinger, "Church's Teaching Authority," 66, n. 13).

121. Rigali, "Uniqueness," 82–84. Rigali argues that Fuchs, by refusing to admit "Christian" to the list of historical and cultural qualifiers that partially determine the method and content of moral thought, has in fact failed to integrate an historical viewpoint thoroughly into his theology. Despite Fuchs's concessions that there are "Christianly human" acts, there is missing from most of his writings "a thematic awareness that the norm of Christian morality is the *Christian* person in history, e.g.,

the late twentieth century western European Roman Catholic"; italics added. A person's religious orientation has, in addition to transcendental significance, meaning as a cultural datum, an element of that person's historical worldview.

122. Ibid., 85.

123. Kenneth R. Himes, "The Contribution of Theology to Catholic Moral Theology," in *Moral Theology: Challenges*, ed. Curran, 66–67. The observation is about McCormick's work, yet it applies even more to Fuchs.

6

Richard A. McCormick and Practical Moral Reason

Richard McCormick and Josef Fuchs represent the same school of moral thought. Fuchs has provided much of the inspiration and theological grounding for McCormick's own practical and methodological work and concurs with him on nearly every concrete application of moral norms, not to mention every debate about their authoritative standing. But there is one significant difference. The motion of Josef Fuchs's corpus has been from fundamental moral theology to practical moral reason, for in his view moral theology's main task is to establish the transcendental ground for the possibility of morality. The motion of McCormick's corpus, on the other hand, has been from practical moral reason to fundamental theology, for from his perspective moral theology's task is to support and develop practical moral reason. McCormick has hammered out the implications of backing norms with values in the process of wrestling with excruciatingly concrete circumstances; he has adjusted his method in light of his practical successes and failures; and he has delved progressively deeper into questions of method and fundamental theology as particular moral issues have required it. This "bottom up" process—reflected in the order of this chapter—reveals out both peaks and fissures in their common landscape that are less visible in Fuchs's top-down approach.

The special benefit and difficulty of examining McCormick is that he is both a transitional figure and a figure in transition. [1] McCormick is a transitional thinker in the sense that he systematically describes and defends a moral tradition in metamorphosis, preserving what is sound in its method and content and yet speaking to contemporary moral sensibilities. [2] Much of his career has been dedicated to redefining issues, clarifying distinctions, refining and regularizing method, and eliminating obscurantism. [3] This conservative presumption makes him a troubleshooting reformer rather than a visionary or a radical. But McCormick also recognizes the revolutionary implications of combining serious, reform-minded casuistry with traditional claims about the perspicuity of natural law.

McCormick is also a figure in transition. His understanding of the Roman Catholic natural law tradition's content, theological ground, and method have undergone important developments at two junctures in his career. The first, to which McCormick himself often refers, was the period following Vatican Council II and the promulgation of *Humanae Vitae;* during this time he ceased merely to defend and apply "prudently and compassionately" Roman Catholic magisterial moral positions, began to explore questions of ecclesiology and method, and developed proportionalism, his hallmark approach to practical moral dilemmas. [4] The second shift, which occurred in the early 1980s, is evident in his more explicitly theological writings on medical and sexual ethics. [5] This later work is cognizant of the link between spirituality and ethics; it also exhibits more systematic efforts to tie moral thought to biblical and theological themes. In what follows, I draw most heavily on the later two periods, in which the themes and tensions implicit in his early work stand out clearly.

PROPORTIONALISM

To understand McCormick is to begin with practical moral reason, the justification and application of moral rules and norms with an eye to determining moral rightness. [6] Although he concurs with Fuchs that moral theology is "to discover the demands of Christian love," [7] for McCormick in practice "moral theology is the scientific study of the behavioral implications of being a Christian, therefore, of the behavioral implications of Christian beliefs about man—his origins, his destiny and his world." McCormick's most widely known contribution to practical moral reason is proportionalism, developed to solve the sorts of dilemmas that arise in a moral system in which norms are unconditionally binding rules and the first task of the moral life is avoiding their transgression.

A classic example is the case of ectopic pregnancy, in which a zygote implants in a woman's fallopian tube. The embryo's normal growth would rupture the tube, causing the embryo's own death but also threatening the woman with death by internal hemorrhage. The only way to save the mother's life is to remove the embryo before rupture occurs. But to remove the embryo is necessarily to cause its death, and to kill an innocent human being is not only to do wrong but to engage in moral evil. What may a doctor do? Moral theologians had presumed that one should refuse to act at all, even if inaction permitted foreseeable harm to occur, when the only means to prevent that harm involved transgressing a moral norm. But tellingly, moral theologians of this century have *not* counseled utter inaction in ectopic pregnancy cases;

rather, in view of the danger to the mother and the embryo's impending death, they have said that the embryo may be removed. Their arguments in favor of this are textbook cases of casuistry: illuminating a difficult case by finding an analogous, more easily solved one. The point of the discussion, it must be noted, is not to *prescribe* intervention but to decide whether intervention is *permissible*, whether it can be seen as an acceptable alternative to the norm that forbids killing.

The traditional escape has been the claim that the decisive factor in judging the morality of the apparently harmful act is the directness or indirectness with which the harm is willed. [8] It matters, in other words, whether the harm is intended or simply foreseen. The British moral theologian Henry Davis held that the intention to remove the section of tube in which the embryo is lodged is merely the intention to excise a dangerously diseased organ and therefore to take lifesaving action; both the death of the embryo inside and the resulting partial sterility (also normally prohibited) are indirectly willed and therefore are morally acceptable side effects of the surgery. But then the question arises why the doctor should not treat the doomed embryo as if it were already dead. Why not simply slice open the tube, "shell out" the nonviable embryo, and repair the tube? This procedure has exactly the same effect on both mother and embryo, except that it does not cause partial sterility and so increases the chance of a later, successful pregnancy. Davis replies that the latter surgery is unacceptable because it involves a moral evil, the *direct* killing of an innocent person; the preservation of fertility, which is a true good, is only an indirect result of the therapy and therefore is not a proper description of the act. For Davis the (prohibited) directness of the intention of death in the second approach depends heavily on the physical directness of the bad effect. If one excises the "diseased" tube, the embryo dies subsequently. If one shells out the embryo, the embryo constitutes the pathology, and its death is the descriptive center of the act. [9]

The example clarifies two points immediately. First, everything depends upon the object, or the boundaries of the action. One could, for instance, accurately call the "shelling" surgery "removing an embryo" and accept the embryo's nearly instantaneous death as an indirect effect. One could also call the removal of the tube—which connects the embryo inside to its sources of nourishment—direct killing. Second, both Davis and McCormick calculate consequences: *not* to perform surgery will result in the death of the embryo and, likely, of the mother. Both believe it permissible to intervene to save the mother through a procedure that inevitably causes the embryo's death. What divides them? Davis skirts the mandate against direct killing by redescribing the act as the removal of a diseased tube in which the embryo happens to reside. McCormick views this as an unhelpfully obscurantist tactic, proof of the unworkability of the criterion of directness. Why not justify the intervention as the least destructive available means of life preservation rather than as clever avoidance of illicit killing? Right away McCormick has a convincing justification for intervention, something Davis lacks. Both therapies result in the woman's life and the embryo's death. What distinguishes them is not the directness of their harm to the embryo but their effect on a condition of further human life, fertility: the good of procreation is better promoted by preservation than by foreclosure of fertility. On this view shelling out the embryo would be not only morally justifiable but—as will become clear below—even morally preferable. [10]

McCormick, and others who distinguish rightness from wrongness in this way, have been dubbed proportionalists. How proportionalism is defined depends upon what is riding on the description. [11] Yet two characteristics are indispensable, each of which should be of interest to feminists and others who connect moral rightness with good consequences. First, all moral judgments involve either implicit (and nearly automatic) or explicit weighing of value and disvalue, most often expressed as good-for or harm-to particular people or humanity in general. [12] These harms and goods and values are variously referred to as nonmoral, premoral, physical, and ontic, to distinguish them from personal moral evil and goodness.

Early in his articulation of the approach McCormick limited the weighing to a single premoral value in each decision: for instance, which of the three approaches—doing nothing, shelling out the embryo, or excising the tube—best advances the single value of human life? [13] But more recently he and others have acknowledged that multiple, incommensurable values must often come into play. [14] This means, second, that one must evaluate concrete circumstances carefully in order to discover precisely which of these values are most at stake and therefore what options are morally permissible. For instance, McCormick believes that the first good at stake in the ectopic pregnancy example is the mother's life; once we have agreed to that, we can discuss what he believes to be the next-important corollary of life preservation, her fertility. The precise shape that the realization of a value will take depends on the description and details of the situation. Thus, like consequentialists, proportionalists are concerned about the likely practical results of actions, and they argue that no action can be judged morally wrong apart from its circumstances and likely results—there are no untransgressable general norms. [15] But proportionalists maintain a connection to the language of deontological norms and absolute rights through *presumptions* against killing innocents, lying, etc.; these actions typically cause such great disvalue—not just materially, but to individual virtue and to community culture—that only very pressing reasons can justify them and only in circumstances in which other weighty values conflict and are at great risk. [16]

McCormick's initial preoccupation with the direct/indirect distinction in this case suggests that even when he challenges the Roman Catholic moral theological tradition, he does so on its terms, fashioning his own moral reflection out of its distinctions and topics. His solution to the dilemma of ectopic pregnancy is clear evidence of his belief that proportionate reason is the mode of traditional Catholic casuistry. He employs old tools designed for avoiding moral evil: the principle of double effect, within which the direct/indirect distinction functions; the distinction between ontic and moral evil; and the conviction that general, objective moral norms stand as universal proscriptions. Here we will investigate them a little more deeply. How is proportionalism continuous with this moral tradition? When McCormick is finished with that tradition, is it in the end still useful and illuminating, or is his account of it transparent for other logics?

McCormick, like Knauer, begins his revisionist project with the theory of double effect, a doctrine that distills general guidelines from Thomas's discussion of self-defensive killing. Suppose, Thomas asked, I am under life-threatening attack. May I kill in self-defense? Thomas believes I may, given the following assumptions and conditions: the desire to preserve my own life is basic, natural, and appropriate; there is no less violent means available; the counterattack itself, and not some subsequent action, stops the attack; and I do not desire the attacker's death. [17] Some of these explanations, of course, are specific to the case. But the moral tradition has drawn more general lessons as well. Grave harms are acceptable as indirect but foreseen effects under the following conditions:

(1) The action is good or indifferent in itself; it is not morally evil. (2) The intention of the agent is upright, that is, the evil effect is sincerely not intended. (3) The evil effect must be equally immediate causally with the good effect, for otherwise it would be a means to the good effect and would be intended. (4) There must be a proportionately grave reason for allowing the evil to occur. [18]

McCormick's proportionalism arose out of a concern to articulate these conditions more precisely. For instance, Thomas assumes that "killing another human being" is not inherently morally evil, but Davis assumes that "killing an embryo" is, so he disqualifies all actions that have embryo killing as their object. McCormick's point is that to begin the investigation with this condition would beg the question, for whether an action is morally evil is exactly what the principle of double effect is meant to establish. [19] This first condition is therefore irrelevant. Second, the distinction between intending a harm and permitting it—between willing harm directly and willing it indirectly—may tell us what the actor intends, but it is not a sufficient criterion of objective moral rightness. [20] Other factors enter the calculus. Besides, he argues, conscious intention is integrated rather than divided; in this sense all foreseen ill effects of an act *are* culpably if regretfully willed and fall properly within its bounds, so that the distinction between direct and indirect willing becomes irrelevant to the judgment of moral rightness. The harm an action produces may simply be justified by the good that it also entails. Third, interpreting equal immediacy temporally misleads; necessity—"this also-harmful action is the only one that can prevent an even graver harm"—is more useful. [21] So, finally, the first three conditions simply restrict the last: what qualifies as a proportionately grave reason?

Two factors must be accounted for. To begin with, it must be determined what sort of harm—or good—is being caused. McCormick brings forward the traditional distinction between premoral or nonmoral (sometimes called ontic or physical) goods and evils on one hand, and moral goods and evils on the other. Premoral goods and evils are benefits and harms to human, often physical, goods, but they are benefits and harms that have not been morally described; they have not yet been labeled right or wrong in the context of circumstances, intentions, and other factors. It is not always right to promote a particular premoral good, and it is not always wrong to cause a particular premoral evil. For example, "killing" is not a full moral description of an act, for death is only a premoral evil. [22] Whether it is morally right depends upon

> the meaning of the action[, which] suggests to us which values (goods) are involved in this or that choice and how they are involved. Knowing this we are positioned to develop a judgment of proportion, namely, a judgment as to whether we are causing harm by performing the action or omitting it. In other words, we are positioned to judge whether the action is describable, all things considered, as an act of beneficence in a conflicting world, or what is the same, whether there is a proportionate reason for performing it even though harm is inevitable. [23]

In a significant departure from early to mid-twentieth-century moral theology, McCormick insists that *inaction* causes harm and therefore is neither passive nor neutral; this judgment anticipates feminist and liberation critiques of "mere" compliance with the status quo.

Further, directly willed premoral evil "is justified. . . . if a genuinely proportionate reason (in the sense stated [below]) is present": [24] "(a) a value at least equal to that sacrificed is at stake; (b) there is no less harmful way of protecting the value here and now; (c) the manner of its protection here and now will not undermine it in the long run." [25] Operating upon a mother suffering from ectopic pregnancy or defending oneself against lethal attack are proportionate life-saving actions. On the other hand, *moral* evil—intentional disproportion—by definition cannot be willed with proportionate reason and therefore cannot be justified by any number of good premoral consequences. [26] Thus bashing over the head someone who is blocking one's view of a movie screen is disproportionate, for human life is too valuable to be squandered for an unobstructed view. Directness and indirectness of intention have nothing to do with these judgments; rather "what was and is decisive is the proportionate reason for acting." [27]

McCormick explicitly connects himself to the moral theological tradition, accepting and painstakingly interpreting its pivotal distinctions and concepts. He also goes to great lengths to demonstrate proportionate reason's origins in the Roman Catholic moral tradition in order to show that, despite the irreducibility of the criterion of proportionate reason, moral norms are both meaningful and indispensable. And McCormick's tendency to organize proportionalism around pursuit of goods rather than around inclinations demonstrates his faithfulness to Thomas's vision. But pedigreed or no, proportionalism wreaks havoc in a system recently accustomed to defining certain sorts of moral acts and their transgression very narrowly. These consequences began to assert themselves above, but they need to be listed explicitly.

First, the move peels a layer off the normative onion, revealing the true meaning of moral wrong to be not disobedience but disproportion: choice, in a complex, concrete situation, to realize a then-trivial value at the expense of a then-important one. The murderous moviegoer is an extreme example. Yet for McCormick value is not only the criterion of immediate moral judgment but, as for Fuchs, the principle of casuistic continuity in a history of dynamic moral norms. Formal norms "enshrine a value without stating concretely or materially what acts embody this value or attack it"; material norms are "contractions of these formal norms to concrete pieces of human conduct," or "statements about value or disvalue," devised in particular historical circumstances. [28] Their form—a "time-conditioned formulation"—merely expresses their content—the "enduring tradition"—and must not be identified

with the latter. [29] This distinction opens the door to development of a hermeneutic of norms in which value is the interpretive criterion.

For instance, McCormick at first explicates and defends the Roman
Catholic church's prohibition of contraception on two assumptions. First,
"total self-giving" (which implies openness to procreation, one of the defining
goods of intercourse) is *the* value at stake in contraception: the ban on
contraception safeguards "the completeness of self-giving. . . . [ensuring] the
integrity of the expression of love and union in one flesh by proscribing
possible counterfeits." [30] Second, nothing can justify the sacrifice of this value.
Reversing his proscription of contraception after the promulgation of *Humanae Vitae*, McCormick implies that his original position was off the mark—
not because it protected an unworthy value, but because it was blind to the
complex of other human values also on the table in sexual relationships:

> Catholic tradition. . . . has insisted that before an action can be branded
> as a *moral* evil, a closer look is demanded. This closer look will reveal
> that, at root, our tradition has been saying that the evils associated with
> human action are *moral* evils precisely in so far as they lack proportionate
> justification. . . . Why can there not be a reason for "taking" the fecundity
> of the sexual act, or even the faculty, at times? . . . To say anything else
> is to say that integral intercourse is in all conceivable situations of
> conflict the highest value, a thing we will not say of human life itself. [31]

Therefore McCormick's challenge to any norm is the question whether it
continues to identify, protect, and promote important values without compromising others inappropriately. Continuously cherished norms are signs not
of the permanence of their formulation but of the significance of "some
particular piece of human conduct." [32] But if a norm is really a cipher—a
modestly useful shorthand for a means of protecting value—then one wonders
why we need to devote so much energy to determining whether we adhere
to them.

Second, the shift to values implied in McCormick's position on ectopic
pregnancy reveals the extent to which his work incorporates a judgment that
moral theology's primary task is no longer either retrospective judgment of
a penitent's past behavior or preoccupation with the "practical problems and
problem-solving" associated with "an ethics of minimal duty." Moral theology
should also be prospective and "aspirational," issuing invitations as well as
obligations: what ideals ought *I*, in Christian love, to *pursue*, and what are
the concrete demands of love on me here and now? How can I embody
moral goodness? [33]

Proportionalism may be seen as an experiment in this new perspective: what would happen if, in situations where harm seems inevitable, one rooted practical moral reason in pursuit of values or goods rather than almost solely in avoidance of evils? As we will see, this transformation rests upon McCormick's anthropology: human beings are perfected in the pursuit and realization of values, not in conformity to predetermined concrete patterns of behavior. [34] This leads in some cases to a radical change of rhetoric: from (on one hand) permission to cause premoral evil to (on the other hand) the question "whether this choice is in *the best possible service of all the values* in the tragic and difficult conflict." [35] But these justifications of questionable acts—"do not directly will evil"—and maximization of value—"seek the greatest good or least evil"—are not synonymous materially or methodologically. As any parent knows, the conversion from a rhetoric of restraining vice to a rhetoric of enabling virtue is a conversion not only of form but of content, habit, timing, and psychology. To prescribe a similar conversion for moral theology is to initiate an equally great transformation.

Third is the effect upon moral theology of juggling incommensurate values. Laying out this point narratively also illustrates nicely McCormick's character as an adjuster, a fixer, a responder-to-critics, a person who returns frequently to the same question until he is satisfied with his answer. The story begins with McCormick's gradual realization that if proportionalism were limited to consideration of the short-term realization of a single value, it would have extremely limited usefulness. Yet admitting many values and considering longer chains of consequences "sentence[s] the discipline to an endless quest for method and content," [36] for it is now necessary to show, in each situation, whether existing norms promote particular real values properly. At worst, as McCormick's critics realized early, opening the door unconditionally to multiple values would lead to a raw consequentialism that would require impractical calculations of an act's eventual effect on infinitely many values—not to mention eroding human rights by removing all absolute protections of human dignity. [37] Does one escape the obligation to consider infinite consequences only by the obligation to avoid the proportionately greater evil of moral paralysis? Clearly the list of morally significant, right- or wrong-making consequences must somehow be limited. Communal criteria based in wisdom—"what a reasonable person would consider to be the meaning or scope of an action"—would likely come into play, as would the recognition that symbolic and expressive actions can be vehicles of premoral evil, but these additions do not solve the theoretical problem. [38]

Awareness of these complications may have contributed to McCormick's simultaneous resistance to and acknowledgment of the need to weigh incommensurables. In places he does his best to narrow the question to one value. His criticism of Grisez's positions on ectopic pregnancy and therapeutic abortion suggests that in these cases a single weighty value is at stake: human life. [39] Likewise, rules against targeting non-combatants in warfare in order to end a present conflict are based in the prudential, teleological judgment that targeting civilians would ultimately harm a single encompassing value, just peace, even if it ended the immediate conflict. [40] But McCormick himself demonstrates, implicitly and explicitly, that the "umbrella values" of human life and just peace shelter many discrete, incommensurable, but interdependent values. For example, the case of ectopic pregnancy really presents at least three practically connected, concrete incarnations of value: the life of a particular child, who cannot be saved; the life of a particular woman, who can be; and future fertility and new children. Likewise, just peace is composed of human life and particular social goods; in practice, in wartime, we must often weigh specific, incommensurable, interdependent harms and benefits against each other. [41] But this admission raises a further question: lacking a medium of exchange among these goods, do we not at least need a sense of their nature and relative importance?

McCormick again obliges, arguing that human beings have, *prior* to acculturation, basic inclinations that tell us "what are the goods or values man [sic] can seek." These inclinations, which closely mirror Thomas's inclinations, are "the values that define our flourishing" concretely, each of which is "equally underived and irreducibly attractive" and "has self-evident appeal as a participation in the unconditioned Good we call God": [42]

> the tendency to preserve life; the tendency to mate and raise children[;] the tendency to seek out other persons and obtain their approval— friendship; the tendency to use intelligence in guiding action; the tendency to develop skills and exercise them in play and the fine arts. In these inclinations our intelligence spontaneously and without reflection grasps the possibilities to which they point, and prescribes them. Thus we form naturally and without reflection the basic principles of practical or moral reasoning. [43]

Moral rightness consists in openness to these basic values, and love of God consists in their realization. [44]

But what constitutes openness to values in our everyday lives depends upon whether those values are practically and theoretically compatible. McCormick holds that they can conflict. How to decide which takes precedence? To argue that any value is absolutely greater than another is to contradict

McCormick's claims about their basic character as well as to foreclose flexibility; for if one always trumps the others, moral discernment amounts to finding the single acceptable action. [45] On the other hand, refusal ever to rank one above another at times consigns moral argument to the insoluble and paralyzing conundrum of the irresistible force and the immovable object. McCormick increasingly shows himself to be blazing a third trail. Value hierarchies exist, but they vary from case to case. One must determine what value is most at stake *in the particular situation one faces.* In some cases, most often at the beginning and end of life, continuing human biological life may not take precedence. [46] If in doubt about which value to pursue, one must remember that all fall under the larger umbrella of the good of the human person, integrally and adequately considered. This holistic end keeps the component values in perspective. Again, the person is the measure of the act. [47]

A fourth transformation is McCormick's dissociation of ontic from moral evil. Certainly Roman Catholic moral theology has never systematically *identified* ontic with moral evil; it has simply established such a close link between them that it becomes impossible to imagine a rational person committing certain ontic evils without moral evil. Richard McCormick has simply followed Josef Fuchs in weakening the connection, highlighting and augmenting the factors that intervene between judgments of grave ontic evil and a verdict of subjective moral evil.

Placing value at the center of the discussion complicates matters in a fifth important way. When ethics is a matter of interpreting rules and morality is a matter of following them, the hierarchy of rules itself mediates conflicts among goods. As soon as morality becomes a matter of the pursuit and realization of value, these conflicts move into the spotlight. We become keenly aware that we cannot realize all values simultaneously and that the trade-offs we make are often not trivial. Anticipating Lisa Cahill's and Martha Nussbaum's recent accounts of right action, McCormick declares that a "good act" is "an act of beneficence in a *conflicting* world." [48]

McCormick's explanation of the origins of these conflicts has been inconsistent; "Ambiguity in Moral Choice" implies that conflict among values is due entirely to imperfection and sin, [49] but elsewhere he intimates that conflict among goods is simply a fact of human finitude and historicity. [50] His most recent work suggests that both are true. Yet far more significant to McCormick than the conflict's origin are its practical consequences for the moral life: acting for one concrete good in fact forecloses, or sacrifices, others. [51] We must learn to live with pursuing one good at the expense of others. Trivially, one cannot attend two weddings in different cities on the same day; more gravely, one may have to choose between taking a low-wage job that entails sending one's children to attend a questionable daycare facility for sixty hours per week and staying at home with them and thereby risking loss of welfare benefits. Or again, the good of the integral whole—be it the person, group, or society—may require that some part suffer a real disvalue; the amputation of a diseased limb is a common example. [52] "Good" actions are not "perfect," only "among the best possible." We should anticipate continual conflict among values, expect to feel regret about even our best decisions, expect to mourn unrealized opportunities, and assume that no option will fulfill all legitimate needs.

Even more arresting, however, may be a sixth factor: among the circumstances that help us to determine, in concrete situations, which values are at stake and what can be required of actors are the sinfulness and developmental imperfection of the moral subject. According to McCormick, the principle of double effect, the precursor of proportionalism, properly applies also to circumstances in which "the preference of a good for or in another at the cost of that good in or for myself should not, in view of human weakness and immaturity, be demanded." [53] McCormick, echoing an older pastoral insight, interprets this as a judgment that a demand for absolute and constant self-sacrifice is so harsh as to drive the sinful or immature Christian from God and so produces a moral evil graver than proportionately justifiable (albeit less than ideal) self-consideration. [54] By the late 1980s he had transformed this criterion from permission to choose between realizing a single value in myself or promoting it in another to the claim that no "ought" binds absolutely where capacity is lacking. For instance, partners' complete inability to resuscitate a dead marriage—which presumably has fallen apart thanks to their own imperfection—frees them from absolute obligation for that marriage and should not stand in the way of their entering new marriages—although presumably after having tried to overcome the faults that led to the demise of the first. [55] McCormick sometimes waffles on whether the criterion of capacity alters objective norms or simply excuses individuals from them; he also gives too little attention to the fact that when we try to apply these criteria to ourselves the line between competent exercise of conscience and self-deception often disappears. For example, the excuse "I just couldn't help myself" must not earn the murdering moviegoer a pastoral adaptation of the commandment against killing; all arguments for pastoral adaptations in concrete situations must demonstrate voluntareity and respect for proportion. Yet despite these difficulties, McCormick's approach acknowledges an important point: the "conflicting world" that conditions beneficent actions encompasses moral and psychological factors *within* the actor as well as circumstances *outside* her.

Taken together, these shifts remind us that the real significance of McCormick's proportionalism is his tentative yet perceptible step toward the transformation—or perhaps even the dissolution—of moral norms. This step is clearest in the essays on particular moral issues in the second half of *The Critical Calling*, especially his essay on teenaged sexuality. At first "a moral statement . . . is a statement of the rightness or wrongness of human actions," but a second, novel element works a change of meaning: "It is a statement embodying the good and inviting to its realization. In this sense it is normative, that is, we all *ought* to try to make our conduct a reflection of the values incorporated in such statements or principles." [56]

What does this mean in the concrete? McCormick begins the reflective part of his article with a personalist, nearly sacramental meditation on monogamous marriage as "the best chance we have to humanize our sexuality, because it is the best chance to develop friendship." Then—apologetically, because "descriptive language . . . *proves* nothing"—he reflects,

> All this means that sexual expression, to have *full* human meaning, to be nourishing and promotive of our personhood, to avoid being trivialized, is not just the present moment. It is both affirmation and promise. As language it celebrates the past and guarantees the future. It is the past and future compressed into the present. It is this past and future which offers us present quality. It is the friendship of the past and future which surrounds sex with loyalty, constancy, fidelity and allows it to speak a fully human language. Sex and eros are fleeting, fickle, and frustrative unless they are supported by *philia*, friendship— the friendship of a permanent covenant. [57]

This description of the sexual ideal provides new grounds for the traditional norm on premarital sex: "intercourse that is genuinely *premarital* is always missing something—or in normative terms, is morally wrong, is to be avoided." [58] The terms "right" and "wrong" remain, but the content, significance, and ground of the norm have changed. The content of the norm is covenanted friendship; the significance is an ideal to be realized (less than full realization is "missing something," not "turning against God"); and the ground is symbolic and personalistic. In this new language of ideals, unions that are not covenants—just as marriages that lack friendship—*fall short* rather than *fail altogether*.

The vision of norm as ideal to be realized pops up—sometimes ambivalently—elsewhere in the volume: for instance, "'abortion is morally wrong' contains the implicit invitation or mandate [which?] to avoid this action in our personal lives and to create a world wherein it is no longer a tragic necessity." [59] The logical conclusion is that, when it is a "tragic necessity," abortion is only imperfect rather than absolutely wrong. Similarly, the indissolubility of marriage is not a metaphysical fact but a "moral ought," an obligation to strengthen, support, and if necessary resuscitate a marriage—with the understanding that it may die despite these efforts. [60] A covenant is not an irrevocable contract. And as McCormick has long held in arguments on contraception, the double values of unity and procreativity are to be realized in relationships rather than acts, and their twin realization is an ideal rather than a mandate. [61] Significantly, McCormick also implies that many of these "oughts" extend to family and society: we all "ought" to encourage covenanted sex, support marriages, create conditions in which unwanted pregnancies occur less often and in which unexpected parenthood does not deepen poverty. We ought, in other words, to ameliorate the conditions that make it hard for others to realize ideals.

Yet glaring contradictions in his treatment of homosexuality confirm the impression that McCormick does not subject all norms to these innovations equally. McCormick clearly believes that homosexuality is neither a mere cultural construct nor a moral evil [62] but a simple fact of created human existence; decisions to enter homosexual relationship often are not wrong and in fact deserve respect. [63] Yet surprisingly—especially so given his excursus on sexuality and friendship—McCormick does not dispute the assertion that homosexual genital acts are "incomplete, flawed and disordered," objectively unjustifiable according to valid moral norms. He concludes, "One can say that homogenital acts always depart from the ideal or the normative. I would have little, indeed no, problem with that. But why not leave it at that? To work back from that tenet to the assertion that the orientation is disordered is neither necessary (to support of the tenet) nor pastorally helpful." [64] This would seem to have been the perfect opportunity to exercise casuistry, to alter either sexual norms or their standard interpretation: the act is not wrong, the orientation is not wrong, so the norm of heterosexual monogamy must need revision. Yet he permits his conviction that homosexuality is not morally aberrant no critical leverage against the ideal of married heterosexual intimacy, even though he has substantially reinterpreted—even relaxed—the latter norm under other pressures. The only consistent way to retain heterosexual intimacy as a norm, then, is to think of it as only a *statistical* norm, an "average" or "mode." But McCormick clearly persists in seeing homogenital relationships as falling short of a *moral* ideal. Mandate has not given way to invitation.

Thus the new shoes still pinch. As William George has pointed out, the same articles in which McCormick seems to transform the meanings of norms reveal his refusal to let go of traditional moral absolutes. [65] McCormick persists in distinguishing general principles from concrete applications, ideals from acceptable realizations, constant substance from changeable form, specific from individual rectitude, and objective requirements from pastoral adaptations, implying that the first member of each pair is higher, better, or more stable than the latter. McCormick's "pastoral" adaptations of general norms have the ambiguous character of being acceptable as perhaps the best possible solution to a problem but still less than fully moral; not "justifiable" by any but the practitioner's own conscience; objectively wrong by the usual measures because they leave the norm itself unchallenged. This contradicts McCormick's insistence that objectively right action is beneficent action in complex circumstances; calls in question the theoretical possibility of using new evidence to transform norms; and suggests that perhaps he has not yet found a way to articulate a rationale for general, universal ideals without toting along language of permission, exception, and transgression.

The roots of this ambivalence may well be political; McCormick knows that reformers stand a better chance than radicals of altering the concrete applications of norms in awkward or oppressive cases. Aware that most members of the Roman Catholic church hierarchy hold many traditional moral norms to be unalterable, he has adopted the strategy of pledging allegiance to these norms but, as in the case of married versus homosexual love-making, arguing painstakingly for the acceptability in particular circumstances of many acts the norms had been assumed to proscribe. The "proportionate, but not ideal" label that results has the practical effect of approving the action without altering the content of the troublesome norm.[66]

But despite the fact that McCormick does not resolve the tension between his new aspirational mandate and the old distinctions with which he attempts to pursue it, the magnitude of the methodological implications of his change in attitude cannot be overestimated. To pursue a value or embody an ideal is to ask different questions than one asks when one intends above all to avoid grave error, and willingness to fit some norms to persons and situations bespeaks a different attitude than willingness only to "excuse" or "dispose" from moral norms.

THEOLOGICAL ANTHROPOLOGY AND THE NATURAL LAW

Like others who fall under the umbrella of proportionalist moral thought described below, McCormick has until recently taken morality's divine ground, and its implications for human reason, largely for granted in his writing on morals. [67] The task here is to distill the anthropological points from the methodological discussion.

McCormick assumes a traditional *exitus-reditus* theology: human beings are sent out from God in creation, and the Christian life is the journey back to God. Within that structure he makes the following claims. Human beings are ontologically good, and their goodness carries a message; they are both work and word of God. The "is" of human being contains the "ought" of divinely determined human goals: God challenges the human person to "become what thou art," to work toward her own inbuilt end. Created humanity— dynamic, rational, and moral—*is* the natural moral law: "man's being as implying his becoming," the inbuilt ordering of the human person toward his or her perfection. [68] As in Thomas and Fuchs, the order of redemption perfects the order of creation: natural law is an interior principle coherent and often synonymous with the law of the new covenant and the law of Christ. [69]

Natural law's ontological, anthropological basis thus encompasses much more than physical nature. People are divinely mandated to organize and create in the world in a way that corresponds to a created order that reason perceives. In addition, as in McCormick's mentor Fuchs, human persons exercise a fundamental option, a basic existential commitment for or against human goods and values. [70] Not surprisingly, then, because basic values are inherently consistent with and conducive to attainment of the ultimate value or good, human perfection—in traditional terms, virtue—is *good pursuit of good or value*. [71] In turn, humanity's ground in God guarantees the unity, cooperation, coherence, and relative stability of human values, of goods-for-human being. Finally, human beings and institutions have an eschatological reference. They are in some sense—apparently partly for developmental reasons, although sin certainly plays a role—imperfect but improving. [72] As we have seen, McCormick takes the radical normative implications of this claim seriously.

But anthropology provides not only an ontological basis for practical moral reason but a set of criteria for its results, guides for human behavior that can be developed from the proximate goods that the inbuilt tendency toward God entails. Thus anthropology gives natural law a positive content: through the basic inclinations it points out human goods for which provision must be made. Yet it does not and cannot specify the precise shape this provision must take. For instance, natural law points out our need for government and dictates that whatever government is formed must not violate certain human values, but it does not declare that a representative democracy is universally the only proper government. [73]

As we have seen, in any concrete discernment the overarching criterion is the good of "the human person integrally and adequately considered." [74] The dimensions of this whole have emerged gradually over the course of McCormick's career. Implicit in his early moral writings is a belief that both biological nature and human relationship are permanent conditions of human existence and constitute values to be protected. We can discern this from his conviction that acts have both "specific" features—nearly always mechanical or physical descriptions or juridical states, like marriage—and "individual" aspects—among others, the subject's particular goals, circumstances, and relationships. [75] This distinction lays the groundwork for McCormick's category of premoral evil, a harm at the specific (often physical) level whose moral status depends partly upon whether it also harms interpersonal values. [76]

Yet specific and individual features of acts—loosely corresponding to physical and interpersonal integrity—proved to be inadequate ethical criteria, prompting McCormick to expand his anthropology. As mentioned above, human beings are reasonable; they have the capacity to act for ends. In addition, especially in sexual ethics, psychological health must be weighed alongside the more traditional value of physical integrity. [77] The same is true for sociality, which McCormick interprets as the capacity for interpersonal relationship. In his later writings, this capacity for relationship becomes, alongside reason, one of the defining characteristics of meaningful human life. [78] Finally, although the essential features of human being may be constant, human experience is inherently historical, and therefore human *knowledge* about human being is changing. In other words, the anthropology upon which both the content and the method of moral thought depend is in flux. [79]

More recently, McCormick has experimented with arranging these elements more formally and intentionally. We have already discussed his inventory of basic values and its resemblance to John Finnis's list. He has also appropriated Louis Janssens's eight aspects of human being. According to Janssens, Vatican Council II's "human person integrally and adequately considered" is a conscious and free subject; a bodily subject; a part of the material or natural world; an interdependent and interpersonal being; a social or institutional being; a religious being; and an historical being. In addition, "human persons, while unique and original, are fundamentally equal." [80] This integral description of the human person is the measuring rod for person-centered moral judgment: "Actions that promote the person adequately considered in this way are morally right; those that attack or undermine the person are morally wrong." [81] Yet it is not clear in either Janssens's article or McCormick's discussion of it precisely how these dimensions are derived, how they function as norms, and what relationship they bear to the basic values whose protection McCormick also considers to be a criterion of right behavior. [82] Reason transcends and orders these other dimensions, without apparently being affected by them; the aspects of human being primarily measure the goodness of actions rather than the adequacy of ethical method. For example, although his more recent writings soften the distinction between reason and other dimensions of human being, human historicity and the capacity for human relationship are still among the factors to be weighed by moral reason rather than among the determinants of that reason's structure. Thus in this sense McCormick's expanded anthropology, despite its radical implications for the content and explication of moral norms, embroiders on traditional natural law anthropology rather than completely overhauling it.

For McCormick is interested in natural law mainly as it explains and validates anthropology's function as source of moral norms. What distinguishes McCormick's work is the unusual degree to which he permits his anthropological commitments to moral development and to historicity to transform the meaning of moral norms. Yet, as we have also seen, he is careful not to step too far outside the bounds of traditional ecclesiastical moral dictates. This leads to the next question: what relative authoritative weight do ecclesiastical moral charism and tough but compassionate reasoning about human being and action possess? What is the church's role as moral teacher?

TRUTH, AUTHORITY, AND INTERPRETATION

Like the feminist thinkers discussed in chapters 1 and 4, McCormick is profoundly aware of the connections between changes in the significance and application of moral norms and shifts in the status of moral authority, institutional and otherwise. The challenge in the Roman Catholic context is reconciling the conviction that the Holy Spirit guarantees the correctness of the church hierarchy's moral teachings with McCormick's belief that all moral judgments—even the hierarchy's—are the products of practical reason and so answerable to all the criteria elaborated in this chapter. For

> An ethics that takes the Incarnation seriously will be the very last to abandon moral reasoning and argument; for the Incarnation, no matter what the depth of its mystery, was, as Vatican II repeatedly noted, an affirmation of the human and its goodness. And this "human," however non-discursive it may be in our future life, is one that presently builds its moral norms, understands exceptions to them, and communicates them through a difficult discursive process known as moral analysis. [83]

Reclaimers of natural law, and all religious feminists, must inquire carefully into McCormick's understanding of the connection between practical reason and ecclesiastical charism. How is the meaning of institutional authority transformed by its accountability to practical reason? [84] How does McCormick solve the conflict between the hierarchical and egalitarian impulses of his tradition?

McCormick's conception of the relationship between rational and institutional authority in ethics rests upon the anthropological conviction that an ontological unity—a common ground and end—underlies human reality. Differing normative descriptions of human being, expressions of truth, and systems of morality are plural only in form, not in substance. [85] As forms intended to reflect this substantive, objective moral order, moral norms are limited truth-claims. [86] But the idea of a moral norm as a concrete, particular expression of objective truth is not necessarily consistent with the idea of a universal authoritative moral teacher. In the Roman Catholic understanding, the magisterium—the hierarchical church in its teaching function—is the repository of a special charism by virtue of which it is the keeper of both doctrinal and moral truth and institutional order. Any self-consciously Roman Catholic ethic, of course, must carefully work out the connections and distinctions between these two sorts of authority, but the project has important implications for relationship between institutional power and truth generally. McCormick diffuses the conflict in two ways. First, he ties ecclesiastical authority to truth in much the same way that Thomas ties civil authority to justice. Second, he links truth to the discipline and practical advantages that position certain people to attain it. Truth—through reason—is the medium of the charism.

How does he arrive at this claim? Given that truth-claims, in moral theology as elsewhere, must be verifiable—it must be possible to determine whether a competent person has reasoned soundly from appropriate premises—if norms proposed by the magisterium bind morally, they bind in their own right, because of their objective truth, regardless of magisterial juridical privilege. Or better, the juridical mandate of the magisterium depends upon its truth-discerning capacity. [87] Yet McCormick does not mean to be a rationalist, for inspiration is not reducible to competent moral reasoning. [88] Rather, he seeks a middle way: [89] magisterial authority best fulfills its office when it permits the Spirit of wisdom to operate freely—that is, when it welcomes and considers all the evidence. This requires collegial attitudes and practices, openness to both old and new information, and dedication to thorough analysis—in short, the traditional attitude of docility, one of the parts of prudence. Thus for McCormick genuine magisterial authority in morals is based not in the independent authority of a mysterious charism but in a *prudential* judgment: hierarchs are institutionally better placed than anyone else to perform these tasks and therefore are best able, when they are disposed to do so, to make room for the Spirit. Where such conditions for reason go, the Spirit follows. [90] Himes summarizes:

> Bishops by virtue of their office and not their scholarly credentials or personal qualities are afforded the best opportunity to gather the church's wisdom. If they merely perform their job well as pastors of the local church and collegial pastors of the universal church the hierarchy has a special advantage through their openness to the Holy Spirit present and active throughout the church. In short, the faithful execution of the responsibilities of episcopal office places the hierarchy in an advantageous position to make judgments assisted by the Holy Spirit. [91]

Such judgments will be marked by tight, convincing arguments. Says McCormick baldly, "one may legitimately expect that this 'light of the Holy Spirit' will manifest itself concretely in the 'way the question itself is handled. That means in the solid presentation of proofs from human experience and with good arguments.'" [92] By implication, then, bad arguments, contrary experiences, and erosion of confidence in magisterial teaching raise questions about the magisterium's openness to the Spirit. Conversely, the Spirit's operation is inhibited to the degree that the gathering or assessing of evidence—including that which emerges from the wider church's response to proposed norms— is foreclosed; [93] in these cases, conclusions are suspect, and error can occur. [94]

But if magisterial teaching is only as good as its reasons, the ultimately binding moral authority is a well-informed, critical conscience. Responsible acceptance of a norm that has been presented as truthful—as corresponding to the objective moral order rooted in human being—involves more than "immediate, unquestioning assent"; it requires a stance of sympathetic "docility and deference" from which the thinker gathers evidence and arguments that transform the norm from a formal or abstract rule to a concrete, textured guide backed by historical, theological, philosophical, scientific, and other claims. [95] In this process of conscientious appropriation, sympathetic, competent reasoners may also find logical errors or other deficiencies—implicit and explicit—in norms. If so, their responsibility to truth and conscience obliges them to reject it—that is, dissent from it. Dissent—in this primary sense of conscientious disagreement, not the secondary sense of organized protest— is thus "the terminus of an open, arduous and docile attempt to understand and appropriate authentic teaching," a result of "the human process of growth in understanding." [96] Dissent is a judgment that the "form" of a given norm expresses the substance of moral truth inauthentically. [97] Because dissent thus serves the same truth that ecclesiastical authority also serves and from which it gains its power to set norms, dissent does not undermine or deny genuine ecclesiastical authority in morals. In fact, because *widespread* dissent among well-informed, competent persons casts considerable doubt on the quality of reasoning behind a proposed norm, the dissenting opinion deserves to be considered by the proposing authority and may also be weighed in personal conscience formation. [98] If this is a prudential claim it has a theological ground: human reason is God-given and universal, and arbitrarily cutting any group or individual out of the conversation would limit reason's activity. [99]

Yet legitimate, reasoned dissent is not the only qualifier of magisterial teaching. Changes in the official Vatican approach to some sorts of moral questions, as well as in its formulation of norms, set historical precedents for future change. [100] Also, moral norms are not at the core of the deposit of faith but are practical applications of it to specific, shifting, widely varying situations. Not only, as in Fuchs, is unanimity in (practical) moral matters less relevant to salvation than is unity in (speculative) matters of doctrine, but

> our formulations of behavioral norms are only more or less adequate, and for this reason are inherently revisable. The fact that some theological formulations have been thought useful by the magisterium of the Church does not change this state of affairs. Historical consciousness has made us freshly aware of the fact that it is our onerous theological task to continue to test the validity of theological formulations, even some very hallowed ones. If we do not, we become imprisoned by words and commit the ever fresh *magnalia Dei* to unwarranted risks. [101]

In addition, like human beings themselves, "the Church is a tentative and unfinished reality. It is *in via*. A fortiori, its moral and ethical judgments are always *in via* and share the messy, unfinished, and perfectible character of the Church itself." [102] Thus changes in ecclesiastical norms may be not merely translations but also true corrections or movements toward eschatological perfection. Finally, as we have noted, McCormick's systematic adherence to a version of probabilism dictates that widespread, articulate dissent against moral norms is important evidence in favor of the argument for their continual reformulation and ought, ideally, to be accounted for procedurally (in ecclesiastical reflection) and not merely methodologically (in individual discernment). [103] These varied warrants—methodological, eschatological, and procedural—combine with McCormick's historicism to qualify further the claims of magisterial charism.

Three difficulties arise from this theology of charism. First, despite McCormick's intentions to avoid rationalism, charism seems reducible to reason. That reason is not univocal is unproblematic unless one expects a single, clear, once-for-all answer; the greater loss may be the quelling of magisterial prophecy, which while frequently "unreasonable" in the same sense as McCormick's meditation on sexuality, and seldom directly translatable to public policy, can often speak truth more arrestingly way in compromised situations. Second, McCormick's vision of moral teaching "in via" introduces a new hermeneutic theory. In his most characteristic, simply historical hermeneutic, the church constantly adapts norms to changing times in order to protect perduring values. But this second, eschatological theory contradicts the first, implying that the church grows ever closer to adequate, objective moral truth as it approaches its goal in God. [104] The third difficulty is one that applies to Fuchs as well: in the summer of 1998, a progression of ecclesiastical documents intended to counter the traditional assumption and proportionalist proposition that matters of morals are removed from the core of theological teaching culminated in the apostolic letter *Ad Tuendam Fidem*. This letter altered canon law to declare that all definitive statements of the magisterium "concerning the doctrine of the *faith or morals,* that is, each and every proposition required for the sacred preservation and faithful explanation of the same deposit of faith, must also be firmly embraced and maintained." [105] McCormick's likely theoretical answer to this obstacle would be that most teachings on morals are not relevant to the explanation and preservation of the deposit of faith; whether this argument will be accepted in practice remains to be seen. Yet despite these unresolved difficulties we can take from McCormick's reflections one important point: magisterial charism operates through and is confirmed in responsible, consultative moral reasoning, so that moral truth is corporately discerned rather than simply divinely revealed. If so, then, what is the significance of Christian faith to moral discernment?

FAITH AND RELIGION VERSUS MORALITY AND REASON

Like his method, McCormick's conception of the connections between faith and moral reason is in flux. On one hand, he has held the classical position that the methods and conclusions, if not all of the presuppositions, of good moral theology and good secular ethics are identical; his whole intention is to bring structure and rigor to a method of reason that purports to apply universally. On the other hand, his writing of the past fifteen years increasingly suggests that Christians may have something uniquely valuable to contribute to public moral debate after all. In neither case does he tackle the postmodern suggestion that there is no permanent, common standard for secular moral debate, but his evolving vision of particularity does nicely set him up to contribute to a self-consciously pluralistic public discussion.

McCormick accomplishes his alignment with traditional interpreters by carving the "religion-morality" discussion into quadrants. [106] The first, essential human ethics, is the realm of concrete universal norms:

> At this level it has been a Catholic Christian conviction at least since the time of Thomas Aquinas that revelation and the faith experience originate no new concrete moral demands that are in principle unavailable to human insight and reasoning.
>
> This means that there is a *material* identity between Christian moral demands and those perceivable by reason. Whatever is distinct about Christian morality is found essentially in the style of life, the manner of accomplishing the moral tasks common to all men, not in the tasks themselves. Christian morality is, in its concreteness and materiality, *human* morality. [107]

Thus objective moral norms in the strict sense, as well as autonomous ethics, inhabit this level alone. [108] Because neither revelation nor the peculiar outlook of faith provides norms that cannot also be reached through reason, McCormick believes that religious conviction has no influence on moral content at this stage; all of its reflections are fair entries in public moral debate. Yet essential human ethics is only the first stage in moral reflection, [109] a preliminary screening out of actions that impermissibly harm basic human goods, a process of ethical discernment that normally leaves us with several ostensibly acceptable alternatives among whose relative virtues it cannot judge.

If the first quadrant answers the question, What may *human beings* do? the second quadrant responds to the query, What must *I* do? The realm of existential human ethics deals with obligations—goods to be realized—that devolve on individuals as individuals. [110] Here we can feel the influence of Fuchs's beliefs in conscience and concrete objectivity. A person's special circumstances, gifts, and aspirations—including her own hierarchy of values— enter ethics at this level. This confluence of other factors yields variety in moral decisions.

Third is essential Christian ethics, which includes general obligations that fall on one as a member of a Christian community: tithing, worship, prayer, other stewardship, and possibly agreement to abide within a particular institutional structure. Although the earlier rendition of this level, like essential human ethics, simply set out the basic requirements of life in a particular Christian community, McCormick's more recent version has a more aspirational flavor. [111] In either event, a peculiarly Christian outlook *does* yield norms unavailable and irrelevant to others outside the community of faith, although the claims these norms entail are perfectly consistent with essential human morality.

Finally, McCormick argues for existential Christian ethics: Christianity's demands upon individuals, with consideration for their particular gifts and circumstances. Like existential human ethics, existential Christian ethics is aspirational—if uniquely concerned with the prayerful selection and pursuit of ideals—rather than minimalistic or conventional. Institutional religious vocation also belongs here, along with many other life-shaping commitments.

In the end, then, essential and existential Christian ethics are what James Gustafson would call true "remainder" ethics; that is, they contain obligations that are incumbent upon Christians over and above those that bind humanity generally. [112] These levels of ethics further narrow the options that the essential human level deems acceptable, but they do not venture outside the latter list of possibilities. No Kierkegaardian Abraham is possible here. As in Fuchs, a *truly* exceptional or "unreasonable" divine commandment would contradict God's intentions for human reason. [113]

For the Christian worldview is neither irrational nor separatist. [114] Faith marks the process of moral reasoning simply by illuminating the knowledge available to all. Not only can the data, insights, and conclusions of moral thought at the essential human level be had from secular sources, but because the sources of faith do not "provide direct answers" to practical questions of means, methods, and applications, human practical reason must work out precisely what it might mean, for example, to respect and nurture God's creation or to love one's neighbor. [115] True to the natural law tradition, McCormick's Christian morality makes common cause with secular morality against amorality.

Be that as it may, McCormick also signals that in practice Christians do in fact have something unique to say at the essential human level. To begin with, McCormick's claim that religiosity is a basic inclination—to him, as to Thomas, a matter of essential human ethics—may be self-evident only to a religious person. Thus this stage is not impermeable to religious insight after all. Second, even at this basic level,

> a person within the Christian community has access to a *privileged articulation*, in objective form, of this experience of subjectivity [human

ethical self-understanding]. Precisely because the resources of Scripture, dogma and the Christian life ("the storied community") are the *fullest available objectifications* of the common human experience, "the articulation of man's image of his moral good that is possible within historical Christian communities remains privileged in its access to enlarged perspectives on man." [116]

The Christian perspective is quintessentially human; the Christian thinker has an "inside line" on the human condition; the Christian story "profoundly stamps" moral theologians and their analyses and judgments; [117] the Christian tradition contributes "perspectives, themes, and insights associated with the story, that aid us to construe the world." [118]

McCormick's most recent work gives us a sense of the *de facto* power of this claim. It is profoundly infused with a sense that the "secular" world, out of touch with the precepts of essential human reason, is in fact straying dangerously from the path, cannot be trusted to support human dignity and values, and cannot recover equilibrium on its own. [119] For example, the brand of secular reason that produced the current health care system cannot be depended upon to reform it; meaningful change "will require something akin to a cultural conversion." [120] The Christian community's theological story, in contrast, "aids us in staying human by underlining the truly human against all cultural attempts to distort the human." [121] This story supplies the vision and the motivation without which we not only might not know what values to pursue—e.g., is medicine primarily a ministry or a business?—but also lack the motivation to pursue them.

Yet Christian community is as important as Christian content. McCormick is convinced that visions that have the power to form and transform action must be communally held. He continually returns to the practical examples of the disastrous consequences of the individualization of tasks and goals and of the need for cooperative, "bottom up," communally inspired innovations of medical bureaucracies. Christians, as a community with social and eschatological vision, seem particularly well-suited to keeping human values alive and therefore to calling others back to them. [122] It is in this sense—as a corrective to a secular society that has lost its natural moral bearings—that Christianity might indeed say something that is de facto distinctive in our culture.

This claim, of course, raises serious questions about the fundamental perspicuity of natural law. It also tellingly echoes the spirit of recent Vatican documents, suggesting that the need to harness reason more explicitly to revelation is not felt only by defenders of absolute moral norms. But it may maroon McCormick oddly, given that his—and the tradition's—typical justification for entering the public fray to debate moral issues is the detachability of Catholic moral reason from Catholic theological conviction. [123] In order to enter the debate in this new guise he would have to accept a conversation in which the religions bring their whole traditions, rather than the parts that can be expressed in "neutral" terms, to the table.

McCORMICK'S SUCCESS AS AN INTEGRATIVE THINKER

McCormick's greatest contribution to the contemporary retrieval of the moral theological tradition has been his courageous habit of pressing Catholic practical moral reason to its limits, reflecting systematically on his uses of it, and adjusting his approaches in light of criticisms, further reflection, and new information. For McCormick as for Fuchs, norms are protectors of values, means to both material and spiritual ends. [124] But McCormick more than Fuchs has given this insight a relentless workout on concrete moral problems, making practical, thoughtful efforts both to reach behind specific moral norms to discover the goods or values they are intended to promote and to account for the capacities of particular moral actors to fulfill them. This evolving notion of moral norms as tools, means to the ends of social justice and personal moral integrity, may be the most uniquely important not only for natural law revival but for feminist critique of customs, laws, and institutional policies.

But if norms are transparent for goods and values, the burden of the discussion shifts to their identification and organization; hence both the importance of anthropology to McCormick's thought and its explicit development as a sort of afterthought. [125] As in the historical natural law tradition, "is" maps to "ought," but McCormick's map is more resistant than some others to the charge of crude naturalism. Not precisely or only the observable needs of human beings but also their universal basic inclinations comprise the "is" that gives content to the "ought." He thus aims for a universal formal description of integral human flourishing and inclination that may be filled out in culturally specific ways; here he, like Fuchs, must acknowledge the tentativeness of even formal descriptions and must take care that they are broad enough to be universally acceptable.

Yet we must distinguish between the content and inductive generation of McCormick's anthropology on one hand and its use on the other. With the exception of his acknowledgment of the properly social character of moral reason, his "person integrally and adequately considered" is more a measure of objective rightness than a subject whose depths are to be plumbed or a blueprint for a new method of moral reasoning. Further, inclinations and criteria of flourishing seem to be interchangeable sources for values and goods, although they imply quite different anthropologies, epistemologies, and methods.

What of individual integrity? Throughout his career McCormick's insistent banging on the door of moral rightness seems to have been inspired by a desire to show that (for example) people who practice contraception may be not only conscientious but also morally good. Proportion, however, does not get us moral goodness. Unlike Fuchs, who concentrates on the subject's attitude toward ultimate ends and assumes that practical moral reason will function smoothly to accomplish them once they are chosen, McCormick takes for granted the subject's transcendental openness toward the good and aids virtue by clarifying the guidelines a prudent person follows in working out the thorny details of practical action. Yet this emphasis can obscure the self-creative character of moral action, whose principal significance, some of his critics argue, "is soul-making," [126] causing "the acting *person* to be morally good or bad, better or worse." [127] McCormick believes that the principal meaning of an action lies instead in its connection to objective values; the actor's integrity is preserved *indirectly*, precisely through choosing well and acting upon that choice. But this connection is more asserted than argued for. A more explicit treatment of the significance of objective rightness for moral goodness would help to explain, for instance, why objective rightness matters at all if "pastorally" acceptable but objectively unjustifiable actions are compatible with moral goodness. McCormick's version of natural law will be inadequate until he develops such a link—say, in an explicit virtue theory. This is especially important because a narrow focus on actions and decisions can eclipse their place within the moral history of the acting subject. [128]

McCormick's success as a social ethicist is mixed. His early accomplishments in this field were in social policy ethics: identifying basic goods and values that society should protect and appropriate rules and laws for guaranteeing these protections within the existing system. A prophetic critique was difficult to construct from this point of view, for preoccupation with the morality of a particular act or policy in a given set of circumstances distracted attention from the question whether the circumstances themselves might not be the more proper objects of change, or, even more radically, whether the good that the act or policy intended to advance was even appropriate. His attention to acts discouraged the brainstorming—the search for new ways of viewing the nature and scope of a moral problem—that often shows apparent either-or dilemmas to be false. For instance, in an early article on the ethical code for Catholic hospitals, the presenting moral problem was the apparent inability of a hospital's obstetrical department to remain solvent unless it performed tubal ligations. McCormick's focus on the "rightness" of acts (tubal ligation, in this circumstance) left a foundational, systematic question inadequately explored: whether Catholic hospitals, or at least Catholic obstetrics departments, fulfilled any needs unmet by other health care facilities— whether, in other words, Catholic health care still had a purpose. [129] Still, his act analysis usefully highlighted the gap between the moral acceptability of a particular act in itself and that of the public policy that permitted, restricted, or forbade it. Some acts may be perfectly acceptable *in limited circumstances*, but the values at stake in them are too grave and the possibility of abuse too great for them to be permitted as a matter of policy. Here de facto protection of values is the central moral criterion of any policy. [130]

McCormick's more recent thought contains further resources for the development of a full-blown social ethic. He not only is increasingly aware that moral reflection is a social, communal process of teaching and learning [131] but also practices moral reflection in this way, at least within the academy. He is theoretically committed to an egalitarian, democratic view of the truth, in the sense that all human beings are more or less outfitted to perform the tasks of moral reasoning and that moral wisdom resides in the community as a whole. [132] And more recent essays on the doctor-patient relationship and the appropriate uses of medical technology exhibit the prophetic confidence that evolves from a judgment that existing systems are out of line with basic human goods. [133] Here McCormick's account of "the human person integrally and adequately considered" has acquired enough critical power to mount a trenchant institutional critique. Tellingly, this new criterion has raised the question of whether the Roman Catholic Church ought to be a health care provider and, if so, what distinguishes it from others. [134]

Yet the most significant questions that McCormick's ethic poses issue from his serious attention to the great challenge of yoking the Roman Catholic moral theological tradition—especially its methods of moral reasoning—to the moral issues that arise in a plural, democratic, capitalist culture. McCormick's success in holding the two together is spectacular. At the same time, many of the connections are sketchy, and showing whether they can in fact be filled in is a project that remains to be pursued.

The first of these incomplete links lies within McCormick's understanding of moral norms. Tying norm to value establishes casuistic continuity ingeniously. Yet it also reveals value as the power behind the norm. Norms are not therefore useless, for they can articulate values for a concrete place and time. But they have no inherent authority. It seems odd, then, to continue to seek moral rightness ("justification" of acts against norms) and to compare this favorably to mere "pastoral adaptation" of norms when in every case the question of what ought to be done is the question of pursuit or protection of *value*. This tactic both undercuts McCormick's own method of practical reasoning and misses the chance to exploit the full power of value for moral theological discernment. In addition, as William George has pointed out, if a legitimate adjustment of an existing norm is "merely" pastoral adaptation, then the opportunity for the new situation to transform the old norm is lost, for treating new situations as permanent exceptions to the rule actually forestalls the casuistic process that adjusts norms so that they continue to express values accurately. [135] Thus as illuminating as McCormick's treatment of norms may be, it will be of limited use until he grants value full authority in practice as well as in theory.

Perhaps the most intriguing but—to the Roman Catholic moral tradition—most threatening class of ambiguities in McCormick's work is the complex of issues that revolves around the relationship between faith and reason, between Christianity and secular thought, between existential invitation and essential obligation. [136] McCormick himself opines that his "greatest failing as a moral theologian (others will certainly note many others) has been the failure to explore and make clearer and more persuasive Vatican II's statement: 'faith throws a new light on everything, manifests God's design for man's total vocation, and thus directs the mind to solutions that are fully human.'" [137] This failing might seem unimportant to an ethic that proceeds on the basis of natural knowledge, but in fact it is essential for two reasons. First, for Christians, all concrete moral decisions involve all four of McCormick's levels of moral deliberation. Theology, communal religious experience, religious literature, and spirituality may make very great material differences at the two Christian levels and will certainly have more diffuse influence upon the human ones. But McCormick has not explained how exactly these religious factors should enter ordinary moral deliberation. For example, what is meant by the requirement that morally right actions be consistent with the Christian story? If "actions that promote the person adequately considered . . . are morally right; [and] those that attack or undermine the person are morally wrong," then "an action consistent with the Christian story" apparently simply means "an action promoting the human person." [138] What has Christianity contributed here? Might its real gift be an answer to the existential question, Who ought I to be, and what ought I to accomplish? The gap between identifying permissible actions and discerning which of them is the true "ought" has not been bridged. This lack is all the more glaring because more of our daily moral struggles occur over what is demanded of us at the existential level than over what is permissible to us at the essential level. [139] Likewise, there is an apparent gap between reason and love of the good. In Thomas, love grounds practical reason; but McCormick rarely mentions this ontological ground for practical reason. Although he occasionally uses the language of charity when he speaks of aspiration and vocation, it is often difficult to see how love of the good or of a person affects a concrete decision about the permissibility of a seemingly wrong act.

Second, a credible version of natural law theology needs continually to demonstrate that theology and human experience still support religious use of *natural* moral reason. McCormick's most recent work confirms both his conviction that God means us to reason and debate on the world's terms and his growing suspicion that Christian reason does not resemble worldly reason at all. If the inconsistency owes to the world's sin or ignorance, then we have to question the tradition's assumptions about the perspicuity of natural law to "pagans." If the inconsistency owes to the fact that the Christian perspective is simply radically different from other points of view, we must question not only natural law's perspicuity but its de facto universality. Without these characteristics natural law cannot claim to be the neutral discourse of all thoughtful people. It becomes self-consciously sectarian. This, as I have shown, is not the death knell it seems to be. But natural law's continued relevance for Christian moral debate depends on the success of thinkers like McCormick in articulating its precise significance within a much larger, more varied conversation.

A refined explanation of the role of reason in Christian moral reflection would also aid McCormick in his recasting of the relationship between ecclesiology and epistemology. McCormick's belief—shared by Fuchs and Curran—is that doctrine's divine basis in revelation rather than reason protects the magisterium's charismatic doctrinal privilege against the sort of "democratization" that moral theology has undergone. Yet once again McCormick's practice seems to run ahead of his theory, pointing to a way out of this contradiction. For instance, he has reasoned from dilemmas in moral theology backwards to issues of systematic theology. This *moral* critique of *dogmatic* theology suggests that the magisterium's dogmatic authority, and not only its moral authority, may in fact be limited by and answerable to the experience of the wider church. [140]

Disharmony is also evident in the contrast between McCormick's clear intention to inspire lay moral reflection and his own insistence on retaining a methodological distinction that makes little sense rhetorically to the moral actor: the distinction between moral norm and pastoral adaptation. The language of pastoral adaptation not only is paternalistic but also shifts attention from the actor's interpretation of a particular norm to the moral counselor and what he or she can conscionably recommend to the actor. [141] For instance, when a troubled person cannot "assimilate and appropriate the values incorporated into moral statements,"

> the moral counsellor . . . can reach a point when it is fruitless to insist on or invite to a course of action that he knows to be fully right. Not being able to change matters or alter perspectives, we try to wrest from a tragic situation the maximum of good—or what is the same, we minimize the evils that we cannot change or prevent. [142]

For example, when teenagers are "determined" to be sexually active, counseling contraception is "pastorally," though not "objectively," acceptable. But McCormick's description of the hypothetical counselor's stance ("if you are determined on this course of action—with which I disagree—and I cannot dissuade you, I want to accept you where you are and help you to make of this situation the best we can") [143] reveals that it is the moral counselor's moral integrity that is at stake, not the advisees'. Underlying the disclaimer is the question, What can I, as counselor, in good conscience advise? If we transpose the subjects, this impression—together with McCormick's opinion of the advisees' moral incompetence—becomes plainer. In the first person one might say, for instance, "I am a married person who is equally determined to have no more children and to continue having sex with my husband when I please. Since I am morally immature and incapable of appreciating the values ensconced in the norms that encourage periodic abstinence, I will make the best of a bad situation, avoiding the need for future abortions by using contraception." This sort of reasoning may satisfy the counselor's conscience, but it is not very satisfying to the agent. When McCormick persists in the model of norm and adaptation, with its implicit preoccupation with what the counselor or confessor may permit, he advances the impression that pastors are the true "adapters" of norms and that it is their own moral culpability, not that of their advisees, that is at stake. Consequently he misses the opportunity to provide individuals with tools appropriate for examining their own capacities and obligations. In contrast to Fuchs, who places the responsibility for discernment squarely on the agent, McCormick has made an incomplete transition from penitential moral theology to contemporary moral empowerment. [144]

The task of choosing values gives rise to other questions. McCormick has resolved his early lack of a means for weighing goods by gradually specifying the content of the criterion—"the good of the human being integrally and adequately considered." This does not solve all problems, of course, but it clearly allows for issues of life cycle, health, spirituality, and social and family context to play a role in determining which of the basic human goods are at stake in a concrete situation. If, as Garth Hallett argues, proportionalism is more an ethical criterion than a comprehensive method of moral discernment, this fix may be adequate (although it depends of course on reaching consensus on a description of the human good). [145] For objective, systematic proportionalist analysis at the essential levels is not meant to guarantee that one who behaves "rightly" is "good" or has chosen the "best" course of action. It is simply meant to show that she has not egregiously violated goods. [146]

Yet when we move on to juggling the aspirational, existential levels of ethics we discover that there is constant tension between the good to which we should aspire and the (nearly) absolute norms that sometimes seem to condemn these aspirations. Here faith seems opposed to reason. McCormick's difficulty in articulating how it is that we determine whether an essential norm holds up against a particular Christian existential calling would be alleviated by a theory of value. If my judgment of what I am called to do is to rest on more than internal intuition or external authority, I need to know not only what values to *protect* but what values to *pursue*. I therefore need to know more clearly what a value is and how it differs from a good. For instance, Paul Quay defines an ontic good as something whose perfection or completeness evokes "a willed response of love, complacency, or desire." A value is "that which can be, is, or ought to be prized, esteemed, or thought to have worth by some human agent. ... more abstractly, a value is that formal aspect of a being which is the ground of its being thus prized." Most significantly, for Quay things are valuable not in themselves but to agents, as potential fulfillments of their chosen or given goals. [147]

I am suggesting not that McCormick adopt Quay's distinction uncritically; in fact, Quay employs his definition against the proportionalist project. Nevertheless, McCormick's arguments would benefit from some similar more careful distinction between goods per se and values as aspects of goods-for-me-and-others-here-and-now. [148] This is especially the case because many goods for which McCormick has deep respect—say a strong spiritual life—are difficult to describe compellingly in public discourse as ontic goods. [149] Certainly spirituality can be argued to have benefits measurable in this forum—psychological and physical health, for instance—but if these premoral benefits are seen as the true point of its pursuit, spiritual fulfillment cannot be accomplished, just as making a sacrifice for a child out of a desire to increase one's own virtue rather than out of love for her cancels the virtuous intention. Once again, McCormick's insight is solid but his details, incompletely worked out.

McCormick's efforts to refine the practice of moral reasoning are unparalleled. He opens new horizons, revealing the "norms behind the norms" to which we can have recourse when norms "fail." He reinvigorates old terms and distinctions and adjusts them in light of both contemporary and traditional standards. Yet in many ways his theory is out of step with his example. He makes compelling use of casuistry, yet at crucial points he is unwilling to permit his cases to transform norms. He espouses a democratic, egalitarian notion of truth, and yet he assumes the role of the pastoral counselor or confessor. He sees Christianity as in some sense countercultural, and yet he believes that Christianity adds nothing new to essential human ethics. He sees the moral life as aspiration and pursuit of value, but he relies heavily on a moral tradition designed for the avoidance of transgression. He argues that goodness is a matter of pursuit of the right, or even the best, but he lacks the virtue theory that might give unity to human actions or connect them more explicitly to a person's ultimate telos in God. Some of these paradoxes are contradictions; others are points of appropriate tension that simply need to be connected more explicitly. Yet McCormick's proportionalism does seem to rest upon an assumption that the interpretation and application of constant norms ought to remain the central task of moral theology. It is this assumption—not entailed by a commitment to natural law or even to casuistry—that leads to awkwardness. Likewise, his as yet only partial success in effectively linking his brand of casuistic practical reasoning to an aspirational theology, to a rich understanding of the moral subject, and to the larger purposes of social ethics limits the usefulness of that endeavor—especially given that a more successful integration of these elements would almost certainly alter the foundations of the very structure of practical reason he has been attempting to perfect. For a version of ethics still indebted to natural law but somewhat more cognizant of these connections, we must turn to Gustavo Gutiérrez.

NOTES

1. See William C. Spohn, "Richard A. McCormick: Tradition in Transition," *Religious Studies Review* 13 (January 1987): 39–42.

2. See Richard A. McCormick, "Self-Assessment and Self-Indictment," *Religious Studies Review* 13, no. 1 (January 1987): 37.

3. See Richard A. McCormick, "The Shape of Moral Evasion in Catholicism," *America* 159, no. 8 (1 October 1988): 183–88.

4. McCormick, "Self-Assessment," 37–38.

5. Richard A. McCormick, *Health and Medicine in the Catholic Tradition: Tradition in Transition* (New York: Crossroad, 1984); and Richard A. McCormick, "Theology and Biomedical Ethics," *Logos* 3 (1982): 25–45. The latter article appears, with revisions and additions, as a chapter in the book. See also the topical essays in Richard A. McCormick, *The Critical Calling: Reflections on Moral Dilemmas Since Vatican Council II* (Washington, DC: Georgetown University Press, 1989).

6. Richard A. McCormick, "Personal Conscience," *Chicago Studies* 13 (Fall 1974): 241.

7. McCormick, "Human Significance," 235.

8. Richard A. McCormick, "Ambiguity in Moral Choice," in *Doing Evil to Achieve Good: Moral Choice in Conflict Situations*, ed. Richard A. McCormick and Paul Ramsey (Chicago: Loyola University Press, 1978), 38.

The contemporary debate on double effect is typically thought to have been started by Peter Knauer, who argued that what makes for a wrongful intention of harm is not directness but lack of proportionate reason for causing it. The ensuing discussion has concentrated upon the legitimacy of weighing consequences, the possibility of commensurating them, and the validity of the distinctions between causing harm, acting wrongfully, and committing moral evil. Proportionalists conclude that the distinction between indirect and direct willing is superfluous because it is transparent for the latter issues. For a history of the debate over intention, see Hoose, *Proportionalism,* chapter 5. For Knauer's position see Peter Knauer, S.J., "The Hermeneutic Function of the Principle of Double Effect," in *Moral Norms and the Catholic Tradition,* Readings in Moral Theology, ed. Charles E. Curran and Richard A. McCormick, no. 1 (New York: Paulist Press, 1979), 1–39.

9. Davis, *Moral and Pastoral Theology,* 2: 171–86.

10. See McCormick, "Ambiguity," 24–28.

11. For example, Peter Knauer, Josef Fuchs, Bruno Schüller, and Charles Curran. For descriptive discussions of proportionalism, see, for example, Richard McCormick's essays in *Doing Evil to Achieve Good*; Hoose, *Proportionalism*; and Hallett, *Greater Good*.

12. Peter Knauer, S.J., "Zu Grundbegriffen der Enzyklika 'Veritatis Splendor,'" *Stimmen der Zeit* 212 (1994): 14–26; see also idem, "Hermeneutic Function," 35.

13. See McCormick, "Ambiguity," 265; and Knauer, "Hermeneutic Function."

14. See for example Hallett, *Greater Good,* 131. Oddly, Hallett does not engage McCormick in any detail. Good hands-on examples in McCormick's writing include chapters 14 and 21 of *Critical Calling*.

15. Odozor, *Richard McCormick,* 110.

16. For an example of such presumptions, see McCormick, *Critical Calling,* 227. McCormick's work suffers to the degree that he does not make this point systematically. See B. Andrew Lustig, "*Veritatis Splendor*: Some Implications for Bioethics," in *Veritatis Splendor: American Responses,* ed. Michael E. Allsopp and John J. O'Keefe (Kansas City, MO: Sheed and Ward, 1995), 252–68.

17. *ST* II-II 64.7.

18. McCormick "Ambiguity," 7.

19. See for example ibid., 11. Because of the potential confusion between evil-as-bad-result and evil-as-personal-moral-failing, I substitute "harm" for evil in the first sense throughout the following discussion.

20. McCormick, "A Commentary on the Commentaries," in *Doing Evil to Achieve Good,* ed. McCormick and Ramsey, 263–4; see also McCormick, "Ambiguity," 41. Yet psychological intention does have bearing on the moral state of the actor. If one can justify a killing in self-defense, but secretly enjoys it, then one performs a morally evil but morally right action.

21. Odozor, *Richard McCormick,* 115–16; McCormick, "Commentary," 237–39.

22. See note 16 above.

23. McCormick, "Commentary," 263.

24. McCormick, "Ambiguity," 45.

25. McCormick, "Ambiguity," 45.

26. The claim of worried critics that proportionalists justify morally evil actions by their premorally good consequences is, from the proportionalist viewpoint, oxymoronic. See Cristina L. H. Traina, "Developing an Integrative Ethical Method: Feminist Ethics and Natural Law Retrieval," Ph.D. diss., University of Chicago Divinity School, 1992, 169–71.

27. McCormick, "Ambiguity," 41. See also 38. This need not alter the significance of psychological directness for *personal* moral evil.

28. McCormick, "Human Significance," 245.

29. Richard A. McCormick, "Aspects of the Moral Question," *America* 117 (9 December 1967): 716; see also Himes, "Contribution," 63–66; and McCormick, "Shape of Moral Evasion," 186.

30. Richard A. McCormick, "Conjugal Love and Conjugal Morality: A Reevaluation of the Catholic Position in Terms of Total Marital Commitment," *America* 110 (11 January 1964): 39.

31. McCormick, "What the Silence Means," 290.

32. McCormick, "Human Significance," 256.

33. McCormick, *Moral Theology in the Year 2000*, 15–16; see also idem, *Critical Calling*, 11; Odozor, *Richard McCormick*, 109.

34. McCormick, "Human Significance," 242. This phrasing of the issue echoes Louis Janssens: "Ethics . . . serves the purpose of improving as much as possible the well-being and the development of persons and social groups" (Louis Janssens, "Norms and Priorities in a Love Ethics," *Louvain Studies* 6 [1977]: 213).

35. McCormick, "Ambiguity," 46; emphasis added. See also McCormick, "Commentary," 265; and the latter half of *Critical Calling*.

36. Odozor, *Richard McCormick*, 178.

37. This is one of John Finnis's central arguments against proportionalism (Finnis, *Fundamentals of Ethics*, 83). Finnis, like Grisez and May, sees moral absolutes as the only alternative to the crippling consequentialism that he believes McCormick's proportionalism to entail. See May, *Moral Absolutes*; Grisez, "Against Consequentialism"; and Grisez, *Abortion*, 286–321, especially 293, 305. In addition, Curran observes, "man does not have the same control over his life that the artisan has over the raw material out of which he is fashioning his product" ("Moral Theology: The Present State," 453). The many variables that enter the mix are the inherent context of human moral reason, not unfortunate obstacles to it. For instance, McCormick's discussion of war, to which I referred above, does not directly consider any moral claims that civilians may have on an enemy. See Finnis, *Fundamentals*, 105; Finnis, *Natural Law and Natural Rights*, 111–18; Paul M. Quay, "Morality by Calculation of Values," *Theology Digest* 23 (Winter 1975): 347–64; Porter, *Recovery*, 130–31; Grisez, *The Way*, vol. 1, chapter 6; Bartholomew M. Kiely, "The Impracticality of Proportionalism," *Gregorianum* 66 (1985): 669–76; Hoose, *Proportionalism*, 85–86. In response to criticism McCormick has dropped the long-term element; for a discussion of this issue, see Cahill, "Teleology," 619–21.

See also Finnis, "Natural Law and Unnatural Acts." Finnis understands conflicts to be facts, not chimeras. He too argues that the goods that human beings can reasonably and appropriately pursue are incommensurable; he further claims, following *Humanae Vitae,* that sexual intercourse necessarily entails the meanings of friendship and procreation (387). To act against these—or to prefer one to the other—is therefore to act against (a) basic human good(s) and deny the inherent meaning of human sexual intercourse. Therefore both contraception and forced marital intercourse are forbidden. But he is unwilling to carry this concern to its logical conclusion in all cases, holding on to the direct/indirect distinction by describing acts narrowly: "one should never choose to do any act which *of itself does nothing but* damage or impede a realization of or participation of any one or more of the basic forms of human good" (*Natural Law,* 118).

38. On the latter, see Hoose, *Proportionalism,* 92; see also Cahill, "Teleology," 629.

39. McCormick, "Ambiguity," 29.

40. McCormick, "Commentary," 265. Plain meanspiritedness is always culpable.

41. McCormick, "Ambiguity," 227–28, 251–53.

42. McCormick, "Theology and Biomedical Ethics," 27; Richard A. McCormick, *How Brave a New World? Dilemmas in Bioethics* (Garden City, NY: Doubleday, 1981), 5. McCormick leans heavily here on John Finnis, "Natural Law." Finnis lays out the basic values in more detail—omitting procreation from the list—in *Natural Law,* 86–90.

43. Ibid., 27. This list comes largely from Finnis, "Natural Law," 367, and closely resembles those drawn up by John Finnis and Germain Grisez elsewhere. See Finnis, *Natural Law,* 86–90; and Grisez, *Abortion,* 312–13.

44. McCormick, "Theology and Biomedical Ethics," 27.

45. For this argument see Finnis, *Fundamentals,* 136–42; Grisez, *Abortion,* 311; Grisez, "Against Consequentialism," 50; and May, *Moral Absolutes,* 53–54. Yet as Cahill notes, "the equal status of [Finnis's, and by implication Grisez's] values is not as self-evident as their general fundamentality" (Cahill, "Teleology," 622–23). Grisez himself places human life—specifically, promotion of this particular human life—above all other goods in a situation of conflict. Yet for him and for Finnis a personal hierarchy akin to McCormick's personal existential ethics—special stress, dictated by one's skills or vocation, on one or a few values—is not only permissible but virtually necessary (Finnis, *Natural Law,* 92–93; and Grisez, *Abortion,* 318). Therefore the conversation on moral hierarchy is far from closed.

46. See, e.g., McCormick, "Nutrition-Hydration: The New Euthanasia?", in *Critical Calling,* 369–88; and idem, "AIDS: The Shape of the Ethical Challenge," in *Critical Calling,* 315–28.

47. McCormick seems more and more to follow Janssens in grounding justice in obligation to seek others' good, one condition of which is respect for their dignity. *Personalism* saves proportionalism from utilitarianism. See for example Janssens, "Norms and Priorities," 219–28.

48. McCormick, "Commentary," 263, italics added.

49. McCormick, "Ambiguity," 47–49.

50. Richard A. McCormick, "Method and Moral Decision-Making," in Richard A. McCormick, *Notes on Moral Theology, 1981 through 1984* (Lanham, MD: University Press of America, 1984), 1–17. Charles Curran's work exhibits some of the same ambiguities; see Secker, "Crisis," 157–59.

51. "Every human choice, as limited, represents a sacrifice, and in this sense the resolution of a conflict" (McCormick, "Moral Norms: An Update," *Theological*

Studies 46 [March 1985]: 62). McCormick approvingly paraphrases Janssens. The reference appears to be to Janssens, "Norms and Priorities," 212. Janssens quotes Henri Bergson, without citation: "Every choice is a sacrifice."

52. Edward V. Vacek, "Proportionalism: One View of the Debate," *Theological Studies* 46 (June 1985): 308–9.

53. McCormick, "Ambiguity," 47–48.

54. Ibid., 48–50.

55. McCormick, *Critical Calling*, 248–51.

56. McCormick, *Critical Calling*, 396.

57. McCormick, *Critical Calling*, 393.

58. McCormick, *Critical Calling*, 393.

59. McCormick, *Critical Calling*, 303.

60. McCormick, *Critical Calling*, 249.

61. McCormick, *Critical Calling*, 19.

62. McCormick, *Critical Calling*, 302, 308–9, 311.

63. McCormick, *Critical Calling*, 309.

64. McCormick, *Critical Calling*, 312. On the anthropological appropriateness of objective disorder as a moral criterion, see Jack A. Bonsor, "Homosexual Orientation and Anthropology: Reflections on the Category 'Objective Disorder'," *Theological Studies* 59 (March 1998): 60–83.

65. William P. George, "Moral Statement and Pastoral Adaptation: A Problematic Distinction in McCormick's Theological Ethics," in *The Annual of the Society of Christian Ethics, 1992*, ed. Harlan Beckley (Washington, DC: Georgetown University Press, 1992), 135–56. For instance, in an article on homosexuality McCormick insists that the application of a norm—the description of the moral meaning of an act and the determination of subjective culpability—is a matter of *objective morality*, applied to an individual case. Yet *pastoral adaptations* "include circumstances affecting both culpability (for what is clearly [objectively?] wrong) and the determination itself of wrongfulness at the personal level" (McCormick, *Critical Calling*, 305). If both are true it is difficult to see what is gained by the distinction. See also McCormick, *Critical Calling*, chapter 8 and p. 293. In a similar vein, Paulinus Odozor approvingly adds that for McCormick concrete statements of norms "never capture [the] good totally or formulate its significance with complete accuracy"; "they are only approximations of truth based on our limited insights and judgment" (Odozor, *Richard McCormick*, 40, 151).

66. Thanks to James Keenan for this observation.

67. Vacek, "Proportionalism," 313.

68. McCormick, "Human Significance," 237–40. McCormick never labels natural law participation in divine reason, but the identity can be inferred; natural law is rooted in the divinely intended structure of human being.

69. McCormick, "Human Significance," 235–37, 239–40.

70. Ibid., 254. This option is not, as in Fuchs, equated with salvation.

71. In "Human Significance," McCormick claims that "man as man is perfected by the *pursuit* of value" (244; emphasis added). Yet elsewhere he claims that "the *realization* of these [basic] values in intersubjective life is the only adequate way to love and attain God" (McCormick, "Theology and Biomedical Ethics," 27, emphasis added). The difference in meaning is significant. The second quote implies that a person's moral goodness depends upon the *accomplishment* of values and the first,

that it consists of *openness to* them. One could point out, as Fuchs does, that moral goodness—loving God—entails concern for effective action. But if *realizing* basic human values is the only way to attain God, moral goodness is tied to consequences. It seems clear from the context of the discussion on proportionalism that good pursuit of values entails attention to probable consequences rather than successful realization of values. Charity, "a way of being" that follows from being "seized by the divine grasp," must "burst forth in different forms of virtuous action" (McCormick, "Human Significance," 234–35). See also Janssens, "Norms and Priorities," 216–17. Charity is the criterion of moral norms, but charity is instantiated in the pursuit of value, according to which rightness and wrongness are judged.

72. McCormick, "Ambiguity," 47–50.

73. McCormick, "Human Significance," 247–48.

74. *Gaudium et Spes*, Part II; quoted in McCormick, *Health and Medicine*, 15; see also Himes, "Contribution," 56–59.

75. See for example Richard A. McCormick, "Practical and Theoretical Considerations," chapter in *The Problem of Population: Educational Considerations* [no ed.] ([Notre Dame:] University of Notre Dame Press, 1965), 3: 51–57; idem, *Critical Calling*, 302–3.

76. In his early work, these levels are fairly coherent; what violates the specific often vitiates the individual and is wrong at least in part because of this vitiation. See Richard A. McCormick, "Family Size, Rhythm, and the Pill," in *The Problem of Population: Moral and Theological Considerations*, ed. Donald N. Barrett (New York: Joseph F. Wagner, Inc., 1965), 71, 80; and Richard A. McCormick, "The Council on Contraception," *America* 114 (8 January 1966): 47. Yet no act can be evaluated on one level—e.g., interpersonal or physical—alone; see Richard A. McCormick, *Notes on Moral Theology, 1965 through 1980* (Lanham, MD: University Press of America, 1981), 678. Over the course of his career, the criterion of interpersonal integrity has increasingly displaced physical integrity.

77. E.g., McCormick, "Human Significance," 249.

78. See McCormick, "Theology and Biomedical Ethics": "in christian [sic] perspective, the meaning, substance and consummation of life are found in human relationships" (36); "the potential for human relationships [is] that aspect of physical life to be valued" (41); great efforts are to be made to preserve a person's life only if there is potential for human relationship (37). See also McCormick, *How Brave a New World?*, 14. For the embodied human being, love of God is impossible outside the context of love for others.

79. See, e.g., McCormick, "Human Significance," 249; Himes, "Contribution," 63–66, on form and substance; and McCormick, *Notes, 1981–1984*, 181–82.

80. McCormick, *Health and Medicine*, 15–17; taken from Louis Janssens, "Artificial Insemination: Ethical Considerations," *Louvain Studies* 8 (1980): 3–29.

81. McCormick, *Health and Medicine*, 17.

82. For instance, Janssens's arguments for the limited acceptability of homologous artificial insemination (AIH) rely only loosely upon the eight-fold criteria he has set up; mediating principles are needed, as one could argue against AIH on the basis of his eight dimensions as well.

83. McCormick, *Critical Calling*, 67.

84. See Avery Dulles, *The Survival of Dogma: Faith, Authority, and Dogma in a Changing World* (New York: Crossroad, 1982 [1971]), 109–11. For other post–Vatican

II treatments of this issue, see Ladislas Orsy, *The Church: Learning and Teaching* (Wilmington, DE: Michael Glazier, 1987); Hans Küng, *Infallible? An Inquiry*, trans. Edward Quinn (Garden City, NY: Doubleday, 1971).

85. McCormick, *Critical Calling*, 132–33.

86. McCormick adopts the traditional natural law tenets of moral objectivity as Keane outlines them: an objective moral order, "in which some actions are right and other actions are wrong," exists; this order is accessible to human persons; knowledge of it is potentially universal; but "human persons do not always actualize their fundamental ability to know the objective moral order" (Keane, "The Objective Moral Order," 260–62). So truth, in the sense of correspondence to reality, is at stake in all moral debates.

87. Himes notes that the question of papal authority in morals is not "what power does the pope as primate have but what conditions permit the pope to exercise his power wisely. It is an ecclesiological, not juridical, concern" ("Contribution," 61).

88. McCormick, *How Brave a New World?*, 225. The following argument is based in my own reading of McCormick and is largely corroborated by Himes, "Contribution," 59–63.

89. Proper moral reason is "informed by" faith, not "without" or "replaced by" it (McCormick, *Critical Calling*, 50).

90. The same potential advantage would accrue to clergy at each level of the hierarchy—bishops in dioceses, priests in parishes, etc. Of course good moral reasoning at the Vatican level depends not only upon an attitude of openness to wisdom among the Roman hierarchy, but also upon the candor of other bishops in their communications to Rome, of priests and laypeople in their communication with bishops, etc.

91. Himes, "Contribution," 60–61.

92. McCormick, *Notes, 1965–1980*, 264. McCormick quotes Bernard Häring, "The Encyclical Crisis," in *The Catholic Case for Contraception*, ed. Daniel Callahan (Toronto: Macmillan, 1969), 82.

93. McCormick, *Notes, 1965–1980*, 263–65.

94. Himes, "Contribution," 61–62.

95. McCormick, "Loyalty and Dissent," 675. The phrase is meant to clarify the phrase from *Lumen Gentium*, "religious submission of will and mind" (quoted in *Health and Medicine*, 69–72). "Docility" should be read in the context of the traditional parts of prudence; see chapter 1. See also McCormick, "Personal Conscience," 244; and McCormick, *Notes, 1965–1980*, 245–46. McCormick describes docility as (1) "a respect for the teacher and his office; (2) a readiness to reassess one's own opinion and therefore a shedding of obstinacy; (3) reluctance to conclude prematurely to error because one realizes (or presumes) that the wisdom of the entire Church has gone into the teaching; (4) a public behavior that fosters respect for the authentic magisterium" (McCormick, *Critical Calling*, 48). To perform for oneself, for all moral norms, the thorough research and analysis that is required for their appropriation would be impossible. One may bypass the process as long as the norms cohere with experience and the proposing authority's past behavior leads one to believe that it makes a habit of responsible reasoning. But significant or repeated experience of incompetence erodes this presumption of trustworthiness and with it, the spirit of sympathy or docility toward new proposals (see McCormick, *Notes, 1965–1980*, 259; and Komonchak, "Authority in Morals," 103–14).

96. McCormick, "Loyalty and Dissent," 675; and Richard A. McCormick, "L'Affaire Curran," *America* 154 (5 April 1986): 266.

97. McCormick, *Critical Calling*, 35.

98. See McCormick, *How Brave a New World?*, 226; McCormick, *Notes, 1981–1984*, 48; McCormick, "Loyalty and Dissent," 675; and McCormick, "Personal Conscience," 247.

99. This claim has close ties to both probabilism—the teaching that one may follow the guidance of any respected moral thinker—and probabiliorism—the teaching that one must follow the opinion of the thinker whose position seems soundest and most compelling. See Jonsen and Toulmin, *Abuse*, 260–61, 166–67. The former two positions rely on the external criterion of a proposing authority (albeit an authority recognized precisely for reasoning well); proportionalism relies upon the internal criterion of value.

100. See Richard A. McCormick, "*Laborem Exercens* and Social Morality," in *Official Catholic Social Teaching*, Readings in Moral Theology, ed. Richard A. McCormick and Charles E. Curran, no. 5 (New York: Paulist Press, 1986), 226–27.

101. McCormick, *Health and Medicine*, 130. Although the language is ambiguous, the context clearly implies *moral* theological formulations.

102. Richard A. McCormick, "Moral Theology 1940–1989: An Overview," *Theological Studies* 50 (1989): 8.

103. Secker notes that this approach, which broadens the magisterial function beyond the hierarchy, requires a new understanding of the role of experience in ethics; that is, it requires a change in ethical method (Secker, "Crisis," 120–25).

104. Himes describes the latter as "an asymptotic understanding of moral truth" ("Contribution," 66).

105. McCormick lays out these levels in *How Brave a New World?*, 8–9, and *Critical Calling*, 194–96. Charles Curran credits Norbert Rigali with this division. See Norbert Rigali, "On Christian Ethics," *Chicago Studies* 10 (1971): 227–47; and Charles E. Curran, "Catholic Social Teaching and Human Morality," in *One Hundred Years of Catholic Social Thought*, ed. John Coleman (Maryknoll, NY: Orbis Books, 1991), 84–85. Curran and Rigali concur that the important question is whether there is a *morality* particular to Christians; pluralism in *ethics* may or may not accompany universal morality. The distinction is not as clear in McCormick, who uses the term "ethics" in his description of the four levels despite his claim that it is morality that concerns him.

106. Pope John Paul II, *Ad Tuendam Fidem*, trans. Ladislas Orsy, in *Origins* 28, no. 8 (16 July 1998): 113, 115–16, at 115, par. 4, emphasis added.

107. McCormick, *How Brave a New World?*, 9; see also Spohn, "Richard A. McCormick." McCormick maintains this position in the more recent "Theology and Biomedical Ethics," 25.

108. McCormick, *Critical Calling*, 195–96.

109. McCormick, *Critical Calling*, 196. For connections between this articulation of "moral minimums" and the possibility of moral absolutes, see Traina, "Developing an Integrative Ethical Method," 183, n. 118.

110. McCormick, *Critical Calling*, 194–95.

111. McCormick, *Critical Calling*, 195.

112. James M. Gustafson, *Can Ethics Be Christian?* (Chicago and London: University of Chicago Press, 1975), 164–68.

113. See also Curran, "Catholic Social Teaching," 85.

114. McCormick, like Fuchs, Rahner, and others, insists upon the existential goodness and even salvation of non-Christians as "anonymous Christians." See Rahner, "Anonymous Christians."

115. See McCormick, "Theology and Biomedical Ethics," 35, 42.

116. McCormick, "Theology and Biomedical Ethics," 43. McCormick cites James F. Bresnahan, "Rahner's Christian Ethics," *America* 123 (1970): 354.

117. McCormick, "Theology and Biomedical Ethics," 25.

118. Ibid., 33.

119. Richard A. McCormick, "Blastomere Separation: Some Concerns," *Hastings Center Report* 24 (March-April 1994): 16.

120. Richard A. McCormick, *Hidden Persuaders: Value Variables in Bioethics* (Bloomington, IN: The Poynter Center, 1993), 9.

121. McCormick, "Theology and Biomedical Ethics," 29; "Christian warrants are confirmatory rather than originating" (ibid., 42).

122. Richard A. McCormick, "Beyond Principlism Is Not Enough: A Theologian Reflects on the Real Challenge for U.S. Biomedical Ethics" in *A Matter of Principles? Ferment in U.S. Bioethics*, ed. Edwin R. DuBose, Ronald P. Hamel, and Laurence J. O'Connell (Valley Forge, PA: Trinity Press International, 1994), 344–61.

123. See McCormick, *Critical Calling*, 203.

124. McCormick acknowledges his debts to Fuchs in "Self-Assessment," 38.

125. See Himes, "Contribution," 49, 54.

126. "Morality is primarily concerned with the fulfillment of human persons in their existential dimension," not with the achievement of values (Grisez, *The Way*, 1:155, 161).

127. Paul M. Quay, "The Disvalue of Ontic Evil," *Theological Studies* 46 (1985): 278. Self-fulfillment automatically accompanies the right choosing of goods because the divine economy is set up so that "goods rightly chosen fulfill persons existentially just by being chosen" (Grisez, *The Way*, 1:160). It would be important to know whether he means here "just by being chosen well and rightly" or simply "just by being chosen—period"—the latter is Grisez's caricatured position, and the former is closer to McCormick's position. Hoose points out that proportionalism's proponents—among them McCormick—confuse personal moral goodness and objective or worldly moral rightness of action (Hoose, *Proportionalism*, 50).

128. The criticism of act-centered ethics is James Gustafson's. See Gustafson, "The Focus and Its Limitations," 179–90.

129. Richard A. McCormick, "The New Directives and Institutional Medico-Moral Responsibility," *Chicago Studies* 11 (1972): 305–14.

130. See for example Richard A. McCormick, "Christian Morals," *America* 122 (10 January 1970): 5–6; Richard A. McCormick, "A Moralist Reports," *America* 123 (11 July 1970): 22–23; and Richard A. McCormick, with Andre Hellegers, "The Ethics of In Utero Surgery," *Journal of the American Medical Association* 246 (2 October 1981): 1550–55. McCormick understands politics as the art of the possible; political activism often involves the prudential judgment that it is better to settle for inadequate protection of a value than to risk losing protection entirely. See for example Richard A. McCormick, "Fetal Research, Morality, and Public Policy," *The Hastings Center Report* 5 (June 1975): 26–31; and Richard A. McCormick, "The Social Responsibility of the Christian," *The Australasian Catholic Record* 52 (July 1975): 253–63. For a

helpful analysis of McCormick's specific contributions to public policy debate, see Leslie Griffin, "The Church, Morality, and Public Policy," in *Moral Theology: Challenges for the Future*, 347–51.

131. McCormick, "Human Significance," 255–57. McCormick views Pope John XXIII as the initiator of the conviction that "laypersons do not simply apply the Church's social teaching; they must share in its very construction" (McCormick, *Health and Medicine*, 5).

132. McCormick, *How Brave a New World?*, 12–14.

133. See especially McCormick, "'A Clean Heart Create for Me, O God.' Impact Questions on the Artificial Heart," in *Critical Calling*, 255–60; idem, "Beyond Principlism"; idem, *Hidden Persuaders*. Yet he does not apply this social critique to all questions; see for instance, in "Therapy or Tampering: The Ethics of Reproductive Technology and the Development of Doctrine" (*Critical Calling*, 329–52).

134. McCormick, "Beyond Principlism," 346.

135. See note 65.

136. See McCormick, *Moral Theology in the Year 2000*, 15–16. McCormick describes aspirational ethics as dealing with "the 3 a.m. questions" of "guilt, personal integrity, of what is my life becoming, of God in my life, of genuine love, of mortality. . . . They are much more invitational than obligational."

137. McCormick, "Self-Assessment," 39; McCormick quotes *Gaudium et Spes*, par. 11. For instance, like Fuchs's, McCormick's excurses into practical moral reason connect awkwardly with his more theological moments. His practical moral discussions are almost devoid of the richly theological language which characterizes his discussions of grace, Christology, and spirituality, and the practical implications of these themes for former questions are rarely worked out (Himes, "Contribution," 66–69).

138. See McCormick, *Health and Medicine*, 17.

139. See Himes, "Contribution," 67–68. For instance, McCormick holds that the central moral challenge posed to the church by the suffering of (at that time, mostly gay) AIDS patients is the question, What would Jesus do? (vocation) rather than, What *may* we do? (permission) (McCormick, *Critical Calling*, 327). The issue here may finally be the relationship between Christian and human morality: not the question of essential Christian norms—rules and practices that make communal Christian life possible—but the question of the extent and definition of universal human aspirations. Gustafson argues that Christian commitment may really impose rigorous moral obligations on those who have committed themselves to a Christian way of life. This does not mean that the obligations are senseless in or incoherent with other perspectives—they may be narrowings or intensifications of general human norms—but it does mean that they are not necessarily *persuasive* from within those other perspectives. Gustafson would argue that they also are not even implicitly binding on those who do not choose the Christian "way." See Gustafson, *Can Ethics Be Christian?*, 165–68. McCormick's aspirational inclinations may lead at times to the claim that "rigorous" obligations hold even for non-Christians.

140. McCormick, like Fuchs, distinguishes doctrinal from moral truth, but others, like Joseph Ratzinger, argue that authority in *moral* matters is a matter of *doctrinal* purity as well, and not a separate or secondary issue (Ratzinger, "The Church's Teaching," 69–70).

141. See, e.g., McCormick, *Critical Calling*, 401. The examples that follow come from an essay specifically addressed to doctors as moral counselors, but the point

holds in his other work. As Odozor notes, McCormick began his career by asking whether a doctor could justifiably remove a probably dead fetus from a woman surgically, not how a woman was to make this decision for herself. See Odozor, *Richard McCormick*, 22.

142. McCormick, *Critical Calling*, 397.

143. Ibid. The example under discussion is divorce.

144. This form of reasoning may be useful in situations in which the mitigating factors are mainly external to the agent—for instance, for women on the lookout for an opportunity to leave an abusive relationship, the argument, "My physical and economic security depend on my permitting my partner sex when he wants it, and I cannot support another child on my own, so I will use contraception," does not require "doublethink" because it does not require the agent to describe herself as morally deficient. This is not to imply that contraception is wrong but to illustrate the logic.

145. Hallett, *Greater Good*; and Hoose, *Proportionalism*, 89.

146. Yet in this regard McCormick's critics gain support from his defenders. For example, Cahill's description of the classical double effect dilemma seems to me not to capture this quality. She claims that "double effect envisages moral dilemmas in which the best outcome concretely possible can be realized only by an action which will be accompanied by some undesirable results" ("Teleology," 608). This may be a conclusion, not the premise, of the process: the judgment whether "the best outcome concretely possible"—more properly, an *acceptable* outcome—*is* the one that entails a harm-causing action.

147. Quay, "Morality," 350–51.

148. Because McCormick stresses the participation of all goods in God, an anthropology of fulfillment, and the obligation to bring goods about, good and value will likely be even more closely harnessed for him than for his critics. Secker notes that McCormick occasionally also muddies the distinction between basic values and the norms or principles that are transparent for them ("Crisis," 271).

149. Hoose points out that proportionalists do not generally limit their consideration to material consequences and ends (Hoose, *Proportionalism*, 87, 92).

7

Gustavo Gutiérrez and Social Solidarity

Gustavo Gutiérrez, "widely considered to be the 'doyen' of Latin American liberation theology," [1] makes almost no explicit use of traditional natural law thought and in fact criticizes it sharply. [2] Yet his work is so strongly informed by natural law assumptions that it is every bit as significant to the contemporary natural law discussion as that of self-conscious revisionists. [3] Of the three theologians we have examined, he is the most systematically dependent on the universal human capacity for moral insight. Yet Gutiérrez also leaves an opening toward evangelical theology by embracing a more explicitly religious motivation for moral commitment than either McCormick or Fuchs; and he builds a bridge to feminist ethics by placing a moral hermeneutic and a historicist theological anthropology at the center of his work. Sorting out the connections among these apparently disparate elements, then, is crucial to an understanding of Gutiérrez's unique contribution.

GUTIÉRREZ'S THEOLOGICAL METHOD [4]

It bears repeating that, for Gutiérrez, liberation theology's social justice insights ultimately serve its evangelical mission: theology is the church's proclamation of the Word to the world. [5] In Latin America the theological project is to answer the question, "How are we to talk about a God who is revealed as love in a situation characterized by poverty and oppression?" [6] According to Gutiérrez, liberation theology makes two indispensable methodological contributions to this task: a moral hermeneutic, which dictates theology's order of proceeding, and the epistemological bias toward the poor. [7] Even more important to this discussion is a fact on which he does not dwell: both of these contributions pivot on traditional natural law convictions.

MORAL HERMENEUTIC. The passage that leads to the moral hermeneutic is experience—not the orderly and easily classified experience of traditional moral theology, but the wild and unpredictable experience visible from within an historical worldview. [8] Gutiérrez begins with the assumption that experience varies widely over time and place. Since the role of theology is to interpret the significance of revelation for particular historical communities, all theology—even and especially natural law thought, with its claims to universality— is shaped by its historical situation. Therefore theology, taken in the broad sense, is inevitably plural and historical. [9] Liberation theology's difference is its awareness of this fact. So for Gutiérrez, as for other liberation thinkers, human historicity is not merely another feature of human being to be reflected upon from a neutral standpoint; it impresses itself upon the method and content of theological reflection.

In fact it would not be too much to say that Gutiérrez traces most theological error to the failure of classically trained theologians to understand the violence they do to a foreign experience by imposing their own theological categories upon it, failing to recognize that others' difference from them may not be the result of ignorance or inferiority. The error is often inadvertent because it is systematized in an apparently impartial method. According to the so-called classical European model of theological reflection, Gutiérrez argues, the Scriptures inspire systematic theology, which lays the universal groundwork for moral theology, which in turn develops moral norms, applying and occasionally adjusting them in light of circumstances. The difficulty is that these tightly woven theories tend to screen out variety in circumstances, and transmission of information about circumstances over a great distance also damps the amplitude of its variation from the baseline of the foreign thinker's own experience. As a consequence, suppositions both overly general and just plain wrong can slip in undetected. For example, Francisco de Vitoria theorizes generally and from a distance about the Spanish right to colonize the Americas, basing his argument simply upon the inherent right of superior people to govern inferior and upon biased reports and assumptions about the Indians' crudeness.

Gutiérrez's own answer to Vitoria is a moral hermeneutic that reorders moral reflection. Gutiérrez takes a cue from Bartolomé de Las Casas, who bests Vitoria by developing an argument "rooted in the truth of the facts"— that is, beginning with the *Indians'* experience. [10] Gutiérrez still begins with faith—theological reflection "sinks its roots" in spiritual experience [11]—but thorough understanding of the cultural situation in which one evangelizes is the first rather than the last intellectual task of theology. [12] The first question must be, what is the *human* issue or experience of which the gospel must make sense here and now? [13] For the scholars of the Northern Hemisphere, the question has been how to make faith credible in an increasingly skeptical and drifting modern world. But this question barely registers on the Latin American consciousness. There, to Gutiérrez's mind, the great stumbling block to faith has always been the poverty and oppression suffered by the majority at the hands of professed Christians. [14] Therefore in Latin America theological reflection must begin with comprehensive analysis—drawing on a variety of disciplines, but largely the social sciences—of the structure of that oppression. This analysis reveals that the Latin American poor live in a situation of oppression or "nonpersonhood" created and reinforced by unjust social, political, economic, and even ecclesiastical structures of international proportions and driven by a combination of greed and apathy. The injustices are of such magnitude that the only possible Christian response, even on the level of unreflective faith, is a moral indictment of oppression accompanied by a Christian praxis of liberation. [15] Thus the moral claim grounds and precedes all epistemic claims.

The last step of theological reflection, arriving at theological truth, thus requires both an active moral commitment—a stance of discipleship [16]—and a sophisticated understanding of social, political, and economic power. Anselm Min argues that for Gutiérrez, these two conditions are inextricably linked: "commitment to the oppressed" is "a necessary condition of theology" not only because the scriptural God opts for the poor but also because in contemporary Latin America only such a perspective captures the overwhelming crisis of poverty driven by oppression. [17] Other commitments—for example, to order, to conversion of the modern world, etc.—are inadequate and even false because they not only miss but actively obscure this crisis.

Theological reflection thus follows social analysis, faith, and praxis, translating the central crisis from a social to a religious context. It meditates on the Word, for and within the church, in the light of concrete active spirituality, linking it to the doctrine and symbols of Christian faith. [18] The Word, accepted by a "faith that is lived and shared in the communion of the church," is the ultimate criterion of praxis. [19] For instance, "if the issue raised by the poverty of the majority of humankind is, in the last analysis, the choice between life and death, then the challenge facing us is not simply that of a "social problem". . . . [but] something contrary to the kingdom of life that Jesus Christ proclaims." [20] The theological question is, What significance does the gospel have for the oppressed? The theological answer is salvation, seen as encompassing liberation. [21]

To be sure, although social science analyzes the causes of political, economic, and social injustice, and concrete social ethics suggests possible avenues for change, the influence does not flow only from social analysis and judgment to theology, nor do political and economic justice exhaust liberation. [22] Gutiérrez's model of Christian thought is cyclic, circulating constantly in faith among theological, practical, and ethical moments, rather than moving solely from (a necessarily fairly abstract) theology through (a likewise abstract) ethics to practice. It is a dialectic designed for the Latin American situation. [23] But for our purposes the crucial point is that in Gutiérrez, as in traditional natural law thought, *concrete moral judgment and the discovery and implementation of concrete, just solutions can occur independently of theological reflection.* This independence is relative in both cases, of course, because natural law ethics' functional independence from theology relies on theological warrants, and liberation ethics' independence from theology is a moment in the dialectical movement between theology and committed praxis rooted in unreflective faith. But in both cases moral knowledge must in some sense be "written on the hearts" of human beings. Gutiérrez speaks of "the ethical reaction . . . which we experience in the face of a situation that we analyze and, above all, live through"; [24] so this moral sense includes, if not principles, at least a moral instinct capable of approval, horror, and other moral reactions. United with faith and active virtue, this moral sense grounds theology; for where there is no commitment to justice, there can be no faith, and the Word of God—and theology as that Word's expression—is dead also. [25]

Gutiérrez's reliance upon a prereflective grasp of morality is all the more obvious in light of Stephen Pope's observation: Gutiérrez "offers no substantive and systematically explicated theory of justice" despite the fact that justice is his central critical criterion. [26] He assumes, in other words, that justice does not have to be explained—our own instincts, sharpened by the results of honest social analysis, will make plain to us what justice is and requires. We have or can generate provisional definitions of justice and other moral principles before we begin to reflect theologically. This ability is the equivalent of Thomistic participation in the eternal law.

But the prereflective sense of justice is not the only pre-theological factor Gutiérrez trusts. Marxist analysis serves as "handmaid" to his theology, furnishing it with social scientific descriptions of history in much the same way Aristotelian philosophy harnessed scientific understandings of human nature and society for Thomas. Does Gutiérrez's attempt to gain critical leverage against current Christian theology and practice then dissolve the authority of faith and revelation? Gutiérrez has checked this erosion by subordinating social analysis to the task of evangelization. Like Thomas, Gutiérrez—especially in more recent writings that respond to Vatican criticisms—insists on keeping a methodological "critical distance" from his analytical aid. [27] For theology—and here the dialectical side of Gutiérrez's method comes into play—does not simply endorse the ideologies or the solutions proposed by the social sciences. [28] Marxist analysis may be the perfect tool to reveal the corruptness of the contemporary ideology of Christendom and the false theology Christians have generated to justify it, but it can and should be dropped when injustice is no longer the central human crisis defining theological reflection. [29] Gutiérrez distances himself as well by refusing to accept Marx's reduction of history to an explanation of "the formation of ideas from material practice." For Marx "the real process of production" is "the basis of all history," and the "sum of productive forces, capital funds and social forms of intercourse, which every individual and generation finds in existence as something given, is the real basis of what the philosophers have conceived as 'substance' and 'essence' of man." [30] Gutiérrez rejects this exclusively material understanding of human activity, history, and nature. [31] *Christian* praxis is rather contemplation and practical activity arising out of deep faith in God; theology is critical reflection, not upon economic practice, but upon an active and contemplative faith, in light of the gospel, and within a social and economic context; and history is the gratuitous salvific activity of God. So if social analytical tools are indispensable to theology, they are also qualified by revelation.

PREFERENTIAL OPTION. The potential for circularity—in the inconclusive, not only dialectical, sense—is obvious. Where does authority lie if neither Marxism nor traditional Christian reflection is completely trustworthy? In modern terms (which sit uneasily with both Thomas and Gutiérrez) we would ask, what guarantees objectivity? If Gutiérrez's simultaneous concern for evangelization and reliance on Marxist analysis do not obviate the need for an overarching critical principle, they do at least generate one. Marxist analysis grants epistemological privilege not to an intellectual elite or to a neutral, uninvolved observer but to the politically and socially powerless on whose labor society is built; and the gospels demonstrate God's overriding concern for the welfare of the poor. These combine in the preferential option for the poor. In its simplest, moral sense, the preferential option simply means that we must imitate God's concern for the poor, meeting immediate needs and transforming the institutions and practices that cause poverty. [32] In its epistemological dimension it is a commitment to social and theological reflection from the perspective of the disenfranchised and in friendship with them. Gutiérrez makes this plainest in his recent work on Bartolomé de Las Casas: only by raising his practice of seeing things as if he were an Indian to a methodological principle could Las Casas fully articulate the injustice of Spanish colonization. [33]

The preferential option is partly a matter of finding the best vantage point—the intellectual equivalent of taking a seat behind home plate—but, as in Thomas, it is also a matter of the optimal alignment of moral and intellectual virtue: to know well one must be rightly disposed, and right disposition entails active love for the neighbor. This is so much the case that intellectual rigor must be a side effect of, not a motivation for, the preferential option:

> The ultimate reason for commitment to the poor and oppressed is not to be found in the social analysis we use, or in human compassion, or in any direct experience we ourselves may have of poverty. These are all doubtless valid motives that play an important part in our commitment. As Christians, however, our commitment is grounded, in the final analysis, in the God of our faith. It is a theocentric, prophetic option that has its roots in the unmerited love of God and is demanded by this love. [34]

God, by being "born into a concrete historical situation of poverty and oppression" and suffering with humanity on the cross, has both chosen the poor and extended saving grace to all. [35] If the preferential option is a faithful, graced response to this unmerited love then it is evidence of neither unbending ideology nor pride. [36] Rather, as Stephen Pope has pointed out, Gutiérrez's recent focus on God's gratuitous love suggests that the preferential option is his version of infused charity: the mode of the virtues and the source of the power to surpass the minimal moral demands of human life. [37] Its precise relationship to justice is not always clear, but otherwise it reflects a very traditional understanding of the function of grace in moral virtue and of the connection of the virtues in a life of Christian prayer and action:

> liberation theology is not simply . . . a theology that emphasizes the social dimension. It is that, but it is more; we are trying to take our stand at a point where it is impossible to separate solidarity with the poor from spirituality, brotherly and sisterly love from prayer, human beings from God. That is what it means to be a Christian, a disciple of Christ who is both God and man. [38]

At the same time, the preferential option for the poor answers some of the democratic concerns of contemporary revisionist authors by recognizing the theological authority of groups who have not been represented in the theological academy—an academy that traditionally draws from oppressive classes and cultures. So although the method responds to local need, it has universal implications for the structure and procedure of theological reflection, for the poor are revealed as agents of liberation and coauthors of theology rather than mere objects of almsgiving or theological rumination. [39] Indeed an authentic liberation theology exists "only when the oppressed themselves can freely raise their voice and express themselves directly and creatively in society and in the heart of the People of God, when they themselves 'account for the hope' which they bear, when they are the protagonists of their own liberation." [40] Similarly, the preferential option gives the content of Latin American theology global significance because the structural causes of the crisis of poverty and oppression overflow Latin American borders.

Fuchs and McCormick draw explicit connections between their own ideas and the central symbols of the natural law tradition. Although Gutiérrez does not, the implicit reliance on natural law methods and assumptions is clear. Like traditional natural law theory, Gutiérrez's liberation theology both appropriates and criticizes scientific descriptions of reality, and like traditional natural law ethics it places concrete ethical deliberation outside the theological task. Gutiérrez believes firmly in extra-biblical moral knowledge, the primacy of grace and charity, and the interdependence of the moral and intellectual virtues, and he points the way to new uses of some of the most central of these old convictions. They find a place in a new systematic structure that sets up a self-conscious, two-way connection between theology and social ethics and establishes new safeguards against witting and unwitting collusion of moral thought, dogmatic theology, and oppression.

THEOLOGICAL ANTHROPOLOGY

Other religions think in terms of cosmos and nature; Christianity, rooted in Biblical sources, thinks in terms of history. [41]

*   *   *

It is important to keep in mind that beyond—or rather through—the struggle against misery, injustice, and exploitation the goal is the *creation of a new man*. [42]

With these bold claims Gutiérrez again seems to turn his back on the natural law anthropology that has sustained even revisionists and head straight for process theology, Marxist materialism, or a general postmodern affirmation of humanity's infinite malleability. But we must be careful what we read into "history" and the "new humanity." Gutiérrez's anthropology, like his method, is really quite traditional in many ways. He in fact embraces a traditional *exitus-reditus* theology of fulfillment. He simply holds that every moment on the human continuum—not just creation, incarnation, resurrection, and judgment—is a point of active contact between graced humanity and divine action, that every material event and social movement of human history is relevant to salvation. This point of view yields important but complex and overlapping claims for theological anthropology.

SALVATION HISTORY. The traditional *exitus-reditus* anthropology emphasizes the individual's origin and end in God. Gutiérrez, while embracing this vision of individual calling, also applies it macrocosmically: history is the story of *humanity's* journey, as an historical and social whole, back to God—in other words, of God's execution of a gracious plan of salvation for the whole human race and the world as well. [43] So, for example, creation is not a perfect, complete divine act but the first and ongoing event in the salvific process; God's creative power is "something that abides," preserves, continues to act. [44] Similarly, salvation is not a remediation God dreams up for an unanticipated problem but the completion and true end of creation and all the events in between. [45] Every divine event points toward the eschaton.

Yet if Gutiérrez rejects God the watchmaker, he also rejects God the sporadically present landlord. Gutiérrez does not limit divine salvific action to obvious events like creation and resurrection. God's relationship to humanity is decidedly historical, immanent, and even interventionist: God is continuously active in human history. The witness to this claim is the history itself, described in Scripture, especially in accounts of God's promise and fulfillment, self-revelation in saving action, and preferential option for the poor: "The entire Bible, beginning with the story of Cain and Abel, mirrors God's predilection for the weak and abused of human history." [46] Gutiérrez recalls Exodus, the story of God's promised rescue of the oppressed people of Israel from slavery and eventual deliverance of them to the promised land. Even more important is the promised and still-unfolding saving action of Christ. [47]

If human history is shot through with God's salvific purpose and continuous action, then humanity collectively is guided, sustained, and perfected by grace. Not only are nature and grace compatible and continuous; there is no nature without grace, only nature intended for, and abiding in, and transformed by grace. Gutiérrez does not, therefore, do away with the traditional distinction between nature and grace. [48] But grace, not nature, comes first in the order of God's intentions: nature was created for grace, and not vice versa. Grace is no mere extension of nature; it transforms nature rather than coexisting with or even merely fulfilling it. Their dynamic interpenetration

254 Gustavo Gutiérrez and Social Solidarity

flows from their common origin and end in God's gratuitous, salvific acts of love. Thanks to this love, we belong individually and collectively to the order of grace. [49]

A SINGLE HISTORY. If God acts continuously in human history, if humanity as a whole participates in divine grace, and if salvation history points inexorably toward the eschaton, then human and divine history are not on parallel trajectories bridged by occasional momentous divine initiatives. Rather the history of salvation and human history are a single history united in Jesus Christ, "the irruption of God into human history": [50]

> There is only one human destiny, irreversibly assumed by Christ, the Lord of history. His redemptive work embraces all the dimensions of existence and brings them to their fullness. The history of salvation is the very heart of human history. . . . All reflection, any distinctions which one wishes to treat, must be based on this fact: the salvific action of God underlies all human existence. . . . Although there may be different approaches to understanding it, however, the fundamental affirmation is clear: there is only one history—a "Christo-finalized" history. [51]

What does this "Christo-finalized" history of transforming grace imply for anthropology? Above all, human beings live in the graced flow of a common divine and human history, moving individually and collectively toward the eschatological fulfillment for which they were created. More specifically, they occupy a place after the Fall, after the Resurrection of Christ, but before the eschaton. They are graced, sinful, forgiven, but not yet fulfilled or whole; they are existentially free to work with or against the universal, divine process of salvation, but often not practically free to realize their dignity in all ways. In fact one of the proofs of the unity of history is the direct correlation between their eschatological position and their concrete lives: sin, "the ultimate root of all disruption of friendship and of all injustice and oppression," manifests itself in widespread poverty and social injustice. [52] Likewise, eschatological hope thus includes freedom not only from sin but from its concrete effects. The "old man" contains the promise of the "new man," [53] called, through the incarnation, to fullness of being. [54] The fulfillment of the promised-but-incomplete Kingdom of God is both immanent and transcendent. [55]

LIBERATION, SALVATION, AND THE NATURAL LAW. The price to pay for Gutiérrez's integral salvation is that although in its potency the Kingdom is an outright gift, it does not spring, instant and ready-made, from the hand of God. "When the grace of God's reign is not accepted, when God's demands are not met, the God of the kingdom is absent." [56] The Kingdom "is also a demand": human history moves toward the promised Kingdom only where and when human beings cooperate with God's salvific grace. Both concrete fulfillment and the eschatological "gift of sonship or daughterhood" wait upon graced human efforts toward "authentic brotherhood and sisterhood." In sum, human efforts to establish justice and accomplish liberation truly advance the Kingdom's progress. [57]

> The growth of the Kingdom is a process which occurs historically *in* liberation, insofar as liberation means a greater fulfillment of man. Liberation is a precondition for the new society, but this is not all it is. While liberation is implemented in liberating historical events, it also denounces their limitations and ambiguities, proclaims their fulfillment, and impels them effectively toward total communion. This is not an identification. *Without liberating historical events, there would be no growth of the Kingdom.* But the process of liberation will not have conquered the very roots of oppression and the exploitation of man by man without the coming of the Kingdom, which is above all a gift. Moreover we can say that the historical, political liberating event *is* the growth of the Kingdom and *is* a salvific event; but it is not *the* coming of the Kingdom, not *all* of salvation. It is the historical realization of the Kingdom and, therefore, it also proclaims its fullness. This is where the difference lies. It is a distinction made from a dynamic viewpoint, which has nothing to do with the one which holds for the existence of two juxtaposed "orders," closely connected or convergent, but deep down different from each other. [58]

Both the startling uniqueness and the ambiguity of Gutiérrez's position are evident here. The eschatological Kingdom of God, like any other divine salvific intervention, must occur in and through concrete human history; yet he also wishes to avoid exaggerated Pelagian assertions that human beings can not only save themselves but also bring about the eschaton. If the union holds, it is thanks to Gutiérrez's doctrines of Christo-finalized history and of grace: following Saint Ignatius, "we are to do everything as if it depends on our work, and afterward recognize that it was a gift." [59] Human cooperation with the process of salvation is graced cooperation in the advancement of salvation history designed by God, not human accomplishment of salvation per se.

From one point of view Gutiérrez's universal salvation history is perfectly traditional: it is the Thomistic view of individual salvation history writ large. In Thomas, for instance, justifying grace does not immediately impart moral perfection or union with God. One must still work out one's own salvation in free cooperation with grace through the doing of good works and the accumulation of merit. Salvation is still gratuitous; works and merit are elements within an enveloping economy of salvation grounded in grace, without which they would be impossible in the first place. Analogously, Gutiérrez's work of liberation is part of the graced process God intends humanity to follow between the historical events of the Resurrection (Thomas's justification) and the eschaton (Thomas's beatitude). In both cases perfection occurs entirely through grace and at the end of a long life in which virtue has been increasingly evident in outward acts. In both cases virtue contributes to the common good. And in both cases beatitude does or can break into human history under the force of grace.

Yet Gutiérrez's extension of the Thomistic model of individual salvation to fit humanity does diverge from the anthropology outlined in chapter 1 and adopted by Fuchs and McCormick. In the latter tradition human society is simply the context or substrate for the growth of individual spirituality and of the church. People live in material and cultural interdependence with the larger human community, which fosters their growth in the acquired virtues, encouraging civic virtue but punishing vice's practical fruits. But the significance for salvation of a just and orderly society is only indirect: that people may more easily pursue their own spiritual union with God. Establishment of a just society is desirable, and is an outgrowth of the collectivity of individual virtue, both acquired and infused, but it is neither a salvific act nor a prerequisite for individual or collective salvation. [60] In any case individual union with God, in all but a few instances, occurs only outside human history, in death.

Gutiérrez, on the other hand, does not even treat the question of individual beatitude before the eschaton. His whole emphasis is upon the coming of the Kingdom to the earthly historical community. Society is not just the nourishing substrate and concrete context of individual conversion and spiritual growth but also and necessarily the locus of the salvation of the human community as a whole. The end of history is within history, not outside it. Salvation is society's proper and direct end. Truly human life, and authentic theology and spirituality, occur only in human community straining toward full communion with God in the world. [61]

> When we assert that man fulfills himself by continuing the work of creation by means of his labor, we are saying that he places himself, by

this very fact, within an all-embracing salvific process. To work, to transform this world, is to become a man and to build the human community; it is also to save. ... Building the temporal city is not simply a stage of "humanization" or "pre-evangelization" as was held in theology up until a few years ago. Rather it is to become part of a saving process which embraces the whole of man and all human history. Any theological reflection on human work and social praxis ought to be rooted in this fundamental affirmation. [62]

The individual's obligation to work for a just community evolves not merely from an overflowing of infused virtue or an extension of habit but an intentional response to the eschatological demand for graced human participation in the building of the Kingdom. [63] People are co-saviors.

Gutiérrez intends his contrast between the cosmic Christ and the historical Jesus to reflect just this juxtaposition between the scholastic vision of cosmic, systematic nature, perfected but not profoundly disturbed by grace, that functions predictably within a set of constant physical and soteriological laws, and contemporary historical understandings of human nature, in which surprise, struggle, and genuine directed change occur. Revelation does not interrupt the smooth functioning of the cosmos; it can overturn and redirect human history. [64]

THE DIMENSIONS OF LIBERATION. But Gutiérrez's vision of the person as an agent and beneficiary of social, historical liberation within the divine project of salvation does not exhaust his anthropology. His further development of the dimensions of human nature draws yet additional clear connections to both traditional and revisionist natural law thought. Liberation is, as always, the starting point; as Schubeck notes, liberationist anthropology is generated from the search "for the meaning of the human in the context of the real struggles of oppressed people." [65] This experience suggests that *genuine* liberation must engage humanity on three distinguishable but interdependent and interpenetrating levels. [66]

The first level of liberation—social, political, economic liberation—we have already encountered: the righting of institutional injustices and the creation of institutions that meet social and material historical needs more fairly. [67] Important to note here is the further implied claim that, in addition to being political and social creatures—this point has been made many times—human beings are embodied. The body, Gutiérrez insists, "is not something the human person *has*, but something it *is*." [68] Serious attention to the body prohibits the romanticizing or excusing of involuntary poverty and suffering. [69] Implicit, then, in Gutiérrez's integration of salvation and concrete, historical liberation is a rejection of a severe body-soul dualism. [70] In a context of abject poverty the first task of liberation is to meet basic, physical human demands for food, clothing, and shelter in a dignified way, not—as in the extreme case of the Spanish conquistadors—to save souls through mass baptism while killing people through overwork, malnutrition, and disease.

If the first level of liberation recalls Thomas's nature, especially in its vegetative and animal dimensions, the third touches on traditional doctrines of the salvation of the soul. Salvation is spiritual liberation—liberation from the sin that feeds oppression—in order to free humanity for communion with God and each other. [71] The most comprehensive political and economic advances do not fulfill, and must not eclipse, the human need to overcome "interior, personal fracture" through *individual* conversion to discipleship and to participate in a vibrant ecclesial life: [72] "a social transformation, no matter how radical it may be, does not automatically achieve the suppression of all evils." [73] Throughout *We Drink from Our Own Wells*, for instance, Gutiérrez mentions spirituality and salvation in the same breath with church, community, or communion. Genuinely liberative praxis and authentic theological reflection are rooted in a deep spirituality. [74]

The second level is the theoretical and practical keystone, analogous to Thomas's reason in both its fully theological and deeply practical dimensions. Here theological and religious commitment take on rational and political characteristics in the creation of "a new man in a new society of solidarity." [75] Gutiérrez describes it variously as the level of history, freedom, and utopian imagination. [76] Liberation at this level is liberation to freedom for self-determination, a good that guards against a reduction of liberation to either its spiritual or its material dimensions. [77] Here is utopianism in the Peruvian tradition, cooperatively analyzing and passionately denouncing injustice, constructing a common vision for the future, and devising means to cross from here to there. [78] Freedom presupposes a hard-headed analytical and practical rationality that is attentive to experience and flexible enough to change course in response to it. Liberation, after all, must *work.* Success is not ideological loyalty but advancement of the communal, historical, concrete, spiritual human good here and now. One can make this judgment only in the field, in the midst of the practical effort to create a just society. [79]

Utopian rationality is therefore practical, relying heavily on prudence. It would be wrong to call it natural law, for in the sense that natural law is participation in divine reason, it still calls for the application, however creative, of eternal law to practical circumstances; utopian thought rather mediates dialectically between revelation and experience. [80] But like natural law, utopian rationality abides in and serves God's providential plan for humanity and counts upon the human capacities for discernment and for free cooperation with grace.

These levels yield a list of basic, interdependent, unrankable goods, a practical and theological anthropology that both arises out of and grounds concrete action and moral discernment. Human beings are constructed of interdependent dimensions that, unlike Maritain's planes of existence, can be neither separated nor ranked. We come to know them not by meditating on our inclinations but by engaging in committed practical action, discovering what seems crucial to life and fulfillment and what brings death and suffering. [81] Human persons are historical (in the sense of living in concrete places and times and "working out their salvation" in a single "Christo-finalized" history); political; called to salvation and liberation; sinful and graced; rational; and both physical and ensouled. But, most of all, they are communal. This, more than anything else, characterizes Gutiérrez's anthropology: the human being is engaged in a *communal* pursuit of the Kingdom of God, and that goal entails historical, concrete fulfillment of human being in all of its dimensions.

Yet even this departure from Thomas's soteriology and anthropology is clearly inspired by Thomas's telic anthropology. Many other departures reveal themselves as at most historical updates. Gutiérrez amplifies and extends Thomas's observations about cultural variations in moral perspective to allow for a modest anthropological open-endedness, an expectation that his anthropology will require rearrangement or addition in the future. Similarly, even in his earliest writings, Gutiérrez introduces the "new man" not to replace the natural law *exitus-reditus* scheme but to define and integrate its content. The "new man" is a humanity we have not *yet* known: renewed in grace, converted, genuinely self-determined toward the true human end of integral liberation. But this novelty resembles Pauline renovation more than absolute otherness. It is grounded in a divine salvific action that begins with creation. Even in Gutiérrez the freedom to create the new humanity "by means of [our] labor" is a freedom not of license but of cooperation with divine grace toward our final end: "man *fulfills* himself by *continuing* the work of creation." [82]

RELIGION AND REASON

Gutiérrez's profound integration of sacred and profane does not cancel his reliance on the moral judgments of "untutored" human reason. It does, however, interestingly qualify their power. In fact, Gutiérrez in many ways has less confidence in raw human reason than do the scholastics and the revisionists. Thus questions of "human" and "Christian" reason or "human" and "Christian" ethics work out differently in his thought. For instance, for the whole scholastic and revisionist tradition, the world abides in God's provident grace, and every human capacity—even if it does not aim directly at salvation—is intended to advance some divinely determined end. Moral reason is one of these capacities, for natural law is human participation in God's eternal law. This amounts to a theological justification for carrying out moral reflection at times without explicit reference to Christian revelation or spirituality. Concerned in addition to develop arguments that do not jar in a world of nonbelievers, Fuchs and McCormick find the points of reconnection to religion especially awkward: for instance, working out the distinctions between the demands of reason and the call of charity or the relationship between autonomous moral reason and ecclesiastical authority. Gutiérrez too assumes enveloping grace but, in self-conscious deference to his circumstances, also assumes a culture of faith. [83] Divine salvific grace is at the explicit center of his reflection. He is also the most thoroughly concerned with the pervasive implications of ethics for theology and of theology for ethics, the weak connection that sometimes stymies Fuchs's ethics and McCormick's theology. Except for the initial crucial prereflective movement toward solidarity with the poor— admittedly inspired partly by faith, but by prereflective faith—moral and theological reflection are a seamless whole. His awkward moments come at the interface of religious reflection with nonreligion, as in his careful qualification in *The Truth Shall Make You Free* of his use of Marxist analysis.

Not surprisingly, Gutiérrez's solution to a "modern" sticky question, the place of non-Christian others in salvation history, is ambiguous. Gutiérrez clearly believes in religious freedom and lauds Las Casas's profound respect for the Indians in their difference, but he also points out that this respect rests on a Christian interpretation of their poverty, which implies that "Jesus Christ is present in them." [84] In other words, the other can be loved precisely because she is caught up in the single sweep of salvation history. In the rare instances when the case of the "good pagan" arises for Gutiérrez, the criterion is identical to that for Christians: "we will be definitively judged by our love for men, by our capacity to create brotherly conditions of life"; [85] for if even among the baptized "there is no salvation without the practice of justice," committed (graced) action must be the central criterion of salvation. [86] Thus as in Las Casas, the "faithless faithful" are in greater danger of perdition than upright nonbelievers. [87] Revisionism's fundamental option for the Absolute appears as the concrete option for (or against) the poor and powerless.

But here a contradiction begins to surface. Even if universal salvific grace can work an *implicit*, unthematic conversion, truly liberative action depends upon utopian reflection; and because one side of the utopian dialectic rests explicitly upon faith and revelation, full cooperation with salvation in history seems to require *explicit* Christian belief. The position implies an aim at eventual Christian, albeit liberative, hegemony. Gutiérrez's silence about religious pluralism—painfully obvious in his passing over the influence of Indian spirituality and ethics upon Las Casas in favor of a lengthy treatment of his European interlocutors—confirms this impression. [88]

But if a more explicitly Christian outlook makes interreligious relations problematic, it also gives an extra edge to Gutiérrez's critique of the institutional church. For instance, the colonial Latin American church reduced Jesus Christ almost entirely to his passion, heavily emphasizing passive suffering as a spiritual virtue, a way of gaining merit toward salvation. The image is obviously a useful ideological tool: work hard, accept poverty, receive a reward in heaven. The vision of integral, salvific, historical fulfillment, however, condemns it on theological as well as moral grounds, for it violates Christian doctrine as well as human dignity. To the extent that the institutional church has colluded in this injustice or refused to risk redressing it, it comes under prophetic indictment. [89] But the critical power of solidarity with the poor reaches deeper than ecclesiastical iconography or even social programming. It entails politically significant changes in viewpoint (toward the oppressed), theological-ethical method (toward liberationist dialectic), and theological-ethical procedure (toward communal theological reflection in local communities). [90] Gutiérrez has in mind Latin American basic Christian communities, or CEBs, whose authority comes by a slightly different route than that of McCormick's democratic moral debaters and has a wider range. It is rooted not only in the universal perspicuity of natural law, as for Fuchs and McCormick, but also in the universal need to reflect from within one's concrete experience, and it extends not just to moral questions but, through its more fully developed critical hermeneutic, to theology as well.

In addition, Gutiérrez makes more explicit than any revisionist—except perhaps Bernard Häring—moral commitment's indivisibility from biblically rooted, communally nourished spirituality. Gutiérrez's theology of spirituality is nascent in *A Theology of Liberation* and receives deeper treatment in the later *We Drink from Our Own Wells* and *The God of Life*. For Gutiérrez spirituality is the way of life entailed by faith: [91] "the following of Jesus," the "dominion of the Spirit," "a vital attitude, all-embracing and synthesizing, informing every detail as well as the totality of our lives," "a manner of life that gives a profound unity to our prayer, thought, and action." [92] This way requires a break with the "old man" on all levels. Given that Gutiérrez assumes a culture of nominal Christian faith, the conversion is not to God simply but

to the realization that "'the union with the Lord,' which all spirituality proclaims, is not a separation from man; to attain this union, I must go through
man, and the union, in turn, enables me to encounter man more fully"; in
essence, "conversion to the Lord implies this conversion to the [exploited]
neighbor." [93] Fuchs's and McCormick's conviction about the religious centrality of the fundamental option appears in even starker terms: either one is
determined to take the gospel's gift and demand of liberation seriously in
one's whole person, or one is a hypocrite. [94] But if spirituality encompasses
morality, action is prayer:

> What we do to the poor we do to Christ himself. It is this fact that
> gives action in behalf of the poor its decisive character and prevents it
> from being taken simply as an expression of the "social dimension" of
> faith. No, it is much more than that; such action has an element of
> contemplation, of encounter with God, at the very heart of the work
> of love. And this encounter is not "merited" by any work; it is the
> gratuitous gift of God. [95]

Prayerful solidarity with the poor also requires Matthean spiritual poverty
(detachment from material goods combined with protest against material
poverty), spiritual childhood (complete and humble openness to God), and,
most of all, the genuine friendship with the poor modeled in the gospels. [96]

Finally and most importantly, the church is the context for any authentic
Christian spirituality—that is, *for all authentically liberative cooperation with
salvific grace.* [97] The following of Christ, the search for union with God, is a
"collective adventure," a journey of the whole people of God. [98] Gutiérrez has
in mind here local communions like the CEBs, in which the holistic Christian
life of prayer, worship, action, and theological reflection is vibrant. This point
cannot be overstressed. Although most critics of Gutiérrez at least nod toward
the CEBs, some tend oddly to underestimate their importance in Gutiérrez's
thought to the integral life of faith that nourishes both action and genuine
and rigorous theological reflection. [99] Gutiérrez's impression of the role of the
church as a global institution is a bit harder to define. If no longer the
exclusive conduit for sacramental grace and salvific truth, the church is still
the sacrament of the world and the appropriate mediating center of the
historical salvific process. Yet Gutiérrez clearly believes that it has at times
refused to cooperate with salvific grace. [100]

But reflection on the significance of faith for the method of moral reason
can go only so far, given that Gutiérrez devotes much more attention to moral
reason's spiritual context and to theological dialectic than he does to concrete

ethical reflection. What else can be said? To begin with, in Gutiérrez's thought, attitude and perspective are not just *dispositionally* but *methodologically* significant. Judgments depend upon facts, and—as Gutiérrez's analysis of the Spanish debates on colonization handily demonstrates—facts arrange themselves differently before the eyes of a person committed to solidarity with the poor than they do before a person committed to turning a profit. Good moral judgment depends as much upon religious life—"prayer, celebration, the knowledge of God's word and a taste for it" [101]—as it does upon clear theological reflection. In other language, we would say that charity perfects moral judgment.

What is the relationship between "human" and "Christian" requirements? Does Gutiérrez recognize Fuchs's and McCormick's distinction between minimal standards of human ethics and Christian or existential ideals? The integration of human and Christian history makes sustaining a distinction between Christian and simply human standards nearly impossible. But Gutiérrez does not conflate minimal requirements with standards of perfection. Like Fuchs and McCormick, he employs an essential human ethic as a screen or filter for clearly wrong acts, a basis for prophetic social critique. This screen identifies violations of the first level of liberation: social, political, and economic justice. But when we shift our focus to the individual, the demands of charity—literally, of *gratuitousness*—outstrip the requirements of justice. In an analysis of Paul's letter to Philemon, Gutiérrez writes, "'Do even more than I say' is a formula for limitless demands. The point is that Christian love is to find expression *in works without limitation*." Genuinely selfless love—not driven by a hope for quid pro quo reward—lies "at the heart of the behavior of a follower of Jesus." [102] To ask merely about what is objectively "right" or "acceptable" is a failure of love, a revelation of hypocritical unwillingness to harness the power of salvific grace. For people of active, reflective faith, the language of minimal requirement is superfluous.

GUTIÉRREZ AS A NATURAL LAW THEOLOGIAN

We have seen that Gutiérrez's efforts to distance himself from the ivory-tower scholastic theorizing of Vitoria and Juan Ginés de Sepúlveda do not imply wholesale rejection of the infrastructure of natural law. First and most important, Gutiérrez bases both his individual and his social anthropologies in Thomas's *exitus-reditus* scheme. This scheme, and all that it entails for the human capacity for cooperation with salvific grace, leads to surprisingly substantive agreement on the unity of moral and intellectual virtues. It is especially important to point out that Gutiérrez's grounding of reflection in praxis in fact recalls the parts of prudence, especially docility, circumspection, caution, and memory. And like Thomas, Gutiérrez founds his reflective method solidly in his anthropology and its attendant epistemology. Understandable divergences in epistemological choices—Thomas fixing on constant physical and psychological human conditions of knowledge, and Gutiérrez, on dynamic cultural conditions—must not obscure their common starting point.

Second, while Gutiérrez's stress on the indivisibility of historical liberation and the progress of salvation history is hardly Thomistic (except that Thomas would agree that an increase in social justice is likely a sign of grace and true virtue in individuals) Gutiérrez's vision of the integral effects of grace is quite traditional. In Thomas grace has practical consequences: the grace of infused charity refers all one's action toward one's last end, God, and brings with it all moral virtues, which bear fruit in good works. [103] Likewise, in Gutiérrez, the grace of genuine conversion infuses human behavior in all contexts and on all levels. It is impossible to be truly grace-filled and intentionally unjust, for instance.

Third, in the liberationist as in the natural law tradition, the true individual and common goods are ultimately compatible and interdependent. Gutiérrez never uses the existence of class conflict in the contemporary world as an argument against the theory of the common good. It is possible for people to pursue and fulfill their true needs and interests harmoniously and cooperatively. [104] But Gutiérrez's notion of the contiguity of salvation history and human history extends the notion of common good to spiritual goods; the spiritual health of the community depends upon that of its members, and vice versa. The journey to the Kingdom is necessarily a common, not a private, venture; the individual is saved with and as a member of the community. This claim appears in Thomas only negatively: an individual's spiritual downfall might infect the community, but there is no direct commerce between individual and corporate grace.

Gutiérrez's extension of the common good also completes the circle of interdependence among the dimensions of human flourishing, a circle left unfinished by Thomas; physical want can have an ill-effect upon the spiritual dimension of human flourishing, and vice versa. Yet Gutiérrez claims not that living in deprivation prevents a person from being saved but that it stands in the way of the historical realization of the Kingdom. Gutiérrez's moral outrage is directed not just at deprivation in itself but primarily at the sinful injustices that cause it. The failure of love that lies behind the injustice, not deprivation in itself, is the true impediment to the coming of the Kingdom. A social and political system that distributes resources justly is both a prerequisite for and sign of corporate growth in the spirit, but this corporate growth also depends upon and aids individuals' conversions to God and to the concrete task of justice. Thus Gutiérrez does alter the Thomistic notion of the common good in two ways: individual and communal spiritual growth are interdependent in a universal sense, not just case-by-case; and spiritual and material goods are inextricably intertwined. Yet the spiritual good is dependent not simply upon the material good but upon the justice with which the material good is produced and distributed.

Occasionally Gutiérrez moves on from implicit affirmations of human beings' pretheological moral knowledge to dalliances with traditional natural law methods of concrete moral discernment. Precisely because Gutiérrez lacks a full-blown ethic, and lacks especially a means of managing the conflicts and compromises that properly prophetic and realistic utopian reflection is bound to require, we need to ask whether these overtures could develop into a more comprehensive, explicit development of natural law method. To begin to formulate an answer, we must move from the genre of analysis to the more tentative genre of thought-experiment. How might Gutiérrez contribute to natural law reconstruction? First, implicit in the foregoing discussion is a respect for prudence, in Thomas's sense: considered judgment based in gathered wisdom. Thomas's dimensions of prudence have resonance in Gutiérrez's writings.

Another promising opening to natural law—telling because it addresses a problem that preoccupies feminist ethics as well—is casuistic: Gutiérrez's mitigation of charity's demand for limitless selflessness. On one hand, as we have seen, Gutiérrez disabuses us of the illusion that charity requires only a fairly clear and minimal level of action; if we think we have done enough, then we have misunderstood gratuitous love. But what about the fact that relatively powerless people are often exploited further precisely through the religiously couched demand to give without limit? Gutiérrez's response is that among the poor

> the form [that love of God and love of self] take bears the mark of an intolerable poverty, of the struggle for basic human survival, of boundary situations. Thus it is often difficult to pronounce definitive judgment with categories belonging to other contexts. This is one more reason to enter the world of the poor with the greatest respect. [105]

Gutiérrez, following Las Casas, begins by thinking from the viewpoint of the powerless person. One must not condemn the poor if they appear to fail to give limitlessly or perhaps even if they fall short of the standards of historical justice. Circumstances dictate the form liberatory action takes. This concession is a fine opening for genuine casuistry, but it contains no solid standards for prophetic judgment of oppressed people or, in fact, of anyone acting in imperfect circumstances. Is self-protection permitted only when it helps me to advance the cause of liberation? Is martyrdom to a cause or apparently hypocritical self-protection more liberatory? [106] Thus exactly what this overture toward casuistry permits and proscribes would need to be clarified.

A clearer opening toward prophetic use of natural law method is Gutiérrez's enthusiasm over the brilliant extended syllogism that Las Casas constructs to show why human sacrifice, a crucial point in Spanish arguments for Native American depravity, does not in fact violate the natural law. Las Casas counters the apparent evilness or irrationality of Native American human sacrifice by deftly rearranging natural law premises to yield an unexpected conclusion: if people have a natural knowledge of and desire to worship God, and if they accordingly want to offer God the best possible gift in worship, then the sacrifice of a human being is completely normal and natural—absent, of course, knowledge of revealed proscriptions. [107] This use of natural law renders the strange discomfittingly familiar, intentionally inspiring both an awareness of common humanity and common moral logic and an urgent need to revisit the effects of other, unshared assumptions upon the "obvious" conclusions one draws from this common logic. The "view from the other's shoes" cannot so easily be dismissed if the other is simply making use of divinely granted, universal moral knowledge.

But these are only openings. Fuller parsing of moral judgment would require versions of three other traditional tools: a clear if revisable list of prophetic standards and goods to be sought; a crisper distinction between the pairs good/bad and right/wrong; and a set of guidelines for reasoning casuistically. Together, these tools would give liberation ethics the capacity to answer the following sorts of questions. What constitutes deprivation? How do standards of rightness or the demands of love change when our lives and livelihood are threatened? If we inadvertently make bad judgments based on poor information, are we good but wrong? At what level does context affect judgment? The challenge—as in traditional natural law reflection, but also in other contemporary liberationist approaches—would be to bring precision to moral reflection but avoid the sort of overuse and legalism that tended to create absurd loopholes and stifle prophetic insight, love, and utopian flexibility.

We are at the end of our hypothetical limb. What can we now claim? It is fair to say both that Gutiérrez leaves a few openings for systematic casuistical reflection and that his theological method can thrive only if it adopts some rigorous method of moral reflection. I have claimed that natural law methods, especially given their rootage in an anthropology so closely related to Gutiérrez's, are the right size and shape to fill the gap.

This does not mean that liberationist ethics could not go forward on some other model; for example, Philip LeMasters suggests that it adopt Barth's *analogical* connection between political progress and salvation and, presumably, develop moral discernment along Barthian lines as well. [108] Even more important, I do not claim that Gutiérrez is convinced that entangling oneself in the fine points of natural law solves any practical issues that the preferential option does not. Again, Las Casas's argument on natural law and human sacrifice proves the point. Its purpose was to dissuade the Spaniards from attacking the Indians, whom he hoped to evangelize peacefully and noncoercively. At stake, Gutiérrez argues, were the Indians' salvation and Las Casas's preferential Christian love for them, not the purity of the just war doctrine. Las Casas's clever rebuttal of it was likely simply a means to defeat his enemies at their own game rather than an affirmation that natural law provides unique guidance to well-disposed moral reasoners. [109] By implication there are significant basic negative moral norms—like "do not sacrifice human beings"—that only the gospel can teach. If so, then Gutiérrez may count the precepts and methods of the natural law inadequate to *Christian* moral discernment.

But these caveats leave a wide berth for a more general and significant claim: as liberationism—including feminism—develops its ethical method, it could comfortably draw upon natural law for theories of good and value, or models of casuistry, or guidance in mediating conflicts.

GUTIÉRREZ'S SUCCESS AS AN INTEGRATIVE THINKER

Gutiérrez's common ground with feminism—a critical epistemology yoked with a liberationist approach to systematic thought—calls for an especially careful evaluation of his approach. For his success or failure, if it does not determine the success or failure of Christian feminist thought, at least gives warnings of potential strong points and trouble spots in feminist theology and ethics.

Gutiérrez incorporates most of the elements we have come to see as essential to Thomistic ethics, but he orders them differently, as stages in a practical-reflective dialectic: action springs from unreflective faith, inspires social analysis, and leads to theological reflection. This reordering forces him to relate all the elements much more closely than do Fuchs and McCormick, forbidding him ever (for example) to lay theology aside once he believes he understands his moral mandate. In turn, his fundamental theology—reflection on the conditions for the possibility of evangelization—rests upon historical and moral factors. So moral reflection is integrated with faith and theology from the beginning, and prereflective ethical knowledge plays a pivotal role in both. Similarly, the material, social, and spiritual flourishing of persons are distinguishable but indivisible. Human beings are created, graced, and intended for integral fulfillment in community; their eschatological expectations include not simply spiritualized, transcendent individual beatitude but completion of a concrete, historical Kingdom of God in the world. These claims connect the eschatological and temporal ends that coexist so awkwardly in Fuchs and McCormick.

These reorderings give each familiar element of his ethic a new twist. Individual integrity begins, for Gutiérrez, not with a formal virtue theory but with a description of the root of human virtue: the preferential option for the poor, expressed in liberating praxis and nourished in ecclesial community. Just as liberation is a dimension of the larger movement of salvation, individual integrity is a dimension of a comprehensive spirituality, the root of the project of liberation. [110] Fuchs's and McCormick's fundamental option may logically entail all of this, but their Absolute has a much more abstract face, and their passages among religious experience, theology, and ethics are not as facile.

The social appears in Gutiérrez's thought in nearly every guise: ecclesial reflection, social praxis, social solidarity, social analysis, and the communal and historical aspect of every dimension of human experience. Communal cooperation in analysis, critique, and constructive planning is presupposed in Gutiérrez's keystone practice of utopian reflection. All that is missing is what might traditionally be labeled a social ethic: broadly applicable norms, principles, and models for just social organization. Gutiérrez leaves this gap intentionally: his social analysis and moral hermeneutic are meant primarily to serve the ecclesial, evangelical task of theology. [111] They are not in themselves social ethics.

But, on the other hand, for Gustavo Gutiérrez theology presupposes at least a rudimentary social ethics; its integrity rests on our ability to make reliable, *pretheological* moral judgments. In fact this task is so urgent that it is often better for the church to risk error in a hasty analysis than to wait for a more studied opinion. [112] Although he assumes that Christians begin from a simple faith, he does not have them consult the exegetical or moral theological traditions to discover whether humanly imposed poverty and oppression are morally wrong, and he can be interpreted as assuming that non-Christians also possess a fundamental moral sense. Extreme violations of the human good are so glaring that systematic listings of fundamental moral principles or human goods are unnecessary. In order to protect the gospel, the church must engage in public, "prophetic *denunciation* of every dehumanizing situation, which is contrary to brotherhood, justice, and liberty. . . . [and of] every sacralization of oppressive structures to which the Church itself might have contributed."[113] Still, this lack of explicit social ethical criteria explains others' worries that liberationists seek material goods at the expense of basic political freedoms.[114]

However, where liberation ethics seems too sketchy to prevent excess, liberation theology steps in with force: evangelization, which can succeed (especially in those places where Christianity has been compromised and has betrayed or ill-served the people) only through development of an integral, credible Christian message; and the promise and mandate of graced cooperation in the building of the Kingdom of God. Because theological and ethical reflection are moments in a unified process rather than activities of separate disciplines, these guidelines are not so easily forgotten. Yet they do not eliminate the methodological bind: on what are prereflective judgments of violation grounded? Only a version of natural law, with an epistemological emphasis on experience as well as on participation in divine reason, could perform this task. Articulating this connection more clearly is in fact essential to the success of the liberationist project as a whole, for the more refined the critique, the more pointed the prophecy and the more specific the utopian reflection. A request for expansion and precision is not necessarily a call for an antihistorical stance. It *is* a call for descriptions of human being and flourishing, and of the grounds for human knowledge of being and flourishing, that stand up to the demands of a particular place and time.

Gutiérrez does eventually make room for constructive Christian social ethics, but it is a task he assigns the community: utopian reflection. This brand of social ethics is potentially more compelling than anything Fuchs or McCormick might be able to develop, for in addition to the goals of fulfilling one's own end, meeting the neighbor's concrete need, and developing a just society it pursues the eschatological goal of cooperating in the elimination of sinful oppression. Methodological and procedural barriers protect it from three fatal faults: carrying out exegetical and theological reflection in detachment from social analysis and concrete action; developing constructive social ethics in detachment from Scripture and socially engaged religious community; and pursuing individual moral discernment and social ethics in detachment from each other. Utopian reflection does not keep well; it must be concocted on site.[115]

Practical moral reason, like social ethics, is anticipated rather than outlined. An adequate practical moral reason would be concerned with means for achieving concrete liberating ends in liberating ways—e.g., consistent with a theologically responsible use of social science analysis—but Gutiérrez does not provide technical guides for accomplishing this. He has little theoretical patience for applying casuistry on the microscopic level—to refine concrete norms—because he has no confidence that highly particular norms developed by the Latin American church ever had any genuinely liberatory intent; even if they had, it would be their liberatory character, not their status as traditional norms, that recommended them. He does, however, congratulate Las Casas for besting his opponents at the casuistical game, and he himself employs casuistic metaphors rhetorically if not systematically. Gutiérrez's concern is instead theological: what does a general situation of economic and political oppression imply for faithful proclamation of the gospel?

Despite all of this, because the moral acts of participating in a concrete liberative praxis and a focused social analysis precede theology in the order of reflection, Gutiérrez's theological success depends on his eventual ability to develop a clearer description of liberative practical moral reasoning; a weakness at this point in his method would jeopardize not only his ethics but his theology. Feminist theological reflection, likewise dependent on a moral hermeneutic, is subject to the same limitation: its ethical house must be in order if its theology is to succeed.

Gutiérrez has responded with similar impatience to other intervening pressures on natural law thought. He depends upon personalism's doctrine of human dignity, but he rejects Maritain's separation of the eschatological and political as well as the tendency, especially in Latin America, for personalist emphasis on authenticity in interpersonal relations to exclude issues of political and economic inequity. Gutiérrez is largely uninterested in theoretical questions of juridical ecclesiastical authority; rather, his emphasis is upon the responsibility of the church, including its most powerful members, to be the church of and for the poor. Just as in Thomas the unjust ruler has abdicated the responsibility to the common good that justifies his rule, in Gutiérrez the unconverted bishop abandons the true mission of the church. Gutiérrez, however, is seeking conversion rather than defrocking. Neither is he drawn in by debates over moral absolutes and virtually exceptionless norms. This demurral owes partly to the prophetic character of his ethic, which permits him to sidestep the issue, and partly to his insistence that the only absolute is God's preferential option for the poor. All else depends on this truth.

Perhaps the most instructive dimension of his approach to ethics is the dimension least commented upon: the relation between Christian and other ethics in a pluralistic world. Gutiérrez, like Thomas, organizes his account of the world and human history under the protective umbrella of Christian accounts of creation, redemption, and the eschaton. This choice raises the specters of triumphalism and cultural hegemony. The difference, as Gutiérrez himself points out, is that his purpose is not to develop a Christian cosmology for export or even to create a "Theory of Everything" for Christians. Rather, he is speaking intentionally of and to a Christian culture about a disease that he believes to be eating away at the core of Christian belief and practice in that place. The self-consciousness of this choice, far from condemning Gutiérrez as intolerant, sets him up perfectly for interreligious and cross-cultural conversations. Fuchs and, during most of his career, McCormick have assumed that basic Christian and universal human norms (or at least values) are always, already, and necessarily interchangeable; Christian theological claims are therefore irrelevant to public discussion and ought to be kept out of it. This complex of assumptions puts them in an awkward theological and practical position when they find themselves contradicting apparently strong secular ethical claims. Gutiérrez, by prescinding from premature claims about the international currency of Christian morals, sets himself up much more aptly for a pluralistic debate about basic norms in which the participants' worldviews and fundamental commitments are highly visible. The Fuchs/McCormick model of public discourse then seems to be a nonconflictual model, in which all participants distill their moral traditions to first principles, subscribing implicitly to the expectation that they will emerge with one coherent worldview and vision of moral truth. The model of discourse that fits Gutiérrez's stance is a conflictual model, in which participants bring their entire traditions to the table. The immediate goals for such a decision would be mutual respect, self-critical assessment of one's own tradition in light of other traditions, and consensus on important practical issues. Wide agreement on general norms is of course a hope, but particularity of worldviews and cultural character should not be sacrificed to meet it.

In the end, Gutiérrez's theological method illuminates contemporary possibilities for natural law ethics not because it is an ethic—his ethic is clearly and intentionally underdeveloped—but because an ethic of a natural law sort is pivotal for the praxis in which his method's self-consciously theological project and self-consciously holistic anthropology are rooted. Liberationist thought keeps intellect, spirituality, and morality in view simultaneously, softening even further than revisionism the divisions among the dimensions of theological moral reflection.

CONTRIBUTIONS

For traditionalists and radicals alike, Gutiérrez's theology is something of a Trojan horse into which he has slipped questionable novel methods under the guise of pure traditionalism, or vice versa. [116] But this metaphor seems inept in light of the way in which ideas recombine and are transformed in concrete human reflection. The more useful question—especially in light of a proposal for feminist appropriation of natural law—is whether Gutiérrez builds a serviceable bridge from Thomas and scholastic theology to a self-consciously interdependent world that has given up on modern assumptions about objectivity, neutrality, and univocal truth but still professes esteem for the human right to self-realization. Does Gutiérrez's historical perspective work well with his traditional anthropological and moral assumptions?

All of Gutiérrez's particular contributions to this task come into focus under one deceptively modest lens: to read Gutiérrez carefully is to enter an exercise in expressing deeply ingrained traditional theological themes—like the *exitus-reditus* anthropology, or the primacy of charity, or the interdependence of moral and intellectual virtue—meaningfully from within a situation of oppression and an historical worldview. The conversion is compelling precisely because he integrates theological and moral inquiry so thoroughly. Gutiérrez asks not only "What does this norm mean today?" but "What does this doctrine mean today?" and even "What does this gospel mean today?" Thanks to this deeper treatment, foundational elements of natural law theology—sullied in the eyes of some by their long connection to the confined range of Thomas's cultural imagination or the even narrower assumptions of neoscholastic moral theology—in fact survive the transition. As a result, natural law's holistic anthropology and confidence in the innate human capacity for moral judgment retain their potency.

At the center of Gutiérrez's contributions to this conversion are two crucial claims: that all theological viewpoints are biased by the interests and locations of their proponents and that this admission, rather than throwing open the door to utter relativism, equips us with new critical tools for scrutinizing theology's faithfulness to the gospel. As Johann Baptist Metz points out, "the question of truth" is now the question whether there are "any interests capable of truth. . . . Thus, the question of truth and the question of justice are interrelated. . . . Interest in undivided justice belongs to the premises of the search for truth." [117] The crucial challenge is thus not establishing a neutral viewpoint—there is none—but choosing an appropriate particularism. The option for the poor eliminates outright some moral and theological perspectives as untruthful or—like theological existentialism—ultimately irrelevant. [118] It is, Gutiérrez believes, *the* interest capable of truth in Latin America and possibly also in our interdependent global society.

The critical power of the preferential option is unmistakable when we consider the contrast between Gutiérrez's apparently deferential insistence that theology subordinate itself to the evangelical function of the church and his sharp criticism of the Roman Catholic Church's official theology and policies. The church may have relieved suffering, but it has also frequently supported and benefited from the social and political structures that cause suffering and, with some recent exceptions, shaped its official theology according to their interests. Such divisions and injustices are obstacles to proclamation. [119] This moral and ultimately theological criticism of the institutional church subjects the church's public affairs—and even more radically, its internal dealings—to the same standards of justice and love that apply to other public institutions. Gutiérrez's recent less combative—some would even say docile—stance toward hierarchical theological authority has not dulled the critical power of this moral hermeneutic. [120]

Gutiérrez's insistence that all knowledge is interested knowledge implies that the prereflective ethical judgments he expects of human beings are not ideally neutral or disinterested. Especially because Gutiérrez is addressing an already nominally Christian context, he assumes that initial "ethical reactions" are based in experience filtered through some combination of reason, intuition, general cultural influence, and peculiarly Christian knowledge; like feminist epistemologists, Gutiérrez would not mistake prereflective moral judgment for moral judgment unformed by culture and religion. In fact this is why Gutiérrez is so concerned about the practical shape of Christian life: people's early experiences shape their deep senses of right and wrong. Here his thought is resonant with that of feminist thinkers like Nancy Chodorow, who has argued that early experience ingrains in children their sense of what roles are "right" and "wrong" for men and women to fill. [121] The intimation that even preanalytical judgments are learned rather than innate may separate Gutiérrez from Thomas slightly, but not completely. Thomas holds natural law's first principles to be innate, but their articulation and application occur gradually, through the training of the will and the intellect. In addition, Thomas's insistence that human beings naturally love their own good and love most their ultimate good, God, reminds us that Thomas's prereflective person is no more "neutral" than Gutiérrez's. Thomas, too, roots theological reflection and moral judgment in the interest capable of truth.

Another of Gutiérrez's contributions is his transfer of individual salvation history onto the screen of collective human history. Although some theological details of this shift are incomplete—for instance, Gutiérrez believes on one hand in the rootage of oppression in individual sin and in the continuing need for individual conversion and redemption from sinfulness, and on the other in collective, historical movement toward the Kingdom of God [122]—

274 Gustavo Gutiérrez and Social Solidarity

the insights it permits into the connections between individual agency and collective responsibility are indispensable to contemporary theological and moral reflection.

First, Gutiérrez employs the hallmark liberationist category of collective agency, and yet he implicitly distinguishes between perduring and contemporary collective agents. Gutiérrez never relies exclusively on the idea of perduring corporate agency to make a moral point. For example, in the same day he used two rationales to recommend that the quincentenary of the arrival of Europeans in the Americas be marked by the forgiveness of Latin American foreign debt. The first was rooted in *perduring* collective European (and North American) agency; here he argued for restitution for past and continuing decimation of Native American lands and peoples. The second was rooted in the responsibility of *current* collective agents for suffering; here he argued for immediate relief of contemporary injustices toward the Latin American poor. Adding that the events of the sixteenth century are not all that relevant in the changed world of today, he insisted that what really mattered was the responsibility of contemporary individuals and institutions toward each other. [123] The theologically troubling idea of a perduring, collective moral actor was therefore unnecessary to the logic of his moral judgment, even if it did provide compelling prophetic images.

But this example also illustrates that for Gutiérrez corporate sin is not merely the summation of individual sins but entails corporate accountability. We make use of a similar notion of corporate responsibility all the time, especially in law, [124] but Gutiérrez pushes it further. To begin with, every time we do something so simple as buy a soft drink, we participate in the evils of the corporation that produced it. Our purchase may not be unjust in any immediate sense—maybe we paid a fair price, purchased it from a local grocer rather than a chain store, and bought other wholesome foods for our children first—but by supporting the corporation's injustices, we help to perpetuate them. Even though we do not intend evil, we genuinely advance oppression. Yet we cannot completely avoid this sort of participation in evil, for if we want to be engaged in the process of liberation, "we cannot opt out of our being present in this sinful society." We can denounce injustice, but we cannot avoid participating in it. [125]

Is this collective entanglement in injustice sin or an inculpable side effect of virtue? Thomas and the revisionists imply that there is always at least one objectively acceptable option. If one chooses it with proper intention, even though it may entail undesirable side effects, one does not sin, for one cannot be condemned for having to act in imperfect circumstances.

This response avoids determining human beings to morally evil acts. But its emphasis on the inculpability of the subject obscures the fact that even the "good" person performing objectively "right" actions is profiting from sinful structures, getting her hands dirty, and inflicting or tolerating others' suffering; to the extent that she does these things even under the guise of "objectively correct" actions she should feel regret and a need of God's grace and forgiveness. This regretful entanglement is certainly different from serious sin, which is a choice against the poor and therefore a conscious refusal to follow God. The spiritual risk and deficit of charity entailed by getting one's hands a bit dirty in the fight for justice is miniscule compared to the spiritual risk and deficit of charity entailed by knowingly turning one's back.

How are we to understand morally this regretful infliction of harm? The scholastic and neoscholastic tradition can view it only as psychological or chimeric guilt, for there is no real fault involved. Thomas's discussion of culpable and inculpable ignorance plays a small supporting part here; [126] actions performed in innocent ignorance of their oppressive effects are excused, and actions performed in culpable ignorance are not. But this is a question of the authority and formation of conscience. The further point—that objectively "right" actions can still cause harm and therefore in some sense demand forgiveness and reconciliation—requires an explanation that the natural law tradition is less well prepared to give.

One solution to the problem is to define a new category of sin, social sin. Anselm Min suggests that Gutiérrez and other liberationists distinguish social sin from personal sin without reducing it to a superpersonal, deterministic force. Just as in Thomas the common good consists of goods that individuals can produce only corporately, in liberation thought corporate sin consists of sins that individuals can commit only in groups, through creation of or participation in oppressive institutions:

> Social sin is committed by individuals in their socialized existence who *together* produce consequences that go beyond their separate individual intentions and wills and thus their separate individual responsibilities. The mere fact that individuals are not responsible for such sins as separate individuals, however, does not mean that they can simply disown their responsibility. What they are not responsible for as separate individuals they are responsible for as associated individuals, for they remain the subject of social sin, which expresses their "collective will" and which is objectified and often reified into degrading institutions and oppressive structures. This means that social sin is sin in the most

proper sense of the term, not merely by analogy with personal sin, with its own subject of freedom and responsibility. [127]

It is imperative, of course, to continue to refine the ethical and eschatological meanings of collective agency. For instance, there is a fine line—articulated more powerfully in Protestant theological traditions than in Catholic thought—between observing that no one can be innocent of social sin and declaring that human beings lack moral freedom. But this need for refinement does not lessen the interpretive power of the category.

The liberationist concept of social sin also entails a transformation of doctrines of salvation. If social sin is committed by individuals as associated beings (rather than by individuals in themselves or by systems or institutions), salvation from social sin is salvation of individuals as associated beings (in their institutionalized relationships). This argument acquires even more power against the backdrop of liberationist convictions about the interdependence of the levels of liberation: through corporate sin I not only participate in the material oppression of others but contribute to their spiritual corruption as well. The point echoes the traditional prohibition against the moral evil of cooperating in another's sin. If oppression can dispose its victim to sin by encouraging her to refuse the preferential option for the poor, then my cooperation in her oppression amounts to my cooperation in both her deprivation (material or premoral evil) and, potentially, her sin (moral evil). [128] Conversely, the work of transforming oppressive institutions has salvific and not just material significance. [129]

CRITICISMS

Gutiérrez excels at the task he sets himself: redesigning theology to fit a spiritually vibrant but unjustly impoverished people. This means we cannot expect him to have all details filled in, to possess a comprehensive ethic, or to satisfy all the demands that might reasonably arise in other social locations. For instance, there are the additions that his theology would require if it were to become a liberation ethic. First, as Stanley Hauerwas points out, the devil is in the details. [130] A general blueprint for a just, selfless, liberated life would contradict Gutiérrez's emphasis on local analysis; but lacking examples of concrete utopian reflection in operation one cannot even be sure how he would order his priorities in practice. The practical objections of critics like Paul Sigmund and Michael Novak, based largely on problems they detected during their own attempts to construct Gutiérrez's absent social ethic, can be answered only through further examples of concrete moral reflection. [131] Second, Gutiérrez's crucial insight into the influence of moral stance upon knowledge is unaccompanied by philosophical or theological explanations of the sources and mechanisms of knowledge. But if pretheological judgments are judgments that genuinely defend the integrity of the historical human person, it is not perfectly clear how that person is known in specific, how that knowledge is converted into concrete moral principles, or how exactly it should be related to revelation. Finally, the transition from prophetic voice to ethic requires mediating principles. For example, the demand to seek out the poor can run counter to the traditional natural law preference for near neighbors, others with whom we have bonds of blood or affection. [132] The moral preferential option for the poor is a way of life within which we carry out all sorts of responsibilities, and how it orders these—especially for those who are not celibate—is not clear.

Three other difficulties arise from an ambiguity in the scope of Gutiérrez's stance. Because all seem endemic to local, historical, dialectical ethics, they deserve some attention here. First, there is an uncomfortable tension in Gutiérrez's work between his call for a theology *of* the oppressed and his effort to do theology *for* the oppressed, a tension that arises from the need to define more precisely the method for exercising the epistemological preferential option for the poor. [133] Gutiérrez must walk a fine line, evangelizing the oppressed—thus risking speaking down to them from a problematic position of neutral omniscience—and letting the oppressed evangelize him— thus risking baptizing the false elements in their theology. On one hand, despite his efforts in *We Drink from Our Own Wells* and *On Job* to ground liberation thought more explicitly in lived spirituality, Gutiérrez's is still a theologian's theology, answering the concerns of the professional theological community. [134] On the other, this care and his unwillingness to make the oppressed the absolute arbiters of orthodoxy protect him from romanticism. The faith of the poor too has been adulterated by adaptation to unjust social structures, [135] and the poor also must be converted. [136] But where does authority lie, if not with the outside expert, with the oppressed, or in the viewpoint of the oppressed? Good method and good sources are essential, but they do not guarantee authenticity. Truth surfaces and can be confirmed only in the process of active, open, loving engagement with particular poor people. [137] For Gutiérrez, the Gospel and Exodus accounts of God's solidarity with the poor are exemplary in this respect.

Second, on one hand Gutiérrez claims to have tailored a theology specifically to fit Latin America and to be reluctant to apply it to events or ideas that arise outside its boundaries. [138] Liberation theology itself is impermanent. [139] For the preferential option for the poor, and really Gutiérrez's whole historical approach, arise from the particular theological problems caused by the local scandal of Latin American poverty. [140] Cultures facing other crises will generate different theologies. On the other hand, as Jeffrey Siker notes, Gutiérrez also implies that the preferential option for the poor has universal critical currency based not only on the contemporary interdependence of Latin America with the rest of the world but on its eternal centrality in biblical revelation. [141] From this perspective, the preferential option ought to lie at the center of all theological reflection. This is a bold statement for one who is so keenly and systematically aware of the pervasiveness of sinful bias in moral and theological reflection. Is Gutiérrez only staging a raid on local theological reflection and then returning to a stance of universal omniscience? Siker declares that he is not: he is open to other hermeneutics, to voices from other cultures. But the more interesting question this raises is one that feminists must answer as well: once we have discarded a belief in a universal, objective viewpoint, how do we make a case that a truth or method we have worked out in a particular historical situation has universal critical power? For Gutiérrez Scripture is the final guarantee of the permanent validity of the preferential option for the poor. But what about oppressive biases that might have influenced the writing and redaction of the biblical text? Gutiérrez's hermeneutic seems better outfitted to organize the liberating themes that may already be found there in abundance than to champion those that have been excluded. [142]

Finally, while Las Casas—and by transitive property, Gutiérrez—speaks of respecting the other in her difference, Alejandro García-Rivera points out that Las Casas's arguments for the dignity of the other are actually based in a presumption of similarity; they move to the level of shared universals before they have explored particular differences adequately. [143] Clearly communal moral and theological reflection cannot proceed without some understanding of what people hold in common. But the criticism reminds us that, in a culture of pluralism, we must not list these factors prematurely but must give others the opportunity to define themselves. [144]

Despite these gaps, however, Gutiérrez's theology of liberation has managed to disengage many traditional elements of natural law theology from corollaries that had led to oppression and connect them instead with a much more historical, experientially driven, dialectical theological method. So although he has not developed an ethic, he has left two important signs for ethical reflection to follow. The first is to pursue the openings left by the traditional elements of his theological anthropology: for instance, his belief in the perspicuity of justice and oppression. The second may seem contradictory, but in a self-consciously pluralistic world the way to avoid making premature claims to universality is to articulate even more precisely how

Christian spirituality and Scripture refine initial moral insight and social analysis in particular communities. Before an ethic can claim to have universal insight, it must make a good case for its ability to speak the truth locally.

NOTES

1. Editor's introduction to Gustavo Gutiérrez, "Option for the Poor: Assessment and Implications," *ARC: The Journal of the Faculty of Religious Studies, McGill* 22 (Spring 1994): 61.
2. See for example Gustavo Gutiérrez, *Las Casas: In Search of the Poor of Jesus Christ*, trans. Robert Barr (Maryknoll, NY: Orbis Books, 1993), chapter 1.
3. See for example Thomas L. Schubeck, "The Reconstruction of Natural Law Reasoning: Liberation Theology as a Case Study," *Journal of Religious Ethics* 20 (Spring 1992): 149–78.
4. A discussion of Gutiérrez's theological method must acknowledge the debate over its development. On one hand, his theological writings show a clear progression from an emphasis on Marxist categories of social analysis to an emphasis on Latin American spirituality; recent years have also seen an apologetic, a new attempt to justify his use of Marxist critical categories. Examples of the latter attempt are his changes to the fifteenth anniversary edition of *A Theology of Liberation*, including a new, extensive introductory essay and replacement of one controversial section. See Gustavo Gutiérrez, *A Theology of Liberation: History, Politics, and Salvation*, trans. and ed. Sr. Caridad Inda and John Eagleson (Maryknoll, NY: Orbis Books, 1973); rev. ed. (Maryknoll, NY: Orbis Books, 1988). Except where noted, all references will be to the first edition of this work.

European and North American demands that Latin American theology justify itself in "traditional" theological terms, especially the demands set forth in the 1984 *Instruction on Certain Aspects of the Theology of Liberation*, have led to much "repetitive apology" by Latin American authors, Gutiérrez among them (in Juan Luís Segundo, *Theology and the Church: A Response to Cardinal Ratzinger and a Warning to the Whole Church*, trans. John W. Diercksmeier [Minneapolis: Winston Press; London: Geoffrey Chapman, 1985], 169–88). See also Congregation for the Doctrine of the Faith, *Instruction on Christian Freedom and Liberation*, in *Origins* 17 (1986): 713, 715–28. This means that Gutiérrez addresses some ideas repeatedly at least partly because others have called upon him to clarify them for the benefit of the northern theological discussion. See Segundo, "Shift." Three of these "repetitive apologies" are gathered in Gustavo Gutiérrez, *The Truth Shall Make You Free: Confrontations*, trans. Matthew J. O'Connell (Maryknoll, NY: Orbis Books, 1990).

On the other hand, Gutiérrez insists that his later writings merely develop ideas that were (intentionally) only nascent in the earlier ones and that he has recanted nothing. However, to the degree that Gutiérrez treats Marxist historical and social analysis as a tool rather than as a foundation, the shift may at most signify a change in approach to social analysis. Because it is method that concerns me here, and because—as will be argued below—Gutiérrez's method does not stand or fall on the integrity of Marxism, this debate over methodological evolution will not affect my argument here.

5. See for example Gutiérrez, "The Truth Shall Make You Free," chapter in *The Truth*, 174; or "A Discussion of Gustavo Gutiérrez's Work," in Gutiérrez, *The Truth*, 4.

6. Gustavo Gutiérrez, *On Job: God-Talk and the Suffering of the Innocent*, trans. Matthew J. O'Connell (Maryknoll, NY: Orbis Books, 1987), xiv.

7. Gustavo Gutiérrez, *The Power of the Poor in History: Selected Writings*, trans. Robert R. Barr (Maryknoll, NY: Orbis Books, 1983), 200.

8. For a sympathetic but useful discussion of the role that Gutiérrez's experience has played in the development of his thought, see Robert McAfee Brown, *Gustavo Gutiérrez: An Introduction to Liberation Theology* (Maryknoll, NY: Orbis Books, 1990).

9. See for example Gutiérrez, *The Truth*, 7, 11; and (on liberation theology generally, but especially Gutiérrez) Anselm K. Min, "Praxis and Theology in Recent Debates," *Scottish Journal of Theology* 39 (1986): 540, 546–47.

10. Gutiérrez, *Las Casas*, 347; see all of chapter 12. See also Gutiérrez, *Truth*, 43.

11. See Gutiérrez, *Theology of Liberation*, 3. The "prereflective" faith that grounds practical commitment is prereflective only in the sense of being uncritical; it *is* theologically expressed (Gustavo Gutiérrez, "Latin American Spirituality," The Albert Cardinal Meyer Lectures [Mundelein, IL: University of St. Mary of the Lake, 25 April 1992]).

12. See Gutiérrez, *The Truth*, 58, 64; idem, *Theology of Liberation*, 6–15.

13. Min, "Praxis and Theology," 540. The position is Min's but is an interpretation of Gutiérrez.

14. Gutiérrez's litmus test for theology is its adherents' participation in the liberation or oppression of the poor: "one of the best ways to refute a theology is to look at its practical consequences" (Gutiérrez, *The Power of the Poor*, 196).

15. For a helpful discussion of the meanings of praxis in liberation theology generally, see John J. Markey, O.P., "Praxis in Liberation Theology: Some Clarifications," *Missiology* 23 (April 1995): 179–95.

16. Gutiérrez, *The Truth*, 66; see also ibid., 104–5; Gutiérrez, *Theology of Liberation*, ix; and Gustavo Gutiérrez, *We Drink from Our Own Wells: The Spiritual Journey of a People*, trans. Matthew J. O'Connell (Maryknoll, NY: Orbis Books, 1984).

17. Min, "Praxis and Theology," 545. In Gutiérrez's earlier writing, "Truth, for the contemporary human being, is something *verified*, something 'made true.' Knowledge of reality that leads to no modification of that reality is not verified, does not become true" (Gutiérrez, *The Power of the Poor*, 59). In Gutiérrez's more recent work he has shifted from a simple claim that truth is created to the more sophisticated epistemological concern to gain a perspective from which liberative truth can be grasped.

18. Gutiérrez, *Theology of Liberation*, 145; See also Gutiérrez, *The Truth*, 174; ibid., 19. In more recent writings Gutiérrez has added that the practice of theology presupposes on the part of the practitioner not only active work for social change but also "the silence of contemplation and commitment" (Gustavo Gutiérrez, *The God of Life*, trans. Matthew J. O'Connell [Maryknoll, NY: Orbis Books, 1991], 145).

19. Gutiérrez, *The Truth*, 101–2.

20. Gutiérrez, *The Truth*, 159–60; and Gutiérrez, "Preferential Option for the Poor," *SEDOS Bulletin* 24 (June–15 July 1992): 179.

21. Gutiérrez, *Theology of Liberation*, rev. ed., xl.
22. This fact qualifies the analytic and constructive use of the social sciences. See Gutiérrez, *The Truth*, 64–65. See ibid., 59, 132; and Gutiérrez, *Theology of Liberation*, 103, 177.
23. See, e.g., Gutiérrez, *The Truth*, 60.
24. Gutiérrez, *The Truth*, 78.
25. Gutiérrez, *The God of Life*, 75. Therefore theology's task is to indicate not only the presence but also the absence of God in human history (Gutiérrez, *The Truth*, 157).
26. Pope, "Christian Love for the Poor," 308.
27. See Gutiérrez, *The Truth*, 53–84. Critics disagree over the degree to which Gutiérrez embraces Marxism. Criticisms fall roughly into three categories. The first sees Marxism as wrong—and hence a poor choice of analytical tools—on either theological or practical grounds. See the 1984 and 1986 *Instructions* on liberation theology; and Joseph Ratzinger, *Church, Ecumenism, and Politics: New Essays in Ecclesiology*, trans. Robert Nowell (New York: Crossroad, 1987), chapters 11–14; idem, "The Church's Teaching," 70–72; Michael Novak, *Will It Liberate? Questions about Liberation Theology* (New York/Mahwah: Paulist Press, 1986); and Paul E. Sigmund, *Liberation Theology at the Crossroads: Democracy or Revolution?* (New York, Oxford: Oxford University Press, 1990), especially 195–98. At the opposite extreme, a second set of critics faults Gutiérrez for failing to embrace Marx's critique comprehensively. See Alistair Kee, *Marx and the Failure of Liberation Theology* (London: SCM Press; Philadelphia: Trinity Press International, 1990); and Marsha Hewitt, "Liberation Theology and the Emancipation of Religion," *Scottish Journal of Religious Studies* 13 (Spring 1992): 21–38. A third group weighs in on Gutiérrez's side, finding his critical use of Marxist categories both sufficiently trenchant and appropriately guarded. See McGovern, *Liberation Theology*, and Anselm Kyongsuk Min, *Dialectic of Salvation: Issues in Theology of Liberation* (Albany: State University of New York Press, 1989), 117–69.
28. Gutiérrez, *The Truth*, 64.
29. Gutiérrez, *The Truth*, 70.
30. Karl Marx, *The German Ideology*, trans. S. Ryazanskaya, in *The Marx-Engels Reader*, 2nd ed., ed. Robert C. Tucker (New York: W. W. Norton and Company, 1978), 164–65.
31. Gutiérrez, *The Truth*, 67–80; and Gutiérrez, *Theology of Liberation*, rev. ed., 157–58.
32. Pope, "Christian Love," 301.
33. Gutiérrez, *Las Casas*, 208, 456, and elsewhere.
34. Gutiérrez, *Theology of Liberation*, rev. ed., xxvii. See also Gustavo Gutiérrez, "Joy in the Midst of Suffering," in *Christ and Context: The Confrontation between Gospel and Culture*, ed. Hilary D. Regan and Alan J. Torrance with Antony Wood (Edinburgh: T&T Clark, 1993), 84; idem, *We Drink*, 125.
35. Jeffrey R. Siker, *Scripture and Ethics: Twentieth-Century Portraits* (New York: Oxford University Press, 1997), 130, 142.
36. Siker, *Scripture and Ethics*, 145. One must choose the poor because God has chosen them (see Gutiérrez, *The God of Life*, 19–20). See also Philip LeMasters, "Christian Social Ethics and Gutiérrez' *The God of Life*," *Encounter* 54 (Summer 1993): 233–47.

37. Pope argues that the preferential option surpasses the already rigorous requirements of charity (Pope, "Christian Love").

38. Gutiérrez, *The Truth*, 52.

39. Pope, "Christian Love," 302–6.

40. Gutiérrez, *Theology of Liberation*, 307.

41. Gutiérrez, *Theology of Liberation*, 174.

42. Ibid., 146; emphasis in original.

43. Gutiérrez, reply to Jürgen Moltmann, in *Christ and Context*, ed. Regan and Torrance, 204.

44. Gutiérrez, *The God of Life*, 18, 78.

45. Gutiérrez, *Theology of Liberation*, 154.

46. Gutiérrez, *Theology of Liberation*, rev. ed., xxvii.

47. Gutiérrez, *Theology of Liberation*, 155–59; see Siker, *Scripture and Ethics*, 128.

48. LeMasters, "Christian Social Ethics," 236–38; Schubeck, "Reconstruction," 164.

49. Gutiérrez, *Theology of Liberation*, 172.

50. Gutiérrez, *The God of Life*, 85.

51. Gutiérrez, *Theology of Liberation*, 153.

52. Gutiérrez, *Theology of Liberation*, 37; see also ibid., 175. The number and welfare of the poor serve as a sort of "Kingdom gauge" in Scripture; widespread poverty and oppression are signs that the eschatological promise of the Kingdom is far from fulfilled. See Gutiérrez, *The Truth*, 94–95, 155–58; and Gutiérrez, *Theology of Liberation*, 160–68.

53. Gutiérrez, *Theology of Liberation*, 146; and Gutiérrez, *The Power of the Poor*, 29.

54. Gutiérrez, *Theology of Liberation*, 172.

55. Ibid., 162.

56. Gutiérrez, *The God of Life*, 75.

57. Gutiérrez, *The God of Life*, 101–2, 118. See also Gutiérrez, *Theology of Liberation*, 176–77.

58. Gutiérrez, *Theology of Liberation*, 177; emphasis added.

59. Gutiérrez, "The Fifth Century of the Discovery of America," The Albert Cardinal Meyer Lecture Series (Mundelein, IL: University of St. Mary of the Lake, 25 April 1992). See also Gutiérrez, "New Evangelization—A Theological Reflection on the Latin American Church—Santo Domingo," *SEDOS Bulletin* 24 (June–15 July 1992), 188: "I have some faith in history. A lot depends on our commitment, our action."

60. See also Ratzinger, *Church, Ecumenism and Politics*, 207–8.

61. See for example Gutiérrez, *We Drink*, 42: following Christ is a "collective adventure." See also Gutiérrez, *The God of Life*, 34.

62. Gutiérrez, *Theology of Liberation*, 159–60. Concretely responding to this call by participating in liberating events is not *sufficient* for salvation. For salvation, and ultimately true liberation as well, requires the conversion of individuals to God and the neighbor. Because grace is the prerequisite for this conversion, both salvation and true liberation require grace; neither can be achieved by human power.

63. For Gutiérrez historical human community asymptotically approaches the Kingdom of God, ever growing closer to it but not becoming identical with it until

the eschaton; in more traditional theology, the human community may also grow more just, but this progress is not considered an approach to God or a contribution to salvation. In either case the eschaton interrupts history's trajectory, but the "leap" is much greater in the traditional than in the liberation model.

64. Gutiérrez, *The God of Life*, 85.

65. Schubeck, "Reconstruction," 165.

66. Gutiérrez, *The Truth*, 14; Gutiérrez, *Theology of Liberation*, 36–37. See also James B. Nickoloff, "Church of the Poor: The Ecclesiology of Gustavo Gutiérrez," *Theological Studies* 54 (1993): 512–35.

67. Gutiérrez, *Theology of Liberation*, 36; idem, *The Truth*, 128–32.

68. Gutiérrez, *We Drink*, 65.

69. See Gutiérrez, *We Drink*, 125.

70. Gutiérrez, *We Drink*, 55–71. Gutiérrez does juxtapose flesh and spirit, but the flesh is a power of weakness and death, not a synonym for the body, which on the contrary implies life.

71. Gutiérrez, *The Truth*, 138; idem, *Theology of Liberation*, 37.

72. Gutiérrez, *Theology of Liberation*, 175.

73. Gutiérrez, *Theology of Liberation*, 35.

74. Gutiérrez, *We Drink*, especially chapter 6; idem, *The Truth*, 56. Gutiérrez has devoted two books—*We Drink from Our Own Wells* and *The Truth Shall Make You Free*—to this point, not to mention his revisions of *Theology of Liberation*.

75. Gutiérrez, *Theology of Liberation*, 232–39.

76. See Gutiérrez, *Theology of Liberation*, 36–37, 232–39; idem, *The Truth*, 132–35.

77. Gutiérrez, *The Truth*, 132–35.

78. Nickoloff argues that Gutiérrez's "focus on the future, passionate love for the people (the poor), and the search for a meaningful unity within the constant flux of the popular movement" are typical of the Peruvian utopian tradition (Nickoloff, "Church of the Poor," 521).

79. Gutiérrez, *Theology of Liberation*, 234–35. This sort of self-conscious flexibility is the essential but subtle barrier between institutional idolatry and the materialist reductionism that is feared, for example, by Joseph Ratzinger (*Church, Ecumenism and Politics*, 243, 253–54).

80. Schubeck, "Reconstruction," 163–64. Schubeck suggests that the experience of natural moral reflection runs in a single direction, from inclinations and right reason to an inductive knowledge of God. My point here is the opposite: methodologically described, it moves from principle to application, and theologically it originates in the divine mind and percolates down to the level of articulate principle.

81. Schubeck, "Reconstruction," 155–59; Gutiérrez, *Theology of Liberation*, chapters 4 and 5; and Patricia McAuliffe, *Fundamental Ethics*, on a similar strategy in Schillebeeckx.

82. Gutiérrez, *Theology of Liberation*, 159; emphasis added.

83. See *The Power of the Poor*, 212–13 and chapter 8; also Clifford Green, "Bonhoeffer, Modernity, and Liberation Theology," *Union Seminary Quarterly Review* 46 (1992): 117–20; and Philip LeMasters, "'Theology from the Underside of History' as a Theory of Theology," *Perspectives in Religious Studies* 19 (Spring 1992): 45–47.

84. Gustavo Gutiérrez, "The Quincentenary," *SEDOS Bulletin* 24 (15 June–July 1992): 169–75.

85. Gutiérrez, *Theology of Liberation,* 198–99.

86. Gutiérrez, *Las Casas,* 239.

87. Gutiérrez, *Las Casas,* chapter 8. Gutiérrez accepts a version of Rahner's anonymous Christianity and its fundamental, athematic option for God and the good. See Gutiérrez, *Theology of Liberation,* rev. ed., 84; and LeMasters, "Christian Social Ethics," 238.

88. Francis Patrick Sullivan, review of *Las Casas, Gregorianum* 76 (1995): 613.

89. Gutiérrez does not regard the Roman Catholic Church's record as an unbroken failure. For instance, Bartolomé de Las Casas's early defense of the dignity of native Latin Americans is extremely important to Gutiérrez, and the documents of official gatherings of the Roman Catholic hierarchy in Medellín and Puebla are also benchmarks, occasions of Christian and ecclesial faithfulness to the gospel. On Las Casas see Gustavo Gutiérrez, *Dios o el Oro en las Indias: Siglo XVI* (Lima, Peru: Instituto Bartolomé de Las Casas/CEP, 1989); and idem, *Las Casas.*

90. See Gutiérrez, "Preferential Option," 179.

91. Gutiérrez, "New Evangelization," 186. Belief in God means living life as a gift from God, for example (see Gutiérrez, *We Drink,* 110).

92. Gutiérrez, *We Drink,* 1; Gutiérrez, *Theology of Liberation,* 203; and Gutiérrez, *We Drink,* 88. See also Gutiérrez, *The God of Life,* 33–64.

93. Gutiérrez, *Theology of Liberation,* 205; see also ibid., 207.

94. See Gutiérrez, *The God of Life,* 125–26.

95. Gutiérrez, *We Drink,* 104.

96. Gutiérrez, *We Drink,* 122–27. Openness is a check against a triumphalistic, inflexible attitude toward liberation. See also Siker, *Scripture and Ethics,* 129. On friendship see Gutiérrez, "Preferential Option," 180–81, and "New Evangelization," 193.

97. Gutiérrez, *We Drink,* 128–35.

98. Gutiérrez, *We Drink,* 72–89.

99. See Hewitt, "Liberation Theology"; LeMasters, "Christian Social Ethics"; and Markey, "Praxis in Liberation Theology."

100. See Gutiérrez, *Theology of Liberation,* chapters 7 and 12.

101. Gutiérrez, *The God of Life,* 137.

102. Gutiérrez, *The God of Life,* 135–36; emphasis added.

103. *ST* I-II 65.3.

104. See for example Gutiérrez, *Theology of Liberation,* rev. ed., 156–61.

105. Gutiérrez, *We Drink,* 125.

106. See, e.g., Paul Ramsey, *Basic Christian Ethics* (Chicago and London: University of Chicago Press, 1950; reprint, Chicago: University of Chicago Press, Midway Reprints, 1978), 176–77; and John Howard Yoder, *The Priestly Kingdom: Social Ethics as Gospel* (Notre Dame: University of Notre Dame Press, 1984), chapter 4.

107. Gutiérrez, *Las Casas,* 175–81, 209–16.

108. LeMasters, "Christian Social Ethics," 244–46.

109. Gutiérrez, *Las Casas,* 177; see also Sullivan, review of *Las Casas,* 614.

110. Gutiérrez's early call for a spirituality of liberation supports this conclusion. See *Theology of Liberation,* 203–8. I suspect that the capacity for the preferential option for the poor is an analogue of Thomas's infused virtue, in the sense that all other virtues—moral and intellectual—seem to depend on it. Unlike Thomas, Gutiérrez seems to hold that it is accessible to everyone who desires it, a matter of commitment rather than gift.

111. Gutiérrez, *The Truth*, 155; see also 141, 152–53. In this sense Gutiérrez is, surprisingly, in agreement with Neuhaus's argument that the church should not create blueprints for liberation. See Richard John Neuhaus, "Liberation Theology and the Cultural Captivity of the Gospel-Political Kingdoms," in *Liberation Theology*, ed. Ronald Nash (Milford, MI: Mott Media, 1984), 232.

112. Gutiérrez, *The Truth*, 271–72.

113. Gutiérrez, *Theology of Liberation*, 267.

114. See Novak, *Will It Liberate?*; and Sigmund, *Liberation Theology at the Cross-roads*.

115. See for example Gutiérrez, *The Truth*, 64; idem, *The Power of the Poor*, 69.

116. Compare Ratzinger and Hewitt, respectively.

117. Johann Baptist Metz, "Theology in the Struggle for History and Society," in *Expanding the View: Gustavo Gutiérrez and the Future of Liberation Theology*, ed. Marc H. Ellis and Otto Maduro (Maryknoll, NY: Orbis Books, 1990), 96.

118. Gutiérrez, *The Truth*, 51–52.

119. Gutiérrez, *Theology of Liberation*, rev. ed., 160–61.

120. Hewitt argues otherwise, but she overestimates Gutiérrez's initial dedication to Marxism and underestimates his hope in a liberative religious praxis. See Hewitt, "Liberation Theology."

121. Nancy Chodorow, *The Reproduction of Mothering: Psychoanalysis and the Sociology of Gender* (Berkeley: University of California Press, 1978).

122. Traina, "Developing an Integrative Ethical Method," 236–39.

123. The first argument was made in Gutiérrez's lecture "The Fifth Century of the Discovery of America." The second was made in general discussion following the lectures.

124. Legally nations and corporations are persons in a sense; they can be held responsible for past actions. If the law considered only the persons who composed the governments or managements liable, a quick change of leadership would absolve the *nations or corporations* (but not the deposed leaders) of legal responsibility for past actions. But often both are considered liable, as long as the leaders were really acting as representatives of the corporation.

125. Gustavo Gutiérrez, "Questions," *SEDOS Bulletin* 24 (June/July 15, 1992): 192.

126. See *ST* I-II 6.8, 19.5-6.

127. Min, *Dialectic*, 107.

128. This may be the fundamental difference between orthodox personalism and liberationism: liberation theology must argue that oppression discourages freedom in its victims in an existential, not merely practical, sense (Min, *Dialectic*, 137). Min's position is theologically problematic unless—again, as in traditional theology—the oppressed share moral responsibility for their own moral failings with their oppressors. Otherwise the oppressed person is fated to sin by her circumstances. See Kay, "Getting Egypt Out."

129. Min highlights the connection: "structural change does not automatically abolish all personal sins, but it does abolish the effect of social, collective sin and provides a positive incentive and wholesome pressure for doing good as well as a

negative pressure for avoiding evil" (Min, *Dialectic,* 108). That participation in just social structures would incline one toward virtue is a thoroughly orthodox view. For Thomas Aquinas "the proper effect of law is to lead its subjects to their proper virtue: and since virtue is *that which makes its subject good,* it follows that the proper effect of law is to make those to whom it is given, good, either simply or in some particular respect" (*ST* I-II 92.1). Human laws lead persons to virtue with respect to the common good, and just institutions conduce to virtue.

130. Stanley Hauerwas, "Some Theological Reflections on Gutiérrez's Use of 'Liberation' as a Theological Concept," *Modern Theology* 3, no. 1 (October 1986): 67–76.

131. Sigmund, *Liberation Theology,* especially 196–98.

132. Pope, *Evolution of Altruism,* 300–301.

133. On this distinction see Segundo, "Shift," 23; and Leonardo Boff, *Church: Charism and Power—Liberation Theology and the Institutional Church,* trans. John W. Diercksmeier (New York: Crossroad, 1985). This need to make space for a theology of the oppressed is a challenge for feminists as well. North American Christianity is a female phenomenon in the same way that Latin American Christianity is a phenomenon of poverty; in both cases the church and popular piety are simultaneously oppressive, consoling, and empowering.

134. For example, a section labeled "The Right of the Poor to Think" condemns "bourgeois Christianity" rather than calling for a new theology developed by the poor (Gutiérrez, *The Truth,* 115–16). See also Sullivan's review of *Las Casas,* above.

135. Gutiérrez argues that "an authentic theology of liberation" will arise only in the expressions of the *liberated* oppressed—or at least in the oppressed in whom the hope of liberation has been awakened (*Theology of Liberation,* 307). Gutiérrez is under no illusions that the poor are saintly or that their opinions should be accepted uncritically—they themselves, for instance, might not be committed to the poor (see for instance Gutiérrez, "Joy," 84; Nickoloff, "Church of the Poor," 527; and Pope, "Christian Love," 304).

136. See also Kay, "Getting Egypt Out." A theological interpretation of internalized oppression would add that oppressive self-understandings are reinforced specifically by religious views of God, the world, and salvation—from which a tenacious low estimation of oneself, one's abilities, and one's aspirations follows. Gutiérrez notes that the Israelite people were not ready to develop their own liberation thought when they departed from Egypt. It took Moses, and a forty-year desert retreat, for them to begin to understand the significance of their slavery and of God's actions toward them (Gutiérrez, *Theology of Liberation,* 156).

137. See Terrance G. Walsh, review of Gutiérrez, *Las Casas,* in *Theological Studies* 56 (June 1995): 367–69.

138. In response to questions during the 25 April 1992 Cardinal Meyer Lecture Series, he insisted that "I have nothing really interesting to say" about the significance for Mexican illegal aliens in the United States of theological reflection on the Latin American conquest because "I have not the experience" of the North American situation. See also Gutiérrez, "New Evangelization," 183.

139. Gutiérrez, "Option for the Poor," 69.

140. "Perhaps it is this very last point—living in the situation—that makes the difference in outlooks" (Gutiérrez, *The Truth,* 78). See also Green, "Bonhoeffer," 120.

141. See Siker, *Scripture and Ethics,* 147–48; Gutiérrez, "Option for the Poor," 69; and Gutiérrez, *Theology of Liberation,* rev. ed., 160.

142. Kee suggests beginning with the "slaughter" of Egyptian children and the violent, obscure, selectively benevolent God who carries it out (*Marx*, 173).

143. Alejandro García-Rivera, review of *Las Casas*, in *Journal of Hispanic/Latino Theology* 2 (May 1995): 70–71.

144. See LeMasters, "Theology from the Underside," 49; and Amy Jessica Rosenbaum, "Uncommon Ground: Using Martin Buber's Philosophy to Set the Parameters of Jewish-Christian Dialogue," Ph.D. diss., Northwestern University, 1997.

8

Feminism and an Adequate Contemporary Natural Law

Reformers of existing traditions are typically judged against two standards: their faithfulness to what is arguably the core of the tradition and their ability to express that core in ways that meet contemporary intellectual and practical demands. It is generally assumed that these two impulses are in conflict and that a successful amalgamation therefore requires intense negotiation and precarious compromise. But in the case of the natural law tradition, preservation of its central impulses entails serious engagement with feminism rather than resistance to it. It should come as no surprise that the converse is also true: the success of constructive feminist ethics depends on its ability to make use of claims and methods like those that are traditional in natural law. Our project is to make a substantive case for these claims and then, in the final chapter, to demonstrate how a self-consciously dual approach—a "natural law feminism"—illuminates contemporary ethical issues. The first part of the project depends upon an evaluation of revisionism's success in fulfilling the criteria established for natural law and feminist ethics.

As we have seen, Josef Fuchs, Richard McCormick, and Gustavo Gutiérrez revise natural law theology from slightly different viewpoints. Fuchs and McCormick are consciously engaged in reform of the moral side of that tradition and in reattachment of this moral side to central symbols and doctrines of contemporary Roman Catholic theology; Gutiérrez's project begins from a completely different premise—ethical praxis and social analysis as sources and prerequisites for an entirely new sort of theological reflection— and so in the end relies, in true traditional form, upon the capacity of human reason for ethical analysis and judgment.

ADEQUACY TO THOMAS

Each of the three picks up most of the threads of traditional Thomistic method, though sometimes with significant variations from the original. For instance, all three imitate Thomas's telic anthropology formally, but all discard the beatific vision and replace it with something else. Fuchs and McCormick bypass consideration of the afterlife for what resembles Thomas's theological virtue of charity: the fundamental option, an existential orientation toward the Absolute expressed in actions that promote temporal flourishing. Gutiérrez merges the human transcendent and immanent ends in his vision of the Kingdom of God, so that pursuit of the true temporal good is already and always pursuit of the ultimate end. Yet all three have in common the belief that persons have a divinely ordained end that is consistent with the promotion of the temporal common good and that should guide and judge their moral lives.

Likewise, each makes a serious effort to address the practical and theological conditions of moral integrity for social, historical persons. Fuchs and Gutiérrez especially convert neoscholasticism's preoccupation with actions to a preoccupation with actors. Yet they risk falling into different traps. Fuchs's judgments of moral goodness are so highly contextual that he can be accused of promoting situationism, while Gutiérrez draws such a sharp line between faithfulness and apostasy that he sometimes seems to eliminate the possibility—especially for the poor—of reluctantly cooperating with unjust structures when survival demands it. Even McCormick shifts his focus to some degree from the morality of acts to the morality of agents by experimenting with ways of understanding apparently imperfect actions as "right" in the individual's circumstances and therefore as potentially consistent with "goodness" or integrity. Both he and Fuchs depend heavily on the theology of the fundamental option, a commitment to the Absolute that is realized in concrete acts and echoes virtue theory. This theology helpfully shifts attention away from discrete acts and toward the integrity of the social, embodied, developing person. Yet in one sense the fundamental option for the Absolute is less satisfying than virtue theory: Although Fuchs's version in particular carefully connects a person's discrete acts with her existential stance before God without identifying the two, it does not knit final and proximate ends, moral attitudes, grace, and soteriology so closely together as does scholastic virtue theory. McCormick echoes Fuchs's helpful account of an agent whose actions express and compose a fundamental option, but his comparative inattention to conscience and his practical emphasis on the evaluation of acts reinforce the neoscholastic image of a fragmented subject seeking guidance from experts on minute, discrete issues.

McCormick's weakness in one department is his strength in another. Although Fuchs and Gutiérrez have roles and even criteria for a solid, comprehensive theory of practical moral reason, the latter receives direct attention only from McCormick, who has developed a method for interpreting moral norms in situations in which faithfulness to norms and promotion of the integral human good seem to be at odds. His theory of proportional reason expands on Fuchs's claims about norms as protectors of values and anticipates Gutiérrez's claim that integral temporal flourishing is a measure of virtue. McCormick's attention to what he would call essential human ethics—universal principles of human moral reason—lends itself well to the project of renewing practical moral reason; this is also the sort of project for which Fuchs makes room in his theology, even though he does not engage in it himself. Yet all three, especially McCormick and Gutiérrez, do insist on the theoretical importance of the communal context of moral reason. Because isolation breeds error and bias, the truth is best pursued in community. If human moral reason is a communal, not individual, project, *Christian* moral reason is an ecclesial venture. That is, it is carried on within, responsible to, and intended (not exclusively) for the Christian community. Gutiérrez most closely approaches this ideal in practice, but none fulfills it absolutely.

Finally, each makes an effort to describe either the content or the parameters of a social ethic: norms for guiding life in society, methods for determining how the norms may be met, and means for fulfilling them. Fuchs and McCormick largely adhere to the traditional natural law model: maintenance of a justly ordered society is, on one level, simply carrying out the secular role that God intended for human society: advancement of the common good through provision of the necessities of human communal and individual flourishing. This goal can also be met by the spilling over of infused charity into the everyday activities of the faithful and, in fact, is completely fulfilled only in this way. Social justice is thus a divinely ordained and assisted task but has purely temporal significance for all but the actor who promotes it. In contrast, Gutiérrez adds that the condition of the social order itself is of consequence for God's plan; human society is not just the substrate but the object and locus of God's project of salvation. The theological significance of the social order is elevated and with it, social ethics. Yet none is a social ethicist per se. Fuchs's transcendental ethic takes him farthest from this role. McCormick takes up biomedical public policy, but not general social ethics. Gutiérrez's interest is theological, even though his transformation of the traditional understanding of social justice and its theological significance shows the way to a new ground for social ethics.

ADEQUACY TO THE POST-THOMISTIC NATURAL LAW TRADITION

A successful revision of natural law must provide an adequate response to the historical and cultural pressures that have produced casuistry, personalism, and other important developments in the tradition. At each stage, success depends not on mimicking earlier solutions but on accounting adequately today for the pressures that produced them then.

CASUISTRY. As we saw in chapter 3, contemporary proponents of casuistry contend that the time is ripe for casuistic argument: cultural change is occurring too quickly for ethical "business as usual" to be a responsible or responsive option, but no stable new worldview has evolved to suggest a new order for moral reflection. Stanley Hauerwas and, more recently, James F. Keenan have also touted casuistry's usefulness for evaluating and improving the coherence of both our acts and our characters with the Christian community and the story that shapes it. [1] Yet of the three figures we have examined, only Richard McCormick argues casuistically, and even he frequently stops short of permitting his insights to alter the use and interpretation of norms. Fuchs, like McCormick, updates the theoretical justification for casuistry: it is for the protection of goods and values. But his invitation to casuistry is compromised by his refusal to demonstrate its use in concrete cases. Gutiérrez tends simply to condemn false principles in favor of true ones. This is prophetic and effective rhetoric, and it may even reflect the truth more accurately than the seeming compromises of a person who tries to salvage something of worth out of a clearly corrupt principle. But it ignores the fact that the same intention— preservation of a value—drives the condemnation of a norm as inspires casuistic reinterpretation of it. It also overlooks the fact that the solid norms that replace the corrupt ones will eventually have to be interpreted—most likely, casuistically.

PERSONALISM. Personalism's attention to the integral, social person yields indispensable criteria for the person both as an object of moral analysis and, more importantly, as a moral subject. Fuchs and McCormick inherit both the strengths and the weaknesses of personalism. Their visions of the moral subject escape the Marxist extreme of determination by economic forces and the liberal extreme of absolute individualist autonomy. Their personalist version of self-legislation is attention to the innate natural law: it is free, yet consistent; it points to the person's ultimate end, and yet it directs her to uphold the common good. Yet the tendency of Fuchs, especially, to speak of "the person" or "man" reveals a still artificially abstract anthropology in which no difference between persons is more than skin deep. This claim is true eschatologically, perhaps, but not temporally. The cost, for both Fuchs and McCormick, of moving the integral person to the center is the marginalization of political, economic, and social forces; they reappear in discussions of the contexts for personal action, but they rarely either themselves become the object of moral analysis or are suspected of worrisomely and subtly corrupting a person's moral outlook. For Gutiérrez, as we have seen, personalism is a springboard: he accounts for personalist insights in most cases by arguing that liberationism supersedes them. He accepts personalism's emphasis on individual dignity, justice, and integrity in interpersonal relations, but he rejects its confidence that personal conversions alone will effect social transformation, and he replaces its traditional version of salvation history with a liberationist vision of the Kingdom of God on earth.

In addition, all three authors are concerned to return what had become rigid divisions in anthropology to their former status as distinctions. Yet in at least two cases their success is compromised by an ambivalence toward the body inherited from the larger personalist tradition. Fuchs's incarnational approach, which locates human experience of the transcendental and universal solely in categorical, particular beings and acts, raises esteem for the body; yet he is suspicious of emotions, traditionally seen as connected with the body and as clouding reason. Indication of the seriousness with which McCormick has taken embodied experience is his attention in his early work on contraception to the sexual experience of married couples. On the other hand, his treatment of the body contains enormous gaps; for instance, women's perspectives on nongenital sexuality are largely absent, evidence that he begins his ruminations with existing norms rather than with general consultations on embodied sexual experience. McCormick integrates the elements of intention as well: willing and permitting—intending and allowing to occur—are part of the same motion of the will. Thus for McCormick as for Gutiérrez, inaction is a form of intentional action and has moral consequences. Of the three, Gutiérrez goes furthest in making embodied social relationships part of the definition, and not just the context, of the human subject; bodiliness enters in Gutiérrez's concern to meet basic human needs and in his vision of integral, historical liberation. It is a rare treat to read a Roman Catholic account of embodiment in which sexuality is not the prominent element, and yet because Gutiérrez rarely touches on these traditionally controverted questions, their important implications for flourishing and for psychology are missing from his work. None, therefore, deals adequately with the bodily dimension of human being or with the related phenomenon of commitment to those to whom, through biology, proximity, or choice, one has a special but perhaps not institutionalized relationship. They are particularly susceptible to feminist criticism on these counts.

Finally, all three authors concur with the personalist observation that to be good is to desire to do right and consequently affirm its impulse to relate moral judgments of persons and actions—of the morally good and the ethically right—without completely identifying them. But the precise way in which the distinction is drawn makes all the difference to judgments about the rightness of acts and the morality of actors in a compromised, conflicted world.

The impulse works out very differently in the three authors. Fuchs and McCormick exhibit traces of the impression (created by neoscholasticism and the moral theology of the manuals) that the first concern of the moral life is to avoid sin, so that it is imperative to explain how an apparently compromised act may be wholly right and therefore not entail sin. Fuchs concentrates on moral goodness, an ultimately soteriological interest. For Fuchs the acceptance or rejection of grace "in the centre of the person," not the "many daily sins and good works which remain only on the edge of personal commitments," is the central concern. [2] The point is that a person of moral integrity is concerned to act well. In the form in which Fuchs expresses it, this laudable concern for integrity—for second-order moral goodness—makes him reluctant to illustrate how to evaluate the first-order moral rightness of actions in relation to ontic goods; in addition, Fuchs seems less worried about the ill effects that an agent's well-intended but possibly erroneous actions have on others. Yet the intended advantage of this "hands-off" approach is freedom. The measure of Fuchs's respect for the moral subject is that he refuses to do her thinking for her; in his hands, the fundamental option transfers the power of authoritative moral reflection—conscience—to the individual in the concrete situation.

McCormick's purview is moral rightness, an issue of practical reason. For McCormick moral dilemmas are rooted partly in human finitude, partly in the need to respond to universal human moral imperfection, and partly in an agent's own moral history, and appropriate solutions must take all of these factors into account. The agent's sinfulness and developmental imperfection especially are anthropological facts to be dealt with, conditions to be allowed for when developing and applying norms, for "it would be inconsistent with the charity of the gospel message to assert that its demands exceed the limitations of the human pursuer." [3] This is of course what classical Protestant theology does assert: God's demands do exceed the maturity and virtue of everyone, but justification and forgiveness can restore them to grace. McCormick argues the issue the other way: a God who truly loves humanity judges each person according to her own salvation history. He does not judge her best efforts to be wrong or hold her to be evil. Yet McCormick's detailed attention to ecclesiastical moral teachings sometimes leaves the impression of paternalism: the measure of the moral life is adherence to ecclesiastical moral dicta (albeit painstakingly and liberally interpreted by McCormick and others)

rather than adherence to the free and responsible dictates of one's own conscience, informed love, and by intimate knowledge of the situation.

Gutiérrez, whose emphasis is upon universal rather than personal salvation history, would counter that McCormick's move undercuts the prophetic,
condemnatory power of the ethical ideal and the responsibility of individuals
and societies to move (with the help of grace) closer to it. As in Fuchs and
McCormick, the free person cannot *in practice* avoid complicity in unjust
structures, and because of this she cannot *in fact* avoid doing harm. But for
Gutiérrez this harm is also moral wrong. To deny this is self-deception and
bespeaks an attitude of sin. Yet this prophetic stance does not free Gutiérrez
from the task of differentiating and relating right and good. Any constructive,
theological liberation ethic will have to explain whether for people who are
morally good—committed to liberation—there are any right acts other than
heroic self-sacrifice for liberation. Unless there are, true Christianity becomes
the purview of celibate, unattached people. Gutiérrez's vision of Christianity
is much broader, but until he expands upon his claim that we must not
judge the behavior of the oppressed too harshly, this broader vision will go
ungrounded. All three accounts would profit from a virtue theory, a systematic
articulation of the links between subject and act and between subject and
salvation.

SOCIAL JUSTICE AND LIBERATION.   Although McCormick makes forays into social policy, and Gutiérrez outlines a dialectic that mediates between utopian
vision and contemporary social reality, none of the three has ventured systematically into social ethics. McCormick's social policy writing reveals why Fuchs,
who prefers to deal in abstract, formal norms, and Gutiérrez, who likes to
make clean, prophetic judgments about moral rightness, might shy away from
this sort of reflection. McCormick tacitly recognizes that often an imperfect
policy that improves communal flourishing and can actually garner enough
support to be enforceable aids flourishing more than an idealistic initiative
that has no prayer of passage or enforcement. Thus a genuinely useful social
ethic demands a willingness to accept compromises without altering ideals.

MAGISTERIAL ABSOLUTISM.   Fuchs's and McCormick's preference for virtually
exceptionless over absolute norms reveals a shared opinion that one can never
know in advance what rightness and goodness may permit in a particular
situation. A morally adequate description of an act requires more than a
merely functional or operational account of it. Intention and a host of other
contextual factors enter the field. They do believe in the existence of absolutely,

inherently wrong acts—acts that create or reveal moral evil in actors—but they insist that descriptions of these acts must include all of the details relevant to moral judgment. Thus even though they may reject the simple magisterial version of absolutism, and even though anxiety over error or ignorance may discourage them from exercising prophetic judgment, prophecy is still methodologically possible to them. Gutiérrez in fact reasons similarly, although he is quickest to condemn apparent transgressions that exploit political, economic, or ecclesiastical power; an apparently unjust action performed by a person with interests incapable of the truth is inherently evil. He does, as we have seen, leave small openings for more lenient judgment of victims of oppression, but he has not worked out the theoretical details of this distinction. In the end, then, none accepts a simplistic moral absolutism, but of the three only Gutiérrez both possesses and makes regular use of an alternative prophetic standard.

CHRISTIAN AND HUMAN ETHICS. As we saw in chapter 3, the question, What is the connection between Christian ethics and human ethics? is a modern question, for it assumes that a univocal secular ethics exists. Fuchs, accepting the modern wording of the question, declares Christian and human ethics identical in content, chalking up all apparent deviations to variety in circumstances and making adjustments for them only at the most concrete level of moral deliberation. He recognizes the pluralism in "human" ethics, but it does not disturb the basic structure of his method. McCormick's essential human ethic echoes this insight; basic moral norms of the sort that protect universal and essential human values hold always and everywhere, and Christian ethics are "quintessentially human" ethics. Yet McCormick's more recent work hints that Christian ethics are in fact different from human ethics, even at the essential level. This claim compromises his assumption that Christian moral positions can win the day in secular discussions if translated into religiously neutral language; he recognizes this problem but has not yet addressed it methodologically. Gutiérrez speaks an unabashedly religious language in all arenas, a move that seems methodologically consistent with the postmodern deconstruction of the ideal of a universal human ethic, and yet he retains assumptions about unreflectively perspicuous grounds for moral judgment. Because it is not immediately evident whether this retention reflects flat-footed modern assumptions about secular ethics or more sophisticated postmodern theories about religiosity and limits on constructions of human flourishing, Gutiérrez needs more explicit theoretical support if he is to be said to have solved the postmodern version of the "Christian-human" dilemma.

HISTORICITY AND PLURALISM.   Uniting late-twentieth-century responses to all
of these concerns are deeper themes that reveal the roots of some of the
differences among authors. For instance, a contemporary vision of history
informs their anthropology: human culture and human being—or, what is
the same, human understandings of them—are in flux. But as we have seen,
this vision does not affect their methods identically. Fuchs and McCormick
view historical change in human self-understanding as something to be accounted for primarily in the interpretation and application of traditional
moral norms, which express perduring moral values. The results of practical
moral reasoning may have to change in order to preserve the spirit of the
norms in the new situation, but the methods by which the norms are applied
and developed remain largely the same. Gutiérrez, on the other hand, argues
that historical context affects not only the material on which theology and
ethics reflect but also their methods of reflection. New historical situations
demand not only new conclusions, but new ways of reaching them.

We have also seen that historicist anthropology revives the question of
humanity's place within salvation history. All three authors hold that human
beings are already saved but not yet perfected and that the human community
is also imperfect; the important question is the strength of the connection
between the personal-spiritual and the social-historical dimensions of this
imperfection. Only Gutiérrez makes a strong theological argument for uniting
salvation history and human history.

The idea of historicity—variety and change through time—entails the
idea of pluralism—variety among contemporaneous cultures. All three authors
assume that there will be cross-cultural pluralism in moral thought. Because
in Fuchs's and McCormick's schemes variety influences only the final step of
reflection, the coordination of principle with concrete situation, they can
accommodate pluralism without altering their foundations or methods. In
their view, pluralism is consistent with the idea of a universal basis for morality,
universal standards for practical moral reason, and the secondary, derivative
character of moral norms. In Gutiérrez, pluralism appears to cut deeper. He
argues that the crisis of one's own context dictates one's choice of method
and procedure. Yet what he gives with one hand he appears to take with the
other, for he considers solidarity with the poor to be a universal Christian
epistemological standard, preference for the poor to be a universal Christian
prophetic standard, and economic and political justice to be a universal moral
standard. Here the "interest capable of truth" ceases to be an abstraction—
a fundamental option for the Absolute, realized in all commitments, large
and small—and acquires the face of the poor neighbor. Thus in the end
pluralism opens the door not to an infinite variety of methods and procedures

but to a global correction of the dominant, myopic approach. In Gutiérrez liberation is the concrete telos that screens and organizes other goods, allowing for diversity without loss of focus.

A number of the gaps and unclarities that have emerged in this discussion of Fuchs, McCormick, and Gutiérrez can be filled by elements analogous to Thomas's. For instance, in every case a clearly articulated virtue theory yoked with an equally lucid epistemology would clarify the relations between goodness and rightness and the conditions of appropriate compromise. Yet in other cases the fault arises from a lack in natural law ethics itself—in many cases, from its failure to fulfill feminist standards of moral discourse, discernment, and action.

ADEQUACY TO FEMINIST CRITERIA

As we saw in chapter 4, feminism establishes criteria of adequacy for content and method, but it adds to these what looks to classical natural law ethics like a third category: procedure. Although all three categories of criteria make substantive contributions to the revision of the natural law approach, the procedural criterion is essential to a natural law ethics that can deliver the universally relevant moral reflections it promises. But the importance of procedure is clearest if we begin with method.

Methods of moral reasoning that meet feminist approval must reflect the structure of human being and moral reasoning observed by women and include safeguards that protect vulnerable groups and values. For instance, the constant mutual conditioning of the personal and political dimensions of human life argue for the unification of "public" and "private" ethics, for no moral question falls neatly into one category or the other. All three authors make significant progress in this direction. Gutiérrez's is most like the feminist position, recognizing the public, structural contribution to the shape of private lives; yet because he barely treats issues traditionally classified as personal ethics, like sexuality, it is not clear whether he would approach them through romanticism, proportionalism, or a feminist perspective of relational justice. [4] McCormick argues that "personal" morality is no less conflicted—and no less directed at the achievement of concrete human goods—than social ethics; like Christine Gudorf, he insists that "familial and sexual ethics" should be argued as broadly and inductively as social ethics. [5] At the same time, the influence does not seem to run the other way; although policy decisions— say, on end-of-life treatment—may take into account a person's likely future capacity for attachment, personal factors like care and attachment have no clearly delineated guiding role in social ethics. Fuchs, because he rarely reflects comprehensively on concrete issues, is the least clear on this issue, but his connection to proportionalism suggests an affinity to McCormick. In the end, then, all make motions toward a unified method, but none actually succeeds in creating and applying one.

The feminist caveat to the requirement of consistency in method is a demand that consistency not be reached prematurely or, once accomplished, assumed to be a permanent accomplishment. One must leave methodological openings for recognizing and evaluating existing, functioning models of moral reason that challenge or complement dominant models. None of the three authors suggests, as Gilligan does, the universal existence of complementary orientations; only Gutiérrez proposes the existence of two moral outlooks, and he emphatically rejects one. But there are parallels among the care-justice, Christian-human, and existential-essential rationales; two different sets of reasons and motivations can be given for the same decision, the latter approach in each pair is sometimes inconclusive without specification by the former, and the former approach often relies on the latter for basic human limits like fairness. [6] In addition, all three authors ground moral reason in anthropologies that theoretically invite new information: Fuchs and McCormick base their argument for the free operation of human moral reason upon God's intentions for the integral human person, and Gutiérrez bases his use of historical and social analysis in the historical and social nature of human being. Each is poised, therefore, to account methodologically for expansions or shifts in anthropology. McCormick, for instance, has taken advantage of this opening to argue that a moral theology that respects the actual conditions of human life and thought must be inductive, [7] important evidence that his version of natural law thought is capable of self-transformation. But, as we have seen, he resists accounting methodologically for other similar changes in anthropology. For instance, feminists—among others—argue for a more narrative understanding of the moral subject according to which moral integrity is best evaluated not instantaneously, in one act, but in the context of a moral career; yet McCormick's approach retains an emphasis on acts. [8] The test will be whether McCormick and others are able to account comprehensively for anthropological change.

By contrast, none of the three has fully understood pluralism's radical practical consequences for the structure of moral reason. For instance, an important element of the feminist argument for alternative orientations is the claim that in any given social and historical setting the experience of feminine embodiment may underpin peculiarly feminine moral frameworks. The possibility of a *permanent* difference between the sexes that yields the potential for *ongoing*, experientially based differences in moral outlook is inadequately addressed by all three authors. Yet Gutiérrez may eventually develop such distinctions as he weaves race, culture, and sex increasingly thoroughly into his understanding of oppression. Unlike poverty, the latter differences, and their accompanying differences in moral outlook, would remain in some form even in a just society.

The final methodological criterion is feminism's moral hermeneutic. Feminists argue that a method that leads to the oppression of women is not only morally but theologically inadequate. Interestingly, although all three authors are inspired in part by the belief that their inherited systems of moral reasoning have caused suffering and moral error and therefore require some sort of theoretical, systematic overhaul, only Gutiérrez explicitly incorporates a moral hermeneutic into his theology: a theology (and moral theology) that can be systematically associated with oppression is suspect because of its complicity in that oppression. Put otherwise, a theology and spirituality that permit gross injustice have unrecognizably twisted fundamental truths of Christian faith. Although in practice Fuchs and McCormick employ a moral hermeneutic, only liberationism explicitly supports the feminist position methodologically. [9]

Second, feminist ethics demands *procedural* criteria to protect the *method's* success. McCormick's democratic impulse begins to address this concern, but feminism has in mind more stringent criteria. Feminist procedure and method overlap somewhat, owing partly to the feminist understanding that the activity of moral reasoning is not merely a prelude to moral action; moral reasoning is a moral act that entails moral commitments and moral self-definition. Therefore solidarity with women is essential both epistemologically—a bias toward the oppressed is a prerequisite for correctly seeing the structures and attitudes that oppress them—and morally—in order to be a person of moral integrity one must define oneself as a person who stands with women and their interests. This is the practical dimension of the moral hermeneutic mentioned above. Of the three authors, only Gutiérrez adopts the criterion of active commitment to the oppressed. For Gutiérrez this commitment includes not only *work* on behalf of and with the poor but also a life-encompassing *residence* with the oppressed. This does not necessarily mean establishing one's home in the slums, but it does require genuine friendship with the oppressed as equals, rather than mere arm's length advocacy. [10] In contrast, Fuchs and McCormick draw on the traditional natural law belief that sin—in this context, failure to opt for the oppressed—does not fully compromise human moral reason unless it rejects the Absolute. [11] Fuchs's and McCormick's position that human moral reason is truly trustworthy in the degree that it is a communal project does leave a small opening for the procedural condition of solidarity: in practice individuals and homogeneous groups are unlikely to reach unbiased—or appropriately biased—conclusions. But to the extent that they leave the condition of solidarity undeveloped, Fuchs and McCormick have difficulty connecting individual integrity—one's self-definition as a moral person—with social ethics and social justice—the theory and practice of transformation of the human community. In feminist and liberationist thought, to engage in liberating practice *is* the condition of morality, and for religious liberationists this practice is also the context (although not the whole) of spirituality and of theological reflection. This would be the case even if liberationists, including feminists, made use of something like McCormick's practical reason in order to determine how to fulfill this commitment in practice. [12]

In addition, feminist procedure dictates that only broad participation in ethical debate can provide the checks and balances that overcome the effects of sin and simple human, historical finitude upon human reasoning. This is neither an argument against the perspicuity of natural law principles and human goods nor an argument against the central role of "the wise"—especially, today, the specialist—in communal moral discernment. Rather, it recognizes that without broad participation in moral discussion the parameters, methods, and conclusions of that discussion may be biased—even innocently—in favor of the concerns and perspectives of these wise persons and specialists. For instance, when (male) natural law thinkers have dictated moral norms rather than eliciting broad moral dialogue, they have impoverished their reasoning and even misdirected their discussions by ignoring women's experiences of human being. For this reason the success of natural law *method* is best protected when there is a *procedure* for including the viewpoints of all, especially those who are normally underrepresented among the "wise." Active commitment among all (especially, Gutiérrez points out, among the marginalized themselves) to respect the dignity and reflective opinions of underrepresented people is a crucial element in this procedure. Grace may operate and truth may assert itself even where the moral debate is confined to an elite that is not so committed; but grace and truth most reliably actualize themselves historically in a cooperative, rather than a constrained, setting. Broad participation thus protects not just the logic of moral reasoning, but even more importantly, its liberative epistemological bias. Fuchs and McCormick consider the communal context essential for similar reasons, although factual and logical errors, not systematic self-interest, seem to be McCormick's worry. Gutiérrez, like feminists, fears oppressive bias; only in the (increasing) degree that he actually thinks through the concerns of basic Christian communities with their members does he actually employ the criterion of breadth. Segundo's criticisms are reminders that, despite their aspirations, Gutiérrez and others may not always reach or report moral conclusions that reflect truly communal discernment and application of moral criteria. [13] But in Gutiérrez's case this is an indication that he has fallen short of his own mark rather than, as is at times true for the other authors, that he does not recognize the mark at all.

More important—and here is Hoagland's contribution—broad participation in moral discussion is essential because moral theologians' tendency to cogitate and promulgate treats moral discussion as a means of solving problems rather than as a forum for promoting moral growth. The very small circle of academic moral discussion has thus cut women and many men off from one of the experiences that contributes to moral maturity. [14] For if grace is best actualized as virtue and wisdom in one who is actively engaged in moral debate, all should participate in conversations across lines of profession, gender, class, and culture. Here, for all the authors, theory outruns practice. Fuchs argues that moral egotism among church functionaries leads to moral immaturity among the laity, but his writing contains little evidence of efforts to engage the laity broadly. McCormick makes very traditional arguments for "on-site" moral deliberation, including the decreasing certainty of increasingly specific moral decisions and the special competence of laypeople in disciplines like medicine and law. He also—somewhat uniquely—applies the social justice doctrine of subsidiarity to moral deliberation: decisions should be made at the lowest level at which it is appropriate for them to be made. [15] Proportionalism invites careful moral reflection, bringing us to the penultimate level of deliberation by generating a set of provisionally acceptable solutions, but it declines to provide definitive answers. At some point ordinary persons must bring other difficult-to-formulate factors—attachments and commitments, for instance—into play. All the same, proportionalism itself is the creation of a professional class of theologians. Gutiérrez, drawing on Freire, insists that participation in moral and theological debate is essential to the empowerment of the oppressed; but he normally presents norms and theories as having been inspired rather than generated by ordinary people.

Finally, it is naïve to assume that opening the door to wider discussion will admit only liberating ideas. The content—the norms or guidelines—that an individual suggests or that an ethic generates must pass the test of adequacy to women's integral flourishing and women's knowledge. This means first that the norms must support a "thick," telic description of women's good and of the conditions of their flourishing. This vision of women's good, like Gutiérrez's vision of liberation, must encompass not only the moral and spiritual dimensions of life but also the material and historical—or rather, its understanding of the former dimensions must entail the latter. In Fuchs, theology provides reasons for caring about the human good. [16] Yet although bodily flourishing seems to be increasingly important to Fuchs, his description of the human good has little content, and there is no indication that women's good may have different requirements than men's or that knowledge is gendered. McCormick introduces dimensions of the human good that resonate clearly with feminist contributions and employs them as moral criteria; the good of intimate relationship, for instance, profoundly affects his reasoning on issues as diverse as contraception, abortion, and medical treatment of comatose patients. He also intimates that the "is" that determines the moral "ought" is concrete, not ideal, and therefore contains a sort of caveat; one should pursue the good at one's own level of moral maturity. Yet here too any intimation of gendered knowledge or gendered needs is missing. Gutiérrez is motivated by the "new man," the liberated person in the liberated society created through graced action on behalf of the oppressed. He has in mind integral political/material, historical, and spiritual fulfillment. Unlike Fuchs and McCormick, he possesses a mechanism for discovering "alternative" accounts of flourishing, but he does not typically use it to uncover gender differences in needs or knowledge. Further, his liberationist idealism—focused on the infinite demands of the Kingdom—rests uneasily with the feminist insistence that infinite giving is inappropriate and destructive to oppressed peoples. Both Latin American and feminist liberation thinkers need to find a convincing way to close the gap between their prophetic idealism and their more flexible, *epikeic* expectations of persons who still labor under the physical, psychological, and spiritual effects of oppression.

None of these three, then, develops norms that self-consciously take into account gender differences in the needs that must be met for people truly to flourish, and none explicitly tests his argument against particular other women's or men's experience. This lack makes clear what a revolutionary act it is simply to argue that standard, "neutral" accounts of flourishing may not account for women's needs and experiences; that women (and all others) are and should be responsible moral agents-in-community; that their concrete material, political, and spiritual fulfillment is a criterion of moral judgment; and that they are to have a hand in defining what constitutes this fulfillment.

Second, the central criterion of corporately generated norms and of their proper use is the good of concrete persons, not merely of values in the abstract. The particularity of this norm reminds us that while the formal shape of flourishing is the same for all, the prerequisites of flourishing differ for particular persons; for instance, a person who is HIV-positive needs more medical care in order to remain healthy than does a person with no chronic illnesses. Fuchs, as we have seen, gives few examples of the application of norms to particular situations, preferring to concentrate on the generic realization of values. His intent and achievement are to leave as wide a berth as possible for the ordinary person's moral reflection and action and therefore as much leeway as possible both for freedom of conscience and for fulfillment of concrete needs. Yet because moral reasoning is not an automatic activity but an art or skill learned through critical observation, it is just at this point that it becomes crucial to know how he would reason himself, to be given some models of gritty, concrete moral reflection. What is needed here is not what McCormick sometimes appears to provide—expert determination of what actions are right for all who find themselves in a given situation—but illustrations of the sorts of considerations a wise and prudent person might employ. For McCormick, too, values remain somewhat abstract, but for slightly different reasons. Finnis, for instance, complains that McCormick is more interested in realizing the value of respect for the innocent in war than he is in his duty to protect particular innocent persons. [17] But it is not clear what it would mean to uphold a value in general; a value has to be instantiated in a concrete human good, even if that good is corporate. The most persistent and trenchant feminist criticism of natural law ethics, both traditional and revisionist, resembles this complaint: that the natural law objections to abortion value abstract or potential human life over the lives of particular, pregnant women and, often, their families. Gutiérrez, on the other hand, tries to avoid these sorts of ambiguities and conflicts by pegging corporate, liberative salvation on the corporate definition, pursuit, and achievement of concrete goods by the oppressed. Concrete—but communal and social—justice and flourishing for individuals is at the center of Gutiérrez's project.

Up to this point the question has largely been whether Fuchs's, McCormick's, and Gutiérrez's approaches are compatible with or adverse to the central commitments of feminist ethics. This is a theoretical, structural issue and appropriately so, if the premise is that the natural law and feminist traditions of ethics are linked by their structure and scope of argument. On the other hand, to the degree that these authors fail to advert to women's experience, practical concerns, and theoretical proposals, they fail to submit their own work to the test of universality. They also fail the moral epistemological criterion, the preferential option for the oppressed and excluded; for as an epistemological criterion, the preferential option must be the premise, and not the conclusion, of moral reasoning.

Of the three, Fuchs is least explicitly concerned with women's issues; women, and moral issues that might specially concern them, are rarely mentioned in his work. In keeping with his images of a central core of theological truths and a periphery of shifting moral guidelines, it is possible that differences of sex, like all other pluralisms and circumstances, would simply be part of the complex of worldly factors that make up the context for concrete moral reflection. But Fuchs does not deal separately with the ethical method or the goods proposed by women, and thus he does not deal explicitly with the possibility that their peculiar experiences could challenge his assumptions. The absence of systematic openings for contributions by women and other marginalized men is appropriate in one sense, for their concerns will guide their own reflection; what is lacking is the awareness that theological anthropological reflection should itself systematically take into account minority and marginal accounts of the structure of human being, fulfillment, and reason. It is this omission that counts against him.

McCormick is slightly more successful on this measure in that the topics he treats—especially reproductive and sexual ethics, ecclesiology, and authority in institutions—are of special concern to many women. In addition, he is an enthusiastic supporter of women's ventures in moral theology, and he has recognized their potential impact on the content of moral norms; for example, he contends that the Roman Catholic church's "admission of the sin of sexism. . . . will profoundly affect the understanding of human sexuality and the ethic built on that understanding." [18] Yet it is not clear what material difference this recognition will continue to make in his own writing. Although McCormick's work exhibits a clear trend from a narrow focus on the significance of vaginal intercourse and ejaculation within a properly procreative marriage to a slightly broader interest in the place of genital sexuality within intimate relationships, he has never incorporated into his discussion of sexuality other experiences—among them pregnancy, childbirth, nursing, weaning, and sexual intimacy exclusive of intercourse—that very many women would describe as falling within the constellation of sexual relationship and as having great moral meaning. By failing to discuss women's sexual issues he misses the new angles that might well help him further to redefine the questions that are posed to him: for instance, not only What did the tradition mean to say? on sexual issues as celibate men defined them in the past but What, owing to its neglect of women's experience, does it neglect or say wrongly? on sexual issues as women define them in the present. Like Fuchs, he takes the basic features of his anthropology and ethical method to be independently valid; new information from women is information to be manipulated by the accepted proportionalist method, not information that suggests new methods.

Yet these shortfalls should not eclipse either his warm support for feminist moral theologians or his own methodological overtures to feminism. [19] His increasingly inductive method and his good will combine to admit moral descriptions that reflect feminist articulations of human experience rather than referring immediately to existing norms. For instance, he begins one of his more recent discussions of sexuality by describing a fully committed sexual relationship as an experience of friendship. This "descriptive language . . . *proves* nothing," he admits, and yet its moral significance is clear in the guidelines he spins from it. He continues the discussion with experiences gleaned from "my tradition," not from conversations with particular persons, but the experience of the tradition is still presented as authoritative precisely as accumulated wisdom rather than as a presumptive declaration of an ecclesiastical body. [20] In this case the risk in using self-consciously inductive reasoning was low, given that the norm generated—sex as the sign of intimacy most fully realized within marital friendship—largely supports the traditional marital norm. Thus clearly experience must have more regular and strenuous workouts if it is not to fall into the personalist trap of uncritically generating new justifications for old norms.

Gustavo Gutiérrez's specific treatment of women as women, and not merely in their capacity as receptacles for children, is the most direct of the three authors'. [21] His one-chapter meditation on and retrieval of Mary is of crucial importance to Latin American Catholicism, for here Mary's human strength—and not merely her passivity and her glory—receive new emphasis. Gutiérrez deals with Mary and poor women in general as doubly oppressed; recognizes sex, culture, and race, not only social class, as dimensions of oppression; and argues that "there cannot, in fact, be a just struggle for the rights of those whom society marginalizes, unless the rights of women are included." [22] He also attempts a broad exegesis of Old and New Testament texts on women. Thus his short, introductory treatment is significant not because it reflects a long record of explicit interest in women's issues—it does not—but because it is a clear result of his method, which leads him to identify the oppressed and the structures that cause oppression. This concern has led him to understand that oppression is not merely economic but also sexual. Consequently he has recognized that not only a speaker's class bias, but also her sex bias, has epistemological significance. Yet Gutiérrez has not turned a critical eye, for instance, on the male God of Scripture or on the status of women within the Exodus community. In order to prove a genuine commitment to women, then, he must take care to make critical use even of "sympathetic" or revolutionary strands of the scriptural and theological traditions, and he must recognize that women and men have potentially distinct voices even when women are not doubly oppressed.

From these criteria we can also tailor a few feminist guidelines specifically to fit the natural law paradigm. First, the feminist and natural law criterion of integral flourishing implies that the theological vision of the ultimate human telos must encompass all the concrete goods of which genuine, integral human flourishing consists. Second, although no group has a corner on the experiential wisdom that informs prudence, anyone at all who wants to make a legitimate moral inquiry must begin in solidarity and conversation with the marginalized or oppressed. This criterion reiterates the properly communal character of moral deliberation.

In addition, feminism helps to refine natural law's understanding of the ethical significance of embodiment. As Lisa Cahill has noted, the recent hoopla over "embodiment" seems disingenuous in a culture that has concentrated so intently on sexual and medical ethics. [23] But in Roman Catholicism the strands of ethics of which she speaks have largely treated the body as object. Feminists would not object to this if the body and its parts were not abstracted from the person in the process; integral, embodied flourishing is, after all, feminism's goal. But feminism calls as well for a revival of the Thomistic emphasis upon the embodied subject: the person whose knowledge, pleasure, pain, and relationships are bodily or bodily mediated. For both physical and social reasons women as a class have access to a whole panoply of embodied experiences in which men either cannot participate directly or rarely participate. Thus the feminist—and Thomistic—insistence that the full range of human moral experience can be expressed only through the self-consciously embodied subject. Finally, the body is not self-interpreting; the most self-evident claims about embodied persons' needs require careful and critical analysis.

Against hierarchical, complementary, and dualist versions of natural law, feminism clearly holds that the equal value and dignity of men and women should be interpreted through the lens of their common humanity, not through the lens of their difference. Men do not have other or "higher" ends and capacities than women, either eschatologically or temporally. Yet a feminism genuinely committed to women's welfare also argues that although the general shape of integral flourishing might be the same for all—differences in sexual organs, skin color, or geographic location do not narrow the basic human telos to (say) childbearing, manual labor, or farming—what each person requires in order to move toward this goal varies. The variations can be as simple and immediate as the different nutritional needs of infants and adults, the differing educational needs of children with learning disabilities and diverse learning styles, or the different shelter needs of people who live in tropical and temperate climates. The feminist point is that, no matter how evenly now-gendered work is reassigned, women always and everywhere will have needs that men do not and will not ever have: protection from unwanted sex and pregnancy, good obstetrical care, economic support for childbearing, and (in an affluent society) medical research and treatment of "women's diseases" like breast cancer. Fulfillment of these needs is a basic right of women in the same way that research and treatment of "men's diseases" like prostate enlargement is assumed to be a right of men.

Finally, encouraged by the question-and-response structure of scholastic *summae* and of manuals of moral theology, proportionalist natural law revisionism has been a dilemma ethic, responding to apparent conflicts—between norm and flourishing or between mutually exclusive goods—as they arise. This has had three effects on proportionalism's approach: its initial stance is reactive, not proactive or idealistic; it tends at first to accept the proposition that a perceived problem really is a dilemma, a matter of an "either/or" choice; and it reduces most contextual factors to circumstances, further information about the act. Only if these assumptions prove inadequate to the dilemma does it experiment with new ways of posing the issue.

Yet it is not clear that there really is such a thing as an either/or dilemma. Feminists and many others would counter that the complex of factors contributing to a decision is rarely reducible to "circumstances of the act," nor are there normally only two alternatives. For example, I might want to know whether I should give money to a homeless person, given that it may be used for alcohol or drugs. The classic rhetoric of the dilemma poses this as a yes-or-no question that pits faith in human nature and altruism narrowly defined against skepticism and a guess about the homeless person's ultimate interests. I really have at least four choices: give the money; do nothing; direct her to a soup kitchen; or buy food for her. But the four immediately become eight because in each case I can explain my action as a carefully considered, concrete commitment to this person, or not. The result is a collection of different, somewhat overlapping, moral descriptions, not two mutually exclusive ones; adding options would easily multiply the number.

Feminist ethics, on the other hand, although it sometimes begins moral reflection with a conundrum, is not dilemma ethics. For feminism as for liberationism the conflicts and apparent dilemmas that inspire moral reflection are not discrete problems to be dispatched by measuring and balancing particular harms and goods in context and issuing lists of acceptable solutions. Rather, feminists begin with the assumption that these conflicts are symptoms that something in the context itself is awry and demands critical analysis. Thus the first task of ethics is to discover whether the conundrum has been improperly expressed, contains suspicious hidden assumptions, or dissolves on examination. [24]

What the feminist critique of natural law reveals, in short, is that traditional natural law thought contains two impulses: the egalitarian impulse, supported by the common human telos, and the hierarchical impulse, supported by the assumption that all differences are to be exploited as justifications for hierarchical social relations and strict divisions of social tasks. But if, as Thomas suggests, temporal flourishing and its pursuit are consistent with and demanded by the ultimate telos, then secondary acceptance of radically different degrees and kinds of flourishing is insupportable and must give way before the genuinely primary commitment to a common telos. Far from eviscerating natural law, then, a feminist critique removes a number of internal obstacles that have prevented natural law from realizing its own ends.

The feminist critique shows not that Thomas or natural law revisionists lost sight of the integral person but that they did not always fully understand or articulate the continuing dynamic interdependence of all the dimensions of integral personhood or the inherent and cultural differences in men's and women's experiences of their connection. The barriers to clear vision are methodological and procedural: a truly comprehensive method requires not neutrality but a moral and epistemological preferential option in favor of those who are generally excluded from both integral flourishing and the process of authoritative moral deliberation. This preferential option ensures both broad development of mature moral agency and wide participation in the process of describing the integral human good and the conditions of its pursuit, both of which are essential to the natural law project. It not only empowers natural law to fulfill its own goals more adequately but reflects central natural law claims: justice in the distribution of goods, the universal perspicuity of natural law principles, and the interdependence of the knowledge and pursuit of the good. In our context the preferential option encourages women's wide participation in public moral discourse, which in turn yields a profound integration of physical, social, intellectual, and spiritual dimensions of human being and the resultant elevation of the significance of the material conditions of human life; the body is not accidental but essential to human existence, and its flourishing is an essential condition of integral human flourishing.

Second and consequently, not only the content but the method of moral thought should reflect observed structures of human reason, with special attention to the methods employed by those who, again, generally have been excluded from authoritative moral deliberation. One of feminism's most important contributions in this regard—one that it shares with liberation thought—is its insistence that ethics in the full sense has to do with aspiration and fulfillment. But McCormick's essential human ethics, taken by itself, cannot be aspirational, and existential human ethics are aspirational but individualistic. Human ethics *logically* requires an additional or encompassing, aspirational vision of corporate human activity and a virtue theory (as well as a theology of vocation) if it is to do more than point to universal minimal requirements for human integral flourishing.

Third, because an essential human ethic is nonetheless indispensable to the project of establishing just conditions in the world, it can succeed in that task only if it systematically incorporates new and formerly peripheral understandings of human being and flourishing and recognizes their possible implications for its method.

BRIDGING OTHER GAPS: GROUNDS FOR NORMS AND SOCIAL ETHICS

The critical synthesis of natural law revisionism and feminist critical standards has left two important gaps: the lack of a clear method for creating norms, and the lack of a principled social ethic.

As we saw in chapters 3 and 6, norms that cease to serve their ends well require transformation through casuistry. But casuistry neither tells us all we need to know about methods for creating norms and principles nor responds adequately to the feminist anxiety that many norms, inextricable from their oppressive origins, may be entirely unsalvageable.

The inadequate attention to norms in feminist thought can be traced partly to the fact that feminists have more experience with critical theory than with constructive ethics. In order to bridge this gap we can capitalize on liberationism, the offshoot of the natural law tradition that overlaps methodologically with feminism. Thomas Schubeck notes that critics who have made the same complaints about liberation theology have overlooked the fact that liberation theologians do hold some basic principles firm and have tacit, if not explicit, means for deriving them.

Liberation theologians, Schubeck argues, operate with a combination of categorical principles ("generally and universally valid perspectives") and concrete principles (context-specific, concrete guidelines), all of which serve and are judged by the ultimate end, the Kingdom of God. [25] For instance, among other things, advancing the Kingdom of God entails fidelity to revelation, under which falls a categorical imperative ("Witness to the truth!"), with its concrete commandments (advancing the common good and promoting flourishing generally), and its even more concrete manifestions (condemning the monopolization of land). [26] Schubeck makes clear that the most concrete imperatives are not so much deduced from as connected thematically with the categorical ones, under the umbrella image of the Kingdom of God; [27] thus liberationists are not adhering to neoscholastic ideals of univocal derivation of norms from principles but seeking to organize their concrete—perhaps disparate—judgments theologically.

Likewise, feminist ethics has a goal (the integral flourishing of women); categorical imperatives (respect for embodied persons); concrete imperatives (never force sexual contact); and concrete manifestations (date rape is wrong). Like liberationists, feminists do not derive concrete claims by methodically applying categorical imperatives in specific situations. Rather, they ask how women's flourishing can be accomplished, here and now, and develop general imperatives out of these judgments. So at each level of concreteness principles are inductive, heuristic devices that gather a collection of similar judgments— and eventually, traditions of similar judgments—under a common umbrella. It is not that feminist ethics lacks principles; the important task is to articulate and connect them.

The second gap, social ethics, is an omission not so much in the natural law or feminist traditions broadly but in Fuchs, McCormick (with the exception of his policy initiatives), and Gutiérrez. The natural law demand for social justice, whose radical implications bloom in liberation theology, has yielded both practical and prophetic imperatives for decades. One of the best witnesses to its serviceability is its capacity to adapt to subtle changes in the definition of flourishing; for instance, the transition from preoccupation with hierarchical order to the embrace of democratic freedom has led to some quite remarkable reversals on the moral acceptability of strikes. Feminists also combine critical analysis and constructive reflection with the bond of realist politics: Joan Tronto's *Moral Boundaries* painstakingly works out the details of a political ethic of care, and Susan Moller Okin's *Justice, Gender, and the Family* proposes practical, political means for passing from the ideal of gender equality to its realization within families. [28] Tronto, for instance, emphasizes the connection between the marginalization of women and their voices and the marginalization of "the activities and concerns of care," which is a "central concern of human life" and prerequisite for human flourishing. She combines prophetic condemnations of the "choices our society has made about what to honor" with proposals for avoiding destructively naïve approaches to political transformation. [29]

Theological connections between social ethics and soteriology are nascent in the social justice tradition, which holds that people pursue the common good out of temporal and eschatological self-interest, genuine moral integrity, love for the Absolute, or perhaps even charity. The liberationist theology of history adds a corporate eschatological significance: in advancing the common good we are also cooperating with God to bring about the reign of justice. This new theology of history shifts the focus of social action from meeting one's own eschatological needs, through response to the concrete needs of one's immediate circle, to participation in God's plans for all of humanity.

If feminist ethics is incomplete without these references to liberation theology and the social encyclicals, is feminist ethics essential to natural law revision at all? As we have seen, one significant contribution is procedural: natural law ethics has been developed, organized, and articulated by small, fairly homogeneous groups of scholars, and feminism provides important alternative procedural models. Methodologically, feminism would seem to have little to contribute to natural law that liberationism lacks because feminist method is an application of the liberation hermeneutic to gender difference. Yet it is worth noting both that the male guild of liberation theologians has been very slow to incorporate gender oppression into its analysis and that it can, if it wishes, justify this addition purely on the basis of the economic and political oppression of women. Not only that, but the liberationist God, in whose image humanity is created, remains by and large male. Thus liberation analyses do not necessarily yield the gender analyses of social power and knowledge that form the foundations of feminist ethics.

Liberation theology frequently fails to find gender because it does not begin with inherent and ineradicable difference. The difference upon which liberation theology focuses is the unjust distribution of wealth and power, which is a product not of the natural order of the world but of sin, a human invention that is to be eradicated by the grace of God. Liberation succeeds when it destroys both sin and the differences of power and wealth that define and divide oppressor and oppressed. But as we saw in the introduction and chapter 1, this strategy would ultimately be fatal to feminism because it would destroy the sex difference that an integral, embodied vision of personhood entails. Sex differences will persist, and they will therefore always be susceptible to an oppressive interpretation. Rather than dissolving oppressive differences by labeling them sinful social constructions, as liberationism tends to do, feminism instead must uproot oppression by destroying oppressive interpretations of difference while leaving difference itself intact. Feminism thus has a double message for natural law thought: a liberationist moral hermeneutic that intends to root out sinful victimization and an affirmation that human beings are fundamentally, inexorably different, that there is one sort of pluralism that cannot be erased. Like liberationism, feminism needs its *moral* hermeneutic—its insistence on commitment to oppressed women as an epistemological criterion—only as long as sex difference is used to justify victimization of one sex by the other. But its argument that, even in a perfectly just society, sex difference entails morally significant variation—slight but crucial differences in what men and women require in order to reach the threshold of flourishing, and slight but epistemologically significant divergences in experience—is a case it must make until the end of embodied human existence. No matter what the social position of women, feminism's argument stands: both of these gendered strands of experience must be sought out and represented.

Feminist critical analysis trades on its unique ability to distinguish pure cultural constructions from either just or oppressive cultural interpretations of ineradicable human difference and on its superior capacity to deal justly with difference. Feminism's basic claim is not, therefore, essentialist, romantic, or simplistically naturalist. Feminism need not argue that more divides men and women than unites them; that men and women complement each other or have mutually exclusive skills; that sexual characteristics categorically exclude anyone from just wages, a standard education, or positions of responsibility; or that one sex is superior to another. But it must argue that this almost universal difference in embodied existence is likely to yield differences in experience that affect moral reflection and that these must be explored critically. This is the uniquely important frontier between natural law and feminist thought. It points, as noted in the introduction, to issues crucial to the success of both.

NOTES

1. See Stanley Hauerwas, "Casuistry as a Narrative Art," *Interpretation* 37 (1983): 377–88; and James F. Keenan, S.J., "The Return of Casuistry," *Theological Studies* 57 (March 1996): 123–29. Keenan is primarily interested in the capacity of casuistic moral judgments to renovate communal biases and narratives; and Hauerwas, in the capacity of casuistic moral judgments to make prophetic demands for faithfulness to constant narratives. But this difference amounts to a distinction rather than an opposition, for both anticipate that honest casuistry will transform the standard interpretations of the communal narrative that govern the moral decisions of both ordinary people and church functionaries.

2. Fuchs, *Human Values*, 110–11.

3. McCormick, "Ambiguity," 49–50.

4. Gutiérrez has pointed out the need for liberation thought to deal with the issues of sexuality and sexism but has not done so in any systematic way himself. Others have begun to probe these topics. See José Comblin, *Retrieving the Human: A Christian Anthropology*, trans. Robert R. Barr, Theology and Liberation Series (Maryknoll, NY: Orbis Books, 1990), 76–88, 123–25; and Ana María Bidegain, "Women and the Theology of Liberation," trans. Robert R. Barr, in *Through Her Eyes: Women's Theology from Latin America*, ed. Elsa Tamez (Maryknoll, NY: Orbis Books, 1989), 15–36. Comblin traces the antiprocreative mentality and sexual libertinism to the

degenerate bourgeois class; he links "primitive" or "traditional" attitudes to high valuation of procreation and observance of strict sexual mores rooted, he believes, in a wise and realistic understanding of human being. Bidegain, on the other hand, argues that in fact popular Latin American Christian sexual mores have been repressive and puritanical, idealizing asexuality. She argues for a new, more personalistic theological view of human sexuality (see "Women," 29–30).

5. McCormick, *Moral Theology in the Year 2000*, 13–14.

6. These parallels are not necessarily complete in every instance; for McCormick, for example, the Christian criterion further narrows the choices that are humanly acceptable, but the existential Christian criterion is the narrowest.

7. McCormick, *Moral Theology in the Year 2000*, 13–14: "Whether our actions or policies are supportive of persons or detrimental to them cannot be deduced from general principles. It takes time and experience."

8. On narrative see also Hauerwas, *Community of Character*.

9. McCormick's insight that inaction is a form of act—a decision from which results follow that may be judged morally—does implicitly suggest support for this position (McCormick, "Commentary," 263).

10. Gutiérrez, The Albert Cardinal Meyer Lecture Series, 25 April 1992.

11. This is not to deny that in Thomas the *perfection* of the moral and intellectual virtues is interdependent (*ST* I-II 58.4–5). Behavior that compromises the dignity of the human being as *imago dei* is unacceptable partly because such behavior willfully misrepresents the truth about human being.

12. The structure of Gutiérrez's thought suggests that he would rely largely on historical and social scientific theories for the practical element of this project. An ethic of radical witness, because it prescinds from the direct intention to change human systems, would not in the end be adequate to feminist or liberationist criteria, although radical witness could partially motivate some actions.

13. Segundo, "Shift."

14. Hoagland lacks a theory of moral development. Her ethic is for adults. It is unclear what sort of moral tutelage children should receive, whether particular values could be promoted, and if so, which and how. Clearly an ethic of obedience would be inadequate.

15. The doctrine of subsidiarity was originally developed to justify government involvement in provision for human welfare but protect individuals from invasive versions of state socialism. The criterion was that what could be accomplished at a lower or more decentralized level should not be carried out at a higher one. For instance, the family, not the state, should raise children; but only the state can guarantee family welfare by enforcing a family wage. For an early discussion, see Leo XIII, *Rerum Novarum*, 6, par. 11.

16. The good of the natural environment seems to be a part of this human good, for the natural environment is still a material to be manipulated by humanity, not a value in its own right. See Fuchs, "On the Theology of Human Progress," in *Human Values*, 178–203.

17. Porter points out that for Thomas acts that are evil in themselves do not merely wound basic values but unjustly inflict harm on particular persons (Porter, *Recovery*, 92, and chapter 5). Finnis has a similar complaint; see his criticism of McCormick's treatment of war in chapter 6 of this volume.

18. McCormick, *Health and Medicine*, 102.

19. For the former see McCormick, "Moral Theology 1940–1989," 12–13.

20. McCormick, *Critical Calling*, 393.

21. Gutiérrez, *The God of Life*, 164–89.

22. Ibid., 165–66. It is also for this reason—its identification of women with Mary, and its implicit posing of Mary as the paradigmatic woman—problematic.

23. Lisa Sowle Cahill, "'Embodiment' and Moral Critique: A Christian Social Perspective," in *Embodiment, Morality, and Medicine*, ed. Lisa Sowle Cahill and Margaret A. Farley, 199–215 (Boston: Kluwer Academic Publishers, 1995), 199.

24. Richard McCormick asks similar questions, but generally in a more circumscribed way and only when no coherent solution seems possible within the parameters of existing norms.

25. Schubeck, *Liberation Ethics*, 245.

26. Schubeck, *Liberation Ethics*, 246.

27. Schubeck, *Liberation Ethics*, 241.

28. Susan Moller Okin, *Justice, Gender, and the Family* (New York: Basic Books, 1989).

29. Tronto, *Moral Boundaries*, 179–80. For a Christian feminist analysis of power in social ethics, see Christine Firer Hinze, *Comprehending Power in Christian Social Ethics* (Atlanta: Scholars Press, 1995).

9

From Feminist Critique to Feminist Ethic

Feminism's purpose is practical: to promote women's integral flourishing, including their fully reflective moral agency. Consequently and appropriately, feminism is a social movement, and feminist philosophy and theology have been designed to serve its purposes: criticizing existing moral traditions and practices and galvanizing support behind initiatives in liberal feminist politics. These deconstructive and political moments of feminism are indispensable to its end, and they provide the formal parameters for feminist moral discourse. Yet they are not adequate, existentially satisfying guides for a constructive ethic or for the moral life. The passage from *the* feminist critique to *a* feminist ethic or from *the* feminist vision of integral flourishing to *a* coherent, meaningful life in a particular place and time requires more than formal boundaries and negative criteria. We have seen some of the raw materials that feminism provides for this constructive project. But natural law ethics also provides two indispensable resources and a number of other supports for this journey. Some of these resources and supports apply to feminism generally, but our focus here will be their contribution to a Christian feminist theological ethic.

Natural law's first contribution is the insistence that a comprehensive, existentially compelling ethic demands an all-encompassing telos. The transition from the critical to the constructive stance depends upon recognizing that even a feminist politics like Martha Nussbaum's expresses the end formally rather than substantively: the provision of all that women would need in order to cross the threshold of integral flourishing if they chose to do so. Certainly Nussbaum's list of conditions for free choice contains elements that no feminist ethic can do without: access to medical care and education, for instance. Yet this vision is neither concrete enough to guide an individual's daily moral life nor compelling enough to transform the elements of the threshold from mere options to goods worth pursuing. A constructive feminist ethic must have a telos, an end that envelops and meaningfully connects the many particular dimensions of women's good. The precise shape this encompassing end takes depends on what other goods it includes, how the goods are related to each other, how women's good is related to the goods of men and of the world, and whether women's good is subordinate to or concretizes some larger, transcendent good.

Legitimate feminist ethics will be united by their commitment to two principles: that an ethic adequate to the moral life demands a telos and that an adequate telos encompasses all the elements of women's genuine flourishing. This does not mean that we can expect all feminists to concur on a single vision of the encompassing end and therefore on a single ethic. Rather, in recognition of feminism's beginnings as a critical discipline, we must expect a variety of feminist ethics, distinguished by their precise understandings and orderings of women's ends. Yet as Margaret Farley reminds us, this variety is not endless: "for most feminists 'reality' is not infinitely malleable, not neutrally open to an infinite number of interpretations at any given point in time. . . . there are limits beyond which some constructions will end in deconstruction." [1]

Christian feminist ethics in particular depends on creating a credible connection among Christianity's formal encompassing telos, salvation; concrete flourishing; and the moral life. Together, Thomas's virtue theory and his belief in virtue's benefits to the common good provide an indispensable connection among the individual's ultimate end in God, concrete daily actions, and communal flourishing. As we have seen, the connection is not complete; concrete flourishing is a temporal end, so that the only reference just acts have to the encompassing telos is through the ultimate good of the individual who performs them. Only people who perform good acts derive benefit in an ultimate sense from these acts. Natural law revisionism is only mildly more helpful: salvation entails an existential commitment to the Absolute expressed in loving, careful pursuit of concrete goods for others. The liberationist twist on the ultimate telos connects temporal and transcendent ends: in acting justly a person not only advances her own ultimate end but contributes to the reign of God, the ultimate good for the whole of humanity. By making communal earthly flourishing a dimension of the ultimate end, this claim removes the suspicion that, since temporal flourishing is only a proximate good, the real significance of generous action lies in advancing one's own salvation. Rather, "right" acts that advance flourishing have a directly eschatological reference, for true temporal flourishing is a dimension of the integral end, liberative salvation. Thus Thomas, with the help of a liberationist interpretation of salvation history, provides Christian feminism with the integral telos it needs in order to develop a constructive ethic.

Second, if, as has been argued, feminist ethics needs principles, it also needs methods for managing them. Natural law provides not only a tradition of principles and norms but a method of criticizing and altering them: casuistry. Case reasoning is an inductive, analogical, and therefore methodologically appropriate tool for feminist moral deliberation. Its great strength is that it provides an alternative to condemning an entire moral tradition on the basis of one apparently destructive moral judgment. This sort of condemnation is at times necessary, but one cannot engage in it very frequently and still lead a coherent, directed moral life. When we run across a case in which flourishing appears to demand a solution that contradicts the principles we have developed, casuistry permits us first to ask whether it is the whole moral system, or just one principle or its application, that is faulty. Often, with a little careful creative reflection, a troubling case can be understood justly and consistently by altering a norm to account for it or by relating it to different, more appropriate principles. For instance, just as charging interest migrated from the category "usury" to the category "just profit" without disturbing the assumption that it was possible to establish limits to the fees that could be charged for the use of money, so firefighting might be moved out of the category "work from which women should be protected" to the category "work any able person may perform" without challenging the underlying presumption that flourishing demands that some people be specially protected from harmful work—children from employment as pornographic models, pregnant women from toxins, etc.

Natural law's contributions of telos and practical moral reasoning are unique. But in other cases the natural law tradition reinforces central claims of the feminist tradition. First, and perhaps most important for Christian feminism, natural law anthropology envisions a person who is fundamentally good and whole. She is naturally inclined toward the good and capable of cooperating with divine grace to work toward the fulfillment of her own ends and those of the community around her. Both virtue theory and the feminist hermeneutic of suspicion caution us that sinful biases can corrupt and divert inclinations, but they also teach us that these errors are reversible and that we can corporately trust reasoned reflection on experience to help us identify them.

A telic natural law anthropology also justifies a person's acting in her own genuine self-interest, within the limits of justice, humility, and finitude. Like Cannon's womanist revision of virtue, this criterion softens liberation theology's sometimes extreme prophetic rhetoric. It simply cannot be demanded that everyone, in every situation, vocally condemn and refuse to participate in any way in injustice. This principle is all the more indispensable in an era that recognizes the profound interdependence of all people and institutions: completely extricating ourselves from participation in injustice is literally impossible.

This sort of emphasis on the goods and the goodness of the subject is absent in most other Western theological traditions. Mainstream historical traditions within Protestantism, less optimistic about the human capacity to recognize and pursue the good, tend to espouse an account of human depravity that places all responsibility for human motion toward the ultimate end on God, and none on human will. [2] These therefore are less well-suited theologically to a meaningful feminist integration of temporal communal flourishing and individual self-protection with ultimate ends.

A second source of reinforcement from natural law is virtue theory. Not only does virtue theory knit together goodness with rightness and temporal flourishing, but it reminds us the point of the moral life is not only to act rightly but to act well; this, in turn, entails becoming a good moral reasoner, also one of the chief goals of feminist ethics. In the natural law tradition, prudence is a virtue whose act is acquired gradually, even when its habit is infused. In this claim, as well as in some of Richard McCormick's pastoral exceptions, we have evidence of a developmental view of moral reason. Feminist models of gender-role learning and care ethics likewise presuppose that the capacity for moral reason and action develops slowly; they simply reject the idea that popular psychological models of moral development like Kohlberg's and Erickson's, which usually treat women as deficient reasoners, have captured either the true progression or the variety in human moral growth.

In addition, Thomas's theory of the theological virtues insists that true, integral virtue cannot exist unless powered by divine charity, which infuses a bottomless love for God and, within this love, for all genuine goods. Virtue theory thus provides theological support for the feminist and liberationist insistence that ethical clarity and genuinely liberative action arise only out of love for and genuine solidarity with the oppressed, as well as—for liberationists—out of a strong if sometimes prereflective faith.

Third, the Roman Catholic social justice tradition's detailed analysis of social problems, if sometimes lacking detail or missing sufficient connection to theology, still equips it to be a strong partner in the likewise critically analytical feminist project of ethics. Even more important, its doctrine of the common good confirms the feminist tenet that all flourishing is integral and interdependent, so that a focus on the well-being of the oppressed necessarily entails a concern for the genuine well-being of all, individually and corporately. This acknowledgment does not imply—as neoscholastic and personalist-absolutist accounts sometimes do—that genuine conflicts of goods never occur or that difficult choices among goods never have to be made; but, combined with a hermeneutic of suspicion, it does warn against assuming that what seems good for the part is best for the whole, or vice versa. We are always under the obligation to examine this connection critically. The liberationist version of the doctrine of the common good also reminds us to be on the lookout for the interdependence not only of parts and wholes but also of all the dimensions of flourishing.

Last, but certainly not least, comes the body as condition of temporal human flourishing and as medium of truth. Here McCormick and Fuchs admirably balance a sense of our responsibility to pursue concrete ontic goods with a resolution not to permit physical descriptions of bodily relations to be morally determinative gauges of complex human relationships. But lacking the feminist sense of the body as the site where social forces converge, they miss the causes of the "biologism" they are attempting to refute; they therefore have no good grounds to avoid a new dualism, a vision of moral reason as ideally disembodied, unaffected, or uninformed by particular bodily experiences. As Susan Ross, Christine Gudorf, and others have insisted, in fact the Roman Catholic natural law tradition has systematically ignored women's accounts of their own embodiment and so has failed to consider its moral and epistemological significance.[3] Thomas and Gutiérrez fill out the theoretical picture helpfully. For Thomas, the body is the medium of sense knowledge and of all recognizably human experience in the world. It sometimes leads us astray, but it also brings us the critical knowledge with which we can discover these departures. For Gutiérrez, the body is the whole human being as we know her—either under the power of flesh and evil, or "freed from the forces of death" and ready "to lead a life in the Spirit."[4] The physical body is not even, as it is for Thomas, a current impediment to the direct illumination of the posthumous, intellectual beatific vision; it is the precondition for the operation of salvific grace. Here we have theological reasons to affirm the feminist confidence in the body as channel of knowledge and field of grace.

Natural law thus models elements that any viable, constructive feminist theological ethic must also possess: above all, an overarching telos, as well as an inductive method of matching cases and principles; an eschatology and a developmental virtue theory that connect individual and communal ends at both the immediate and ultimate levels; a tradition of social analysis; an argument for self-preservation; and an integral rather than ambivalent reading of human embodiment. But these elements also provide a constructive Christian feminism the rudiments of a coherent theological ethic.

THE POSSIBILITY OF PROPHECY: THE FATE OF
UNIVERSAL CLAIMS IN A PLURALISTIC AGE

One of the goals that has slipped out of sight repeatedly in the foregoing chapters is the aim of reconciling feminism's prophetic role—the identification and denunciation of universally reprehensible beliefs and practices—with its pluralist presumption that no group truly shares the experiences of, and therefore may speak for, the moral beliefs and practices of another. This conflict between prophetic universals and pluralist relativism stands in for the conflict between modernity and postmodernity. As chapter 3 implied, the ideal of expressing natural law as a universal, neutral ethic is a modern ideal. Feminism's critical deconstruction of natural law's claims to quintessential neutrality seems to destroy its most useful characteristic, but in fact it frees natural law thought to participate more honestly and subtly in contemporary moral debate. For deconstruction reveals the distinctively Christian character of natural law thought, relieves the pressure to make universal, neutral claims, and permits natural law to identify itself as a religious (as well as perhaps liberationist or feminist) ethic. Apparent ideological neutrality is no longer the prerequisite for credibly entering public discussions.

This unexpected new role for natural law confirms the suspicion that we must live in the tension between prophecy and pluralism. The only tidy means to a resolution of this tension would be the wrong-headed elimination of one pole or the other, with its consequent unjustifiable loss. For example, setting up absolute norms or a single prophetic authority destroys egalitarian, participatory thought and risks the introduction of oppressive biases, but utter relativism forbids the establishment of any cross-cultural standards and, in extreme cases, the development of standards within a community or even the formation of community itself.

This does not mean that universal ethical claims are forbidden; they cannot be because making moral sense of one's surroundings involves generalizing about experience, and experience is social and public rather than private. It is to say that all claims about universals must be made with earnest humility; they are hypotheses (though strong ones), must be susceptible to criticism from both inside and outside one's own tradition, and must be made from a position of self-conscious particularity rather than claimed neutrality. For want of a better label, we might call these "revisable universals," a term that expresses their inherent openness to reconsideration better than the proportionalist Roman Catholic "virtually exceptionless norm." For instance, a feminist natural law ethic, as we saw above, might adopt revisable universals along two ubiquitous axes of injustice: political and economic oppression, which are rooted in the universal human capacity to sin through domination, and sexist oppression, which is rooted in sin but also exploits ineradicable universal sex differences. A feminist theological ethic disqualifies as unjust any anthropological telos or principle that depends on either of these sorts of oppression. [5] So, first, institutions, actions, and beliefs that create or justify economic and political oppression are false; and second, institutions, actions, and beliefs that create or justify sexual oppression are false. Conversely, the pursuit of genuine, integral flourishing is not an arbitrary choice; it has a theological mandate.

But once revisable universal claims are made, how can they be tested and defended in cross-cultural conversation? First, often false claims can be eliminated without the need for cross-cultural comparison at all. For the culture in which an oppressive claim is rooted rarely stands in monolithic support of it. One should begin by asking whether critiques of the proposed claim already exist inside the culture. If so, and they also draw upon central cultural traditions, it may not even be necessary to seek a critical standpoint outside the culture. For instance, college students are often fully aware that Christian arguments were marshaled in support of the enslavement of Native Americans and Africans, but they are often surprised to learn that there was also a continuous current of Christian condemnation of forced labor, the slave trade, and forcible conversions—in short, an inside Christian critique of oppressive Christian doctrines and practices.

But a strategy for critique is still not a methodological foundation for a constructive ethic. Here Nussbaum's concept of a threshold comes into play, but not in the way we might assume. The thresholds, as she defines them, are more like revisable universals than like moral absolutes; they shift even within her own thought. The most basic critical criterion is not whether another ethic puts forward Nussbaum's list of thresholds or goals for flourishing but whether that ethic sets the same thresholds or goals for everyone. Standards for flourishing must be universal, not gender-, race-, or class-particular. Although some allowance must be made for age differences and their accompanying developmental needs, we should be suspicious whenever a group seems to be systematically excluded from any dimension of flourishing or given a variant definition of well-being.

Finally, although deconstructionism correctly claims that we have no direct access to others' experience and so cannot reproduce their knowledge exactly, natural law correctly points out that human beings share characteristics—like reason, emotion, and language—that make it possible to communicate our reflections on our own experience. No human beings who possess language are utterly inaccessible to each other in this way. One highly underrated aid to this capacity is imagination. Philip Keane describes imagination as "the basic process by which we draw together the concrete and the universal elements of our human experience," letting these "two sides of our knowing play with one another"; [6] it "is an essential step in the human move toward moral truth" because it "opens levels of experience which we could never achieve through principles alone." [7]

Keane's definition of imagination—a process for mediating between concrete and abstract—seems designed for the casuistic project of classifying cases under norms. Imagination as a tool for creative navigation of the waters of plural experience must be conceived differently, as a way of relating the concrete to the concrete, as the creative capacity to "think ourselves into" the experiences of others. It is not a substitute for dialogue but presumes it; it can never lead one person to have precisely the same experience as another; and it must be employed not in isolation or with paternalism but with humility and under the tutelage of those whose experience one wishes to understand. True moral imagination is not a flight of fancy but the careful effort to carry out moral reflection from within the unfamiliar complex of commitments, experiences, and moral claims of another person's life. [8] Understood as a function of traditional natural law prudence—specifically of docility, or "teachability"—imagination has a twofold benefit: the (never successful) attempt to stand in another's shoes not only enables one to look upon that other's situation with simultaneous intimate understanding and critical distance, as prophetic outside voice and informed sympathizer, but also gives one critical distance on one's own situation. [9]

Christian doctrines of sin and human finitude caution against viewing imagination as a panacea, a guarantee of justice; it is not. It is susceptible to self-deception, and so its effectiveness depends upon its being employed with good will and humility and upon its insights being acted upon creatively. My point here is that if irreducible differences between men and women inevitably yield divergent experiences and prudential judgments, these differences do not doom men and women to separatism, destructive conflict, or oppressive relationship; they can be crossed, though not closed, through the common human capacities for imagination and language. Likewise, imagination must be a crucial element of any successful cross-cultural discussion of moral flourishing and basic rights.

NATURAL LAW FEMINISM IN ACTION: TWO EXAMPLES

How precisely does a natural law feminist treatment of a moral issue differ from the other options available within either the feminist or the natural law traditions of ethics? As Margaret Farley and Paul Lauritzen point out, feminist arguments frequently overlap arguments made from other perspectives; we must not expect utter novelty in content. [10] On the other hand, we should expect characteristically feminist inspirations and methods. As we will see, what distinguishes feminist from natural law analyses is their insistence upon examining issues in their social contexts, their inclusive procedure, and their commitment to women's concrete good. What should distinguish natural law feminism from either of its root traditions is its distinctive combination of feminist convictions with a clear, telic anthropology, a method of practical moral reason, and theories of integrity and social justice that connect all dimensions of social and individual flourishing eschatologically. This is a tall order to fill in a short space, but we can at least begin to see what difference a natural law feminism might make to concrete moral reflection—in this case, to issues dealing immediately with bodily sexuality. We will begin by examining *Donum Vitae,* the 1987 document on reproductive technologies issued by the Congregation for the Doctrine of the Faith (CDF), as well as feminist and natural law feminist writings on reproductive technologies.

THE ETHICS OF REPRODUCTIVE TECHNOLOGY. *Donum Vitae* outlines the still current Roman Catholic magisterial teaching on the use of new reproductive technologies (NRTs). As we will see, the document's anthropology yields conclusions that claim to be universal and eternal. *Donum Vitae* espouses an anthropology that elevates the good of interpersonal intimacy above all other values; it sees the body not just as the symbol or sacramental sign for affection and commitment but as the channel, the necessary means, to committed relationship. It limits promotion of fertility to interventions that simply increase the likelihood that a normal act of marital sex would result in conception. [11] Its objection to all more invasive interventions is rooted in personalism: they interrupt the divinely intended flow of love between husband and wife, making procreation merely a technical production and endangering the emotional ties between spouses and between parents and their children. A family in which the children are not biologically related to both parents or in which children are conceived in some way other than intercourse transgresses in a basic way on the rights and relationships of its members.

Applying the feminist criteria of chapter 4 requires us to point out a number of problematic characteristics of the document and its argument, some of which arise in revisionist critiques and some of which do not. To begin with, its promulgation by the Vatican Congregation for the Doctrine of the Faith immediately contradicts not one but two imperatives of feminist moral reflection. First, rather than reporting consensus or inviting reflection, it unilaterally dictates guidelines for individual behavior and recommends institutional and social policy. Second, not only is it highly unlikely that any of its formulators is either a married person, a woman, or a parent but the authors do not give evidence of having consulted any of these three classes of people or even of having gone to school on reports of parental or marital experience. Any consultation of this sort that may have contributed to the guidelines goes unreported because it is seen as methodologically irrelevant to the validity of the conclusions.

In addition, *Donum Vitae* takes personalism to an extreme, abstracting familial relations from their natural context of supporting relationships and social institutions. It represents marriage as a private, romantic, exclusive covenant between autonomous people, a covenant that gives husband and wife the exclusive "right to become a father and a mother only through each other" and the child "the right to be conceived, carried in the womb, brought into the world and brought up within marriage" by "his" own biological parents. [12] It gives the impression that the conjugal relationship itself is the being whose good is to be pursued, an entity whose good seems to supersede even that of the persons who compose it. The risk this false isolation runs is that, lacking a scale for measuring the relative importance of conjugal flourishing against the other goods that compose the human telos, it may turn us against our true end by absolutizing or idolizing what is really only a constituent, subordinate good. Paradoxically, this is the same complaint Vatican documents typically make against those who contextualize other goods, like that of sexual pleasure.

This exclusive, familial interpretation of personalism cannot easily include the goods of others in its scope. An extreme example is its treatment of surrogacy. Although personalist reasoning should reject the practice of surrogacy outright, because it involves using a person—the surrogate mother—as the means to an end, *Donum Vitae* instead condemns her as an interloper who disturbs marital peace and "offends the dignity and right of the child." [13] In fact the exclusive strength of the marital/genetic connection is so extreme as to call into question for the reader the moral propriety of adoption. Through its attention to the good of individual women as spouses and mothers rather than in themselves, this response to surrogacy also belies the exclusivity of the Vatican document's focus on the eventual good of the embryonic person-in-the-family.

Donum Vitae's particular choice of telic anthropologies allows it to base moral claims on consequentialist arguments, much as liberation theologians do, by arguing backward from social disorder to individual sin: suffering, disorder, and injustice must be the direct results of actions and attitudes that contradict the human telos. Yet two factors separate this argument from genuine feminist or liberationist reflection. First, the claims it produces are absolute and universal, not contextual or provisional. Second, it does not critically examine the links among inclination, virtue, and flourishing or between vice and suffering. For example, it asserts rather than demonstrates the "naturalness" of parents' desire for genetic connection with their children and the dire effects of inserting reproductive technology or gamete donors into a genetically and socially exclusive family system—an error even Richard McCormick repeats in an opinion piece highly critical of the document. [14] There is similarly little attention to the need to determine *which* cause has produced an ill effect. For instance, is a child's identity confusion a product of unclear parentage per se, of society's unjust tendency to link status with "licit" family structures, of parental insecurity, or of the child's own immature desire to place blame for her own anxieties on some external agent?

The odd isolation of all of these considerations from other social forces is repeated in the failure of both the document and the McCormick column to evaluate the intrusive threat of (say) in vitro fertilization (IVF) against other avoidable and unavoidable, potentially divisive forces—many of which are goods in themselves, like genuine professional success or careful attention to children—that threaten the marriage covenant but do not, if the partners are tenacious, destroy it. One has the sense that IVF inherently not only breaches fidelity but removes a couple's future capacity for it, driving husband and wife necessarily and helplessly apart. Yet this intimation contradicts plain, common-sense knowledge gleaned from marital experience: any issue, even a trivial one, can be the occasion of marital failure, if either partner is predisposed in this direction; and no breach, even a weighty one, necessarily destroys marriage if both members of the couple are committed to overcoming obstacles.

The document does forbid arguing from the natural and appropriate desire for genetically related children to a right to have genetically related children: natural inclinations do not automatically establish themselves as absolute goods but must be subject to reason. At the same time, this caveat is based not, as a feminist argument might be, on the need to balance goods and use social resources responsibly but on the assumption that technological intervention in procreation is an absolute evil in itself, never justified even in the best of hypothetical social circumstances. In addition, the document carries out absolutely no critical analysis of the desire for children; this desire merely "expresses the vocation to fatherhood and motherhood inscribed in conjugal love." [15] If genetic connection is as important as the document implies, one element of this drive would be the desire to create a being who will share the parents' genetic material and so cement their bond with a biological adhesive. [16] Yet a feminist must ask what social and historical pressures combine to make this desire seem "natural" to the encyclical's authors. Does it reflect the requirements of human dignity everywhere, or only their approximation in a patriarchal culture? It is equally important to ask what social and theological pressures lead them to assert the "inviolable right of every innocent human being to life," regardless of developmental stage or viability. [17]

Finally, by consigning the entire significance of procreativity to the personal sphere, *Donum Vitae* misses the opportunity to appropriate traditional social justice arguments against procedures like IVF. These procedures erode the common good in two respects. First, they invite social justice and liberationist criticisms of inegalitarian distribution of resources: they are exorbitantly expensive, they are unjustly distributed, and their distribution is tightly controlled by a small class of professionals who also profit generously from them. [18] They also value the desire of well-off couples to have genetically related children over the need of existing parentless children for stable homes.

On balance, then, *Donum Vitae*'s violations of feminist criteria for moral reflection are multiple: it fails to consult widely or to invite creative or novel responses; it erodes the interpretive and critical power of the dialectic between human telos and concrete integral flourishing; it ignores social justice concerns; it makes uncritical assertions rather than analytical arguments; it embraces a questionably narrow telos; and it implies that outward adherence to the exceptionless concrete norms it creates is a condition of moral goodness and of achieving the ultimate end. And all of these errors jeopardize its legitimacy as an argument of natural law as well.

These criticisms of *Donum Vitae* have unearthed a number of important feminist arguments against both the current state of invasive reproductive technologies and the Vatican's refusal to countenance their use in any circumstances. But a few other concerns that do not arise so obviously in *Donum Vitae* are equally indispensable to a thorough feminist analysis of all these issues. The first is what philosopher Susan Sherwin labels "technophilia": a love of technology that converts technical or medical solutions to small, controlled problems into new demands and self-understandings based in new technical possibilities. [19] Sherwin worries about the way in which "helpful" reproductive technologies create demands for themselves, but we can see the pattern in far more mundane examples. For instance, orthodontia that corrects genuinely functional difficulties with the bite is now a socially accepted, even privately insured, form of self-remaking, even when the motivation is only cosmetic.

But as Lisa Cahill and Bonnie J. Miller-McLemore argue—joined by Richard McCormick—technophilia's tendency to create a demand for more technology also masks a misguided desire to seek medical or technical solutions to decidedly nonmedical problems. [20] Miller-McLemore's feminist analysis and reconstruction of regnant psychological theories of generativity yields a highly credible alternative interpretation of the human "need" (asserted by both users and natural law critics of NRTs) for the procreation of biologically related children. She argues that the generative impulse is rooted, among other places, in the human developmental need to come to terms with death and finitude. One outlet for this need has been the procreation and nurturing of children, who are (in an unfortunate sense) then clear "products" or continuations of their parents. Generativity crises arise because the limited ways in which people are taught socially to deal with this anxiety—for men, primarily through productive work and "siring" children, and for women, primarily through gestation, childbirth, and caretaking—often conflict with both genuine, integral emotional maturity and the now uncertain expectations of a more gender-egalitarian society. Fertility and infertility alike are obvious flash points for explosive, unresolved questions about life goals, social purpose, and society's hidden influence over individuals' desires, and they are frequently made to bear the weight of all of these confusions. Miller-McLemore's analysis suggests that there are important moral differences between the mature, considered desire to raise and even bear a child and the "desperation" that so often passes as evidence for a desire so "natural" and ineluctable that neither natural law traditionalists nor revisionists question it, and both users and advocates of NRTs interpret it as grounding a right to infertility therapy. [21]

Here we can begin to see two differences between the feminist and the personalist-absolutist approaches to NRTs: the feminist treatment is both more expansive and more concrete than the personalist absolutist or, for that matter, the mainline "bioethics" approach. First, feminist ethics investigates the ways in which unexamined social pressures form people's desires and arrays of common-sense choices, the raw material for (in Thomas's language) their inclinations and their prudential judgments. They also examine the ways in which institutions create and order desires, limit the ways in which these may be acceptably fulfilled, or force impossible choices—for instance, the choice between suffering under the shame of infertility and enduring the dehumanizing procedures of the more complex NRTs. Viewing infertility as a technical problem encourages people to articulate the moral question in stark "either/or" terms: are NRTs acceptable or not? This way of framing the question obscures an array of other low-technology remedies for infertility that, as Susan Sherwin notes, treat causes rather than symptoms and so advance the integral well-being not only of women but of everyone: for example, cutting back the rates of infection of sexually transmitted diseases that indirectly cause female infertility, improving nutrition, and reducing exposure to toxins. [22]

Likewise, feminists tend to be more expansive in their choice of sources. For instance, not only medical expertise and traditional moral arguments but discrete, concrete persons' experience play prominent roles. Cahill, Miller-McLemore, and others are not psychologists, anthropologists, or sociologists, and yet they make explicit use of these disciplines' discoveries. They also reflect self-consciously on their own experience or at least explain the ways in which it has inspired their analyses and constructions. [23]

This expansion of sources leads to the second point, the greater concreteness of feminist arguments. Lisa Cahill points out that personalist-absolutist and even some revisionist natural law accounts of sexuality and reproduction are curiously focused on relationships that seem to exist independently of body or society, echoing rather than correcting the error of a larger culture in which "the bodily aspects of parenthood disappear to the moral backstage, while the affective and intentional ones part the curtains to a standing ovation." [24] For feminists, it is concrete, embodied persons in whom—both individually and collectively—the connections among social, physical, psychological, and religious forces acquire meaning and demand response. Bonnie Miller-McLemore illustrates:

> Although on one level I knew that it is God who gives new life and new hope in baptism and communion, on another level I experienced . . . disenchantment when I looked upon a crèche scene of kings, shepherds, and a father, absent of women except for a Mary, who in Protestant sanctuaries fades away into the shadows. Carrying thirty extra pounds of baby, and later bearing the sticky weight of nursing, told me that I knew something about the giving of one's body and blood that did not seem reflected in the way rituals of communion and baptism are enacted. In its most powerful rituals and stories, it seemed as if a male church had forsaken women, and then wrongly appropriated the bounty of female bodily knowledge. [25]

The very particular experience of attending church while pregnant jolts Miller-McLemore to awareness of the misfit between Christian soteriology and moral teachings on one hand and her own experience on the other, inspiring critique and reconstruction. Mary Pellauer's systematic ethical reflection rooted in her own experience of sexual pleasure, and Patricia Beattie Jung's reflection on the moral significance of women's sexual pleasure generally, illustrate the fruitfulness for ethics of an experiential approach and point out the need for more systematic reflection on the experiences of fertility and infertility. [26]

Given all these critical and constructive feminist contributions, what is the point of natural law feminism? What does a new "ism" contribute to the discussion of NRTs? What is unique to natural law feminism is not the elements of its critique but the way in which it assembles and reinterprets these elements. Especially in sexual and reproductive ethics, in which claims about the human telos and embodiment must be so painstakingly criticized and related, natural law feminism walks the line between determinism and deconstruction. Margaret Farley argues that feminist theology promotes freedom from artificial limits derived from bodily gender features. This freedom yields a freedom for healthy embrace of gendered difference and its goods and pleasures:

> A beginning feminist response to past religious and cultural associations of women with their bodies was a rejection of this association. Anatomy was *not* destiny; women were not to be identified with their bodies any more than were men; women could transcend their bodies through rational choices. Such a response paradoxically freed women, however, to take their bodies more seriously. Rather than abstract from bodilyness, reinforcing a dichotomy between body and mind, women soon moved to "reclaim" their bodies—to claim them as their own, as integral to their selfhood and their womanhood. [27]

This means, for example, that adequate natural law feminist accounts of sexual and reproductive ethics must criticize all "self-evident" assumptions about human—especially women's—embodiment and flourishing, refusing to "sacralize" maternity. At the same time, as Paul Lauritzen notes, they must not turn a suspicion of the desire for a child into a devaluing of children and childbearing: "women may legitimately value carrying and caring for children," and these experiences should be "celebrated"—at least in fully egalitarian settings, when they are freely chosen. [28]

Lisa Cahill's natural law feminist treatment of birth technologies not only acknowledges this claim but illustrates its applicability to the more difficult issue of biological relatedness. She argues that

> A Christian perspective on reproductive technologies can appreciate the human and moral importance of biological kinship, without

either absolutizing it or making its level of importance to social parent-hood totally dependent on individual choice. The "need" to have a biologically related child is natural, and its fulfillment is worth pursuit and the support of modern medical technology. Pressures on couples, and especially women, to see biological parenthood as essential to adult identity needs [sic] to be re-examined, however. [29]

For Cahill as for the CDF, the "psychospiritual and social" dimensions of marriage are more important morally than "the physical or embodied aspects," and yet the inextricable connection of biological, social, and spiritual factors forbid the exclusion or ascendance of any single dimension. [30] The criteria of the Kingdom are complex.

This balanced approach allows Cahill to argue on all sides of the question: in favor of limited use of NRTs, as a means of answering some couples' desires for biologically related children; against uncritical use of NRTs, in deference to the preference for biological kinship and in suspicion of the motives behind NRTs, which range from parents' overly selfish desires for self-fulfillment to the questionable or unquestioned goals of medical researchers and doctors. [31]

Cahill does isolate the physical dimension from the others temporarily but with different results than either the CDF document or McCormick's revisionist treatment. She argues that "shared biological parenthood" is a good that must be *respected* in all circumstances but that "what constitutes adequate recognition of the value" in particular circumstances depends on the setting. [32] This claim allows Cahill to argue, for example, that there is a morally significant difference between insemination with a husband's sperm and insemination with donor sperm but prevents her from having to conclude that this difference is morally determinative in every circumstance. This is not precisely the same as arguing, as McCormick does, that (e.g.) homologous artificial insemination is a "second best" solution to the problem of biological parenthood, acceptable only in situations in which the ideal, procreative intercourse, cannot be realized. [33] McCormick's aim here is to seal off the possibility of the use of NRTs by couples who can conceive without them. But this way of stating the issue implies that it is possible to isolate and judge single variables in procre-ative decisions. Cahill's articulation preserves the multivalence of the decision.

Cahill's treatment of kinship is open to argument. For instance, it would not be difficult to object that the need for biological kinship either is much less "natural" than she believes or, even if inherent, carries less moral weight than she presumes; for instance, if controlled studies were unable to correlate developmental or emotional problems with NRTs, one justification for the kinship presumption would weaken considerably. Likewise, an expanded discussion of the implications of NRTs for the relationship between individual choice and the common good, treated only suggestively in her analysis, might eclipse the concern for biological relatedness in a very different way. [34] Serious contemplation of the disproportionate demand an individual born in the first world places on the global ecosystem is one example of this concern for the common good, but there are many others: the social need for "other mothers" (adults with time and energy to nurture children not their own), or the justice of spending money on infertility treatments. And the question of gay and lesbian couples' desires for biologically related children—an important test of the method—is undiscussed. [35] Yet these complaints prove rather than erode the larger points: first, the paths to flourishing are many and depend heavily on circumstances; second, dimensions of human flourishing are interdependent, and it is as erroneous and dangerous to eliminate one dimension from consideration as it is to absolutize it. A clear telos—existential or communal—can help to order these dimensions in a given context, but it rarely solves individual cases conclusively.

A LESS-TRAVELED PATH: BREAST-FEEDING. The advantages of natural law feminism over other versions of feminism and over classical or revised natural law may be clearer if we examine an issue that entails intimacy and embodiment but has received little recent treatment in the natural law tradition: breast-feeding. Our analysis of *Donum Vitae* above suggests how a personalist-absolutist account of nursing and maternal-infant relations might be expressed were they ever recognized as substantive moral issues. On this view, "the mother" and "the child" are an isolated dyad. The self-giving conjugal act and the gestation and birth of her child are physical expressions of the mother's commitment to the procreation and nurture of this particular child. The quintessential expression of this intimate relationship is nursing, an act in which the mother gives herself fully in protection and nurturance, and the child becomes aware of his origin in her, her love for him, and his dependence on her. In the act of nursing, the unitive/developmental dimension (essential to both the child's emotional development and the support of the mother's attentive love during the difficult period of infancy) and the nutritive dimension are morally and psychologically inseparable. In fact we can even say that the child has a right to be nursed by his own mother. Some think that the nutritive and psychological/developmental dimensions of nursing can be separated and that a wet-nurse or technological intervention, in the form of formula, can be substituted without damage to the child or to the relationship. But this act would cause a fundamental rupture ultimately harmful to both mother and child and contradict the intimate and exclusive character of mother-infant love. Conversely, for a woman to feel the intense physical pleasure of contact with her child without the nutritive element would be selfish, lacking in the proper maternal quality of total self-gift. [36]

Not surprisingly, these very arguments have been made, both by medieval theologian-critics of wet-nursing and by contemporary advocates of breast-feeding, including some feminists. Psychologist D. W. Winnicott's language of the nursing couple also illustrates the connection between the conjugal dyad and the nursing dyad arrestingly. [37] And nearly all contemporary arguments in favor of breast-feeding mention the psychological, physical, and developmental advantages for infants and the physical and psychological benefits to mothers. [38] In short it would not be hard to construct an inductive argument in support of breast-feeding very like the CDF's encomium to "natural" conception: breast-feeding is the appropriate way to advance the God-given ends of both mothers and infants. In fact perhaps the only divergence of this not-so-hypothetical argument from the model above is that contemporary advocates at least are often themselves women who breast-feed or men who have long experience with mothers and their nursing infants.

Although many Western feminists have adopted an ideal very like this, others have objected that the ideology of the "nursing couple" commits two related, fatal errors: it abstracts women and babies from their social contexts, and it therefore—like *Donum Vitae*—either elevates the good of a relationship above the goods of the partners who compose it or—when the emphasis is on the benefits to the child—values the child's flourishing over the mother's. [39] The work of Vanessa Maher, Catherine Panter-Brick, and others suggests that the benefits touted by Western breast-feeding advocates apply only to well-nourished, married Western women who have the luxury of staying home with their infants while their husbands earn—and share—an adequate income. Mothers who suffer undernourishment (often a result of unjust distribution of food within the family), heavy physical work, and frequent pregnancy actually harm themselves by breast-feeding, and inadequate milk production and the difficulty of caring for a child while working often leads to dangerously early use of less nutritious or harder to digest solid foods, endangering the life of the child. By contrast, women in patriarchal households in which there is enough money to purchase formula can both lessen their health risks and gain some small degree of control over their husbands' earnings by refusing to breast-feed. [40] Diane Eyer has also deconstructed the myth of maternal-infant bonding, one of the strongest developmental arguments in favor of breast-feeding. [41] And Jules Law's analysis of the claims behind the rhetoric of contemporary breast-feeding advocates reveals most of those claims to be either groundless or inflated. [42] The obvious conclusion is that blanket advocacy for breast-feeding, because it necessarily ignores the social context of the practice, is at best ignorant and at worst oppressive; some authors even imply that the contemporary breast-feeding advocacy movement is an example of antifeminist backlash, a ruse to limit women's social and economic power.

Natural law feminism mediates this dispute by refusing to reduce the good to psychological, social, or physical flourishing. Rather, it insists upon the identification of an integral good under which all these elements fall, declining to condone any person or principle that calls for the disproportionate pursuit of one or two at the expense of the others. Again, the choice of telos will have some effect on the appearance of the integral good because it arranges and relates the goods that compose it; but no telos that categorically excludes or ignores any dimension of women's good can be acceptable. Goods must be judged against each other and against integral flourishing. [43]

Thus just as biological kinship is an insufficient criterion for procreative decisions, a narrow examination of pleasure and psychological benefits to affluent women and their children, "all other things being equal," is an inappropriate and inadequate measure of breast-feeding's value. It would be cruel and short-sighted to press these advantages on an undernourished woman in her late thirties trying to nurse her eighth or tenth child. But this fact does not, as some gender studies approaches might suggest, imply that the benefits wealthy Western women and their children experience are morally irrelevant. These benefits too fall under the umbrella of the integral good, if at a slightly less urgent level than basic nutrition. If the point of feminism is to move from a world in which most women survive to a world in which all of them flourish, then the goal is for all mothers to be able to choose or reject breast-feeding freely. To create this world would be to move to a new plane, one on which women choose for or against breast-feeding, without great cost to their own physical or economic welfare, on precisely the same bases as wealthy Western women do: convenience, psychological benefits, nutritional value, physical pleasure, etc. Women—and based on their experiences, feminist natural law ethics—must examine rather than discard these "natural" arguments, preserving them in anticipation of a time when they will not be used oppressively.

In addition, women who can speak about their experiences of mothering in very particular economic and social settings, and not only theorists who examine discrete effects of breast-feeding in controlled situations, must be the creators of this "rich vision" of the practice of breast-feeding. And women themselves must be able freely to choose, especially in compromised circumstances, among the feeding methods available. This is so not because choice is the ultimate value, and not merely because it is women who are most aware of their own concrete options, but also because reasoning well about their own goods and those of people near to them is a crucial dimension of women's own integral and ultimate good.

Finally, the criterion of integral flourishing is a judgment on the social and economic oppression under which so many women live. It is not enough, as the logic of some eras of natural law thought might have demanded, to say merely that "using formula is permissible when no adequate alternative is available." Rather, a feminist/liberationist perspective prophetically condemns a world in which women routinely have to weigh harming themselves against feeding their children. It also commits itself substantively to the liberation of this world and these people. In fact, a strong, telic, soteriological anthropology coupled with a critical hermeneutic has more liberative potential than either a one-dimensional or an "atelic" anthropology. Rather than isolating or absolutizing dimensions of persons or acts, natural law feminism analyzes the context to discern which of many apparent routes to the good actually advance integral flourishing here and now.

These discussions of the sexual body highlight the challenges facing a feminist version of natural law. The Roman Catholic natural law tradition, like feminism, is generally comfortable reflecting on the contingencies and complexities of social ethics, and natural law feminism should gladly inherit these capacities. But the body is a different matter. The natural law tradition holds that the embodied person has a telos, and the body and all its parts are divinely created specifically with this telos in mind. This is often interpreted to mean that each part has its own purpose and that to turn that part away from its purpose would be to act against one's larger end by disordering desire and disrespecting the wisdom of one's maker. Feminism's properly deconstructive impulse, on the other hand, forbids us to think of anything as "pure nature." Any apparently "natural" feeling or attribute is actually socially constructed, taught and learned so thoroughly that it seems inevitable. One continuing challenge for natural law feminism is thus to articulate ever more carefully the moral meaning of gendered embodiment and of "nature" in general.

The telic natural law and critical feminist perspectives combine to suggest that nature is neither determinative of nor irrelevant to ethics. As Stephen Pope says of biological nature, it "constitutes one important basis for human flourishing and indicates certain goods that will be included in lives lived well," but this does not imply that the "biologically natural" is always "the normatively good." [44] The "natural" person has a telos, but "natural" desires have no inevitability or ends or even independent existence that exert moral authority over the wisdom and freedom of the person whom they inhabit.

Human nature in the fullest sense is the whole range of capacities and powers, interpreted differently everywhere, that we can marshal for pursuit of our ends. Neither fixed nor arbitrary, it is the field of possibility within which we construct and pursue concrete visions of integral flourishing.

The balance and comprehensiveness of a natural law feminist approach to even these narrowly drawn questions of sexuality and parenthood suggests its potential fruitfulness both for systematic moral reflection and for the moral life. At this point a small but growing group of thinkers—Lisa Cahill, Jean Porter, Margaret Farley, and Cynthia Crysdale, among others—is making regular use of it. The finely textured, careful analysis the approach permits is evident in their writing, but much remains to be done. Natural law feminism faces two continuing challenges: in Margaret Farley's words, "to attend to reality and to care for it justly." [45] The first, explored briefly here, is the challenge of analyzing integral, social, embodied experience and articulating its implications for both the content and method of ethics. The other, shared with liberationists generally, is the challenge of turning institutional critiques into designs for the just distribution of political and economic power and for the attentive provision of the prerequisites for flourishing. [46] Feminists' own formidable criteria will be the most exacting measures of their success.

NOTES

1. Farley, "Feminism and Universal Morality," 185.
2. Notable exceptions are Quakers and Mormons.
3. Susan A. Ross, "God's Embodiment and Women: Sacraments," in *Freeing Theology: The Essentials of Theology in Feminist Perspective,* ed. Catherine Mowry LaCugna (San Francisco: HarperSanFrancisco, 1993), 185–209; Susan A. Ross, "Extravagant Affections: Women's Sexuality and Theological Anthropology," in *In the Embrace of God: Feminist Approaches to Theological Anthropology,* ed. Ann O'Hara Graff (Maryknoll, NY: Orbis Books, 1995), 105–21; and Christine E. Gudorf, *Body, Sex, and Pleasure: Reconstructing Christian Sexual Ethics* (Cleveland: The Pilgrim Press, 1994).
4. Gutiérrez, *We Drink,* 68.
5. Lisa Sowle Cahill, "Feminism and Christian Ethics: Moral Theology," in *Freeing Theology: The Essentials of Theology in Feminist Perspective,* ed. Catherine Mowry LaCugna (San Francisco: HarperSanFrancisco, 1993), 211–34, at 216–18; for the difficulties in finding affirmation in Thomas for political applications of this principle see Paul J. Weithman, "Complementarity and Equality in the Political Thought of Thomas Aquinas," *Theological Studies* 59 (1998): 277–96.
6. Philip S. Keane, *Christian Ethics and Imagination: A Theological Inquiry* (New York/Ramsey: Paulist Press, 1984), 81. Keane is concerned with the tension between the principles of a moral tradition and changing human experience and with developing new rationales for altering or following the former. My proposal adds to this description the necessity of attempting to understand a concrete situation from

another's viewpoint rather than assuming that one has all the relevant "facts" and needs only to interpret them in a creative way. I propose, in other words, to add an affective element to the cognitive exercise of imagination. This additional condition is not consistently apparent in Keane's discussion.

Keane argues several points which are compatible with feminist convictions and goals: imagination is not antirational but is an aspect of human rationality which serves the need to move beyond discursive moral thinking (13–16, 172); imagination can be an aid to opening discourse on, e.g., scientific and medical ethics to others besides technical experts (146); it is also an invaluable tool for awakening people who are accustomed to viewing sin as a private matter to the moral significance of social justice (11–13, 165–69). For Keane imagination is an indispensable means of moral pedagogy. Feminists and liberationists must exploit it more broadly if they really want to engage "mainstream" scholars and laypeople.

7. Ibid., 90.

8. Cristina L. H. Traina, "Sympathetic Imagination: Experience, the Other, and the Feminist Argument for Pacifism," in *Festschrift for Edmund Perry* [working title], ed. George D. Bond and Thomas Ryba (Evanston, IL: Northwestern University Press, forthcoming).

9. This latter condition invalidates the "petition and response" and "promulgation" styles of ethical discourse; I must confirm my dialogue partner's image of my experience in order for my partner's moral judgment based upon that image to be valid. The necessity of humility here is clear: without it one cannot resolve the conflict between the promulgator's view that my (different) experience is not relevant to a particular moral decision, and my belief that it is.

10. Margaret A. Farley, "Feminist Theology and Bioethics," in *Feminist Theological Ethics: A Reader*, ed. Lois K. Daly (Louisville: Westminster/John Knox Press, 1994), 192–93; and Paul Lauritzen, "Whose Bodies? Which Selves? Appeals to Embodiment in Assessments of Reproductive Technology," in *Embodiment, Morality, and Medicine*, ed. Lisa Sowle Cahill and Margaret A. Farley (Boston: Kluwer Academic Publishers, 1995), 113–26.

11. Congregation for the Doctrine of the Faith, *Donum Vitae*, in *Gift of Life: Catholic Scholars Respond to the Vatican Instruction*, ed. Edmund D. Pellegrino, John Collins Harvey, and John P. Langan (Washington, DC: Georgetown University Press, 1990), 1–41.

12. *Donum Vitae*, 21, italics removed.

13. *Donum Vitae*, 23.

14. Richard A. McCormick, "Surrogate Motherhood: A Stillborn Idea," *Second Opinion* 5 (1987): 128–32. In 1991 Joseph Boyle opined that there was not yet any satisfactory account of the connections *Donum Vitae* draws between "flawed" marital acts and dire concrete consequences or affronts to dignity. See Joseph Boyle, "The Roman Catholic Tradition and Bioethics," in *Bioethics Yearbook*, volume 1: *Theological Developments in Bioethics, 1988–1990* (Boston: Kluwer Academic Publishers, 1991), 10.

15. *Donum Vitae*, 30.

16. For others seen Pope John Paul II, *Love and Responsibility*.

17. *Donum Vitae*, 13.

18. For these criticisms of the "industry" of new reproductive technologies, see Sherwin, *No Longer Patient*, 126–30.

19. Sherwin, *No Longer Patient*, 119.

20. Cahill, "'Embodiment,'" 202–3; Bonnie J. Miller-McLemore, "Produce or Perish: Generativity and New Reproductive Technologies," *Journal of the American Academy of Religion* 59 (1991): 39–69; see also McCormick, "Surrogate Motherhood," 132.

21. On desperation and infertility see Sherwin, *No Longer Patient,* 131; and Cahill, *Sex, Gender,* 244–45.

22. Sherwin, *No Longer Patient,* 135. Sherwin adds cures for male infertility, indirectly helpful in that they remove the blame from women and protect them from needless medical intervention.

23. See Miller-McLemore, "Produce or Perish," 39–40; and Cahill, *Sex, Gender,* 246–49.

24. Cahill, *Sex, Gender,* 217; see 232–33.

25. Bonnie J. Miller-McLemore, *Also a Mother: Work and Family as a Theological Dilemma* (Nashville: Abingdon, 1994), 129.

26. Mary D. Pellauer, "The Moral Significance of Female Orgasm: Toward Sexual Ethics that Celebrates Women's Sexuality," *Journal of Feminist Studies in Religion* 9 (Spring–Fall, 1993): 161–82, and Patricia Beattie Jung, "Good Sex: A Catholic Perspective on Women's Sexual Pleasure" [working title; forthcoming].

27. Farley, "Feminist Theology," 199–200.

28. Lauritzen, "Whose Bodies?", 125.

29. Cahill, *Sex, Gender,* 252. See also Pope, *Evolution of Altruism.*

30. Cahill, *Sex, Gender,* 254.

31. Cahill, *Sex, Gender,* 252–54.

32. Cahill, *Sex, Gender,* 252–53.

33. McCormick, *Critical Calling,* 348.

34. Cahill, *Sex, Gender,* 251–52.

35. Cahill and Shannon say elsewhere that as long as reproductive decisions are seen as private decisions and as long as society has no formal criteria for parenthood, "the exclusions of gays and lesbians from clinics may be inappropriate, if not impossible"; the same applies to single adults and unmarried couples. The context of the discussion is the development of a consistent policy. See Thomas A. Shannon and Lisa Sowle Cahill, *Religion and Artificial Reproduction: An Inquiry into the Vatican "Instruction on Respect for Human Life in Its Origin and on the Dignity of Human Reproduction"* (New York: Crossroad, 1988), 100.

36. On approaches to the moral interpretation of maternal pleasure in nursing, see Traina, "Passionate Mothering."

37. D. W. Winnicott, *The Family and Individual Development* (London: Tavistock Publications, 1965), 15. For critiques of medieval and contemporary popular versions of this argument, see Law, "The Politics of Breastfeeding," and Clarissa Atkinson, *The Oldest Vocation: Christian Motherhood in the Middle Ages* (Ithaca: Cornell University Press, 1991).

38. See for example La Leche League, *The Womanly Art of Breastfeeding,* 5th rev. ed. (New York: Plume, 1991).

39. For feminist embrace of breast-feeding, see Sheila Kitzinger, *The Experience of Breastfeeding,* new ed. (New York: Penguin Books, 1987); and Sheila Kitzinger, *Woman's Experience of Sex* (New York: Penguin Books, 1983).

40. See Vanessa Maher, "Breast-Feeding and Maternal Depletion: Natural Law or Cultural Arrangements?", in *The Anthropology of Breast-Feeding: Natural Law or*

Social Construct, ed. Vanessa Maher (Providence, RI: Berg Publishers, 1992), 151–80; and Catherine Panter-Brick, "Working Mothers in Rural Nepal," in *Anthropology of Breast-Feeding,* 133–50.

41. Diane E. Eyer, *Mother-Infant Bonding: A Scientific Fiction* (New Haven: Yale University Press, 1992).

42. Law, "Politics."

43. See, e.g., Pope, *Evolution,* 155.

44. Pope, *Evolution,* 155. On ecosystematic interdependence as a natural limit on ethical behavior, see William C. French, "Ecological Concern and the Anti-Foundationalist Debates: James Gustafson on Biospheric Constraints," in *The Annual of the Society of Christian Ethics 1989,* ed. Diane M. Yeager, 113–130 (Georgetown University Press, 1989).

45. Farley, "Feminism and Universal Morality," 185.

46. Schubeck, *Liberation Ethics,* 242.

Bibliography

Adams, Robert Merrihew. "Religious Ethics in a Pluralistic Society." In *Prospects for a Common Morality*, ed. Gene Outka and John P. Reeder, Jr., 93–113. Princeton, NJ: Princeton University Press, 1993.

Addelson, Kathryn Pyne. "Knowers/Doers and Their Moral Problems." In *Feminist Epistemologies*, ed. Linda Alcoff and Elizabeth Potter, 265–94. New York: Routledge, 1993.

Alcoff, Linda and Elizabeth Potter, eds. *Feminist Epistemologies.* New York: Routledge, 1993.

Alfaro, Juan. "Nature: The Theological Concept." In *Sacramentum Mundi.*

Allsopp, Michael E. and John J. O'Keefe, eds. *Veritatis Splendor: American Responses.* Kansas City, MO: Sheed and Ward, 1995.

Arbuckle, Gerald A. "Inculturation Not Adaptation: Time to Change Terminology." *Worship* 60 (1986): 511–20.

Arntz, Josef Th. C. "Die Entwicklung des naturrechlichen Denkens innerhalb des Thomismus." In *Das Naturrecht im Disput: Drei Vortrage beim Kongress der deutschsprachigen Moraltheologen, 1965 in Bensberg*, ed. Franz Böckle, 87–120. Dusseldorf: Patmos-Verlag, 1966.

Atkinson, Clarissa. *The Oldest Vocation: Christian Motherhood in the Middle Ages.* Ithaca: Cornell University Press, 1991.

Atkinson, Clarissa, Constance H. Buchanan, and Margaret R. Miles, eds. *Shaping New Vision: Gender and Values in American Culture.* The Harvard Women's Studies in Religion Series, no. 5. Ann Arbor: UMI Research Press, 1987.

Babbitt, Susan E. "Feminism and Objective Interests: The Role of Transformation Experiences in Rational Debate." In *Feminist Epistemologies,* ed. Linda Alcoff and Elizabeth Potter, 245–64. New York: Routledge, 1993.

Baier, Annette C. "Hume, the Reflective Women's Epistemologist?" In *Moral Prejudices: Essays on Ethics.* Cambridge, MA: Harvard University Press, 1994.

————. *Moral Prejudices: Essays on Ethics.* Cambridge, MA: Harvard University Press, 1994.

Bar On, Bat-Ami. "Marginality and Epistemic Privilege." In *Feminist Epistemologies,* ed. Linda Alcoff and Elizabeth Potter, 83–100. New York: Routledge, 1993.

Battaglia, Anthony. *Toward a Reformulation of Natural Law.* With a Foreword by James P. Mackey. New York: The Seabury Press, 1981.

Baum, Gregory. "Faith and Liberation: Development Since Vatican II." In *Vatican II: Open Questions and New Horizons,* Theology and Life Series, no. 8, ed. Gerald M. Fagin, 75–104. Wilmington, DE: M. Glazier, 1984.

Beauvoir, Simone de. *The Second Sex.* Translated and edited by H. M. Parshley. New York: Vintage Books, 1974.

Belenky, Mary Field, Blythe McVicker Clinchy, Nancy Rule Goldberger, and Jill Mattuck Tarule. *Women's Ways of Knowing: The Development of Self, Voice, and Mind.* New York: Basic Books, 1986.

Benhabib, Seyla. "Autonomy, Modernity, and Community: Communitarianism and Critical Social Theory in Dialogue." In *Cultural-Political Interventions in the Unfinished Project of Enlightenment,* ed. Axel Honneth, Thomas McCarthy, Claus Offe, and Albrecht Wellmer, 39–59. Cambridge: MIT Press, 1992.

————. "Feminism and Postmodernism: An Uneasy Alliance." In *Feminist Contentions: A Philosophical Exchange,* ed. Linda Nicholson, 17–34. New York: Routledge, 1995.

————. "The Generalized and the Concrete Other: The Kohlberg-Gilligan Controversy and Feminist Theory." In *Feminism as Critique: On the Politics of Gender,* ed. Seyla Benhabib and Drucilla Cornell, 77–95. Minneapolis: University of Minnesota Press, 1987.

Benhabib, Seyla, and Drucilla Cornell, eds. *Feminism as Critique: On the Politics of Gender.* Minneapolis: University of Minnesota Press, 1987.

Bergmann, Sheryle. "Feminist Epistemology." *Eidos* 6 (December 1987): 201–14.

Bernardin, Joseph Cardinal. "The Consistent Ethic of Life: An American-Catholic Dialogue." In *Consistent Ethic of Life,* ed. Thomas G. Fuechtmann, 1–11. Kansas City, MO: Sheed and Ward, 1988.

Bettenhausen, Elizabeth. "The Moral Landscapes of Embodiment." In *Feminist Theological Ethics: A Reader,* ed. Lois K. Daly, 262–70. Louisville: Westminster/John Knox Press, 1994.

Bidegain, Ana María. "Women and the Theology of Liberation." Translated by Robert R. Barr. In *Through Her Eyes: Women's Theology from*

Latin America, ed. Elsa Tamez, 15–36. Maryknoll, NY: Orbis Books, 1989.

Böckle, Franz. "Einfuhrung." In *Das Naturrecht im Disput: Drei Vortrage beim Kongress der deutschsprachigen Moraltheologen, 1965 in Bensberg*, 7–14. Dusseldorf: Patmos-Verlag, 1966.

Böckle, Franz, ed. *Das Naturrecht im Disput: Drei Vortrage beim Kongress der deutschsprachigen Moraltheologen, 1965 in Bensberg*. Dusseldorf: Patmos-Verlag, 1966.

Boff, Clodovis. *Theology and Praxis: Epistemological Considerations*. Translated by Robert R. Barr. Maryknoll, NY: Orbis Books, 1988.

Boff, Leonardo. *Church: Charism and Power—Liberation Theology and the Institutional Church*. Translated by John W. Diercksmeier. New York: Crossroad, 1985.

Bordo, Susan. "The Cultural Overseer and the Tragic Hero: Comedic and Feminist Perspectives on the Hubris of Philosophy." *Soundings* 65 (Summer 1982): 181–205.

Børreson, Kari Elisabeth. *Subordination and Equivalence: The Nature and Rôle of Women in Augustine and Thomas Aquinas*. Translated by Charles H. Talbot. Washington, DC: University Press of America, 1981.

Boyle, Joseph. "The Roman Catholic Tradition and Bioethics." In *Bioethics Yearbook*. Volume 1: *Theological Developments in Bioethics, 1988–1990*, ed. Baruch A. Brody, B. Andrew Lustig, H. Tristram Engelhardt, and Laurence B. McCullough, 5–21. Boston: Kluwer Academic Publishers, 1991.

Bresnahan, James F. "Rahner's Christian Ethics." *America* 123 (1970): 351–54.

———. "Rahner's Ethics: Critical Natural Law in Relation to Contemporary Ethical Methodology." *Journal of Religion* 56 (January 1976): 36–60.

Brink, David O. *Moral Realism and the Foundations of Ethics*. Cambridge Studies in Philosophy. Cambridge: Cambridge University Press, 1989.

Brown, Robert McAfee. *Gustavo Gutiérrez: An Introduction to Liberation Theology*. Maryknoll, NY: Orbis Books, 1990.

Bruch, Richard. "Das sittliche Naturgesetz als Gottes- und Menschenwerk bei Thomas von Aquin." *Zeitschrift für Katholische Theologie* 109 (1987): 294–311.

Butler, Christopher. *The Theology of Vatican II*. London: Darton, Longman and Todd, 1967.

Butler, Judith. *Bodies That Matter: On the Discursive Limits of "Sex"*. New York and London: Routledge, 1993.

———. "Contingent Foundations: Feminism and the Question of 'Postmodernism.'" In *Feminist Contentions: A Philosophical Exchange*, ed. Linda Nicholson, 35–57. New York: Routledge, 1995.

———. *Gender Trouble: Feminism and the Subversion of Identity*. New York: Routledge, 1990.

Byrne, Patrick. "The Thomistic Sources of Lonergan's Dynamic World View," *The Thomist* 46 (1982): 108–45.

Cahill, Lisa Sowle. *Between the Sexes: Foundations for a Christian Ethics of Sexuality*. Philadelphia: Fortress Press; New York and Ramsey: Paulist Press, 1985.

———. "The Catholic Tradition: Religion, Morality, and the Common Good." *Journal of Law and Religion* 5 (1987): 75–94.

———. "'Embodiment' and Moral Critique: A Christian Social Perspective." In *Embodiment, Morality, and Medicine*, ed. Lisa Sowle Cahill and Margaret A. Farley, 199–215. Boston: Kluwer Academic Publishers, 1995.

———. "Feminist Ethics." *Theological Studies* 51 (1990): 49–66.

———. "Feminist Ethics, Differences, and Common Ground: A Catholic Perspective." In *Feminist Ethics and the Catholic Moral Tradition*. Readings in Moral Theology 9, ed. Charles E. Curran, Margaret A. Farley, and Richard A. McCormick, S.J., 184–204. New York: Paulist Press, 1996.

———. *Sex, Gender, and Christian Ethics*. New Studies in Christian Ethics. Cambridge: Cambridge University Press, 1996.

———. "Teleology, Utilitarianism, and Christian Ethics." *Theological Studies* 42 (1981): 601–29.

———. "Women, Marriage, Parenthood: What Are Their 'Natures'?" *Logos* 9 (1988): 11–35.

Cahill, Lisa Sowle, and Margaret A. Farley, eds. *Embodiment, Morality, and Medicine*. Boston: Kluwer Academic Publishers, 1995.

Callahan, Sidney. "Abortion and the Sexual Agenda: A Case for Pro-Life Feminism." *Commonweal* 113 (25 April 1986): 232–38.

———. *In Good Conscience: Reason and Emotion in Decision Making*. San Francisco: Harper and Row, 1991.

Calvez, Jean Yves, and Jacques Perrin. *The Church and Social Justice*. Translated by J. R. Kirwan. London: Burns and Oates, 1961.

Calvin, John. *Institutes of the Christian Religion*. Vol. 1. Translated by Ford Lewis Battles. The Library of Christian Classics, vol. 20, ed. John T. McNeill. Philadelphia: Westminster Press, 1960.

Camenisch, Paul F. *Religious Methods and Resources in Bioethics*. Theology and Medicine, vol. 2. Boston: Kluwer Academic Publishers, 1994.

Cannon, Katie G. *Black Womanist Ethics*. American Academy of Religion Academy Series, no. 60. Atlanta: Scholars Press, 1988.

Cardman, Francine. "The Church Would Look Foolish without Them: Women and Laity Since Vatican II." In *Vatican II: Open Questions and New Horizons.* Theology and Life Series, no. 8, ed. Gerald M. Fagin, 109–19. Wilmington, DE: M. Glazier, 1984.

Carnes, John R. "Christian Ethics and Natural Law." *Religious Studies* 3 (October 1967): 301–11.

Carr, Anne E. *Transforming Grace: Christian Tradition and Women's Experience.* San Francisco: Harper and Row, 1988.

Cates, Diana Fritz. "Taking Women's Experience Seriously: Thomas Aquinas and Audre Lorde on Anger." In *Aquinas and Empowerment: Classical Ethics for Ordinary Lives*, ed. G. Simon Harak, 47–88. Washington, DC: Georgetown University Press, 1996.

Charvet, John. *Feminism.* Modern Ideologies Series. London: J. M. Dent, 1982.

Childress, James F. "Ethical Theories, Principles, and Casuistry in Bioethics: An Interpretation and Defense of Principlism." In *Religious Methods and Resources in Bioethics.* Theology and Medicine, vol. 2, ed. Paul F. Camenisch, 181–201. Boston: Kluwer Academic Publishers, 1994.

Chodorow, Nancy. *The Reproduction of Mothering: Psychoanalysis and the Sociology of Gender.* Berkeley: University of California Press, 1978.

Chopp, Rebecca. "Feminism's Theological Pragmatics: A Social Naturalism of Women's Experience." *Journal of Religion* 67 (April 1987): 239–56.

———. "Seeing and Naming the World Anew: The Works of Rosemary Radford Ruether." *Religious Studies Review* 15 (January 1989): 8–11.

Code, Lorraine. "Credibility: A Double Standard." In *Feminist Perspectives: Philosophical Essays on Method and Morals*, ed. Lorraine Code, Sheila Mullett, and Christine Overall, 64–88. Toronto: University of Toronto Press, 1988.

———. "Taking Subjectivity into Account." In Linda Alcoff and Elizabeth Potter, eds., *Feminist Epistemologies*, 15–48. New York: Routledge, 1993.

Code, Lorraine, Sheila Mullett, and Christine Overall, eds. *Feminist Perspectives: Philosophical Essays on Method and Morals.* Toronto: University of Toronto Press, 1988.

Coleman, John, ed. *One Hundred Years of Catholic Social Thought.* Maryknoll, NY: Orbis Books, 1991.

Comblin, José. *Retrieving the Human: A Christian Anthropology.* Translated by Robert R. Barr. Theology and Liberation Series. Maryknoll, NY: Orbis Books, 1990.

Congregation for the Doctrine of the Faith. *Instruction on the Ecclesial Vocation of the Theologian.* In *Origins* 20, no. 8 (1990): 117–26.

Cooey, Paula M., Sharon A. Farmer, and Mary Ellen Ross, eds. *Embodied*

Love: Sensuality and Relationship as Feminist Values. San Francisco: Harper and Row, 1987.

Copleston, F. C. *Thomas Aquinas.* Harmondsworth, Middlesex: Penguin Books, 1955; reprint, London: Search Press; New York: Barnes and Noble, 1976. Original title: *Aquinas.*

Crowe, Michael Bertram. *The Changing Profile of the Natural Law.* The Hague: Nijhoff, 1977.

———. "The Pursuit of the Natural Law." *Irish Theological Quarterly* 44 (1977): 3–29.

Crysdale, Cynthia S. W. "Horizons That Differ: Women and Men and the Flight from Understanding." *Cross Currents* 44 (Fall 1994): 345–61.

———. "Revisioning Natural Law: From the Classicist Paradigm to Emergent Probability." *Theological Studies* 56 (1995): 464–84.

Culpepper, Emily Erwin. "Philosophia: Feminist Methodology for Constructing a Female Train of Thought." *Journal of Feminist Studies in Religion* 3 (Fall 1987): 7–16.

Curran, Charles E. "Catholic Social Teaching and Human Morality." In *One Hundred Years of Catholic Social Thought,* ed. John Coleman, 72–87. Maryknoll, NY: Orbis Books, 1991.

———. *Directions in Catholic Social Ethics.* Notre Dame: University of Notre Dame Press, 1985.

———. *Faithful Dissent.* Kansas City, MO: Sheed and Ward, 1986.

———. "How My Mind Has Changed, 1960–1975." *Horizons* 2 (Fall 1975): 187–205.

———. "Is There a Distinctively Christian Ethic?" In *Metropolis: Christian Presence and Responsibility,* ed. Philip D. Morris, 92–120. Notre Dame: Fides, 1970.

———. "Moral Theology: The Present State of the Discipline." *Theological Studies* 34 (September 1973): 446–67.

———. *Ongoing Revision in Moral Theology.* Notre Dame: Fides/Claretian, 1975.

Curran, Charles E., ed. *Contraception: Authority and Dissent.* New York: Herder and Herder, 1969.

———. *Moral Theology: Challenges for the Future: Essays in Honor of Richard A. McCormick, S.J.* New York/Mahwah: Paulist Press, 1990.

Curran, Charles E., and Richard A. McCormick, S.J., eds. *Moral Norms and the Catholic Tradition.* Readings in Moral Theology, no. 1. New York: Paulist Press, 1979.

———. *Official Catholic Social Teaching.* Readings in Moral Theology, no. 5. New York: Paulist Press, 1986.

————. *Natural Law and Theology*. Readings in Moral Theology, no. 7. New York/Mahwah: Paulist Press, 1991.

————. *The Use of Scripture in Moral Theology*. Readings in Moral Theology, no. 4. New York/Ramsey: Paulist Press, 1984.

Curran, Charles E., Margaret A. Farley, and Richard A. McCormick, S.J., eds. *Feminist Ethics and the Catholic Tradition*. Readings in Moral Theology, no. 9. New York: Paulist Press, 1996.

Dalmiya, Vrinda, and Linda Alcoff. "Are 'Old Wives' Tales Justified?" In *Feminist Epistemologies*, ed. Linda Alcoff and Elizabeth Potter, 217–44. New York: Routledge, 1993.

Daly, Gabriel. "Catholicism and Modernity." *Journal of the American Academy of Religion* 53 (December 1985): 773–96.

Daly, Lois K., ed. *Feminist Theological Ethics: A Reader*. Louisville: Westminster/John Knox Press, 1994.

Daly, Mary. *Gyn/Ecology: The Metaethics of Radical Feminism*. Boston: Beacon Press, 1978.

Davaney, Sheila Greeve. "The Limits of the Appeal to Women's Experience." In *Shaping New Vision: Gender and Values in American Culture*, ed. Clarissa W. Atkinson, Constance H. Buchanan, and Margaret R. Miles, The Harvard Women's Studies in Religion Series, no. 5, 31–50. Ann Arbor: UMI Research Press, 1987.

————. "Problems with Feminist Theory: Historicity and the Search for Sure Foundations." In *Embodied Love: Sensuality and Relationship as Feminist Values*, ed. Paula M. Cooey, Sharon A. Farmer, and Mary Ellen Ross, 79–95. San Francisco: Harper and Row, 1987.

Davis, Henry. *Moral and Pastoral Theology*. 4 volumes. 5th ed. (volume 1) and 4th ed. (volumes 2–4). Heythrop Series, no. 2. New York: Sheed and Ward, 1943–46.

Delhaye, Phillip. "Naturrecht—Geschichte." In *Lexikon für Theologie und Kirche*, 2nd rev. ed.

Demmer, Klaus. "Moralische Norm und Theologische Anthropologie." *Gregorianum* 54 (1973): 263–306.

d'Entreves, A. P. *Natural Law: An Introduction to Legal Philosophy*. 2nd ed. Hutchinson University Library Series in Philosophy, ed. S. Korner. London: Hutchinson, 1970.

Donagan, Alan. *The Theory of Morality*. Chicago and London: University of Chicago Press, 1979.

Douglass, R. Bruce, Gerald M. Mara, and Henry S. Richardson, eds. *Liberalism and the Good*. New York: Routledge, 1990.

Duffy, Stephen. "Catholicism's Search for a New Self-Understanding." In

Vatican II: Open Questions and New Horizons, ed. Gerald M. Fagin, Theology and Life Series, no. 8, 9–37. Wilmington, DE: M. Glazier, 1984.

Dulles, Avery. *The Reshaping of Catholicism: Current Challenges in the Theology of Church.* San Francisco: Harper and Row, 1988.

———. *The Survival of Dogma: Faith, Authority, and Dogma in a Changing World.* New York: Crossroad, 1982 [1971].

Ehrenreich, Barbara, and Janet McIntosh. "The New Creationism: Biology under Attack." *The Nation,* 9 June 1997, 11–16.

Eisenstein, Zillah. *The Radical Future of Liberal Feminism.* New York: Longman, 1981.

Ellis, Marc H., and Otto Maduro, eds. *Expanding the View: Gustavo Gutiérrez and the Future of Liberation Theology.* Maryknoll, NY: Orbis Books, 1990.

Elshtain, Jean Bethke. *Public Man, Private Woman: Women in Social and Political Thought.* Princeton, NJ: Princeton University Press, 1981.

Engelhardt, Paulus. "Thomism." In *Sacramentum Mundi.*

Eugene, Toinette. "Moral Values and Black Womanists." In *Feminist Ethics: A Reader,* ed. Lois Daly, 160–71. Nashville: Westminster/John Knox Press, 1994.

Eugene, Toinette M., Ada María Isasi-Díaz, Kwok Pui-lan, Judith Plaskow, Mary E. Hunt, Emilie M. Townes, and Ellen M. Umansky. "Appropriation and Reciprocity in Womanist/Mujerista/Feminist Work." *Journal of Feminist Studies in Religion* 8 (Fall 1992): 91–122.

Eyer, Diane E. *Mother-Infant Bonding: A Scientific Fiction.* New Haven: Yale University Press, 1992.

Fagin, Gerald M., ed. *Vatican II: Open Questions and New Horizons.* Theology and Life Series, no. 8. Wilmington, DE: M. Glazier, 1984.

Farley, Margaret A. "Feminism and Universal Morality." In *Prospects for a Common Morality,* ed. Gene Outka and John P. Reeder, Jr., 170–90. Princeton, NJ: Princeton University Press, 1993.

———. "Moral Discourse in the Public Arena." In *Vatican Authority and American Catholic Dissent: The Curran Case and Its Consequences,* ed. William W. May, 168–86. New York: Crossroad, 1987.

———. *Personal Commitments: Beginning, Keeping, Changing.* San Francisco: Harper and Row, 1986.

Ferré, Frederick. "Boston Personalism." In *Religion and Philosophy in the United States of America: Proceedings of the German-American Conference at Paderborn, July 29–August 1, 1986,* ed. Peter Freese, vol. 1, 197–211. Essen: Die Blaue Eule, 1987.

Finnis, John. *Fundamentals of Ethics.* Washington, DC: Georgetown University Press, 1983.

————. *Natural Law and Natural Rights.* Oxford: Clarendon Press; New York: Oxford University Press, 1980.

————. "Natural Law and Unnatural Acts." *Heythrop Journal* 11 (1970): 365–87.

Finnis, John, and Germain Grisez. "The Basic Principles of Natural Law: A Reply to Ralph McInerny." In *Natural Law and Theology*, ed. Charles E. Curran and Richard McCormick, S.J., Readings in Moral Theology, no. 7, 157–70. New York/Mahwah: Paulist Press, 1991.

Firestone, Shulamith. *The Dialectic of Sex: The Case for Feminist Revolution.* New York: William Morrow, 1970.

————. "On American Feminism." In *Woman in Sexist Society: Studies in Power and Powerlessness*, ed. Vivian Gornick and Barbara K. Moran, 485–501. New York: Basic Books, 1971.

Flannery, Austin, ed. *Vatican Council II: The Conciliar and Post Conciliar Documents.* Northport, NY: Costello Publishing Company, 1975.

Ford, John C., and Gerald Kelly. *Contemporary Moral Theology.* 2 vols. Westminster, MD: Newman Press, 1958–63.

Fraser, Nancy. "False Antitheses: A Response to Seyla Benhabib and Judith Butler." In *Feminist Contentions: A Philosophical Exchange*, ed. Linda Nicholson, 59–74. New York: Routledge, 1995.

Fuchs, Josef, S.J. *Christian Ethics in a Secular Arena.* Translated by Bernard Hoose and Brian McNeil. Washington, DC: Georgetown University Press; Dublin: Gill and Macmillan, 1984.

————. "Christian Faith and the Disposing of Human Life." *Theological Studies* 46 (December 1985): 664–84.

————. *Christian Morality: The Word Becomes Flesh.* Translated by Brian McNeil. Dublin: Gill and Macmillan; Washington, DC: Georgetown University Press, 1987.

————. "Conscience and Conscientious Fidelity." In *Moral Theology: Challenges for the Future: Essays in Honor of Richard A. McCormick, S.J.*, ed. Charles E. Curran, 108–24. New York/Mahwah: Paulist Press, 1990.

————. *Für eine menschliche Moral: Grundfragen der Theologishen Ethik.* 2 vols. Studien zur theologischen Ethik; Études d'éthique chrétienne, 25. Freiburg, Schweiz: Universitätsverlag; Freiburg, Wien: Verlag Herder, 1988–89.

————. "Good Acts and Good Persons." In *Considering Veritatis Splendor*, ed. John Wilkins, 21–26. Cleveland: Pilgrim Press, 1994.

————. *Human Values and Christian Morality.* Translated by M. H. Heelan, Maeve McRedmond, Erika Young, and Gerard Watson. Dublin: Gill and Macmillan, 1970.

————. *Moral Demands and Personal Obligations.* Translated by Brian Mc-Neil. Washington, DC: Georgetown University Press, 1993.

————. *Natural Law: A Theological Investigation.* Translated by Helmut Reckter and John A. Dowling. New York: Sheed and Ward, 1965.

————. *Personal Responsibility and Christian Morality.* Translated by William Cleves and others. Washington, DC: Georgetown University Press; Dublin: Gill and Macmillan, 1983.

————. "The Phenomenon of Conscience: Subject-Orientation and Object-Orientation." In *Conscience: An Interdisciplinary View,* ed. Gerhard Zecha and Paul Weingartner, Theory and Decision Library Series A: Philosophy and Methodology of the Social Sciences, 27–56. Boston: D. Reidel Publishing Company, 1987.

Fulkerson, Mary McClintock. *Changing the Subject: Women's Discourses and Feminist Theology.* Minneapolis: Fortress Press, 1994.

Gadamer, Hans-Georg. *Truth and Method,* 2nd ed. New York: Crossroad, 1982.

Gallagher, John A. *Time Past, Time Future: An Historical Study of Catholic Moral Theology.* New York and New Jersey: Paulist Press, 1990.

García-Rivera, Alejandro. Review of Gustavo Gutiérrez, *Las Casas. Journal of Hispanic/Latino Theology* 2 (May 1995): 70–71.

George, William P. "Moral Statement and Pastoral Adaptation: A Problematic Distinction in McCormick's Theological Ethics." In *The Annual of the Society of Christian Ethics, 1992,* ed. Harlan Beckley, 135–56. Washington, DC: Georgetown University Press, 1992.

Gersh, Gabriel. "Emmanuel Mounier and Christian Personalism." *Religion in Life* 31 (Summer 1963): 436–42.

Gilligan, Carol. *In a Different Voice: Psychological Theory and Women's Development.* Cambridge: Harvard University Press, 1982.

————. "Moral Orientation and Moral Development." In *Women and Moral Theory,* ed. Eva Feder Kittay and Diana T. Meyers, 19–33. N.p.: Rowman and Littlefield Publishers, 1987.

Gilman, Charlotte Perkins. *The Man-Made World: Or, Our Androcentric Culture.* New York: Charlton Company, 1911; Source Book Press, 1970.

Gornick, Vivian, and Barbara K. Moran, eds. *Woman in Sexist Society: Studies in Power and Powerlessness.* New York: Basic Books, 1971.

Grabmann, Martin. *Thomas Aquinas: His Personality and Thought.* Translated by Virgil Michel. New York: Longmans, Green and Co., 1928.

Green, Clifford. "Bonhoeffer, Modernity, and Liberation Theology." *Union Seminary Quarterly Review* 46 (1992): 117–31.

Gremillion, Joseph, ed. *The Gospel of Peace and Justice.* Maryknoll, NY: Orbis Books, 1976.

Griffin, Leslie. "The Church, Morality, and Public Policy." In *Moral Theology: Challenges for the Future: Essays in Honor of Richard A. McCormick, S.J.,* ed. Charles E. Curran, 334–54. New York/Mahwah: Paulist Press, 1990.

Griffith, R. Marie. *God's Daughters: Evangelical Women and the Power of Submission.* Berkeley: University of California Press, 1997.

Grisez, Germain Gabriel. *Abortion: The Myths, the Realities, and the Arguments.* New York and Cleveland: Corpus Books, 1970.

———. "Against Consequentialism." *American Journal of Jurisprudence* 23 (1978): 26–72.

———. *Contraception and the Natural Law.* Milwaukee: Bruce Publishing Company, 1964.

———. *The Way of the Lord Jesus.* Vol. 1, *Christian Moral Principles.* Chicago: Franciscan Herald Press, 1983.

Grosz, Elizabeth. "Bodies and Knowledge: Feminism and the Crisis of Reason." In *Feminist Epistemologies,* ed. Linda Alcoff and Elizabeth Potter, 187–215. New York: Routledge, 1993.

Grundel, Johannes. "Natural Law (Moral)." *Sacramentum Mundi.*

Gudorf, Christine E. "Renewal or Repatriarchalization? Responses of the Roman Catholic Church to the Feminization of Religion." *Horizons* 10 (Fall 1983): 231–51.

———. "To Make a Seamless Garment, Use a Single Piece of Cloth: The Abortion Debate." In *The Public Vocation of Christian Ethics,* ed. Beverly W. Harrison, Robert L. Stivers, and Ronald H. Stone, 271–86. New York: Pilgrim Press, 1986.

Gula, Richard M. *Reason Informed by Faith: Foundations of Catholic Morality.* New York/Mahwah: Paulist Press, 1989.

———. *What Are They Saying About Moral Norms?* New York: Paulist Press, 1982.

Gustafson, James M. *Can Ethics Be Christian?* Chicago and London: University of Chicago Press, 1975.

———. "The Focus and Its Limitations: Reflections on Catholic Moral Theology." In *Moral Theology: Challenges for the Future: Essays in Honor of Richard A. McCormick, S.J.,* ed. Charles E. Curran, 179–90. New York/Mahwah: Paulist Press, 1990.

———. "Nature: Its Status in Theological Ethics." *Logos* 3 (1982): 5–23.

———. *Protestant and Roman Catholic Ethics: Prospects for Rapprochement.* Chicago and London: University of Chicago Press, 1978.

———. *Varieties of Moral Discourse: Prophetic, Narrative, Ethical, and Policy.* The Stob Lectures of Calvin College and Seminary, 1987–88. Grand Rapids, MI: Calvin College and Seminary, 1988.

Gutiérrez, Gustavo. *Dios o el Oro en las Indias: Siglo XVI*. Lima, Peru: Instituto Bartolomé de las Casas/CEP, 1989.

————. "The Fifth Century of the Discovery of America." Paper presented for the Albert Cardinal Meyer Lecture Series. Mundelein, IL: University of St. Mary of the Lake, 25 April 1992.

————. *The God of Life*. Translated by Matthew J. O'Connell. Maryknoll, NY: Orbis Books, 1991.

————. "Joy in the Midst of Suffering." In *Christ and Context: The Confrontation between Gospel and Culture*, ed. Hilary D. Regan and Alan J. Torrance with Antony Wood, 78–91. Edinburgh: T&T Clark, 1993.

————. *Las Casas: In Search of the Poor of Jesus Christ*. Translated by Robert Barr. Maryknoll, NY: Orbis Books, 1993.

————. "Latin American Spirituality." Paper presented for the Albert Cardinal Meyer Lecture Series. Mundelein, IL: University of St. Mary of the Lake, 25 April 1992.

————. *On Job: God-Talk and the Suffering of the Innocent*. Translated by Matthew J. O'Connell. Maryknoll, NY: Orbis Books, 1987.

————. "New Evangelization—A Theological Reflection on the Latin American Church—Santo Domingo." *SEDOS Bulletin* 24 (June–15 July, 1992): 182–88.

————. "Option for the Poor: Assessment and Implications." *ARC: The Journal of the Faculty of Religious Studies, McGill* 22 (Spring 1994): 61–71.

————. *The Power of the Poor in History: Selected Writings*. Translated by Robert R. Barr. Maryknoll, NY: Orbis Books, 1983.

————. "Preferential Option for the Poor," *SEDOS Bulletin* 24 (June–15 July, 1992): 176–81.

————. "Questions." *SEDOS Bulletin* 24 (June/July 15, 1992): 189–97.

————. *A Theology of Liberation: History, Politics, and Salvation*. Translated and edited by Sr. Caridad Inda and John Eagleson. Maryknoll, NY: Orbis Books, 1973.

————. *A Theology of Liberation: History, Politics, and Salvation*. Rev. ed. Translated and edited by Sister Caridad Inda and John Eagleson. Maryknoll, NY: Orbis Books, 1988.

————. *The Truth Shall Make You Free: Confrontations*. Translated by Matthew J. O'Connell. Maryknoll, NY: Orbis Books, 1990.

————. *We Drink from Our Own Wells: The Spiritual Journey of a People*. Translated by Matthew J. O'Connell. Maryknoll, NY: Orbis Books; Melbourne, Australia: Dove Communications, 1984.

Hall, Pamela M. *Narrative and the Natural Law: An Interpretation of Thomistic Ethics*. Notre Dame: University of Notre Dame Press, 1994.

Hallett, Garth L. *Greater Good: The Case for Proportionalism.* Washington, DC: Georgetown University Press, 1995.

Harak, G. Simon, ed. *Aquinas and Empowerment: Classical Ethics for Ordinary Lives.* Washington, DC: Georgetown University Press, 1996.

Harding, Sandra. "The Curious Coincidence of Feminine and African Moralities: Challenges for Feminist Theory." In *Women and Moral Theory,* ed. Eva Feder Kittay and Diana T. Meyers, 296–315. N.p.: Rowman and Littlefield Publishers, 1987.

———. "The Instability of the Analytical Categories of Feminist Theory." *Signs: Journal of Women in Culture and Society* 11 (Summer 1986): 645–64.

———. "Rethinking Standpoint Epistemology: What Is 'Strong Objectivity'?" In *Feminist Epistemologies,* ed. Linda Alcoff and Elizabeth Potter, 49–82. New York: Routledge, 1993.

———. *Whose Science? Whose Knowledge? Thinking from Women's Lives.* Ithaca: Cornell University Press, 1991.

Harrison, Beverly Wildung. "Human Sexuality and Mutuality: A Fresh Paradigm." *Journal of Presbyterian History* 61 (Spring 1983): 142–61.

———. *Making the Connections: Essays in Feminist Social Ethics.* Edited by Carol S. Robb. Boston: Beacon Press, 1985.

———. *Our Right to Choose: Toward a New Ethic of Abortion.* Boston: Beacon Press, 1983.

Harrison, Beverly Wildung, Robert L. Stivers, and Ronald H. Stone, eds. *The Public Vocation of Christian Ethics.* New York: Pilgrim Press, 1986.

Hartley, Thomas J. A. *Thomistic Revival and the Modernistic Era.* Studies in Religion and Theology: Dissertation Series, no. 1. Toronto: Institute of Christian Thought, University of St. Michael's College, 1971.

Hauerwas, Stanley. *A Community of Character: Toward a Constructive Christian Social Ethic.* Notre Dame: University of Notre Dame Press, 1981.

———. "Nature, Reason, and the Task of Theological Ethics." In *Natural Law and Theology.* Readings in Moral Theology, ed. Charles Curran and Richard A. McCormick, no. 7, 43–71. New York/Mahwah: Paulist Press, 1991.

———. "Some Theological Reflections on Gutirrez's Use of 'Liberation' as a Theological Concept." *Modern Theology* 3, no. 1 (October 1986): 67–76.

———. "Casuistry as a Narrative Art." *Interpretation* 37 (1983): 377–88.

Hewitt, Marsha. "Liberation Theology and the Emancipation of Religion." *Scottish Journal of Religious Studies* 13 (Spring 1992): 21–38.

Himes, Kenneth R. "The Contribution of Theology to Catholic Moral Theology." In *Moral Theology: Challenges for the Future: Essays in Honor of*

Richard A. McCormick, S.J., ed. Charles E. Curran, 48–73. New York/ Mahwah: Paulist Press, 1990.

Hirsch, Marianne, and Evelyn Fox Keller, eds. *Conflicts in Feminism*. New York and London: Routledge, 1990.

Hittinger, Russell. *A Critique of the New Natural Law Theory*. Notre Dame: University of Notre Dame Press, 1987.

Hoagland, Sarah Lucia. *Lesbian Ethics: Toward New Value*. Palo Alto, CA: Institute of Lesbian Studies, 1988.

Hofer, Josef, and Karl Rahner, eds. *Lexikon für Theologie und Kirche*. 2nd rev. ed. Freiburg: Verlag-Herder, 1962.

Hollenbach, David. *Claims in Conflict: Retrieving and Renewing the Catholic Human Rights Tradition*. New York: Paulist Press, 1979.

Honneth, Axel, Thomas McCarthy, Claus Offe, and Albrecht Wellmer, eds. *Cultural-Political Interventions in the Unfinished Project of Enlightenment*. Cambridge: MIT Press, 1992.

Hoose, Bernard. *Proportionalism: The American Debate and Its European Roots*. Washington, DC: Georgetown University Press, 1987.

Hope, Ann, and Sally Timmel. *Training for Transformation: A Handbook for Community Workers*. Book 1. Gweru: Mambo Press, 1984.

Hudson, William Donald. *Modern Moral Philosophy*. New York: Doubleday and Company, 1970.

Isasi-Díaz, Ada María. "Solidarity: Love of Neighbor in the 1980s." In *Feminist Theological Ethics: A Reader*, ed. Lois K. Daly, 77–87. Louisville: Westminster/John Knox Press, 1994.

Jaggar, Alison M. "Feminist Ethics." In *The Encylopedia of Ethics*, vol. 1, ed. Lawrence C. Becker and Charlotte B. Becker, 361–70. New York: Garland, 1992.

———. "Love and Knowledge: Emotion in Western Epistemology." *Inquiry* 32 (June 1989): 151–76.

Janssens, Louis. "Artificial Insemination: Ethical Considerations." *Louvain Studies* 8 (1980): 3–29.

———. "Norms and Priorities in a Love Ethics." *Louvain Studies* 6 (1977): 207–38.

John Paul II, Pope [Karol Wojtyla]. *The Acting Person*. Translated by Andrezj Potocki. Dordrecht, Boston: D. Reidel, 1979.

———. *Ad Tuendam Fidem*. trans. Ladislas Orsy. In *Origins* 28, no. 8 (16 July 1998): 113, 115–16.

———. *Blessed Are the Pure of Heart: Catechesis on the Sermon on the Mount and the Writings of St. Paul*. Boston, MA: St. Paul Editions, 1983.

———. *Centesimus Annus*. In *Origins* 21, no. 1 (16 May 1991): 1–24.

————. *Love and Responsibility.* Translated by H. T. Willetts. New York: Farrar, Straus, and Giroux, 1981; first Polish ed., 1960.

————. *Original Unity of Man and Woman: Catechesis on the Book of Genesis* (Boston: Daughters of St. Paul, 1981); idem, *Blessed Are the Pure.*

————. "The Perspectives of Man—Integral Development and Eschatology." Translated by A. N. Woznicki. *Center Journal* 3 (Spring 1984): 127–42. Reprinted from *Wroclawskie Studia Teologiczne* (July 1975).

————. "Thomistic Personalism." In *Person and Community: Selected Essays.* Translated by Teresa Sandok, OSM Catholic Thought from Lublin, vol. 4. New York: Peter Lang, 1993.

Jonsen, Albert R. "Casuistry, Situationism, and Laxism." In *Joseph Fletcher: Memoir of an Ex-Radical: Reminiscence and Reappraisal,* ed. Kenneth L. Vaux, 10–24. Louisville: Westminster/John Knox, 1993.

————. "Foreword." In *The Context of Casuistry,* ed. James F. Keenan, S.J. and Thomas A. Shannon, Moral Traditions and Moral Arguments, ix–xiv. Washington, DC: Georgetown University Press, 1995.

Jonsen, Albert R., and Stephen Toulmin. *The Abuse of Casuistry: A History of Moral Reasoning.* Berkeley: University of California Press, 1988.

Jung, L. Shannon. "Feminism and Spatiality: Ethics and the Recovery of a Hidden Dimension," *Journal of Feminist Studies in Religion* 4 (1988): 55–71.

Kaufman, G. W. "A Problem of Theology: The Concept of Nature." *Harvard Theological Review* 65 (1972): 337–66.

Kay, Judith Webb. "Getting Egypt out of the People: Aquinas's Contributions to Liberation." In *Aquinas and Empowerment: Classical Ethics for Ordinary Lives,* ed. G. Simon Harak, 1–46. Washington, DC: Georgetown University Press, 1996.

————. "Human Nature and the Natural Law Tradition." Ph.D. diss., Graduate Theological Union, 1988.

Keane, Philip S. *Christian Ethics and Imagination: A Theological Inquiry.* New York/Ramsey: Paulist Press, 1984.

————. "The Objective Moral Order: Reflections on Recent Research." *Theological Studies* 43 (1982): 260–78.

Kee, Alistair. *Marx and the Failure of Liberation Theology.* London: SCM Press; Philadelphia: Trinity Press International, 1990.

Keenan, James F., S.J. "The Casuistry of John Mair, Nominalist Professor of Paris." In *The Context of Casuistry,* ed. James F. Keenan, S.J. and Thomas A. Shannon, foreword by Albert R. Jonsen, Moral Traditions and Moral Arguments, 85–102. Washington, DC: Georgetown University Press, 1995.

———. "Catholic Moral Theology, Ignatian Spirituality, and Virtue Ethics: Strange(r Than They Should Be) Bedfellows." *Supplement to the Way on Spirituality and Ethics* (Spring 1977): 36–45.

———. *Goodness and Rightness in Thomas Aquinas's Summa Theologiae.* Washington, DC: Georgetown University Press, 1992.

———. "Proposing Cardinal Virtues." *Theological Studies* 56 (1995): 709–29.

———. "The Return of Casuistry." *Theological Studies* 57 (March 1996): 123–39.

———. "William Perkins (1558–1602) and the Birth of British Casuistry." In *The Context of Casuistry*, ed. James F. Keenan, S.J. and Thomas A. Shannon, foreword by Albert R. Jonsen, Moral Traditions and Moral Arguments, 105–30. Washington, DC: Georgetown University Press, 1995.

Keenan, James F., S.J., and Thomas Shannon, "Contexts of Casuistry: Historical and Contemporary." In *The Context of Casuistry*, ed. James F. Keenan, S.J. and Thomas A. Shannon, foreword by Albert R. Jonsen, Moral Traditions and Moral Arguments, 221–31. Washington, DC: Georgetown University Press, 1995.

Keenan, James F., S.J., and Thomas A. Shannon, eds. *The Context of Casuistry.* Foreword by Albert R. Jonsen. Moral Traditions and Moral Arguments. Washington, DC: Georgetown University Press, 1995.

Key, Ellen. *Love and Ethics.* New York: B. W. Huebsch, 1912.

———. *War, Peace, and the Future: A Consideration of Nationalism and Internationalism, and of the Relation of Women to War.* Translated by Hildegard Norberg. New York: G. P. Putnam's Sons; London: Knickerbocker Press, 1916.

Kiely, Bartholomew M. "The Impracticality of Proportionalism." *Gregorianum* 66 (1985): 655–86.

Kittay, Eva Feder, and Diana T. Meyers, eds. *Women and Moral Theory.* N.p.: Rowman and Littlefield Publishers, 1987.

Kitzinger, Sheila. *The Experience of Breastfeeding*, new ed. New York: Penguin Books, 1987.

———. *Woman's Experience of Sex.* New York: Penguin, 1983.

Knauer, Peter, S.J. "The Hermeneutic Function of the Principle of Double Effect." In *Moral Norms and the Catholic Tradition*, Readings in Moral Theology, ed. Charles E. Curran and Richard A. McCormick, no. 1, 1–39. New York: Paulist Press, 1979.

———. "Zu Grundbegriffen der Enzyklika 'Veritatis Splendor.'" *Stimmen der Zeit* 212 (1994): 14–26.

Komonchak, Joseph. "Authority and Magisterium." In *Vatican Authority and American Catholic Dissent: The Curran Case and Its Consequences*, ed. William W. May, 103–14. New York: Crossroad, 1987.

Kopfensteiner, Thomas R. "Science, Metaphor, and Moral Casuistry." In *The Context of Casuistry*, ed. James F. Keenan, S.J. and Thomas A. Shannon, Moral Traditions and Moral Arguments, 207–20. Washington, DC: Georgetown University Press, 1995.

Korsgaard, Christine M. *The Sources of Normativity*. Edited by Onora O'Neill, with responses by G. A. Cohen, Raymond Geuss, Thomas Nagel, and Bernard Williams. Cambridge: Cambridge University Press, 1996.

Langan, John. "Beatitude and the Moral Law in St. Thomas." *Journal of Religious Ethics* 5 (Fall 1977): 183–95.

———. "The Christian Difference in Ethics." *Theological Studies* 49 (March 1988): 131–50.

Lauritzen, Paul. "A Feminist Ethic and the New Romanticism—Mothering as a Model of Moral Relations." *Hypatia* 4 (Summer 1989): 29–44.

———. "Whose Bodies? Which Selves? Appeals to Embodiment in Assessments of Reproductive Technology." In *Embodiment, Morality, and Medicine*, ed. Lisa Sowle Cahill and Margaret A. Farley, 113–26. Boston: Kluwer Academic Publishers, 1995.

Law, Jules. "The Politics of Breastfeeding." *Signs: Journal of Women in Culture and Society*. Forthcoming.

Lawler, Ronald D., OFM, Cap. *The Christian Personalism of Pope John Paul II*. The John Paul Synthesis: The Trinity College Symposium I. Chicago: Franciscan Herald Press, 1982.

Lefebure, Leo D. "John Paul II: The Philosopher Pope." *Christian Century* 112, no. 5, 15 February 1995, 170–76.

LeMasters, Philip. "Christian Social Ethics and Gutiérrez' *The God of Life*." *Encounter* 54 (Summer 1993): 233–47.

———. "'Theology from the Underside of History' as a Theory of Theology." *Perspectives in Religious Studies* 19 (Spring 1992): 39–51.

Lester, Rita Marie. "Ecofeminism in a Postmodern Landscape: The Body of God, Gaia, and the Cyborg." Ph.D. diss., Northwestern University/ Garrett-Evangelical Theological Seminary, 1997.

Lindbeck, George A. *The Nature of Doctrine: Religion and Theology in a Post-liberal Age*. Philadelphia: Westminster Press, 1984.

Lisska, Anthony. *Aquinas's Theory of Natural Law: An Analytic Reconstruction*. Oxford: Clarendon Press, 1996.

Longino, Helen E. "Subject, Power, and Knowledge: Description and Pre-scription in Feminist Philosophies of Science." In *Feminist Epistemolog-*

ies, ed. Linda Alcoff and Elizabeth Potter, 101–20. New York: Routledge, 1993.

Luijpen, William. *Phenomenology of Natural Law*. Translated by Henry J. Koran. Pittsburgh: Duquesne University Press, 1967.

Lustig, B. Andrew. "*Veritatis Splendor:* Some Implications for Bioethics." In *Veritatis Splendor: American Responses*, ed. Michael E. Allsopp and John J. O'Keefe, 252–68. Kansas City, MO: Sheed and Ward, 1995.

Luther, Martin. "Freedom of a Christian." In *Martin Luther: Selections from His Writings*, ed. John Dillenberger. Garden City, NY: Doubleday, Anchor Books, 1961.

MacIntyre, Alasdair. *After Virtue: A Study in Moral Theory*. 2nd ed. Notre Dame: University of Notre Dame Press, 1984.

———. "Natural Law as Subversive." *Journal of Medieval and Early Modern Studies* 26 (Winter 1996): 61–83.

Maguire, Daniel C. "The Feminist Turn in Ethics." *Horizons* 10 (Fall 1983): 341–47.

———. "The Feminization of God and Ethics." *Christianity and Crisis* (15 March 1982): 59–67.

———. "Moral Inquiry and Religious Assent." In *Contraception: Authority and Dissent*, ed. Charles E. Curran, 127–48. New York: Herder and Herder, 1969.

———. "*Ratio Practica* and the Intellectualistic Fallacy." *Journal of Religious Ethics* 10 (1982): 22–39.

———. "Service on the Common." *Religious Studies Review* 10 (January 1984): 10–14.

Maher, Vanessa. "Breast-Feeding and Maternal Depletion: Natural Law or Cultural Arrangements?" In *The Anthropology of Breast-Feeding: Natural Law or Social Construct*, ed. Vanessa Maher, 151–80. Providence, RI: Berg Publishers, 1992.

Maher, Vanessa, ed. *The Anthropology of Breast-Feeding: Natural Law or Social Construct*. Providence, RI: Berg Publishers, 1992.

Mahoney, John. *The Making of Moral Theology: A Study of the Roman Catholic Tradition*. The Martin D'Arcy Memorial Lectures 1981–82. Oxford: Clarendon Press, 1987.

Malloy, Edward A. "Natural Law Theory and Catholic Moral Theology." *American Ecclesiastical Review* 169 (1975): 456–70.

———. "Problems of Methodology in Contemporary Roman Catholic Ethics." *St. Luke's Journal of Theology* 22 (December 1978): 20–42.

Maritain, Jacques. *The Person and the Common Good*. Translated by John J. Fitzgerald. New York: Charles Scribner's Sons, 1947.

Markey, John J., O.P. "Praxis in Liberation Theology: Some Clarifications." *Missiology* 23 (April 1995): 179–95.

Marshall, G. J. "Human Nature Changes." *New Scholasticism* 54 (1980): 168–81.

Marx, Karl. *The German Ideology*. Translated by S. Ryazanskaya. In *The Marx-Engels Reader*, ed. Robert C. Tucker, 2nd ed., 146–200. New York: W. W. Norton and Company, 1978.

Matthews, Eric. *Twentieth Century French Philosophy*. Oxford and New York: Oxford University Press, 1996.

Maurer, Armand. *St. Thomas and Historicity*. The Aquinas Lecture, 1979. Milwaukee: Marquette University Press, 1979.

May, William E. *Moral Absolutes: Catholic Tradition, Current Trends, and the Truth*. Milwaukee: Marquette University Press, 1989.

———. "The Moral Meaning of Human Acts." *Homiletic and Pastoral Review* 79, no. 1 (October 1978): 10–21.

May, William W., ed. *Vatican Authority and American Catholic Dissent: The Curran Case and Its Consequences*. New York: Crossroad, 1987.

McAuliffe, Patricia. *Fundamental Ethics: A Liberationist Approach*. Washington, DC: Georgetown University Press, 1993.

McCool, Gerald. *Catholic Theology in the Nineteenth Century*. New York: Seabury Press, 1977.

McCormick, Richard A., S.J. "L'Affaire Curran." *America* 154 (5 April 1986): 266–68.

———. "Ambiguity in Moral Choice." In *Doing Evil to Achieve Good: Moral Choice in Conflict Situations*, ed. Richard A. McCormick and Paul Ramsey, 7–53. Chicago: Loyola University Press, 1978.

———. "Aspects of the Moral Question." *America* 117 (9 December 1967): 716–19.

———. "Blastomere Separation: Some Concerns." *Hastings Center Report* 24 (March–April 1994): 14–16.

———. "Beyond Principlism Is Not Enough: A Theologian Reflects on the Real Challenge for U.S. Biomedical Ethics." In *A Matter of Principles? Ferment in U.S. Bioethics*, ed. Edwin R. DuBose, Ronald P. Hamel, and Laurence J. O'Connell, 344–61. Valley Forge, PA: Trinity Press International, 1994.

———. "Christian Morals." *America* 122 (10 January 1970): 5–6.

———. "A Commentary on the Commentaries." In *Doing Evil to Achieve Good: Moral Choice in Conflict Situations*, ed. Richard A. McCormick and Paul Ramsey, 193–267. Chicago: Loyola University Press, 1978.

———. "Conjugal Love and Conjugal Morality: A Re-evaluation of the

Catholic Position in Terms of Total Marital Commitment." *America* 110 (11 January 1964): 38–42.

———. "The Council on Contraception." *America* 114 (8 January 1966): 47–48.

———. *The Critical Calling: Reflections on Moral Dilemmas Since Vatican Council II.* Washington, DC: Georgetown University Press, 1989.

———. "Exchanges on Fundamental Theology." *Theological Studies* 47 (March 1986): 69–88.

———. "Family Size, Rhythm, and the Pill." In *The Problem of Population: Moral and Theological Considerations*, ed. Donald N. Barrett, 58–84. New York: Joseph F. Wagner, Inc., 1965.

———. "Fetal Research, Morality, and Public Policy." *The Hastings Center Report* 5 (June 1975): 26–31.

———. *Health and Medicine in the Catholic Tradition: Tradition in Transition.* New York: Crossroad, 1984.

———. *Hidden Persuaders: Value Variables in Bioethics.* Bloomington, IN: The Poynter Center, 1993.

———. *How Brave a New World? Dilemmas in Bioethics.* Garden City, NY: Doubleday, 1981.

———. "Human Significance and Christian Significance." In *Norm and Context in Christian Ethics*, ed. Gene H. Outka and Paul Ramsey, 233–61. New York: Charles Scribner's Sons, 1968.

———. *"Laborem Exercens* and Social Morality." In *Official Catholic Social Teaching*, Readings in Moral Theology, ed. Richard A. McCormick and Charles E. Curran, no. 5, 219–32. New York: Paulist Press, 1986.

———. "Loyalty and Dissent: The Magisterium—A New Model."*America* (27 June 1970): 674–76.

———. "Moral Norms: An Update." *Theological Studies* 46 (March 1985): 50–64.

———. *Moral Theology in the Year 2000: Reverie or Reality?* The Nash Lecture. Regina: Campion College, University of Regina, 1988.

———. "Moral Theology 1940–1989: An Overview." *Theological Studies* 50 (1989): 3–24.

———. "A Moralist Reports." *America* 123 (11 July 1970): 22–23.

———. "The New Directives and Institutional Medico-Moral Responsibility." *Chicago Studies* 11 (1972): 305–14.

———. *Notes on Moral Theology, 1965 through 1980.* Lanham, MD: University Press of America, 1981.

———. *Notes on Moral Theology, 1981 through 1984.* Lanham, MD: University Press of America, 1984.

———. "Personal Conscience." *Chicago Studies* 13 (Fall 1974): 241–52.

———. "Practical and Theoretical Considerations." Chap. in [no editor] *The Problem of Population*. Vol. 3, *Educational Considerations*, 50–73. Notre Dame: University of Notre Dame Press, 1965.

———. "Self-Assessment and Self-Indictment." *Religious Studies Review* 13, no. 1 (January 1987): 37–39.

———. "The Shape of Moral Evasion in Catholicism." *America* 159, no. 8 (1 October 1988): 183–88.

———. "The Social Responsibility of the Christian." *The Australasian Catholic Record* 52 (July 1975): 253–63.

———. "Surrogate Motherhood: A Stillborn Idea," *Second Opinion* 5 (1987): 128–32.

———. "Theology and Biomedical Ethics." *Logos* 3 (1982): 25–45.

———. "What the Silence Means: Richard A. McCormick Answers His Critics." *America* 129 (20 October 1973): 287–90.

McCormick, Richard A., and Andre Hellegers. "The Ethics of In Utero Surgery." *Journal of the American Medical Association* 246 (2 October 1981): 1550–55.

McCormick, Richard A., and Paul Ramsey, eds. *Doing Evil to Achieve Good: Moral Choice in Conflict Situations*. Chicago: Loyola University Press, 1978.

McGovern, Arthur F. *Liberation Theology and Its Critics: Toward an Assessment*. Maryknoll, NY: Orbis Books, 1989.

McInerny, Ralph. "The Principles of Natural Law." In *Natural Law and Theology*. Readings in Moral Theology, ed. Charles Curran and Richard A. McCormick, no. 7, 139–56. New York/Mahwah: Paulist Press, 1991.

McIntosh, Janet. Letter to the editor. *Atlantic Monthly* 281, no. 6, June 1998, 8–9.

McLaughlin, Eleanor Commo. "Equality of Souls, Inequality of Sexes: Woman in Medieval Theology." In *Religion and Sexism: Images of Women in the Jewish and Christian Traditions*, ed. Rosemary Radford Ruether, 213–66. New York: Simon and Schuster, 1974.

Metz, Johann Baptist. "Theology in the Struggle for History and Society." In *Expanding the View: Gustavo Gutiérrez and the Future of Liberation Theology*, ed. Marc H. Ellis and Otto Maduro, 94–101. Maryknoll, NY: Orbis Books, 1990.

Midgeley, Louis C. *Beyond Human Nature: The Contemporary Debate over Moral Natural Law*. Charles E. Merrill Monograph Series in the Humanities and Social Sciences, vol. 1, no. 4. Provo, UT: Brigham Young University Press, 1968.

Milby, T. H. "Natural Law, Evolution, and the Question of Personhood." *Quarterly Review: A Scholarly Journal for Reflection on Ministry* 6 (Summer 1986): 39–47.

Miller, Richard B. *Casuistry and Modern Ethics: A Poetics of Practical Reasoning.* Chicago: University of Chicago Press, 1996.

Miller-McLemore, Bonnie J. *Also a Mother: Work and Family as a Theological Dilemma.* Nashville: Abingdon, 1994.

———. "Produce or Perish: Generativity and New Reproductive Technologies." *Journal of the American Academy of Religion* 59 (1991): 39–69.

Mills, Charles W. "Alternative Epistemologies." *Social Theory and Practice* 14 (Fall 1988): 237–63.

Min, Anselm Kyongsuk. *Dialectic of Salvation: Issues in Theology of Liberation.* Albany: State University of New York Press, 1989.

———. "Praxis and Theology in Recent Debates." *Scottish Journal of Theology* 39 (1986): 529–49.

Mitchell, Basil. *Morality: Religious and Secular: The Dilemma of the Traditional Conscience.* Oxford: Clarendon Press, 1980.

Mondin, Battista. "Faith and Reason in Roman Catholic Thought from Clement of Alexandria to Vatican II." *Dialogue and Alliance* 1 (1987): 18–26.

Morgan, Marabel. *The Total Woman.* Old Tappan, NJ: Revell, 1967.

Mounier, Emmanuel. *Personalism.* Translated by Philip Mairet. London: Routledge and Kegan Paul, 1952.

The Mud Flower Collective [Katie G. Cannon, Beverly W. Harrison, Carter Heyward, Ada María Isasi-Díaz, Delores S. Williams, Mary D. Pellauer, and Nancy D. Richardson]. *God's Fierce Whimsy.* New York: Pilgrim Press, 1985.

Nash, Ronald, ed. *Liberation Theology.* Milford, MI: Mott Media, 1984.

National Council of Catholic Bishops. "Called to be One in Christ Jesus: Third Draft of Pastoral on Concerns of Women." *Origins* 21 (23 April 1992): 761–76.

Nelson, Lynn Hankinson. "Epistemological Communities." In *Feminist Epistemologies,* ed. Linda Alcoff and Elizabeth Potter, 121–59. New York: Routledge, 1993.

Neuhaus, Richard John. "Liberation Theology and the Cultural Captivity of the Gospel-Political Kingdoms." In *Liberation Theology,* ed. Ronald Nash, 45–67. Milford, MI: Mott Media, 1984.

Newton, Niles. "Interrelationships between Sexual Responsiveness, Birth, and Breast Feeding." In *Contemporary Sexual Behavior: Critical Issues in the 1970s,* ed. Joseph Zubin and John Money, 77–98. Baltimore: Johns Hopkins University Press, 1973.

———. *Maternal Emotions.* New York: Hoeber, 1955.

Nicholson, Linda, ed. *Feminist Contentions: A Philosophical Exchange.* New York: Routledge, 1995.

Nickoloff, James B. "Church of the Poor: The Ecclesiology of Gustavo Gutiérrez." *Theological Studies* 54 (1993): 512–35.

Noonan, John T., Jr. "Development in Moral Doctrine." In *The Context of Casuistry,* ed. James F. Keenan, S.J. and Thomas A. Shannon, Moral Traditions and Moral Arguments, 188–204. Washington, DC: Georgetown University Press, 1995.

Novak, Michael. "Traditional Pragmatism: An Ethic Both Practical and Wise." *Journal of Ecumenical Studies* 5 (Spring 1968): 284–307.

———. *Will It Liberate? Questions about Liberation Theology.* New York/Mahwah: Paulist Press, 1986.

Nussbaum, Martha C. "Aristotelian Social Democracy." In *Liberalism and the Good,* ed. R. Bruce Douglass, Gerald M. Mara, and Henry S. Richardson, 203–52. New York: Routledge, 1990.

———. "Human Functioning and Social Justice: In Defense of Aristotelian Essentialism." *Political Theory* 20, no. 2 (May 1992): 202–46.

———. "Non-Relative Virtues: An Aristotelian Approach." *Midwest Studies in Philosophy,* vol. 13: *Ethical Theory: Character and Virtue,* ed. Peter A. French, Theodore E. Uehling, Jr., and Howard K. Wettstein, 32–53. Notre Dame: University of Notre Dame Press, 1988.

O'Brien, David J., and Thomas A. Shannon, eds. *Renewing the Earth: Catholic Documents on Peace, Justice and Liberation.* Garden City, NY: Doubleday, Image Books, 1977.

O'Connell, Timothy E. *Principles for a Catholic Morality.* Foreword by Charles E. Curran. San Francisco: Harper and Row, 1978.

O'Donovan, Leo J. "Was Vatican II Evolutionary? A Note on Conciliar Language." *Theological Studies* 36 (September 1975): 493–502.

Odozor, Paulinus Ikechukwu. *Richard A. McCormick and the Renewal of Moral Theology.* Notre Dame: University of Notre Dame Press, 1995.

O'Malley, John W. "Developments, Reforms, and Two Great Reformations: Towards a Historical Assessment of Vatican II." *Theological Studies* 44 (September 1983): 373–406.

———. "Reform, Historical Consciousness, and Vatican II's Aggiornamento." *Theological Studies* 32 (December 1971): 573–601.

Outka, Gene H., and Paul Ramsey, eds. *Norm and Context in Christian Ethics.* New York: Charles Scribner's Sons, 1968.

Outka, Gene, and John P. Reeder, Jr., eds. *Prospects for a Common Morality.* Princeton, NJ: Princeton University Press, 1993.

Overall, Christine. "Feminism, Ontology, and 'Other Minds.'" In *Feminist*

Perspectives: Philosophical Essays on Method and Morals, ed. Lorraine Code, Sheila Mullett, and Christine Overall, 89–106. Toronto: University of Toronto Press, 1988.

Panikkar, Raimundo. *El Concepto de la Naturaleza—Análisis Histórico y Metafísico de un Concepto*. Madrid: Consejo Superior de Investigaciones Científicas, Instituto "Luís Vives" de Filosofía, 1951.

Panter-Brick, Catherine. "Working Mothers in Rural Nepal." In *The Anthropology of Breast-Feeding: Natural Law or Social Construct*, ed. Vanessa Maher, 133–50. Providence, RI: Berg Publishers, 1992.

Parsons, Susan Frank. *Feminism and Christian Ethics*. New Studies in Christian Ethics. Cambridge: Cambridge University Press, 1996.

———. "The Intersection of Feminism and Theological Ethics: A Philosophical Approach." *Modern Theology* 4 (April 1988): 251–66.

Pascal, Blaise. *The Provincial Letters*. Translated by A. J. Krailsheimer. New York: Penguin Books, 1967.

Patrick, Anne E. *Liberating Conscience: Feminist Explorations in Catholic Moral Theology*. New York: Continuum, 1996.

Paul VI, Pope. *Humanae Vitae*. In *Humanae Vitae and the Bishops: The Encyclical and the Statements of the National Hierarchies*, comp. by John Horgan, 33–56 (Shannon: Irish University Press[, 1972]).

———. *Populorum Progressio*. In *Renewing the Earth: Catholic Documents on Peace, Justice and Liberation*, ed. David J. O'Brien and Thomas A. Shannon, 307–46. Garden City, NY: Doubleday, Image Books, 1977.

Pegis, Anton Charles. *At the Origins of the Thomistic Notion of Man*. The St. Augustine Lecture, 1962. New York: Macmillan, 1963.

———. *The Middle Ages and Philosophy: Some Reflections on the Ambivalence of Modern Scholasticism*. James Roosevelt Bagley Lecture, Seton Hall University. Chicago: Henry Regnery Co., 1963.

Perry, Michael J. *Love and Power: The Role of Religion and Morality in American Politics*. New York: Oxford University Press, 1991.

Pieper, Josef. *The Four Cardinal Virtues*. Various translators. Notre Dame: University of Notre Dame Press, 1966.

Pierce, Christine. "Natural Law Language and Women." In *Woman in Sexist Society: Studies in Power and Powerlessness*, ed. Vivian Gornick and Barbara K. Moran, 160–72. New York: Basic Books, 1971.

Pinckaers, Servais. *Les Sources de la Morale Chrétienne: sa Méthode, son Contenu, son Histoire*. Etudes d'éthique chrétienne (Studien zur theologischen Ethik), no. 14. Fribourg: Editions Universitaires; Paris: Editions du Cerf, 1985.

Pincoffs, Edmund L. *Quandaries and Virtues: Against Reductivism in Ethics*. Lawrence, KS: University Press of Kansas, 1986.

Pope, Stephen J. "Christian Love for the Poor: Almsgiving and the 'Preferential Option.'" *Horizons* 21 (1994): 288–312.

———. *The Evolution of Altruism and the Ordering of Love.* Moral Traditions and Moral Arguments. Washington, DC: Georgetown University Press, 1994.

Porter, Jean. "At the Limits of Liberalism: Thomas Aquinas and the Prospects for a Catholic Feminism." *Theology Digest* 41 (Winter 1994): 315–30.

———. "Contested Categories: Reason, Nature, and Natural Order in Medieval Accounts of the Natural Law." *Journal of Religious Ethics* 24 (1996): 207–32.

———. *Moral Action and Christian Ethics.* Cambridge: Cambridge University Press, 1995.

———. *The Recovery of Virtue: The Relevance of Aquinas for Christian Ethics.* Louisville: Westminster/John Knox Press, 1990.

Potter, Elizabeth. "Gender and Epistemic Negotiation." In *Feminist Epistemologies*, ed. Linda Alcoff and Elizabeth Potter, 161–86. New York: Routledge, 1993.

Quay, Paul M. "The Disvalue of Ontic Evil." *Theological Studies* 46 (1985): 262–86.

———. "Morality by Calculation of Values." *Theology Digest* 23 (Winter 1975): 347–64.

Rabuzzi, Kathryn Allen. "The Socialist Feminist Vision of Rosemary Radford Ruether: A Challenge to Liberal Feminism." *Religious Studies Review* 15 (January 1989): 4–8.

Rahner, Karl. "Anonymous Christians." In *Theological Investigations*, vol. 6, *Concerning Vatican Council II*, trans. Karl-H. and Boniface Kruger. Baltimore: Helicon Press; London: Darton, Longman and Todd, 1969.

———. "Dogma." In *Sacramentum Mundi.*

———. *Foundations of Christian Faith: An Introduction to the Idea of Christianity.* Translated by William V. Dych. New York: Seabury Press, 1978.

———. *Theological Investigations.* Vol. 2, *Man in the Church.* Translated by Karl-H. Kruger. Baltimore: Helicon Press, 1963.

———. *Theological Investigations.* Vol. 6, *Concerning Vatican Council II.* Translated by Karl-H. and Boniface Kruger. Baltimore: Helicon Press; London: Darton, Longman and Todd, 1969.

———. *Theological Investigations.* Vol. 9, *Writings of 1965–67.* Translated by Graham Harrison. New York: Herder and Herder, 1972.

———. "Toward a Fundamental Theological Interpretation of Vatican II." Translated by Leo J. O'Donovan. *Theological Studies* 40 (December 1979): 716–27.

————. "Transcendental Theology." In *Sacramentum Mundi.*

Rahner, Karl, et al., ed. *Sacramentum Mundi: An Encyclopedia of Theology.* New York: Herder and Herder; London: Burns and Oates, 1969.

Ramsey, Paul. *Basic Christian Ethics.* Chicago and London: University of Chicago Press, 1950; reprint, Chicago: University of Chicago Press, Midway Reprints, 1978.

Ratzinger, Joseph Cardinal. *Church, Ecumenism, and Politics: New Essays in Ecclesiology.* Translated by Robert Nowell. New York: Crossroad, 1987.

————. "The Church's Teaching Authority—Faith—Morals." In *Principles of Christian Morality,* Heinz Schurmann, Joseph Cardinal Ratzinger, and Hans Urs von Balthasar, 47–73. Translated by Graham Harrison. San Francisco: Ignatius Press, 1986.

Reeder, John P., Jr. "Foundations without Foundationalism." In *Prospects for a Common Morality,* ed. Gene Outka and John P. Reeder, Jr., 191–214. Princeton, NJ: Princeton University Press, 1993.

Regan, Richard J. *American Pluralism and the Catholic Conscience.* Foreword by John Courtney Murray. New York: Macmillan Company; London: Collier-Macmillan Limited, 1963.

Regan, Hilary D., and Alan J. Torrance with Antony Wood. eds. *Christ and Context: The Confrontation between Gospel and Culture.* Edinburgh: T&T Clark, 1993.

Rhonheimer, Martin. *Natur als Grundlage der Moral: die personale Struktur des Naturgesetzes bei Thomas von Aquin: eine Auseinandersetzung mit autonomer und teleologischer Ethik.* Innsbruck: Tyrolia-Verlag, 1987.

Rigali, Norbert J. "Artificial Birth Control: The Impasse Revisited." *Theological Studies* 47 (December 1986): 681–90.

————. "The Moral Act." *Horizons* 10 (Fall 1983): 252–66.

————. "On Christian Ethics." *Chicago Studies* 10 (1971): 227–47.

————. "Toward a Moral Theology of Social Consciousness." *Horizons* 4 (Fall 1977): 169–81.

————. "The Uniqueness and Distinctiveness of Christian Morality and Ethics." In *Moral Theology: Challenges for the Future: Essays in Honor of Richard A. McCormick, S.J.,* ed. Charles E. Curran, 74–93. New York/Mahwah: Paulist Press, 1990.

Romelt, J. Review of *Natur als Grundlage der Moral: Die personale Struktur des Naturgesetzes bei Thomas von Aquin: Ein Auseinandersetzung mit autonomer und teleologischer Ethik,* by Martin Rhonheimer. *Zeitschrift für Katholische Theologie* 3 (1989): 211–16.

Ross, Susan A. "The Bride of Christ and the Body Politic: Body and Gender in Pre-Vatican II Marriage Theology." *Journal of Religion* 71 (July 1991): 345–61.

————. *Extravagant Affections: A Feminist Sacramental Theology.* New York: Continuum, 1998 [forthcoming].

Rossi, Alice S. "Maternalism, Sexuality, and the New Feminism." In *Contemporary Sexual Behavior: Critical Issues in the 1970s,* ed. Joseph Zubin and John Money, 145–73. Baltimore: Johns Hopkins University Press, 1973.

Ruddick, Sara. *Maternal Thinking: Toward a Politics of Peace.* Boston: Beacon Press, 1989.

Ruether, Rosemary Radford. "The Development of My Theology." *Religious Studies Review* 15 (January 1989): 1–4.

————. "The Feminist Critique in Religious Studies." *Soundings* 64 (Winter 1981): 388–402.

————. "The Future of Feminist Theology in the Academy." *Journal of the American Academy of Religion* 53 (December 1985): 703–13.

————. *Gaia and God: An Ecofeminist Theology of Earth Healing.* San Francisco: Harper and Row, 1992.

————. *Liberation Theology: Human Hope Confronts Christian History and American Power.* New York: Paulist Press, 1972.

————. *New Woman/New Earth: Sexist Ideologies and Human Liberation.* New York: Seabury Press, 1975.

————. *Sexism and God-Talk: Toward a Feminist Theology.* Boston: Beacon Press, 1983.

————. *Women-Church: Theology and Practice of Feminist Liturgical Communities.* San Francisco: Harper and Row, 1985.

Ruether, Rosemary Radford, ed. *Religion and Sexism: Images of Women in the Jewish and Christian Traditions.* New York: Simon and Schuster, 1974.

Russell, Letty M. *Human Liberation in a Feminist Perspective: A Theology.* Philadelphia: Westminster Press, 1974.

Saiving, Valerie. "The Human Situation: A Feminine View." *Journal of Religion* 40 (1960): 100–12.

Schaef, Anne Wilson. *When Society Becomes an Addict.* San Francisco: Harper and Row, 1987.

Schoof, Mark. *A Survey of Catholic Theology 1800–1970.* With a Foreword by Edward Schillebeeckx. Translated by N. D. Smith. Paramus, NJ and New York, NY: Paulist Newman Press, 1970.

Schubeck, Thomas L., S.J. *Liberation Ethics: Sources, Models, and Norms.* Minneapolis: Fortress Press, 1993.

————. "The Reconstruction of Natural Law Reasoning: Liberation Theology as a Case Study." *Journal of Religious Ethics* 20 (Spring 1992): 149–78.

Schüller, Bruno. *Wholly Human: Essays on the Theory and Language of Morality.* Translated by Peter Heinegg. Dublin: Gill and Macmillan; Washington, DC: Georgetown University Press, 1986.

Schurmann, Heinz, Joseph Cardinal Ratzinger, and Hans Urs von Balthasar, eds. *Principles of Christian Morality.* Translated by Graham Harrison, 47–73. San Francisco: Ignatius Press, 1986.

Secker, Susan. "The Crisis within Official Catholic Sexual and Biomedical Ethics and American Revisionist Moral Theology: The Relationship between Selected Methodological and Ecclesiological Aspects." Ph.D. diss., University of Chicago, 1989.

Segers, Mary C. "Feminism, Liberalism, and Catholicism." In *Feminist Ethics and the Catholic Tradition,* Readings in Moral Theology No. 9, ed. Charles E. Curran, Margaret A. Farley, and Richard A. McCormick, S.J., 586–615. New York: Paulist Press, 1996.

Segundo, Juan Luís. *Berdiaeff: Une Reflexion Chrétienne sur la Personne.* Paris: Aubier, 1963.

———. "The Shift Within Latin American Theology." *Journal of Theology for Southern Africa* 52 (September 1985): 17–29.

———. *Theology and the Church: A Response to Cardinal Ratzinger and a Warning to the Whole Church.* Translated by John W. Diercksmeier. Minneapolis: Winston Press; London: Geoffrey Chapman, 1985.

Selling, Joseph A. "Introduction." *Personalist Morals: Essays in Honor of Professor Louis Janssens,* ed. Joseph A. Selling, 1–7. Leuven: Leuven University Press, 1988.

Seuss, Dr. (Theodore Seuss Geisel). "The Sneetches." In *The Sneetches and Other Stories.* New York: Random House, 1953.

Shannon, Thomas A., and Lisa Sowle Cahill. "The Instruction and Roman Catholic Moral Teaching." In *Religion and Artificial Reproduction: An Inquiry into the Vatican "Instruction on Respect for Human Life".* New York: Crossroad, 1988.

Sherwin, Susan. "Feminism and Medical Ethics: Two Different Approaches to Contextual Ethics." *Hypatia* 4 (Summer 1989): 64–68.

———. *No Longer Patient: Feminist Ethics and Health Care.* Philadelphia: Temple University Press, 1992.

Sigmund, Paul E. *Liberation Theology at the Crossroads: Democracy or Revolution?* New York, Oxford: Oxford University Press, 1990.

Siker, Jeffrey R. *Scripture and Ethics: Twentieth-Century Portraits.* New York: Oxford University Press, 1997.

Simons, Eberhard. "Personalism." *Sacramentum Mundi.*

Snitow, Ann. "A Gender Diary." In *Conflicts in Feminism,* ed. Marianne Hirsch and Evelyn Fox Keller, 11–43. New York and London: Routledge, 1990.

Sommers, Christina Hoff. *Who Stole Feminism: How Women Have Betrayed Women.* New York: Simon and Schuster, 1994.

Sperry, Roger W. "Changed Concepts of Brain and Consciousness: Some Value Implications." *Perkins Journal of Theology* 36 (Summer 1983): 21–32.

Spohn, William C. "Notes on Moral Theology: 1992, The Magisterium and Morality." *Theological Studies* 54 (1993): 95–111.

————. "Richard A. McCormick: Tradition in Transition." *Religious Studies Review* 13 (January 1987): 39–42.

————. "The Use of Scripture in Moral Theology." *Theological Studies* 47 (March 1986): 88–102.

————. *What Are They Saying about Scripture and Ethics?* New York: Paulist Press, 1984.

Storrie, Kathleen. "Contemporary Feminist Theology: A Selective Bibliography." *TSF Bulletin* 7 (May–June 1984): 13–15.

Stout, Jeffrey. *Ethics after Babel: The Languages of Morals and Their Discontents.* Boston: Beacon Press, 1988.

Sullivan, Francis Patrick. Review of *Las Casas. Gregorianum* 76 (1995): 612–24.

Tamez, Elsa, ed. *Through Her Eyes: Women's Theology from Latin America.* Maryknoll, NY: Orbis Books, 1989.

Thiry, L. "Ethical Theory of St. Thomas Aquinas: Interpretations and Misinterpretations." *Journal of Religion* 50 (April 1970): 169–85.

Thistlethwaite, Susan Brooks. *Sex, Race, and God: Christian Feminism in Black and White.* New York: Crossroad, 1989.

Thomas Aquinas, Saint. *The Political Ideas of St. Thomas Aquinas: Representative Selections.* Edited by Dino Bigongiari. New York: Hafner Press, 1953.

————. *Summa Theologiae.* 5 vols. Translated by the Fathers of the English Dominican Province. [N.p.]: Benziger Brothers, 1948; reprint, Westminster, MD: Christian Classics, 1981.

Thomasma, David. *Human Life in the Balance.* Louisville: Westminster/John Knox Press, 1990.

Tinder, Glenn. "Can We Be Good without God? On the Political Meaning of Christianity." *The Atlantic,* December 1989, 69–85.

Tong, Rosemarie. *Feminist Thought: A Comprehensive Introduction.* Boulder and San Francisco: Westview Press, 1989.

Traina, Cristina L. H. "Developing an Integrative Ethical Method: Feminist Ethics and Natural Law Retrieval." Ph.D. diss., University of Chicago Divinity School, 1992.

————. "Oh, Susanna: The New Absolutism and Natural Law." *Journal of the American Academy of Religion* 65 (1997): 371–401.

————. "Passionate Mothering: Toward an Ethic of Appropriate Mother-Child Intimacy." *Annual of the Society of Christian Ethics, 1998,* 175–196. Washington, DC: Georgetown University Press, 1998.

————. "Sympathetic Imagination: Experience, the Other, and the Feminist Argument for Pacifism." In [Festschrift for Edmund Perry], ed. George D. Bond and Thomas Ryba. Evanston, IL: Northwestern University Press. Forthcoming.

Treacy, Gerald C., ed. *Five Great Encyclicals: Labor, Education, Marriage, Reconstructing the Social Order, Atheistic Communism.* New York: Paulist Press, 1939.

Tronto, Joan. *Moral Boundaries: A Political Argument for an Ethic of Care.* New York: Routledge, 1993.

Vacek, Edward V. "Proportionalism: One View of the Debate." *Theological Studies* 46 (June 1985): 287–310.

van Melsen, A. G. M. "Natur und Moral." In *Das Naturrecht im Disput: Drei Vorträge beim Kongress der deutschsprachigen Moraltheologen, 1965 in Bensberg,* ed. Franz Böckle, 61–85. Dusseldorf: Patmos-Verlag, 1966.

Vaux, Kenneth L. *Joseph Fletcher: Memoir of an Ex-Radical: Reminiscence and Reappraisal.* Louisville: Westminster/John Knox, 1993.

Veatch, Henry B. *Swimming against the Current in Contemporary Philosophy.* Studies in Philosophy and the History of Philosophy. Washington, DC: Catholic University of America Press, 1990.

Walker, Margaret Urban. "Moral Understandings: Alternative 'Epistemology' for a Feminist Ethics." *Hypatia* 4 (Summer 1989): 15–28.

Walsh, Terrance G. Review of Gustavo Gutiérrez, *Las Casas. Theological Studies* 56 (June 1995): 367–69.

Warren, Virginia L. "Feminist Directions in Medical Ethics." *Hypatia* 4 (Summer 1989): 73–87.

Watters, Ethan. "Ward Connerly Won the Battle—Now He's Facing the War." *Mother Jones* 22, no. 6, November/December 1997, 71–73.

Weaver, Mary Jo. *New Catholic Women: A Contemporary Challenge to Traditional Religious Authority.* San Francisco: Harper and Row, 1985.

Weinreb, Lloyd L. *Natural Law and Justice.* Cambridge, MA: Harvard University Press, 1987.

Welch, Sharon D. Welch. *A Feminist Ethic of Risk.* Minneapolis: Fortress, 1990.

Westberg, Daniel. *Right Practical Reason: Aristotle, Action, and Prudence in Aquinas.* Oxford: Clarendon Press, 1994.

White, Morton. *What Is and What Ought to Be Done: An Essay on Ethics and Epistemology.* New York: Oxford University Press, 1981.

Wilkins, John, ed. *Considering Veritatis Splendor.* Cleveland: Pilgrim Press, 1994.

Williams, Delores S. "The Color of Feminism: Or Speaking the Black Women's Tongue." In *Feminist Theological Ethics: A Reader,* ed. Lois K. Daly, 42–58. Louisville, KY: Westminster/John Knox Press, 1994.

Winnicott, D. W. *The Family and Individual Development.* London: Tavistock Publications, 1965.

Wojtyla, Karol. See John Paul II, Pope.

Yoder, John Howard. *The Priestly Kingdom: Social Ethics as Gospel.* Notre Dame: University of Notre Dame Press, 1984.

Zecha, Gerhard, and Paul Weingartner, eds. *Conscience: An Interdisciplinary View.* Theory and Decision Library Series A: Philosophy and Methodology of the Social Sciences. Boston: D. Reidel Publishing Company, 1987.

Zubin, Joseph, and John Money, eds. *Contemporary Sexual Behavior: Critical Issues in the 1970s.* Baltimore: Johns Hopkins University Press, 1973.

Index

Abortion, 8, 49n7, 138–39n104, 163n2, 167n64; in Fuchs, 187, 193; in McCormick, 212, 215–16; feminist critique of prohibition, 303; in Gudorf, 141–42

Absolute (divine), existential option for in Fuchs, 169–70, 183; and goodness of subject, 173; and sin, 171, 173; acts as expression of, 172–73; implications for norms, 174–76; and virtue, 177; and telos, 183–84; and Christian particularity, 188–89; in Christ, 190; in revisionism generally, 289, 296, 310, 316; in Gutiérrez, 260. *See also* God

Absolutes, moral, 32, 43, 73, 294–95; in liberalism, 7–8; in personalist absolutism, 110–12; in private ethics, 142; in Fuchs, 173–74, 182, 192; in McCormick, 206–7, 211, 214, 216–17, 234; in Gutiérrez, 270–71

Absolutism, moral, 10, 41–43, 119–22, 127–28, 294–95, 327

Adams, Robert Merrihew, 9, 33

Agency, collective, 30, 147–48; in Fuchs, 185; in Gutiérrez, 274–76. *See also* social sin, solidarity

Agency, individual, in liberalism, 7, 26–27, 100–1; and historical interdependence, 30; and social pressures,

38; and virtue, 76; in feminist thought, 145–49, 160, 165n38; in Gutiérrez, 251–52, 274; in McCormick, 289, 293; and fundamental option, 308; and feminist ethics, 315

Anthropology, as basis for norms and reflection, 6, 55–57; in Thomas Aquinas, 58–63; advantages of telic, 6, 17–18, 57, 85–86, 127–30, 334; liberal and social constructionist, 32–34; and inclinations, 71–75; and personalism, 108–10, 114; formal versus concrete, 191–92; in *Donum Vitae,* 323–24

Feminist, 42–47, 147–58; natural law feminism, 317, 323

In Fuchs, 170–83; formal and concrete, 191–92; connection to Thomas, 194

In Gutiérrez, 252–59; and history, 246, 272; connection to Thomas, 263, 266–67, 272

In McCormick, 211–12, 217–20; and norms, 228–29 In revisionism generally, 288–89, 291–94, 296, 298

Aristotle, influence on moral thought, 10, 45–47, 58, 63–65, 74, 83, 100; versus Plato, in Fuchs, 184

371

Catholic Worker movement, 107, 110

Centesimus Annus, 82, 96n140, 97–98
nn154–55, 125, 135nn61–62

Charism. *See* ecclesiology and epistemology

Charity, 74–81, 117, 125, 157; in Fuchs,
172; in Gutiérrez, 251–52, 260,
263–65, 272; connection to virtue
in Thomas, 318; goal of moral life,
289–90; and human capacity, 293.
See also love

Chodorow, Nancy, 273

Chopp, Rebecca, 43, 50n29, 160–61

Christian ethics, particularity of. *See*
human ethics

Christology and ethics, 107, 114–15,
120–21; law of Christ, 63, 180, 188,
218; imitation of Christ, 190, 251,
261–62; proclamation of the Kingdom, 248; Jesus as savior in history, 253–54, 257

Church, role of, 115–18, 120–21, 125;
Fuchs on role in individual salvation, 170, 184–85; on limits to
moral aptitude of hierarchy, 185;
McCormick on authority in theology and morals, 220–24, 232;
Gutiérrez on church community as
locus of spirituality, reflection, and
action, 248, 258, 262; on ecclesiastical injustice, 261, 273; on church
as agent of prophecy and solidarity, 268–71. *See also* ecclesiology;
magisterium

Circumstances, effects on moral evaluation, 41, 76, 79, 84, 86, 128–29, 156;
connection to prudence, 63–69
In Fuchs, and objectivity of norms,
174, 176, 182; and conscience, 184
In McCormick, as essential to evaluation of acts and norms, 203,
206–10, 214, 217

Code, Lorraine, 30–31

Collective agency. *See* agency, collective

Common good, 45, 59–63, 80–86, 114–
15, 141, 145, 157; in Gutiérrez,
256, 264–65, 271; in revisionism
generally, 289–91, 310; virtue and,
316; interdependence and, 318;
reproductive technology and, 326,
330–31

Comunidades de base. *See* basic Christian communities

Conflict, among norms or goods, 12,
103–4, 108, 111; as context for
moral thought and action, 208,
211–14, 291–92, 318–19; as cause
of proportionate reason, 206–7;
origins of, 174, 213; as model for
moral reflection, 271; and dilemma
ethics, 307–8

Congregation for the Doctrine of the
Faith (CDF), 121, 323

Connerly, Ward, 7–8, 86

Conscience, in Thomas, 65, 78–79; in
feminist thought, 142, 145–46
In Fuchs, 184; as source of objective judgment, 183, 187; conditions of good function, 187; as
locus of moral authority, 191,
194
In McCormick, as locus of authority, 222; and self-deception, 214,
217; and variety in concrete decisions, 225

Consensus, "overlapping," as de facto
criterion for moral norms, 9, 15–16,
33, 41–42, 105; as procedure for
moral reflection, 146; neglected,
323–24. *See also* procedure in
ethics

Consequences, as criteria for moral judgment, 2–3, 84–86, 142; in
McCormick, 205–6, 209; limits of